PEPYS: HIS LIFE AND CHARACTER

OTHER BOOKS BY
JOHN DRINKWATER

Mr. Charles King of England

A Book for Bookmen

The Pilgrim of Eternity: Lord Byron

Victorian Poetry

The Lyric

Oliver Cromwell

Abraham Lincoln

SAMUEL PEPYS

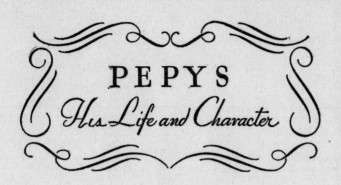

PEPYS
His Life and Character

BY

JOHN DRINKWATER

Published by DOUBLEDAY
DORAN & COMPANY, INC.
Garden City, New York
MCMXXXI

PRINTED AT THE *Country Life Press*, GARDEN CITY, N. Y., U. S. A.

TO ALBERTA
COUNTESS OF SANDWICH
WHOSE TITLE WAS FIRST GRACED
BY PEPYS'S FRIEND
MY LADY OF THE DIARY

PREFACE

MY PURPOSE in this book has been to present a portrait combining in one figure the Pepys known to his own generation as a distinguished civil servant and a connoisseur of liberal tastes, and the Pepys known to later ages as a Diarist of unique attractions.

The names to which in such an enterprise debts have first to be owned are John Smith, Lord Braybrooke, Mynors Bright, Henry B. Wheatley, and J. R. Tanner. It has been impossible, and unnecessary, to record acknowledgments to these sources page by page. The list of authorities given at the end of this volume could have, and has not, been expanded into a litter of footnotes. But to Dr. Tanner I should like to particularise my thanks for his courtesies, and for the invaluable help that I have derived from the many occasional publications which are a splendid prelude to the large-scale life of Pepys upon which he has been engaged for many years, a life which we may expect to bring the full scope of Pepys's naval career into final perspective with his personality. Debts of a more fugitive kind have been acknowledged in the text.

A word should be said as to the spelling adopted in quotations. Consistency here is out of the question. In the first place, neither John Smith nor Mynors Bright in their transcriptions of the Diary and other documents used a spelling that would have been recognisable to Pepys himself. Moreover, Pepys and his contemporaries had no consistent orthographic standard of their own. And, further, a letter may be found in Smith's volumes of 1841, regularised by its editor, and the reply to it in Dr. Tanner's volumes of 1926, printed from the original manuscript. In such circumstances it has been no part of my desire to indulge what Wheatley charmingly calls the modern 'craze for Uniformity.'

In my year dates I have used New Style: treating January 1st as New Year's Day.

My thanks are also gratefully offered to Lord Sandwich for allowing me free access at all times to his Hinchingbrooke papers; to the Master of Magdalene; to Mr. F. McD. C. Turner, the present Pepysian Librarian, for patiently bearing with my enquiries; to Messrs. Ellis of Bond Street for the use of Thomas Baker's MS. Journal in their possession; to Mr. W. F. Ashley, Clerk to the Huntingdon Grammar School; and, for sundry kindnesses, to Mr. Francis Needham, of the Bodleian, Mr. W. Hamilton Fyfe, Headmaster of Christ's Hospital, Mr. P. M. Evans of the Clothworkers' Company; and Mr. F. A. C. Bathurst of Robson and Co., for an unpublished Pepys document. For help in searching various church registers in the neighbourhood of Huntingdon I am grateful to the Rev. H. N. Hadrill of Brampton, the Rev. R. P. Moline of Cottenham, and the Rev. A. L. Grimley of Ellington.

J. D.

Pepys House,
Brampton,
Huntingdon.

CONTENTS

ILLUSTRATIONS

CHAPTER I

EARLY DAYS. LONDON. HUNTINGDON. CAMBRIDGE

S AMUEL PEPYS was born on February 23, 1633. We hardly embroider history if we say that at the time a new England was being born too. The Elizabethan glory was waning, had, indeed, almost become a memory. Shakespeare, Beaumont and Fletcher, John Webster and the rest of them were gone; even Donne, who had tuned, or untuned, English poetry to a new mood, had died a year ago. Herrick was in his prime, but his lyric purpose was not to reflect this age or that. Of the splendid company of poets who made the long turn of the century into a Virginian voyage of the imagination, Ben Jonson alone, in what then passed for old age, was surviving his successes. It was but a year or two since the laureate sent from his neglect and penury to ask the King for an alms. Charles I sent him ten guineas. 'His Majesty has sent me ten guineas because I am poor and live in an alley; go and tell him that his soul lives in an alley.' It is a story worth noting by those who advance Charles's patronage of the arts in his favour.

These men would not have been unknown in the society of middle-class trading folk into which Pepys was born. But other men, and events other than poetry, no doubt more closely claimed their attention. James I had died in 1625, and in the same year Francis Bacon closed the majestic tragedy of his broken fortune and broken honour. The care of England was handed on to the first Charles and to George Villiers, the Buckingham whose assassination three years later was lamented by none but an infatuated master.

The reign of James I, in spite of the sovereign's will, was
largely Elizabethan in character, but with the coming of
Charles, the Stuart influence seemed to be established. By
the time that Samuel Pepys was born there were already
signs that the establishment was infirm. The Tudor power,
brutal and tyrannous as it could be towards persons, had
always had a lively sense of its responsibility to the people.
It worked by an instrument that seems formidable to our
modern theory of liberty, and it may have worked largely
to interested ends, but there it was. And it was a sense that
was now being alienated from the practice of government.
The lives of the people were being threatened by they knew
not what danger; up and down the country the minds of
men were disturbed. And by nobody was the growing
anxiety so deeply realised as by the men in all classes upon
whom rested the burden of the nation's daily work. There
were families too powerful or too well-disposed to be seriously affected by Court meddling, and there were humble
folk who found some security in being beneath Court notice.
But the squires and the farmers, the professional men, the
merchants and the tradesmen were conscious of a menace
that had not yet plainly declared itself. There is nothing to
tell us what were the political views of John Pepys, earning
a modest livelihood as a tailor just outside the city walls,
but in common with his fellow citizens, he must have asked
himself what would come of my Lord Wentworth's accession to Court favour, and when his boy Samuel was two
years old there was matter for more than evening gossip
when 'the Mayor, Commonalty and Citizens' of London
informed the King, with expressions of devoted loyalty,
that they positively would not pay Ship Money. A year
later John Hampden was to say the same thing even more
decisively.

This John Pepys was a tailor who lived in St. Bride's
Churchyard off Fleet Street, two hundred yards or so west
of the City boundary at the old Fleet Ditch. The obscure
London tradesman came of substantial middle-class stock,
with origins at Cottenham in Cambridgeshire. A fourteenth

century Pepys was a protégé of an abbot of Crowland, or Croyland, who had migrated to Huntingdonshire from Scotland. Samuel's cousin Roger told him of a document recording twenty-six householders of the name in Cottenham during Elizabeth's reign. No less than seventeen spellings of the name have been noted. In the Cottenham registers I find what appear to be Pepis, Pepyes, and Pepys. It is clear in any case that there was no family uniformity in the matter, and the same thing no doubt applied to the pronunciation of the name. Samuel, it is reasonably certain, called himself Peeps. Mr. Edward Hoare has recently discovered that in the books of his bank, where Samuel had an account, the name is spelt Pepies, and puts this in as evidence that the pronunciation was Peppis. A rhyme of 1675:

> Him I must praise, who opened hath my lips,
> Sent me from Navy, to the Ark, by Pepys,

suggests also that someone called him Pips. But it is common enough even for acquaintances to be erratic about a difficult name, and the evidence as to Samuel's own use is sufficient. There are three sources of unbroken tradition—the descendants of his sister Paulina, the Sandwich family, and Magdalene College, Cambridge. All are unequivocally for Peeps. The family had an agreeable taste in nomenclature. John's father was Thomas, who, having a brother called Thomas also, was distinguished as Thomas the Black from Thomas the Red. John, further, had an uncle Talbot who became Recorder of Cambridge in 1624, and, better still, an uncle Apollo.

John was born in 1601, and so was over thirty years of age when Samuel, his fifth child, was born. His wife was Margaret Kight, of whose family standing we have a single glimpse in the fact that her brother was a butcher of Whitechapel. There were in all eleven children of the marriage, but Samuel, Thomas, John, and Paulina alone survived childhood. The struggling father of this household was as yet many years from being established in trade by admission to his City Company. He was, in fact, at present regarded as one of those foreigners whose competition was such that the 'Freemen of the said Company using the trade of Cutting Taylors cannot live upon their calling but are necessitated to crave and receive Alms of the said Company so that many poor families of the said cutting taylors are in grievous want and the said Company by relieving so great a number may in time become unable to bear their own or the common charges of the City.' It was not until 1649 that the Court of the Company referred back 'to the favourable consideration of the committee,' the petition of 'John Pepys a foreign tailor dwelling in Bride's Churchyard,' with the recommendation that, 'having lived in the same place for thirty-six years as apprentice and master, and having duly paid all scot and lot,' he should be elected with the caution 'that so as they shall do in favour to him the same to be no precedent for the future for any others.' Samuel's father had to wait until 1653 for admission to the freedom. He celebrated the occasion by presenting the Company with a Silver Tankard and a Trencher Salt.

It needs a somewhat close effort of the imagination to realise what the London of the seventeenth century before the Great Fire in 1666 was like, both within the walls and without. Two or three centuries may make very little difference to the nature of man, but they can make a difference that is almost incalculable to the conditions in which he lives. The London into which Samuel Pepys was born was entirely Elizabethan in character. Its principal thoroughfare was the river, towards which the architectural features of the city fronted. Above this pleasant water-line of buildings rose the spires of over a hundred city churches, dominated by the great mass of St. Paul's. To a distant view the aspect was delightful, with a charming distinction that has been recorded with obvious accuracy by Wenceslaus Hollar. But the enchantment of the view very notably lay in its distance. At close quarters the eye found less satisfaction. but even so it found a good deal more than the nose. Building by building, the Elizabethan houses had in their design no little of the character of a great age, but the design of the city as a whole had disappeared in a congestion that was tightening yearly from wall to wall. The streets were mostly so narrow that the top storeys of opposing buildings allowed but a foot or two of skylight to penetrate faintly to the cobbles below. The over-crowding in the poorer quarters of the town had forced the population of large areas to live in squalid tenement houses at the rate of a family to a room, had even forced it into patchwork hovels and underground, in conditions no better than barbarous. Constantly over this scene, intensifying its gloom and grime, hung a heavily charged smoke cloud, sometimes drifting away to offend the nicer neighbourhood of Whitehall and the west. Evelyn complained of 'the hellish and dismal Cloud of sea-coal' which caused the city of London to 'resemble the suburbs of hell.' The confined thoroughfares were frequently made altogether impassable by trucks and barrows and bales of merchandise that were deposited anywhere at anybody's will. Through the day the crackling of wheels on stones mingled incessantly with the shrill outcry of hawkers and the competitive bidding of apprentices, scolding or persuading the passers-by into their masters' shops. By night the streets were unlit save at a point of vantage here and there where private enterprise or some charitable bequest provided a single candle, with light feebly penetrating its case of horn.

The population within and without the walls was something less than 150,000, according to a census taken by Sir Robert Ducie, the Lord Mayor, in 1630, although a computation of 1636, made during the Lord Mayoralty of Sir Edward Bromfield, gives the figure at that date as being 700,000. In 1681 it was estimated that the numbers had risen to a million and a half. At the time of Pepys's birth, the population, whatever the precise extent of it may have been, was living at a physical pressure that, within the walls at least, must have seemed very near breaking point. If

London is crowded to-day, it was no less crowded then, and in conditions upon which happily we can only speculate. The plague had already made its visitations, and the resources of the city graveyards were already strained. Of sanitary decencies there were none. The great Fleet Ditch had long since become a public offence and scandal, and now the filth of every household was thrown into the street to disperse as it might in the next rain along the gutters. Foul vapours crept through every crevice of the city, laying up everywhere the terrible infection that was to liberate itself in the horror of 1665.

These were the conditions of London citizenship when Samuel Pepys was born. The picturesque traffic of the water front and the habits of life that converged upon it were the escape from what otherwise could hardly have been tolerable. The houses built across London Bridge, which alone connected the city with the south side, looked down upon an unending passage of boats plying for public hire between the Tower and the ampler spaces of the parks beyond Westminster. And within a short walk of the walls lay for the citizens who were so disposed the pleasant fields of Hoxton and Stepney and Islington and Bethnal Green.

From the years 1659 to 1669, that is to say from the twenty-seventh to the thirty-seventh year of his age, Samuel Pepys kept a diary which is in many respects the completest record of a biographical decade that has ever been made. As to the remaining sixty years of his life, our information is scanty, and with regard to the period before he began the Diary we have to shape our portrait from slender strays of evidence. Nevertheless, just enough of fact is ascertainable to leave us, if not with any considerable knowledge of what he did, at least with some not negligible sense of the circumstances and environment that influenced his early life. We know from the records of Magdalene College, Cambridge, that he entered that establishment in 1650, transferring from Trinity Hall, to which College he had gone up in the same year, but our earlier dates must depend upon surmise. In April 1664, Samuel and his wife, 'conquered, with much ado, a desire of going to a play,' and went instead for a drive through Whitechapel and Bethnal Green, and 'so to Hackney, where I have not been many a year, since a little child I boarded there. Thence to Kingsland, by my nurse's house, Goody Lawrence, where my brother Tom and I was kept when young.' And again in May 1667, 'Our dinner cost us 6s., and so my wife and I away to Islington, it being a fine day . . . and walked over the fields to Kingsland, and back again; a walk, I think, I have not taken these twenty year; but puts me in mind of my boy's time, when I boarded at Kingsland, and used to shoot with my bow and arrows in these fields. A very pretty place it is; and little did any of my friends think I should come to walk in these fields in this condition and state that I am.' John Pepys, it is reasonable to suppose, found St. Bride's Churchyard no very suitable place for a crowding family of young children, and was glad enough to have one or two of them taken off his hands by obliging relatives. Kingsland was near enough to home, and there was an aunt Ellen Kight living at Islington. It is assumed by Mr. Wheatley that these Kingsland days were in Samuel's very early childhood, before he went to Huntingdon. I think, however, that they more probably belong to the time when he was attending St. Paul's School. The reference to 'twenty years' in the note of 1667, which seems to overlook the visit of 1664, would take us back to 1647 when Samuel was fourteen, by which date he is likely to have left the Grammar School at Huntingdon for St. Paul's in London. There are difficulties in this conjecture, the chief one being that while St. Paul's School was less than a mile from St. Bride's Churchyard, it was more than two from Kingsland. On the other hand, a careful examination of the passages just quoted lends colour to the theory. When he speaks of his friends not foreseeing the time when he should 'walk in these fields in this condition and state,' Pepys, who uses language precisely, would seem to be referring to a time twenty years ago not when he made a casual visit to Kingsland, but when he was habitually there. Moreover, as a schoolboy of

fourteen he could have had friends to whom his future state
might have been given a thought at least, while he is unlikely to have pictured himself being considered in this connection as a child hardly out of infancy. Further, from the
entry of 1664, we gather that he had lived both at Hackney
and Kingsland, which were adjoining neighbourhoods. He
there says explicitly that he had not been to Hackney since
he boarded there. It is true that he does not use these words
of Kingsland, but he does refer to it merely as the place
'where my brother Tom and I was kept when young.' If,
in fact, he had visited Kingsland since that date, he would
in making his notes have been likely to mention the circumstance as distinguishing in his mind the impressions made
upon him by the two places at the age of thirty-one. That
he does not do so suggests strongly that in 1664 he had
seen neither Hackney nor Kingsland since he boarded there.
As in 1667 he says that he had not been to Kingsland for
twenty years, it follows, if our reasoning be right, that he
had 'boarded there' until 1647, when he was fourteen years
old. The presumption is that between that date and his
admission to Cambridge, he lived again with his father.

As we shall now see, he appears to have left Huntingdon Grammar School when he was eleven. This would leave
a period of three years in the charge of one whom the
man of thirty-five might naturally enough remember as his
nurse Goody Lawrence, and it would be natural, too, for
him, using the Pepysian idiom, to write of himself between
the ages of eleven and fourteen as a little child. Finally,
there is the consideration that Samuel's uncle Robert Pepys,
of whom we shall hear directly, till the end of his life
showed an attachment for this nephew, which must have
been formed during the boy's Huntingdon Grammar School
days. It is reasonable to suppose that Samuel was promoted
from Huntingdon to St. Paul's by his uncle's favour and at
his expense. It may very well have been that it was Robert
rather than John who then thought it better for the boy to
be boarded out away from the congestion of St. Bride's

Churchyard. The proposal would no doubt be readily enough received by the father, but I seem to see the uncle's interest behind it. We may note in passing that there is an entry in the Brampton register, 'Goody Lawrence Widow was buried the 21st day of March 1676.' May this not be the nurse, sent by Robert Pepys to London in charge of his small nephew, and returning in her old age to her native place?

Uncle Robert Pepys in 1630 had married a widow, Anne Trice, of Brampton, a village lying two miles out of Huntingdon. The Trice family was of ancient standing in the neighbourhood. A Thomas Tryce de Godmanchester had been associated with the founding of the free grammar school of that town in 1558, and his genealogy as given by Robert Fox in his history of Godmanchester shows that he had sons, Richard Tryce de Stukely Magna and Jasper Tryce de Brampton. In the marriage papers, the bridegroom is described as Robert Pepys of Hinchingbrooke. Hinchingbrooke, which is situated midway between Huntingdon and Brampton, is the name of a mansion and not of a village, and Robert's designation can mean only that he was in some capacity on the establishment of the house. His office, whatever it was, would be a considerable one. Hinchingbrooke had been bought in 1627 from Sir Oliver Cromwell, the young Oliver's uncle, by Sir Sidney Montagu, whose wife was none other than Paulina Pepys, the sister of the Thomases Black and Red. She was, therefore, Robert Pepys's aunt, and it is to her influence that we may ascribe her nephew's presence in the household. That his position was in a modest way a thriving one we may gather from the respect which his nephew Samuel, who was at no time unmindful of worldly affairs, consistently pays him in the Diary. Again, the evidence is slight, but it leads us to natural and probable conclusions. Robert was now man enough to be able to lend a hand to his not very prosperous brother, the tailor of St. Bride's Churchyard. An offer of keep and schooling in the country to one of the little Lon-

don boys could not fail of a welcome, and somewhere about
1640, when he was not yet ten years old, Samuel came down
to Huntingdon to school.

There are but two entries in the Diary that throw light
on this period, but they place Samuel's early education at
Huntingdon beyond doubt. In March, 1660, he 'met Tom
Alcock, one that went to school with me at Huntingdon,
but I had not seen him these sixteen years.' Here, as always,
we have to bear in mind Pepys's manner of writing. Everything went down direct from his mind to the page. It cannot be said from the evidence of the Diary that he was
always a limpid stylist; indeed, there are many passages
when he is discussing technical or business affairs so ob-
scurely involved as hardly to repay the trouble of elucida-
tion. But, in noting his daily record of events, his method
was not subtle, and if sometimes it was not wholly explicit
it was never deliberately equivocal. When, as often happens, a passage can be read in two ways, the solution will
nearly always be found in following, as is not difficult, the
passage of his thought from the mind to the page. Whether
Pepys really intended that his Diary should never become
public property is a question for later discussion, but it is
clear at least that when he was writing it his purpose was
not to explain himself to other people, but, for his own
amusement, to make a record that, written in shorthand,
was also at times shaped in a shorthand of the mind. This
point need not be further argued, but it is, I think, one always to be remembered when reading the Diary, as helping
us often to place the right construction on Pepys's meaning. When, for example, we read, 'I met Tom Alcock, one
that went to school with me at Huntingdon, but I had not
seen him these sixteen years,' two inferences may reasonably be made. Although Pepys does not precisely say so,
we may conclude that the last time that he saw Tom Alcock
was at school at Huntingdon, and secondly, although again
the precise statement is not made, that the time referred
to was the end of his own Huntingdon schooldays. Had he
seen Alcock since being with him at Huntingdon, he cer-

tainly would not have phrased his note just like that, nor would he be likely in making his notes to calculate nicely the exact term or year in which he and Alcock were together. He would merely, we may be sure, remember that he had not seen Alcock since he was at school with him, and that it was sixteen years since he himself had left Huntingdon. It has seemed worth while to examine this entry with some particularity as showing the way in which doubtful passages in the Diary as a whole will be regarded in this book.

We may take it, then, that Samuel was at the Huntingdon Grammar School until 1644, when he was eleven years old. After his marriage with Anne Trice in 1630, Robert Pepys had moved to Brampton, and it was doubtless at this time that he bought the house which later became his nephew Samuel's property. It is in this house that the present lines are being written. Samuel, in later days, enlarged it, but when he first knew it in his childhood, it was a small affair of six rooms pleasantly situated twenty yards or so back from the Huntingdon turnpike, with a flat expanse of meadows behind it broken by a line of willows on the banks of the quietly drifting Ouse less than half a mile away. Looking from the upper windows across the bend of the road to the east, the roofs of Hinchingbrooke could be seen, now concealed by a later growth of trees. That this was so we know from the following letter written to Pepys in 1697 by the Reverend John Turner of Eynesbury:

Eynesbury, March 4, 1696 [-7].

Sir,

Just now I had a messenger from my Lord Sandwich desiring that I should write to you and request in my Lord's name that you will please to graunt His Lordship leave to cut down the top of an hedge of yours in Brampton field which hinders his Lordship's prospect. Sir, I should give you trouble to no purpose in describing the hedge and circumstances of what my Lord desires. I will say this only, which I am well assured will have creditt with you, Sir; I know that which my Lord desires of you will not be five shillinge damage to yourselfe or your tenant, and that which you would not deny to his Lordship though neither he nor his ancestors had bin known to you.

Sir, my Lord also requires me to request of you a word or two in answer to his Lordship's desire that upon your graunt he may trim 3 or 4 yards of the hedge in right season of the year. Sir, I am gladde of this service to my Lord, which gives me opportunity (without troubling you with a particular letter) to give you most humble thanks for the many great favours which in severall occasions you have most readily conferred on me, and shall be most gratefully remembred as long as I live. Sir, you know I am an old man, but if God prolong my life till summer I shall have a mind once more to see London and wait on my friends there. Sir, I present my most reall and hearty service to you, and am, Sir, Your very much obliged and faithful servant, JOHN TURNER.

Sir, if you write to me let it be by the St. Neotts bagg.

Brampton, which in a distant age had been favoured by Kings Stephen and John and Henry II as a hunting chase, was, as it still remains, an agricultural village straggling away to the north from a church of which the tower, as we know from the date on the porch, was rebuilt in 1635. Hitherto there had been '5 great belles in the Steaple and on littell bell.' It was not until 1927 that Mr. Whitear, working upon Mr. Walter G. Bell's discovery in the St. Bride's registers, dispelled the long-persistent tradition that it was at Brampton that Samuel Pepys was born. One authority after another had accepted the statement, and even Wheatley could do no more than say that as the registers of Brampton church do not go back beyond 1654, it could not be confirmed. Pepys himself makes no reference to the event, but public information on the matter in his own time seems to have been accurate. In the year of his death, 1703, an annual publication, calling itself *A Compleat History of Europe: or, a View of the Affairs thereof,*

Civil and Military, for the Year 1703, published an obituary notice which opens as follows:

Pepys (Samuel) Esq., Secretary of the Admiralty of England to their late Majesties K. Charles and K. James II and one of the greatest ornaments of his Age, departed this Life the 26th instant [May]. He was descended of the Ancient Family of the Pepys's of Cottenham in Cambridgeshire, born in London Anno 1632 [O. S.] and had his maturer Education at St. Paul's school there, and Magdalen College in the University of Cambridge.

Mr. Whitear's evidence on the subject is conclusive, but Samuel was at Brampton early enough to be in contact there with affairs that were of great consequence in the gathering clouds of national life, and destined to be of capital importance in his own career. The Grammar School in Huntingdon was an institution founded with the Hospital of St. John as long ago as the twelfth century. It is a small square building of Norman ecclesiastical style, standing flush up to the foot-walk in the main street of the town. But in Pepys's time its aspect was Elizabethan, the overlay of that later generation having been removed only in recent times. The registers of the school, if, indeed, such ever existed, have disappeared, but one or two facts happily survive to our purpose. I have been able to recover from the school archives a document from which the following is an extract:

This Indenture made the three & twentith day of March [1624] . . . Betweene the Bayliffs and Burgesses of the Towne of Huntingdon . . . Patrons of the Hospitall of Snt John . . . of the one parte And Thomas Beard Dtor in Divinity and Master of the said Hospitall and Robt Cooke of Huntingdon aforesaid Gent. of the other parte.

Whereas there is fower parish Churches wthin the said Towne of Huntingdon, the Liveing belonging to the same being so small as none of them are sufficient or convenient to maintain a learned Preacher by reason whereof all the said Pishes and Towne of Huntingdon were for a long time before the said Thomas Beard became Master of the said Hospitall utterly destitute of a learned Preacher to teach and instruct them in the word of God. But sithence the said Thomas Beard became Master of the said Hospitall being admitted thereunto by the psentacon of the said Bayliffs and Burgesses The said Thomas Beard hath not only maintained a Grammar Schoole in the said Towne according to the foundacon of the said Hospitall, by himselfe and a Schoolmaster by him pvided at his owne charges But hathe allso beene continually ressident in the said Towne & painefully preached the word of God in the said Towne of Hunt on the Saboth day dewly to the great comfort of the Inhabitants of the said Towne And the said Thomas Beard being care-full and desirous that some learned Preacher may suc-ceed him in the said Hospitall who may be resident in the said Towne and preach there so long as he shall hold the said place in like manner as the said Thomas Beard hath done intendeth to doe and maintaine also the said Schoole as he hath done . . . The said Bayliffs and Burgesses have . . . granted . . . unto the said Thomas Beard his Executors and assignes the next psentacon to the said Hospitall when it shall next become voide by any meanes . . . And foreasmuch as he the said Robert Cooke hath a Sonne named Henry Cooke whoe is a faith-full and learned [?] and Minister of God's word who both the said Thomas Beard and all or the most part of the Inhabitants of the said Towne doe very well like and approve off . . . Therefore the said Robert Cooke doth covennt . . . that if the said Henry Cooke shall . . . be psented to the said Hospitall at the next avoydance thereof . . . he shall . . . be resident in the said Towne and ordinarily on the Saboth dayes preach the word of God there . . . And shall also by himself or some other sufficient Schoolemaster by him to be pvided

BRAMPTON CHURCH, APPROACHED FROM PEPYS HOUSE

Photograph by E. S. Whitney.

at his own cost and charges maintain a grammar Schoole
in the same Hospitall . . .

                       Tho: Beard   Ro: Cooke

Sealed and delivered in the presence of us.
    Robert Bernard
    John Turpen
    Henry Cooke
    Henry Bralin
    Sam: Johnson

This Thomas Beard was a person of some consequence in
his day as the author of a now forgotten theological work,
and as a champion of the rights of conscience under Laud's
nose in London, but he takes a more memorable place in
history as the schoolmaster who taught Oliver Cromwell.
We do not know the date at which he handed on his duties
to Henry Cooke; indeed, I find the record of no further
appointment until a document of 1680, when John Matthews was given the mastership of the school at an annual
salary of £20 and the use of the schoolhouse 'upon payment of a peppercorn rent at the Feast of St. Michael the
Archangel if demanded.' Beard died in 1632, and so was
no more than a memory when Pepys was at the school.
Events were moving in the world, however, that must have
made the memory a living one. For the events were rever-
berating to very notable and fateful purpose in Huntingdon. In 1642, old Sidney Montagu of Hinchingbrooke,
seventy years and more of age, suffered imprisonment in
the Tower for refusing to take the oath of allegiance to
the Parliamentary Army under Essex, and crying traitor
on those who did so. He was released after a few days, but
returned to Hinchingbrooke with a heavy heart. For there
his son Edward, a boy of seventeen, who was just marry-
ing Jemimah Crew, the daughter of an ardent Parliamen-
tarian house, was eager with what to his father were treasonable enthusiasms. These were inspired chiefly by that
Huntingdon burgess who, having moved from his native
town to St. Ives and thence to Ely, was now at the age of

forty-three making his first decided bid towards control of the national destinies. Oliver Cromwell, long known among his own people for his resistance to sundry encroachments upon common rights, was now turning his mind and his energies to charters of a wider scope. In 1643, after Edgehill, he was back in his own shire prophesying the wrath and the salvation to come. The enlistment of the Ironsides had begun. The newly formed Eastern Association drew young Edward Montagu into its fiery discipline, and he became a leader among the band of boys of good breeding from whom Cromwell chose his first lieutenants. He raised his own regiment, to join the forces now under command of his cousin the Earl of Manchester of Kimbolton, Major-General of the Associated Counties. The old father could endure these things no longer, and, handing over Hinchingbrooke to his son's keeping, he retired to another estate, consoling an embittered old age with a new wife, whose company he lived to enjoy less than a year.

Pepys, child though he was, cannot have been unaware of these family convulsions, which must have been so freely debated in his uncle's household. Across the fens and the east midlands the excitement was at highest pitch. The long quarrel had declared itself in civil war at last, and in those early days of the struggle Huntingdon was at the very heart of the temper that most firmly took the issue in hand. Troops were moving, rumours flying, oddly clad little groups of men drilling tirelessly on the commons, in the barns, in the streets. Cromwell himself was constantly coming and going from the town where his influence had first been asserted. In the daily course of events, it is certain that the young scholar of the Grammar School must not infrequently have seen the heavily featured man in buff and black, even in buff and steel, riding through the town, and have stood with his companions to watch Mr. Cromwell who once had done his reading and writing in their own classroom. Pepys says nothing of these circumstances in his Diary, but then he says little of any circumstances before its opening. In 1662, then a stout and prospering royalist, he took breakfast at Cambridge in 'the room where Cromwell and his associated officers did begin to plot and act their mischiefs in these counties,' though he had other thoughts to occupy his morning, being served with bad oysters and getting ten miles out of his way on the Royston road. In 1667, however, he agreed one day with his naval friends at dinner, that 'Cromwell was a brave fellow, and did owe his crowne he got to himself as much as any man that ever got one,' and, with a natural taste for horrors, he was, neverthless, shocked when the order for Cromwell's disinterment was made, 'that a man of so great courage as he was, should have that dishonour.'

What all these things were about the Huntingdon schoolboy would be unlikely to ask himself, but he would know that his own family was somehow important on account of them. The house he lived in was a little one, but in the great house that he passed daily on his walk to school there lived a dashing young cousin, hardly older than his own oldest schoolfellows, with an attractive and friendly wife, who herself was just her husband's age, and he would be a little proud of the relationship. Sometimes there would be a visit to the Castle, as it was known in the neighbourhood, and there he would see great preparations going forward, and hear how this Mr. Cromwell was becoming a very great man indeed. Young married couples, and with affairs of such moment on their hands, have not much attention to spare for small cousins who are commonly pickles, but here was the beginning of a friendship that was to mean much to three lives. If Cromwell was to have no more devoted servant than Edward Montagu, Montagu was himself to have no more devoted servant than Samuel Pepys, and Mistress Jemimah, as my Lady Sandwich, was to learn how staunch that devotion could be. Already before he left the Grammar School, Samuel could find occasion for hero worship in the exploits of his cousin Edward. In 1644, Colonel Montagu and his men were in the front of the

attack at Marston Moor, and 'stood as a wall of brasse';
thenceforth the advancement of the Puritan cause was his
own.

The Brampton house, as has been said, was a little one,
and as Anne Trice when she married Robert Pepys was already the mother of seven children, it must have been
sufficiently crowded. We do not know how many of them
came into the new household, but there is evidence to show
that at least six of them survived childhood, and none·to
suggest that most of them were more than children at the
time of their mother's second marriage. There is a record
of a Jasper Trice holding land at Brampton in 1630, who
may have been the eldest of the family, and the 'Jasper
Trice, Gent' who was buried in 1675. If so, we may assume
that he was a very young landowner. It is worth noting
that in 1661, when Pepys and his father inherited the
Brampton house under Robert's will, Samuel, although he
was engaged with Tom and Jasper Trice in a tiresome legal
dispute, speaks of them from the first as though they were
acquaintances of long standing, and with personal intimacy;
'Jasper Trice myself and others at Mother —— over
against the Crown, we sat and drank ale and were very
merry till 9 at night.' And, again, 'I staid with Thos. Trice
and Mr. Philips drinking till noon . . . home to my father,
who could discern that I had been drinking, which he did
never see or hear of before.' It is probable that between
his Huntingdon school days and his inheritance of the
Brampton property, Pepys made occasional visits to the
neighbourhood, particularly as by the date of his marriage
in 1655 his relationship with the Montagus had become intimate. Moreover, there were the three years of his residence
at Cambridge when the sixteen-mile journey to Huntingdon could be made with comparative ease. But it is unlikely
that after his school days he was often at Brampton until
he had property of his own to take him there. In the early
days, when Pepys was young and poor, the cost of the journey from London was not lightly to be undertaken, and
although his uncle Robert may sometimes have indulged

his affection for a respectful and intelligent nephew by standing the expenses, the treat was doubtless an infrequent one. The familiar note in his references to Tom and Jasper in 1662 derives, I think, from his early days when he was living in the same house as the Trices, and, as likely as not, going to school with the younger children.

Pepys was a round-faced stockish little man, and we see him as a round-faced rather fat little boy. That he already had observant eyes is suggested by a single entry in the Diary, when in 1668 after a frolic drinking at Goody Gorum's he took his party on for further refreshment at the Chequers in Huntingdon 'where I observed the same tapster, Tom, that was there when I was a little boy.' Pepys was then thirty-five years of age, when it is not too common to remember a face seen casually at ten. The routine of his school days would not be without adventures other than those of wars, alarms, and the mysterious goings on at the great house. Huntingdon enjoyed a peculiar notoriety as a breeding place of witchcraft, and the public mind reassured itself at intervals by the spectacle of some miserable old creature being consumed by faggots in the public streets. There is record of a double burning in 1646. Samuel, in later days, had an unlovely turn for this kind of thing, and it may well have had instruction thus early in Huntingdon. So strong a hold had this particular brand of fanaticism in the district, that as late as 1808 four men and five women were convicted at Huntingdon assizes for a succession of brutal assaults upon an old farm wife who was accused of throwing people into fits by the aid of magic, and who volunteered to prove her innocence by being weighed against the church Bible. The offenders were locked up for inadequate terms in the Huntingdon gaol, and even then the persecution did not cease. I have been even told that there are witches not a dozen miles away from Huntingdon still.

Less sensational, but not without its allurements, was the daily adventure of the journeys between Brampton and school. The two-mile walk was a simple matter enough in summer, and on occasion a penny or two would enlist the services of a local carrier. But in the winter, when the swollen Ouse, reinforced by the overflow from Bedford Levels, spread across the Hinchingbrooke meadows and made the road impassable, there was the excitement of wading through the floods, or, better still, of not being able to go to school at all. A word should here be added for the honour of Brampton, to one of Lord Braybrooke's notes in his edition of the Diary. Says Pepys in 1667: 'This day coming from Westminster . . . we saw . . . a fisher-boat, with a sturgeon that he had newly catched in the River; which I saw, but it was but a little one; not big enough to prevent my mistake of that for a colt, if ever I become Mayor of Huntingdon.' Braybrooke tells us that during a high flood the men of Huntingdon and the men of Godmanchester fell into dispute as to the nature of an object that was seen floating on the waters. But he does not tell us that certain good men of Brampton also were present. The Godmanchester men declared it to be a black hog, but Huntingdon opinion was fixed that it was a sturgeon. The literal Brampton mind declared it to be nothing but a donkey, and donkey it was. And to-day, after three hundred years, the Huntingdon man who is not quite all he might be may still pass for a Huntingdon sturgeon in the Brampton taprooms. The name was current in Pepys's time.

Of the character of the education given at the Grammar School when Pepys was there we can form some idea from the indenture appointing the John Matthews aforesaid to the mastership. He is

to instruct in Greek & Latin Tongues such ch^n of the s^d Mayor Ald^n & Burgesses of the Boro. as are or shall be fit & capable & as shall for that purpose be sent & to qualify them for the Universities of this Land if their parents or Gov^{rs} shall desire the same . . .

Matthews himself was a Master of Arts, and it is clear that a boy could here be as well grounded for the universities as at the public schools of greater reputation. If its tradition was not adorned, as was that of St. Paul's to which the young Pepys was now to be transferred, by so great a name as that of John Colet, it is clear that the burgesses of Huntingdon took their school very seriously, and that Dr. Beard had set a standard of learning and discipline that was not unworthy of one of the most enlightened centres of the great age of English Puritanism. It may be noted that Edward Montagu, when he was Lord Sandwich, sent his twin sons, John and Oliver, to the school.

In 1644, when Pepys rode back to London to enter St. Paul's School, Laud was about to follow Strafford to the block, and the Parliamentary forces were consolidating from the success of Marston Moor towards the decisive field of Naseby in the following year. The school building that Pepys knew as a boy was destroyed with its records in the Great Fire, but that the five or six years which he spent there were happily employed is suggested by the active and friendly interest that he took in the school during his later life. It is a pleasing circumstance that he should have gone from the school that reared Cromwell to the one that reared Milton. It is not encouraging to find that there is not a single reference to the great Puritan poet in the Diary. It may be mentioned that on retiring from his European tour in 1639 Milton lodged for a short time, in Johnson's words, 'At the house of one Russel a taylor in St. Bride's Churchyard.' The High Master of St. Paul's was John Langley, a licenser of the Press, who was just publishing a treatise on rhetoric for the benefit of his scholars. Pepys makes no allusions to him, but he tells us something of Samuel Crumlum. He was Head Master of the Chapel School belonging to the Mercers' Company, the governing body of St. Paul's Foundation, and was promoted to the sub-mastership of the latter school in 1647, becoming High Master on Langley's death ten years later. Crumlum was a scholar of parts, and Pepys, who used to call on him frequently in later years, when taking his constitutional walks from the Navy Office, admired his learning but formed no

very high opinion of his character. On a September afternoon of 1662, he found his old master considerably flown
with wine much to the impairment of his wit, 'that though I
honour the man, and he do declare abundance of learning
and worth, yet I confess my opinion is much lessened of
him, and therefore let it be a caution to myself not to
love drink, since it has such an effect upon others of greater
worth in my own esteem.' As Pepys 'could not avoid' drinking five glasses with him in the afternoon, and found another friend later in the evening with whom also he could
not avoid a prolonged sitting, we may detect a personal
note in the grievance. The acquaintance did not improve
with time, although it remained civil enough. Pepys liked to
show him the treasures of his collection, and gave him presents of books for the school. He was flattered when on
Apposition Day the Master 'did me much honour by telling many what a present I had made to the school, showing
my Stephanus, in four volumes, cost me £4. 10s.,' and later
he made the gift up to £5 by adding 10s. for 'strings, and
golden letters upon the books.' But in 1665, he breaks out
with 'Lord! to see how ridiculous a conceited pedagogue he
is, though a learned man, he being so dogmaticall in all he
do and say.' Whether these pedagogic aspects had been
acquired when Crumlum first came to the school in 1647
and Pepys was still a scholar we are not told. Mrs. Crumlum is mentioned as a pretty woman, who found some of
the boys more pleasing to look at than her husband.

In 1660, Pepys found himself sitting with official dignity
at the King's Council for Trade in Mercers' Hall, and 'It
pleased me much now to come in this condition to this place,
where I was once a petitioner for my exhibition in St. Paul's
School.' On the Apposition Day above mentioned, he saw
'the head forms posed in Latin, Greek, and Hebrew,' and
assured himself that 'they did not answer in any so well
as we did, only in geography they did pretty well'; the
speeches, also, 'were just as schoolboys' used to be . . .
but I think not so good as ours were in our time.' In 1664,
he spent an evening with 'my old Jack Cole . . . a man

of good parts, but, I fear, debauched . . . talking of old school stories, and very pleasing ones, and truly I find that we did spend our time and thoughts then otherwise than I think boys do now, and I think as well as methinks that the best are now . . . And strange to see how we are all divided that were bred so long at school together, and what various fortunes we have run, some good, some bad.'

Among Pepys's other schoolfellows at St. Paul's was Richard Cumberland, who became afterwards Rector of Brampton, and came within reasonable distance of taking Paulina Pepys with him as his wife to the Bishopric of Peterborough; Thomas Davies, afterwards Lord Mayor of London, and a bookseller credited with the astonishing feat of having forgiven a scrivener a debt of £60,000; Thomas Elborough, 'a silly fellow,' 'a fool,' and 'a simple rogue,' who nevertheless preached as good a sermon in 1666 as Pepys ever heard; and one Christmas, who on a certain occasion was to cause Pepys grave anxiety.

Industry and an aptitude for making the most of opportunities were characteristic of Pepys throughout his life, and the general tone of the scattered references to his schooldays indicates that he took his education seriously. He had a literal enquiring mind, eager for information, and careful of its resources. No man was ever less of a prude, but at least he could claim at the end of a long and ample life that his heart had at no time hardened against repentance. The astonishing self-revelation of the Diary shows us a man who, whatever his indulgences, never lost hold of a certain dry formality, a methodical efficiency, in the conduct of life. Candour need not blush to acknowledge that his drinkings and his rompings were perfectly consistent with an orderly and a provident application to affairs. If he was not proof against private temptations, he did not sacrifice his public utility to them. It is deeply significant of his character that while he was one of those devoted playgoers who can enjoy a bad play almost as much as a good one, who, indeed, are often unable to distinguish one from the other, he was constantly chiding himself for wasting his

time and his money at the theatres. He was never confident
that however engaging the traffic of the stage, and particularly the ladies of the stage, might be, the drama was quite
fit employment for a man of intellectual balance. For poetry
he had, and professed, neither taste nor understanding. He
was attracted to the fashionable portrait painters of the
time, who happened also to be very good painters, largely
by their social interest. He had what later criticism would
regard as a strangely simple-minded taste for pictures of
people and places that he knew. He read widely, but not for
the imaginative elements in literature. It was in music alone
among the arts that the emotional side of his nature found
full scope, and for music he had a genuine passion. For
the rest, he had the curious, elegant inclinations of the
connoisseur. He liked acquiring charming and interesting
things, and liked to display them tidily. He was proud of
his beautiful collection of books, and the prouder because
they were uniformly bound and exquisitely tooled, and to
arrange them in their handsome presses was a delight almost as great as to read them. He pasted his prints and
his scraps into folios with loving care, and indexed them
with a scrupulous eye for the adornment of a page. His
affections, his sense of fun, his musical enthusiasm, and his
social appetites were continually running away with a somewhat austere gentleman of refined taste. Half the differences with his wife arose from her insensibility to these pre-
ciser habits of his mind. He had no objection to a woman
being a baggage, but he could not abide a sloven.

It was this neatly regulated Pepys, the Pepys of the
Royal Society and the Naval Accounts, rather than the
Pepys who was to tousle Deb. Willett and grow faint at
the strains of a favourite air, who was in the making at
St. Paul's School. A knowledge of tongues, a talent for calculation, and some acquaintance with the lessons of history, these were things that could be turned to account in
some career, and these things were cultivated. Good handwriting was by no means to be neglected, and it must have

been in these early days that Pepys began to train himself to the beautiful penmanship of his later life.

Pepys left St. Paul's School in 1650, and in the meantime the Civil War had reached the first of its two great crises with the execution of the King in 1649. Edward Montagu had been prominent in these events, but as the tragedy of Whitehall approached he had misgivings which were shared by many stout Parliamentarians. When Charles was seized by Cornet Joyce at Holmby House, John Crew, Montagu's father-in-law, was one of the commissioners having custody of the King's person. The party rested at Hinchingbrooke on the journey to London, and while it is not known whether Montagu himself was there, his wife was, and 'the King was nobly treated . . . with much honour and affection.' So much, indeed, that for a time some suspicion rested on the master of Hinchingbrooke. But whatever personal regard for the King may have been displayed, the Montagu interest was firmly pledged to the Revolution and to the coming Commonwealth. The example was not lost upon the humbler kinsfolk in London, and in 1660 Samuel confided to his Diary the confession, 'I was a great Roundhead when I was a boy.' It was upon the occasion of this entry that Mr. Christmas caused Pepys no little apprehension. They chanced upon each other's company with several other guests at a country house, not having seen each other since their school days. The moment was a searching one. Charles II had been brought back to his throne, and many old scores were to be paid. Pepys had been greatly up and doing at the Restoration, had, indeed, cut quite a figure in it in a small way. He had accustomed his mind to another turn of thinking since the Roundhead times, and when, dressing of a morning, he fell to singing his own setting of Montrose's verses, *Great, Good and Just,* it was now as 'the fatal day' that he recalled the scene at Whitehall. He saw Harrison hanged, drawn, and quartered at Charing Cross, and 'thus it was my chance to see the King beheaded at White Hall, and to see the first blood shed in revenge.'

No one could impugn the correctness of his speech in these days on the burning question of the hour; even his sentiments were carefully guarded. The authorities were taking note of him, and his prospects were bright. What the man of twenty-seven had said or thought as a boy of seventeen could be nobody's business. But here was just the devil of it; this was the sort of thing that amid the present excitements and felicitations was everybody's business. Since the King came back Pepys could show a very promising record of service; royalty itself had even condescended to make several encouraging observations to him. It might be that if the worst came to the worst his reputation would survive any silly gossip about a boy's chatter, but he was exceedingly anxious to take no risks. And here suddenly he found himself in front of other people, influential people, people who might drop a word in eminent circles, in the company of a talkative fellow—Pepys saw at a glance that he had become very fat and a great drinker—who was with him at St. Paul's on that 'fatal day' when some of the scholars had witnessed the last act of retribution. And Pepys, as they sat talking, remembered with growing uneasiness what he had said. He had said that if he were called upon to preach a sermon on the event, his text should be 'The memory of the wicked shall rot.' What if Christmas should remind him in the presence of these hopeful acquaintances that he had said that he should like to preach upon the late King to the text of 'The memory of the wicked shall rot.' The situation was highly provoking, and, although it was November of the year, Pepys, already rather short in the neck, found the atmosphere very oppressive. And then to his unmeasured relief he found that after all Christmas had left the school before the date of this indiscretion, and so his alarms were groundless. But Pepys was considerably shaken and had to call at two alehouses on the way home.

Pepys was entered with a sizarship from St. Paul's, at Trinity Hall, Cambridge, on the twenty-first of June, 1650. The entry was transferred to Magdalene in October of the same year, but he did not go into residence until the fol-

lowing March. In a list of the members of his family which
he discovered among his papers in 1664, he has attached
to his own name the note, 'Went to reside in Magdalene College, and did put on my gown first, March 1, 1651.' Pepys
in after days made casual references to his acquaintances at
Cambridge, but none to his accomplishments. The records
of the University are silent on the subject, beyond telling
us that he graduated a Bachelor of Arts in 1653, a year in
which he also came into public notice by being solemnly
reprimanded in the presence of all the Fellows of the College by the Registrar for 'having been scandalously over-
seene in drink the night before.' Festivities apart, he seems
to have borne himself with a modest respect for his station;
in after years, when he was a person of more consequence,
he met Sir John Skeffington, 'whom I knew at Magdalene
College, a fellow-commoner, my fellow-pupil, but one with
whom I had no great acquaintance, he being then, God
knows, much above me.' The trifles of daily habit remained
in his mind long afterwards. Rising in the small hours one
summer morning in 1664, he went into St. Dunstan's to
find that prayers were read there every morning at six
o'clock, 'a thing I never did do at a chapell, but the College
Chapell, in all my life.' In 1668, on revisiting Cambridge,
he walked into the buttery of Magdalene as a stranger, and
there drank his bellyful of beer, the best he ever drank,
and gossiped about the old days with the butler's man, 'who
was son to Goody Mulliner over against the College, that
we used to buy stewed prunes of.' There were friends who
came to no great station in the world, but who were pleasantly remembered afterwards; Mr. Nicholson, for example,
with whom in 1662 he consoled himself at home for the
misfortune of a stale sturgeon that had been served at his
table, by playing '3 or 4 things upon the violin and basse,'
and Charles Carter, with whom, in 1667, one day after
dinner he had 'much talk of old acquaintance of the College, concerning their various fortunes; wherein, to my joy,
I met not with any that have sped better than myself.' An
entry of 1663 is disappointing in its brevity. 'In Covent

Garden, to-night, going to fetch home my wife, I stopped at the great Coffee House there, where I never was before; where Dryden the poet (I knew at Cambridge), and all the wits of the town . . . there, I perceive, is very witty and pleasant discourse. But I could not tarry, and as it was late, they were all ready to go away.' Dryden was but two years older than Pepys, and he, too, had family connections with Huntingdon, of which some records still survive in a town charity and a Dryden's Walk.

Pepys's bequest of his library, the most cherished of all his possessions, to Magdalene is sufficient evidence of the satisfaction with which he remembered his university days. During the three years of Pepys's Cambridge residence, the Civil War had passed through its last phase. Cromwell had overwhelmed the Scots at Dunbar on one third of September, and had destroyed the young Charles's last hopes at Worcester on another. Charles's flight has become a classic of romance, and it was the young scholar of Magdalene who was to take down the narrative from its hero's own lips. By 1653, when Pepys went down from Cambridge, Charles was drifting about the continent in exile and penury, Oliver Cromwell was issuing proclamations as Lord Protector, and the Commonwealth had been established. In the Barebones Parliament of this year, Edward Montagu, after a temporary retirement, took his seat again as member for Huntingdon and was made a Commissioner of Customs, given lodgings at Whitehall, and appointed to the Council of State. In the ensuing wrangles between Cromwell and the Parliament, Montagu kept steadily on the windy side of fortune and grew in favour among the little band of lieutenants through whom the Protector exercised the autocratic government to which necessity was driving him. Montagu was now twenty-eight, his young cousin twenty, and in casting about for a career Samuel's attention must have already been fixed upon the public service in which his relative was growing from power to power. It was at this time, as we have seen, that John Pepys became a duly accredited Merchant Taylor; he still had other children to provide for, however, and was in no position to advance his elder son unaided. But of Edward Montagu, prompted perhaps by a timely word from Uncle Robert, much might reasonably be hoped.

For a year or so Samuel seems to have drifted about with undecided purpose. And then with an imprudence strangely inconsistent with the character that was developing, he undertook to support a wife before he had any means of supporting himself. On the 1st of December, 1655, he married Elizabeth St. Michel, a girl of fifteen, of attractive looks, but, like himself, penniless. Her father belonged to a mildly aristocratic French family, whose only connection with a large fortune was that they had lost it. How Pepys met her we do not know. Her father had concluded a series of unprosperous adventures on the Continent by rescuing his own daughter from a convent, where she had been placed by her mother, who was an Irish woman. He had thereupon removed his family to England, at a safe distance, as he hoped, from the papist influences that he abominated. He was a man charmingly insensible to the material needs of life, and always incapable of keeping his affairs in order. He was given to inventions, and patented one for curing smoking chimneys, another for purifying water. If ever he paid a visit to the house at Brampton he no doubt found occasion for the employment of both. In 1667, he petitioned the King for leave to exploit the lost mines of King Solomon, which he was convinced he had discovered. Any misgivings which may have been caused by the vacancy of his new son-in-law's prospects were allayed by the comforting reflection that his daughter had at least married a Protestant. Alexander St. Michel is but a fugitive figure in the Pepys household as we see it in the Diary, but he is one who would have engaged the affections of Cervantes.

The young couple were married at St. Margaret's Church, Westminster. There is, in fact, an unsolved confusion as to the date of the wedding. Pepys himself refers to it as October 10th, while December 1st is recorded in the registers. It is a matter of no consequence. They had no house of their own to go to, and neither John Pepys nor Alexander St. Michel was able to assist them. It was now that the association with Edward Montagu began to take practical effect. The continuance of the Spanish war at sea had brought Montagu into naval affairs, and in the year of his young cousin's marriage he became a Commissioner of the Admiralty. His advancement was unhindered, and early in January, 1656, he was appointed joint Commander of the Fleet with Robert Blake, with the rank of General at Sea. Preparations for joining his ship were at once put in hand, and it became necessary to leave somebody in charge of his personal affairs at home. The time was one for young and eager men, and there was no reason why a man who was commanding the British Fleet at the age of thirty should undervalue the abilities of a cousin because he was only twenty-three. Samuel was civil in his manners, intelligent company, methodical in his habits, and well educated. Moreover, he was very much in need of work, and there were family claims which the head of a great house could not disregard. Accordingly, when Montagu sailed in February to hunt Spaniards and form designs upon Gibraltar that were to materialise fifty years later, he left Pepys with limited powers of stewardship over the establishments at Hinchingbrooke and London, with instructions to keep his patron informed of the course of public and private events. It was part of the arrangement that the young couple should have quarters in both houses, and it is to this time that Pepys looks back, ten years later, when he writes, 'Lay long in bed, talking with pleasure with my poor wife, how she used to make coal fires, and wash my foul clothes with her own hand for me, poor wretch! In our little room at my Lord Sandwich's; for which I ought for ever to love and admire her, and do; and persuade myself she would do the same thing again, if God should reduce us to it.' Whether the little room was at Hinchingbrooke, or at the house in Lincoln's Inn to which Montagu moved from the White-hall lodgings, we are not told.

Montagu returned from his first expedition at the end of October, 1656, and received the thanks of Parliament for services that had not hitherto been very substantial. It was not, however, his fault that he had not been able to bring the Spaniards to decisive action, and if he could take to Westminster no spectacular tidings, he at least had in his hold a substantial treasure of silver that had been captured by one of his rear-admirals in a raid off Cadiz. He appears, during his absence, to have learnt a good deal about the art of navigation, to have kept his command firmly in hand, and to have been distressingly seasick. In any case his reputation had not been diminished. He came back as a man whose stake in the Commonwealth was a high one, and as a public servant securely fixed in the Protector's favour. His fortunes were more eminently than ever worth following, and Pepys assiduously followed them.

The question chiefly exercising men's minds at the moment was whether Oliver should be made King of England. After much voluble disputing, it was decided, at his own direction, that he should not. Instead, his Protectorship was made hereditary, and a great ceremony took place in Westminster, having all the pomp and significance of a coronation. Nothing was lacking of the purple and the ermine, the sceptre and the sword. At the investment, Montagu was given a place of official honour, and where Montagu was there we may be sure was Pepys not far off. It was a scene made for the pen that had not yet begun to write. Three weeks later, Montagu was back at sea. After protracted negotiations with Mazarin, Cromwell had engaged himself with France in joint operations against Spain, and the Spanish Netherlands became the point of attack. Montagu had command of the forces at sea, Turenne of those on land. Early in the campaign the news of Robert Blake's death at Santa Cruz added anxiously to Montagu's responsibility, but the expedition was successful. Mardyke was taken, and Montagu received the Protector's thanks and assurance of yet higher consideration. He returned to England in

October and obtained leave to attend to his private affairs at Hinchingbrooke. During this absence, Pepys had again been looking to his patron's interests at home, and was now a growing influence in the Montagu establishment.

From a series of letters from Pepys to Montagu, to be found in the Carte MSS. at the Bodleian, a few passages may here be given to indicate the relations between the two men at this time. The period covered is from 1656 to 1659. The letters were mostly written from Pepys in London to Montagu at Hinchingbrooke. 'The common vogue is the olde story of the Protector's kingshipp, which is now sayd to bee meerely opposed by the Major Generals and Souldiers in the House.' Pepys, left to dispose of certain prize goods in London, writes: 'I doe not remember every single chest's lading, but they opened them all, and to my best memory, there was 3 of druggs, 2 of tortois shell, one of some small roots, bound up in rowles. . . . Mr. Hetley shall have a chest of Sugar if your Honour thinks fit. . . .' He conducted money transactions for his patron in London: 'I waited upon Mr. Crew yesterday, who tolde mee he thought your Honour might shortly have occasion for the £300 which I pay'd him the last weeke, and consequently desired mee to forbeare endorsing it, for avoiding its crossing out againe, or too great a trouble in procuring such a sum otherways.' Again: 'Your £250 at the Exchequer I have taken up for the last quarter, for there is much feare of a stopp there to the payment of Salarys, as there is at the Excise office and elsewhere.' Also, he had supervision of his Lordship's domestic staff, not always without embarrassment: 'As for my privity to her [a maid's] marriage, if noe duty to yourselfe, a tendernesse to my Credit (as to my employment) obligeth me to avoid such actions which (like this) renders it so questionable. But I shall submitt your opinion of my honesty in this to that which Mr. Barton and Roger shall informe you of from her own mouth. . . . Your commands concerning her removall I shall obey . . . Capt Clerke . . . hath presented you with 6 goodly plantes of Cedar.' And then: 'I am too evidently convinced that Sarah's and this mayd's miscarriage had risen from want of employment at home, and especially from their victualling abroad, under pretense of which 4 houres at least in a day was excused for theyr being abroad, and from thence at Cook's shops comes theyr acquaintance with these fellows,' upon which he proposes that the next maid 'shall diet as well as myselfe and my wife for 4 shill: a weeke, and by that means the disrepute of a mayd's going to a victualling house, and neglect of your Honour's owne doors will bee prevented.' The new maid presenting herself, Pepys had to explain what was expected of her: 'She answered, she never had beene used to make fires, wash roomes, or cloths, scoure, or doe anything like that, and that she expected only to take charge of the goods and oversee other mayds as a housekeeper.' Whereupon she went away, 'and I have not since heard of her.' The incidents caused Pepys some anxiety: 'the losse of your Honour's good word I am too sure will prove as much my undoing, as hitherto it hath been my best friend.' But the trouble blew over.

Matters of all kinds were referred to his care: 'Sir Anthony Cooper lett mee know severall were putting in for Your Lordship's lodgings. [If you desire to part with them] he doth intend to put in for them; but if you have any desires to continue them, hee will wholly desist from any such endeavours of his own, and ... hinder those of others.' Mistress Jemimah has to stay at a doctor's for a time to undergo treatment, and Pepys ascertains that the fee is to be £100, the recovery to be effected in three months: 'I have been sollicitous to him concerning it and I doubt not [he] will speedily provide for the child's cure.' Attention was paid to the domestic requirements of Hinchingbrooke: 'I have sent swords and belts, black and modish, with 2 capps for your Honour and 2 for Mrs. Jemimah, and 2 pairs of spurrs for yourself'; 'This week I shall alsoe send raysors, and battledoors for the children'; 'I have this week sent down one box of Oranges, 2 raysors in a little box ... some shittlecocks alsoe 4 battledoors for the children'; 'The childrens hatts and ratterns for my Lady I sent the last week.'

In these letters are frequent examples of the descriptive gift and the sense of a situation that Pepys was later to employ in the Diary. He tells of a gentleman who, on being released from gaol, 'fell a preaching out of a window towards the streete, protesting he as little knew how he came out as for what he was cast into prison.' Remembering his own experience, he notes with personal interest how 'being this morning (for observation sake) at the Jewish synagogue in London I heared many lamentations made by Portugall Jewes for the death of Ferdinande the Merchant, who was lately cutt (by the same hand with myselfe) of the stone.' A touch of music takes his fancy at once: 'Pagan Fisher hath a solemn speech prepared for the . . . day of His Highnesse inauguration, to be spoaken in the Cockpitt . . . and distrusting by his rhetoriq he should loose the name of the Poet mendicant, he hath fitted a song, which Mr. Hinxton hath sett for six voices, with symphonys between each stanza for as many instruments,' and elsewhere we come upon a strange note of the somewhat freakish humour in which Cromwell could at times indulge: 'Some talke there is of a plott, but I believe it is merely raysed upon the late discovery of so many Jesuit priests, whose copes and other popish vestments the protector yesterday made some of his gentlemen put on to the causing of abundance of mirth.'

In December, 1659, Pepys was an eye-witness of the turbulent civic outbursts provoked by the rising pretensions of the Army; how vividly a witness shall be shown in a final letter taken from the Carte MSS. of this period:

MY LORD,
Yesterday's fray in London will most likely make a great noise in yᵉ Country, and deservedly, as being yᵉ soonest began yᵉ hottest in yᵉ pursuit and the quietest in yᵉ Close of any wee have hitherto known. In yᵉ morning a Comon councell being mett, some young men in yᵉ name of yᵉ

Citty apprentices presented theyr petition (much talked
of of late, and wch ye Comittee of safety sett out a procla-
mation against) to ye Lord May^r and Com. Councell.
This meeting of ye Youth was interpreted as a forerunner
of an insurrection, and to prevent that, ye Souldiers were
all (horse and Foot) drawne into ye Citty, wch ye apprentices by another mistake thought to bee done on
purpose to prevent the delivery of theyr petc̄on. Hence
arose jealouses on both sides we fear, y^y ye Shopps
throughout London were shutt up, ye souldiers as they
marcht were hooted at all along ye streets, and where any
stragled from the whole body, the boys flung stones, tiles,
turnups, etc, wth all ye affronts they could give them, some
they disarmed and kickt, others abused ye horses w^th
stones and rubbish they flung at them; and when Coll.
Huson came in the head of his Reg^t they shouted all
along a Cobler a Cobler; in some places the apprent.
would gett a football (it being a hard frost) and drive
it among ye souldiers on purpose, and they either durst
not (or prudently would not) interrupt them; in fine,
many souldiers were hurt wth stones, and one I see was
very neere having his braines knockt out with a brick batt
flung from ye top of an house at him. On ye other side, y^e
souldiers proclaimed the proclamc̄on against any sub-
scripc̄ons, wch the boys shouted at, in contempt, wch some
could not beare but lett fly theyr musq^ts and killed in
severall places (whereof I see one in Cornhill shott
through the head) 6 or 7, and severall wounded. About
4 of ye Citty traine bands were up, but nothing passed
betweene ye sould^rs and them but soure lookes. Towards
evening ye May^r sent to Alderm. and to Comon Councell
to desire ye remaining of the souldiers out and they would
undertake ye quieting of ye City, wch was not then granted,
soe ye Souldiers tooke possession of ye gates all night, but
by morning they were with drawne out of ye Citty (having only pulled down ye gates at Temple bar) and all
now quiett as ever. Portsmouth stands out for certaine,

Morly is there, and Haslerigg and Walton are believed to bee gone that way.

Yo^r r^{pf} dutif^{ll} Servt

S. PEPYS.

I left Mrs. Jem. well just now.

The letter from Sec. Office for my cheife and ma^{tr} at ye Generall Councill.

But for the present there was a rapidly gathering momentum in public affairs that was beyond the scope of Pepys's experience. Cromwell was deeply engaged in the constitution of his new House of Lords, and falling daily more at odds with the Commons in the process. Many influential leaders of the Commonwealth, Montagu's own cousin Manchester, and his father-in-law John Crew, among them, were distrustful of the new expedient, and would not lend their names to it. Montagu, too, had misgivings, but they were insufficient to destroy his confidence in Cromwell's judgment. When he took his seat in the new Parliament it was as Baron Montagu.

The Commons immediately fell to argument about the validity of Cromwell's new creations, and argument was no longer to Cromwell's taste. In a tone to which they were now becoming accustomed, he bade them be gone about their business, which was not at Westminster, and turned again to government by his own authority. His constitutional right, or lack of it, need not be discussed here, but it is important to observe that whether or not he was governing by any discoverable consent, he was on the whole governing well. It was this circumstance by which he bound to himself the steady loyalty of such men as Montagu, who knew very well that the Protector in all his power was walking on extremely dangerous ground. Early in the new year, 1658, Montagu, who since Blake's death had taken seniority of command at sea, rejoined the French in operations against Dunkirk, and again with success. He was fêted by Mazarin, and his prestige at home was advanced. He was preparing himself for a Spanish offensive on a larger scale, and then, in September, Cromwell died.

On a sudden, the whole aspect of English domestic policy was profoundly changed. Richard Cromwell, nominated to his father's succession, was wholly unfitted for the office. For eight years Oliver, with unexampled determination, had carried through a task of immeasurable difficulty. On his death there was no man in England capable of filling his place, but in his son Richard all the elements of incapacity were perfectly combined. Every thoughtful mind in the Commonwealth was immediately beset by fears, and every faction bubbled with intrigue. Demands were made for a republic, demands for a restored monarchy. For a time Montagu stood firm for a protectorate, though in the person of the Protector it was foredoomed to failure, loyal to the tradition that he conceived himself to have inherited from his great master. To Republican and Royalist seductions alike he turned a deaf ear, retiring when possible from public notice, and active only in his duties as General at Sea. But the situation daily became more hopeless, and when these duties took him on an expedition to the Sound, for the purpose of mediation between Sweden and Denmark in a quarrel that threatened English and French interests, he was beginning to contemplate possibilities as yet but dimly defined. During his absence the Republican party at home reduced Richard Cromwell's powers to a fiction, and threatened to remodel the government to their own desire. Montagu made no secret of his disapproval. For Pepys was in close touch with his master in the Sound, making at least one official visit to the fleet there, and he knew that Montagu was writing to Lenthall, deeply concerned by the fresh developments, knew also that he was telling the King of Sweden of the menace that was looming against the government of England. But what Pepys did not know was that Montagu, feeling that association with the party in power at Westminster was no longer possible, now entered into correspondence with the exiled Charles Stuart. Montagu knew very well how precarious was the design, and took no one into his confidence. It was not until November 1660 that Pepys learnt the truth. 'My Lord . . . did also bless himself with his good fortune, in comparison to what it was when I was with him in the Sound, when he durst not own his correspondence with the King; which is a thing I never did hear of to this day before; I do from this raise an opinion of him, to be one of the most secret men in the world, which I was not so convinced of before.'

In the negotiations that preceded the Restoration of Charles II, Montagu took a part of capital importance. If the deciding influence was Monk's, it was one that could hardly have been exercised without Montagu's support. If the army waited upon Monk's word, the fleet waited upon Montagu's. The General at Sea returned to England at the end of August, and was disconcerted to find that precipitate Royalist risings had gravely endangered the designs to which he was now secretly committed. His name was spoken with suspicion in Republican councils, and he was relieved of his command. He retired to Hinchingbrooke, where frequent letters in cipher arrived from Pepys, who was employed in watching the movement of affairs in London. Montagu for the moment was out of public employment, and was content to let the coming changes shape themselves in their own time. For that change of some kind there must be, he was now convinced. He had no faith in an English republic, and in his heart, whatever immediate appearances might be, he had no fear that it would be established. He was deeply imbued with the traditional belief of his countrymen that government in England must be vested in a hereditary magistrate, and he was convinced that sooner or later the choice must be made between restoration of the House of Cromwell and restoration of the House of Stuart. As the House of Cromwell at present meant Richard, whom he knew to be incapable of governing a parish council, to say nothing of a kingdom, his allegiance drifted steadily towards the little court in Holland, where, after ten years of frustration, hopes were mounting eagerly. Montagu had small enough reason for blind faith in the Stuarts, but there was at least a chance that the lesson of 1649 might have been learnt. And, in any case, there was no alternative, that is to say no alternative worth taking. The royal House of Stuart had been unfortunate in its kings, but it still was a royal house, the only royal house available. So that as Montagu watched and waited at Hinchingbrooke, he knew that he was watching and waiting for the return of Charles. But, like Monk, he was too shrewd to risk all by any ill-timed action. It was no moment for feather-brained enthusiasm. If the King was to come back to his throne, it could only be with a solid weight of responsible and deliberate opinion behind him. Montagu felt that this was being formed, but he knew that it could not be forced.

His belief did not long lack confirmation. The officers of the Fleet let it be known through private channels that they would welcome the return of their old commander. Pepys informed him of rumours that an official petition was to be lodged to this end. Private letters of appeal came to Hinchingbrooke, but Montague was wary; he was confined to his chamber of a distemper; he understood that Parliament had other views on the matter; he was his correspondent's truly affectionate friend, and, indeed, was deeply sensible of the affection shown him by all the officers of the Fleet; but he begged to be excused saying more about it just at present. A little later, the Republican tide seemed to be flowing strongly again, and Montagu even contemplated closing down his London establishment. At the last moment he thought better of it, persuading himself once more that Republican authority was alien to the spirit of England and would show itself to have no foundations. By the end of the year, the crisis was approaching. Montagu knew now that his recall was desired throughout the Fleet. Westminster was in confusion, with the armed forces of the Parliament thoroughly demoralised under Lambert's command. On the northern bank of the Tweed, Monk was waiting at the head of his perfectly disciplined and devoted veterans. The panic-stricken Republicans offered the taciturn soldier anything he would condescend to ask. He condescended to ask nothing; he merely waited. He, like Montagu, was now convinced that Charles must be the choice, but he allowed his mind to be read by no one. At the turn of the year, he knew that he had only to march on London for the situation to be in his hands. Still keeping his intentions to himself, he decided to advance. On January 2, 1660, he crossed the Tweed at Coldstream, and, on the night before, Samuel Pepys at his house in Axe Yard had written the first page of his Diary.

CHAPTER II

THE RESTORATION. CLERK OF THE ACTS

IN THE meantime, Pepys had obtained a clerkship in the office of George Downing, a Teller of the Receipt of the Exchequer, at a salary of £50 a year. The pay was small, but the duties seemed to have been unexacting. Pepys frequently arrived at the office to find that there was no business to be done, and a full day's work is seldom if ever recorded. Throughout his life Pepys paid close attention to his money matters, and already the young clerk was anxiously manipulating his slender finance, paying a small debt here, raising a loan there. He was now twenty-seven years of age, and on his first appearance in the Diary we find him in full exercise of the natural eagerness towards all the daily traffic and business of social life that was to be the secret of his fame. He was actively interested in the great events of his time, but they never dulled his appetite for the unconsidered trifles that made the common round of the clock. Indeed, his distinction first and last was that for him the routine of experience was neither unconsidered nor trifling. On occasion, he could set down memorable records of memorable scenes, but the chief merit of his chronicle is that from page to page it makes memorable the things that none but himself would have troubled to remember. During the first month or two of the Diary, the note is firmly struck that was to dominate the whole. Brave names and brave phrases have their place. 'Mr. Fage . . . told me what Monk had done in the City, how he had pulled down the most part of the gates and chains that they could break

down, and that he was now gone back to White Hall.' 'I
went up to the lobby, where I saw the Speaker reading of
the letter; and after it was read, Sir A. Hazelrigge came
out very angry, and Billing standing at the door, took him
by the arm, and cried, "Thou man, will thy beast carry thee
no longer? thou must fall." ' 'They told me how the Speaker
Lenthall do refuse to sign the writs for choice of new
members in the place of the excluded.' And so on. But in
the midst of these national crises, which were gathering at
the rate of about one a day, Pepys found ample time for the
agreeable little employments of which he never wearied.
Although he could say of himself a little ambiguously, 'My
own private condition very handsome, and esteemed rich,
but indeed very poor,' he was never quite lackpenny when
it came to indulging convivial tastes that were at present
sufficiently modest. He might have to borrow £10 to meet
some pressing claim, but if office business permitted, as it
generally did, the social enjoyments of the day were varied
and finely savoured. The habit of Axe Yard was of necessity
a frugal one, a cut of collared brawn being thankfully received after a day in the city on bread and cheese, and there
is obvious relish in the recollection of turkey pie and a
goose at someone else's table; less relish, however, when
'the venison pasty was palpable beef.' But there is already
pleasure in obliging a friend with a morning draught at
the Axe in King Street, or with an afternoon pint of wine
at the Star in Cheapside. Dining at taverns was a custom
of the day, and Pepys seldom dined alone. There were
houses to be visited too, his father's and others, and hospitality to be returned. And on occasion Mrs. Pepys, now
twenty years of age, could achieve the dignity of a dish of
steaks and a rabbit. Indeed, at one family reunion for which
'My Lord's' lodgings were requisitioned, the exchequer
must have been severely strained, since it provided 'a dish
of marrow bones; a leg of mutton; a loin of veal; a dish of
fowl, three pullets, and two dozen of larks all in a dish; a
great tart, a neat's tongue, a dish of anchovies; a dish of
prawns and cheese,' though it may have been my Lord's

exchequer after all. And after dinner would come cribbage, or, best of all, music; 'and there we sang of all sorts of things, and I ventured with good success upon the part first sight, and after that I played on my flageolet, and staid there till nine o'clock, very merry and drawn on with one song after another till it came to be so late.' Or if it was not the flageolet it might be the viol, for to be a musician was to practise several kinds of mastery. And the day would be diversified by calls at the bookseller's or the haber-dasher's, with a little purchase here and there. If one volume only could be afforded at the bookshop another might be read while waiting, since business was not pressing. Then, there might be the correction of his brother John's Greek speech for Apposition Day at St. Paul's, or a little sermon to be delivered to Sister Pall about stealing his wife's scissors, and then sometimes the necessity of receiving monies or telling out the pay to soldiers at the office, and, perhaps, a game of 'shittlecock.' And then home, prefer-ably by water, since walking on winter evenings was haz-ardous; 'Back to Whitehall, and in the garden, going through to the Stone Gallery I fell into a ditch, it being very dark.' At home, if there was no company, there were accounts to be made up, or an inexpensive print to be hung, and pegs to be contrived for hats and coats, with Mrs. Pepys and the maid washing, perhaps, until near midnight. For it was an irregular household. At times it would be home to bed at nine o'clock, and then again 'I staied up till the bell-man came by with his bell just under my window as I was writing of this very line, and cried, "Past one of the clock, and a cold, frosty, windy morning." '

But neither business nor social engagements were allowed to interrupt the careful association with my Lord and his household. The inducement was a twofold one. Pepys was already genuinely attached to his cousins and their rapidly growing family. The Montagu children were ten in number, born at dates ranging from 1646 to 1664. Two of the girls, Jemimah and Anne, aged respectively fourteen and seven, were at this time living in London in charge of their maids,

and one of Pepys's duties was to supervise their accounts.
'Here I staid and made up Mrs. Ann's [their maid's] bills.'
Jemimah at fourteen seems to have been a very advanced
young lady. She entertained Pepys and his wife in expectation of a sack possett, 'it being a great frost,' but as her
brother Edward, aged twelve, failed to turn up, the possett
did not appear; however, she kindly saved part of it for
Pepys when he called two days later. She came up 'hot and
merry' from the kitchens, Pepys being troubled by a suspicion that she had been given wine by the servants. She
played cards and taught him cribbage, which was well
enough, but she was also apparently breaking the heart of
a Mr. Moore, a lawyer, who came in an extremely melancholy state of mind about it to ask Pepys to put in a good
word for him. When she was threatened with smallpox,
which mercifully turned out to be nothing worse than swine-
pox, Pepys was all anxiety; and in the early part of the
Diary there is almost daily witness of his concern for her
well-being. Anne, at the age of seven, is not so frequently
mentioned.

So that Pepys found the connection an agreeable one,
pleasant in its interchanges and enlivened by such satisfaction as a present from my Lord of a dozen bottles of sack.
But it was more than agreeable. In his little attentions to
the children, and his careful handling of such commissions
as were entrusted to him, he was not only properly grateful for favours received, but humanly sensible of who could
tell what possibilities to come. The Exchequer Clerk with
easy time on his hands, constrained to be elbowed aside by
such as 'had a mind to take the wall,' loitering to see his
stock of pigeons breeding fast in the spring, ordering a barrel of soap or a flock bedding for the young ladies, calling
upon Mr. Hill, 'the instrument maker,' to consult him
about a lute, was an extremely obscure person, without a
suspicion that he was writing an immortal book. But the
confidential amanuensis of Lord Montagu could cherish
hopes. Monk now had the army well in hand, indeed, he
had everything well in hand, though at the end of Febru-

ary he was still making public disclaimers of any Royalist intentions. But Pepys was told by John Crew that Montagu could have employment with the Fleet again for the asking. Pepys dispatched the news to Hinchingbrooke, borrowed £5, and set off to Cambridge to instal his brother John at Christ's. On his return to town rumour was busier than ever. A friend upon whom he called thought it safe to show him concealed at the back of his chimney a lion and unicorn, brightly polished against the King's return. On March 6th, Montagu was back in London. Taking Pepys aside into the garden, he told him that he was again going to command at sea, which was interesting; he also told him that he thought the King would be brought back, which was more interesting still; but most interesting of all to Pepys was my Lord's invitation formally to enter his service as secretary. And the young man lay long awake in bed that night 'in discourse thereupon' with his wife.

All excitement at the proposal, Pepys nevertheless gave it prudent thought before accepting it. There could have been no serious doubt about his answer, but still it was a time of change, other advancement was being hinted at, and after all it was just a little difficult to know that my Lord was on the right side of the gate. For a day or two, Pepys, although he busied himself with his patron's affairs, was undecided, and still had time to spare for rag tag and bobtail, of which he was ashamed, at Mrs. Jem's, or to stop at Adam Chard's to buy a cat-call for three groats; but on the third day all scruples had been dispelled by the prospect of great employment, he told Lord Montagu that he was ready to go to sea, and the bargain was concluded. Then for a fortnight there was a scurry of preparation. The little clerkship was placed in commission with a friend, and arrangements were made for Mrs. Pepys to stay with an old acquaintance in the country, an occasion for some protest. Picking up the first fruits of place in the shape of perquisites from small people applying for small jobs; hiring servants; paying his rent up to the coming Ladyday; laying in a stock of writing materials; indulging his wife to the

extent of three new smocks, while furnishing his own wardrobe on a more generous scale, Pepys found himself suddenly a person of consequence, and prayed God to keep
him from being too much lifted up thereby. On the 3d of
March he embarked at Gravesend with Lord Montagu in
the *Swiftsure,* which was to carry the General's flag until
the *Naseby* was ready for his occupation.

And so Pepys started on his adventure, far from knowing how great an adventure it was to be. Nor did Montagu
himself know. Everyone believed now that Monk was for
the King, and his Majesty's health was being drunk openly
in the City. But while Monk and Montagu might be clear
about the matter in their minds, they could not yet tell
precisely how or when the Restoration was to be effected.
In the meantime, by going to sea again with the Fleet, his
new command of which had been taken over with Monk's
blessing, Montagu placed himself in a position of great
strategic power. He embarked with no specific design, and
the Fleet did not know under what orders they were sailing.
Indeed, there were no orders. All that was necessary in the
present situation was that the Fleet should be at sea, and
under the command of a man whose known inclinations
were not likely to come into conflict with Monk's. Any moment now might be the moment for the decisive movement
to be made, and Montagu was there to make it. As the
ships lay off Gravesend, tidings came of the growing wave
of Royalist sentiment in London. The King's effigy was up
again in the Exchange, the Skinner's Company when entertaining Monk had taken down the Parliament arms in their
Hall and put the King's in its place. Mysterious boats began to slip out in the direction of Holland, and mysterious
letters began to arrive for my Lord that were not shown
even to his secretary. Monk was said to have declared for
Charles, but to have declared also that if the King came
back it should be his doing. The signs were clear enough,
and Pepys noted them, but for several weeks he had no
further enlightenment, and applied himself with steady
efficiency to the duties of his new post.

At the end of a long day, after he had been three weeks at sea, Pepys recorded in his Diary, 'So to sleep, every day bringing me a fresh sense of the pleasure of my present life.' And the picture that he draws of himself at this beginning of his long and distinguished contact with naval affairs is one of unbounded zest and animation. He does his work diligently, is proud of himself and of his master, allows nothing to escape an insatiable observation, and is eager to take every kind of pleasure that comes his way. He sits hours on end writing at his letters and instructions, scrupulous to have all punctual and in order. He begins to experience a pleasing sense of his own dignity. He is much vexed when his clerk, one Burr, goes on shore without his leave, but there is satisfaction in having a clerk to be vexed by. He finds his cabin appointments not placed to his liking, spends the morning in getting them right, and in doing it is infinitely pleased to see everyone so ready to come and go at his command. When he receives a letter addressed Samuel Pepys, Esq., God knows he is not a little proud. But, busy as he was, and exacting to himself in respect of his duties, there was ample time for diversion. Being the General's man meant courtesy and consideration from all ranks, and Pepys, moreover, took genuine pleasure in making himself a likeable fellow. He must already have been uncommonly good company. He had a good average mind, was shrewd and industrious, and had a talent for not confusing great with little things while being intent on both. It says much for the quality of education in his time that a schooling that was within the reach of very moderate means should turn out in the ordinary course of its operation a man so apt and so well equipped in so many directions. Pepys had his innocent vanities, and was ingenuous enough in his little boastings, but for the most part the man revealed in the Diary is one who takes a liberal enlightenment for granted. And from his view of enlightenment, timely levities were by no means to be excluded.

On his second day at sea (a Sunday), he was gratified to find that he 'took place of all but the Captains,' and, dining

handsomely, slept at the service that followed. The next
day there was a special merriment in his cabin at night, it
being the second anniversary of his being cut for the stone,
an occasion that he celebrated with festive piety throughout his life. He was ready to take a hand at ninepins, clown
with the spigot of an ale barrel, or to borrow the lieutenant's glass to look at the women on a passing merchant-
man, 'being pretty handsome.' He was equally at ease taking wine and pickled oysters with the Captain, or a glass of
grog with the barber. He could dispute with the chaplain
on the efficacy of extemporary prayer, and when a prisoner
was brought on board he could question him in French and
Latin. His taste for music found ample scope. He played
the viallin, sometimes alone 'in a melancholy fit,' sometimes
in company. 'He sang a psalm or two' in parts with a friend
before going to sleep, and was offended by a coxcomb who
played 'a bass part upon the viall . . . so like a fool that
I was ashamed of him.' His enthusiasm for music was
shared by his master. 'After that W. Howe and I went to
play two trebles in the great cabin below, which my Lord
hearing, after supper he called for our instruments, and
played a set of Lock's, two trebles, and a base, and that
being done, he fell to singing of a song made upon the
Rump, with which he played himself well, to the tune of
"The Blacksmith." '

His relations with Montagu were unfailingly happy.
Pepys knew his place exactly, and the General was able to
extend to him frequent personal civilities without endangering discipline. And so the young secretary was often at
his Lordship's table, and when he heard likely scraps of
conversation was discreet enough not to offer uninvited
opinions, and the conversation became more likely day by
day. What was going to happen he still did not know, but
he began to suspect that it was something remarkable.
These were untroubled and hopeful days, the only cloud
being his separation from the girl with whom he was, and
in spite of everything was always to remain, in love. 'My
heart exceeding heavy for not hearing of my dear wife,

and, indeed, I do not remember that ever my heart was so apprehensive of her absence as at this very time.' And steadily the composition of the book went on. It may be noted that in 1669, nine years, that is, after this date, Pepys wrote 'Up and to the Tower; and there find Sir W. Coventry alone, writing down his journall, which he tells me, he now keeps of the material things, upon which I told him (and he is the only man I ever told it to, I think), that I kept it most strictly, these eight or ten years, and I am sorry almost that I told it to him, it not being necessary, nor maybe convenient, to have it known'; but on board the *Naseby,* under date April the 11th, there is the entry, 'I staid the lieutenant late, showing him my manner of keeping a journall.'

On Mayday, Pepys heard that the King's flag had been put up on a maypole by the people of Deal, and the next day news came from London that the City had declared its allegiance to a monarchy, and that Charles's proposals for a settlement had been read to the House, which thereupon voted £50,000 for the King's immediate needs. Pepys knew now that the Restoration was in sight, but he still did not know what he himself might see of it. Nor did he know that one of the secret missives received by the General had been from Charles Stuart in these terms:

. . . therefore all I desire of you is, that you will give me your word, that you do and will take my business to heart; and then I shall, with all freedom, consult with you about the time, and other circumstances,

and, as for the past:

I do assure you that I am so far from remembering anything to your disadvantage, that I look upon you as a person to be rewarded.

And he as secretary had not been called upon to take down the reply that had gone off in one of the mysterious boats:

'The gracious reception your Majesty hath vouchsafed to give the humble tender of my Loyaltye unto you, proceedes from the same fountaine,' and so on, concluding, 'My life and fortune shall ever be devoted to your service.' On the next day, May 3d, Montagu showed Pepys the King's declaration and his letters addressed to the Generals at Land and Sea. These were to be communicated to the Fleet, and all the commanders were assembled on board the *Naseby* for the purpose; Pepys, to his immense satisfaction, was ordered to read the documents aloud. This done, the ceremony was repeated on the quarter deck, and as Pepys came to an end, 'the seamen did all of them cry out, "God bless King Charles" with the greatest joy imaginable.' Then the young secretary, in a pardonable flush of excitement, was taken with his documents to the other ships, 'quite through the fleet. Which was a very brave sight to visit all the ships, and to be received with the respect and honour that I was on board them all; and much more to see the great joy that I brought to all men.' On his return to the *Naseby,* Montagu showed him letters from Charles and his brother James 'in such familiar style as to their common friend, with all kindness imaginable. . . . And the Duke offers to learn the seaman's trade of him, in such familiar words as if Jack Cole and I had writ them.' Flags were out, there was a great firing of guns, and there were two pipes of canary. Next morning Pepys woke to find himself a figure of consequence beyond his dreams. Moderation was difficult. Many copies had to be made of the vote by which the Council of War had the day before acknowledged the King, and on all of them he took leave to insert his own name, that 'if it should come in print my name may be at it.' And more was yet to follow. The conviction throughout the country that at last a settlement of long and desperate confusion had been reached found expression in a rush of high spirits that spread to the Fleet, keeping everyone for days on end in a perpetual flutter of affairs and feasting. The excitement grew as preparations went forward for what

Pepys could not now fail to realise was some crowning adventure. He was ordered by the General to 'write for silk flags and scarlett waistcloathes. For a rich barge; for a noise of trumpets, and a set of fidlers.' The King's Gentlemen of the Bedchamber arrived on board and inspected the cabins, and on May 10th, the news at last was out, for 'my Lord called me into his cabin, and told me how he was commanded to set sail presently for the King.'

Here, indeed, was matter enough to turn a young man's head. Rarely has fortune behaved more handsomely to a budding career. Her favours had been granted against all the odds. Pepys owed everything to Montagu, but Montagu himself owed much to chance. He was a man of character and ability, who had proved himself to have a steady nerve, a clear head, and principles. But, sound in quality as he was, and an honour to his country in an age of great Englishmen, he was not a man of whose merits it could be said that in any circumstances they would have raised him to the highest eminence. He was a distinguished naval commander, but he cannot be claimed as one of the great English seamen. At any time he would have been worthily active in the life of his country, but that he took a great part in a great moment of history was due largely to the accident of his association with Huntingdon. For it was there that he had fallen under the spell of Cromwell, and it was his devotion to that great man that had given him all his prosperous opportunities. He had turned them to account with judgment and credit, and there was a pretty element of irony in the fact that he was about to bring them to fulfilment in restoring the House that Cromwell had overthrown. With him was the young cousin, who three months before had been cooling his heels in London on petty employments that seemed to be leading nowhere. And now, at the age of twenty-seven, Pepys found himself in an office of responsibility and esteem on the ship that was putting out to bring Charles home.

We may pause a moment upon those principles with

which we credit Montagu. In *Astræa Redux,* Dryden (the poet, I knew at Cambridge), wrote:

> The *Naseby* now no longer *England's* shame,
> But better to be lost in *Charles* his name
> (Like some unequal Bride in nobler sheets)
> Receives her Lord: The joyful *London* meets
> The Princely *York,* himself alone a freight;
> The *Swiftsure* groans beneath great Glouc'sters weight. . . .

and, contemplating the spectacle, he became rhapsodical upon the enormities of the passing age:

> And as devouter *Turks* first warn their Souls
> To part, before they taste forbidden Bowls,
> So these when their black Crimes they went about,
> First timely charm'd their useless Conscience out. . . .

and,

> Welcom now (*Great Monarch*) to your own;
> Behold th'approaching Cliffes of *Albion;*
>
> .   .   .   .
>
> So tears of joy for your returning spilt,
> Work out and expiate our former Guilt.

This was in 1660. But in 1659, Dryden had written, in far nobler strains of eulogy, stanzas *Consecrated to the Memory of His Highness, Oliver late Lord Protector:*

> Though our best Notes are Treason to his Fame,
>   Join'd with the loud Applause of publick Voice,
> Since Heaven, what Praise we offer to his Name,
>   Hath render'd too Authentick by its Choice.
>
> Though in his Praise no Arts can liberal be,
>   Since they, whose Muses have the highest flown,
> Add not to his Immortal Memory;
>   But do an Act of Friendship to their own.

.   .   .   .

His Grandeur he derived from Heav'n alone,
For he was great, e'er Fortune made him so;
And Wars, like Mists that rise against the Sun,
Made him but greater seem, not greater grow.

.   .   .   .

And yet Dominion was not his Design;
We owe that Blessing not to him, but Heav'n,
Which to fair Acts unsought Rewards did join,
Rewards that less to him, than us, were giv'n.

.   .   .   .

Tis true, his Count'nance did imprint an Awe,
And naturally all Souls to his did bow;
As Wands of Divination downward draw,
And point to Beds where Sov'raign Gold doth grow.

.   .   .   .

Nor dy'd he when his Ebbing Fame went less,
But when fresh Laurels courted him to live:
He seem'd but to prevent some new Success,
As if above what Triumphs Earth could give.

.   .   .   .

His Ashes in a Peaceful Urn shall rest,
His Name a great Example stands to show,
How strangely high Endeavours may be bless'd,
Where Piety and Valour jointly go.

It is not agreeable to reflect that a great poet can be a
shameless time-server. But the evidence unhappily is clear.
To praise Cromwell and welcome Charles was within the
bounds of honour, and honest men did both. But to go
whining to Charles with defamation of the man who a
year before had been the subject of this elegiac splendour
was to lose all sense of decency. In 1659, Cromwell was
for Dryden the hero above reproach; in 1660, to suit the occasion, he became the source and instrument of all treason.

It is here that we have to distinguish Montagu's conduct
from such offending, to show, in fact, that in the most difficult crisis of his life, and in making the most difficult decision, principle was not sacrificed. It is true that at the

Restoration it was a necessity of Charles's position to treat Cromwell's assumption of power as an act of usurpation, and it was part of the formality for men like Montagu to accept the royal pardon for their share in it. It was, moreover, in the nature of things that the King should exclude from this amnesty the men who had been directly responsible for his father's death. But in accommodating himself to the technique of the new situation, Montagu made no gesture dishonouring the great cause that he had served. He said nothing, and in justice to Charles it must be added that he was asked to say nothing that could be interpreted as a confession of error. If asked whether, with his present knowledge, he would have acted as he did in 1642, he would not have hesitated in his answer, and it would have been yes. Indeed, he knew very well the dangers that confronted the Restoration. When men had first begun to talk of Charles's return as a likely event, and his own sympathies were beginning to be known, he had told Pepys that, if it came about, the King could not last long unless he carried himself 'very soberly and well.' Montagu, and those in his position, had shown in service how passionately they believed in the reforms for which Cromwell stood, but at Cromwell's death they believed as passionately that the supreme magistracy could no longer remain an elective office in England. And the answer to the charges that have sometimes been brought against them of bad faith and self-interest is simple. To accuse Montagu of veering to the wind is to overlook the fact that he was one of the men who decided which way the wind should blow. Had Monk and Montagu, and the few men comparable with them in influence, determined that the King's return would be a misfortune for England, the Restoration would not have taken place. It was a fact, whatever the form and ceremony might be, that Charles did not fail to acknowledge.

It is unlikely that Pepys held exalted views upon the matter. He was not a cynic and he was not indifferent to the public interest, but his private interest was not yet sufficiently secure to allow him much time for reflection upon anything beyond it. He was at no height yet for a broad survey of events. Quite unexpectedly he had got his feet rather firmly placed on one of the lower rungs of his ladder, and the ascent in front of him was enough to engage all his energies. There was entertainment in plenty to be derived from the shifting pageant in which he suddenly found himself a humble figure, but it was not now for him to moralise it. He would have been a very good servant to Richard Cromwell, or a President, or any other master into whose service Montagu's decision might have brought him. In the meantime here he was stepping on to the Dutch shore in the entourage of the King's highly esteemed friend, driving by coach into the Hague, and piping on his flageolet for very joy.

There he saw the Prince of Orange, the Queen of Bohemia, the Duke of York, and the King of England, whom he took to be a very sober man, but very active and stirring. He bought a basket for his wife, and three books for himself. He found the women 'very pretty and in good habits, fashionable and black spots.' He was treated by my Lord with more respect than ever he did get. He purchased some 'fine linning stockings and wide canons,' a little envious perhaps of a gentleman who came on board 'like an ass, with his feathers and new suit that he had made at the Hague.' He saw the Princess Royal and the Dowager Queen, Henrietta Maria, and my Lord Chancellor Clarendon, newly in custody of the Great Seal and much afflicted by the gout. He was in great uncertainty of mind about a pretty Dutch woman whom he found sleeping in his lodging bedroom, and on one occasion toasted the King's health so well that waking betimes in the morning he mistook the rising sun for the setting. In the press of affairs and people he mislaid my Lord's eldest son, Edward, a boy of twelve, and was in a fever of concern till he was found.

At length the preparations for the great voyage back to England were complete, and on May 23d, the King embarked in the *Naseby*, the name of which was altered by royal command to the *Charles*. In the afternoon, upon the

quarterdeck, Charles talked at large to the company upon
his escape from Worcester, making Pepys 'weep to hear
the stories that he told,' stories that the young man was
to record at the King's dictation twenty years later at Newmarket. Pepys being instructed to write out a pass in the
King's name, had the honour of presenting it himself for
the royal signature; he had to speak of business to the Duke
of York, who called him Pepys by name. On the morning
of the 25th, Charles landed and was received by Monk
at Dover, Montagu taking leave of the man whom he had
brought back to his throne, and at night Pepys caused a
painter to gild the mark at the head of the table where
the King that day with his own hand had marked his height.

For a fortnight there were affairs to put in order on the
ship. Montagu was invested with the Garter, and given to
expect the Mastership of the Wardrobe, which was conferred upon him three weeks later. Pepys received £30 as
his share of the present given to the ship by the King, and
what with this and eight guineas received elsewhere for
favours done, he was able at the end of the voyage, when
his Dutch purchases had been made, to reckon his account
at near £100, four times the amount of his fortune when he
had left home, for which God be blessed. He thanked the
General for doing so well by him, and was told 'We must
have a little patience, and we will rise together.' And so,
after an absence of eleven weeks, by road to London, carrying the King's 'gittar,' kissing a good handsome wench at
Gravesend, with a future suddenly become bright beyond all
expectations. Pepys arrived in town on June 9th, and, going
to his father's, put himself in 'handsome posture' to wait
upon my Lord at Whitehall. 'Found the King in the Park.
There walked,' and then, upon an almost lyric note, 'Gal-
lantly great.' A fitting close for the prelude to a career.

On returning to London, it was a fortnight before Pepys
could get back into his own house, and in the meantime he
stayed with his wife at his father's. Employment was no
longer desultory, and he was put to it to keep pace with
his master's affairs. For the moment his own were unsettled.

He was receiving £50 a quarter from the Commissioners of the Navy as secretary to the General, which he was augmenting with a not infrequent £5 on the side in the way of business; but he had more thriving hopes. Montagu was as good as his word. On June 29th, Pepys received from the Duke of York his warrant as Clerk of the Acts, an appointment carrying a salary of £350 a year. And on the same day, was issued the Patent for Montagu's elevation to the Peerage. He first thought to take the title of Portsmouth, but changed his mind, and became the first Earl of Sandwich. Pepys's connection with the Navy was thus established on terms of high consequence. The Clerk of the Acts was alternatively styled Clerk of the Ships, and ranked as an officer of the Admiralty. The full Board consisted of the Lord High Admiral, a Treasurer, Comptroller, Surveyor, three Commissioners and the Clerk himself. At the time of Pepys's appointment these offices were held respectively by the Duke of York, Sir George Carteret, Sir Robert Slingsby, Sir William Batten, Lord Berkeley, Sir William Penn and Peter Pett. The Duke, who was Pepys's own age, had a genuine zest and ability for the Navy, his administration of which was the most creditable circumstance of his career. The other members of the Board were all the Clerk's senior by several years, and they were, moreover, all men of experience in naval affairs. Carteret, at the age of sixty, had spent many years at sea, and was described by Clarendon as one of the best seamen in England. Slingsby, ten years younger, had also been bred a sailor, and Batten had been Surveyor of the Navy when Pepys was six years old, and afterwards in command at sea. Berkeley was a soldier; he had held ambassadorial rank under Charles I, and had subsequently seen service with Turenne in France, an adventure that involved some knowledge of the sea. Penn, forty years of age, was a Vice-Admiral, and Peter Pett, fifty, had for some years been Commissioner at the Chatham Dockyards. Into this company, at the age of twenty-eight, was introduced a young man who a year ago had hardly known one end of a ship from the other, and whose knowledge of the Navy was now no more than he had been able to pick up during a few weeks at sea, in what was hardly more than a domestic capacity. Nor was his new post by any means merely that of a scrivener. The duties of the Clerk were responsible and varied. Not only had he to conduct the general correspondence of the Board and keep its accounts, but he also had to attend to the provision of materials for building and repairing ships, and be precisely informed as to the condition and movements of the Fleet. All the details of the civil side of naval administration passed through his hands, and much important secret information was placed in his keeping. He had to be closely in touch with the state of naval supplies and finance, even with such matters as personnel and discipline. 'It is certaine,' says a record of the time, 'no man sees more of the Navye's Transactions than himselfe, and possibly may speak as much of the project if required, or else he is a blockhead, and not fitt for that imployment.' Pepys took up his new duties with a virgin innocence of their complicated nature. He had everything to learn; he knew, for example, even less of accounting than of the Navy. But education had made learning a habit of his mind, and the sufficient assurance of his success lay in the fact that he was decidedly not a blockhead.

He applied himself at once to the task before him with a resourceful wit and unsparing industry. The comprehensive book on Pepys that is being written by Dr. Tanner is to supply us with a detailed account of his career as a public servant. How valuable this is likely to prove we may judge from the important papers which Dr. Tanner has already published. In the present study, we have only to consider Pepys's official life in so far as it enlarges our knowledge of his character, and in this respect it is wholly to his credit. As a public man he was never employed in any service other than that which he now entered, and as he grew in authority he grew also in application and efficiency, a record in itself somewhat unusual. Of the many enigmas presented by the psychology of English history there is

SILVER MEDAL, STRUCK BY JOHN ROETTIER

Commemorating the return of Charles II to England in 1660. On the reverse, the landing at Dover showing Montagu's ship, the NASEBY, *renamed the* ROYAL CHARLES.

perhaps none more perplexing than that of the English Navy. It is a service that is regarded properly with the deepest national pride and gratitude. In valour, in discipline, in loyalty, and in chivalry, it has been an example to the world. Its great names are household words, and its honour is jealously regarded not by seamen alone. And yet, when we turn aside from the authentic splendour of these generalisations, and consider the inner story of its evolution, we find the splendour shot through with perplexing strands of corruption, incompetence, and even horror. During the period of Pepys's administration, he was constantly at odds with conditions that were baffling to the public servant and profoundly distressing to the man. Dr. Tanner says rightly that the source of all evils was the impoverishment of the Treasury, but to explain them does not make it the easier to understand how the service can have survived them. The spectacle of crews rioting in the streets for their pay, sometimes three or even four years overdue, was common; and, hardly less common, that of starving seamen dropping in their tracks with no riot left in them. The contractors, with long scores unsettled, supplied short rations and unwholesome rations, until, tired of waiting, they refused to supply anything at all. The King's government at one time could not buy a bundle of candles for the ships at Gravesend unless the money was paid across the counter. The press gang, at its wit's end, sent cripples and children to the ships. Commanders secretly let themselves out for public hire, stuffing their ships with merchandise that made rapid clearing of the decks in an emergency impossible. Captains were constantly absent from their ships without leave, trusting them to the irresponsible charge of untrained lieutenants who had been commissioned by Court favour. The treatment of the sick and wounded was grossly inadequate, and of prisoners of war, barbarous. In these circumstances discipline was maintained with the utmost difficulty, and reform was beyond any but the stoutest determination. Pepys was determined. He laboured incessantly to check extravagance, pay debts, enforce regu-

lations, establish credit, see that contracts were completed,
decide disputes by justice and not by interest, and deal
fairly or even generously by the common seamen. And in
the face of endless discouragement he made his impression
upon this most intractable material. By 1665, he was able
to write in his Diary, 'Thence to the Cockepitt and there
walked an houre with my Lord Duke of Albemarle
[Monk] alone in his garden, where he expressed in great
words his opinion of me; that I was the right hand of the
Navy here, nobody but I taking any care of anything therein; so that he should not know what could be done without
me. At which I was (from him) not a little proud.' In his
will he could speak modestly and sincerely of 'my more
than four and twenty years publick and painful service
faithfully performed to the Crown,' service, be it said, for
which the Crown owed him some £28,000. His friend
Evelyn could say of him at his death, 'None in England
exceeding him in knowledge of the Navy, in which he had
passed through all the most considerable offices . . .
which he performed with great integrity.' In an obituary
notice contained in the Annual of 1703, to which reference
has already been made, are the words:

. . . it may be affirm'd of this Gentleman, without Exception, That he was the greatest and most useful Minister
that ever fill'd his Posts in England; the Acts and Registers of the Admiralty, and Navy vouching this Character
beyond Contradiction. . . . In a Word; as for his
Standing, he was esteem'd the Father, so far his Abilites,
Experience, and true Concernment for its Prosperity extended, as he was justly rever'd (even after his Retirement) as the Oracle of the Navy.

We shall see that in the flourish of these periods eulogy was
hardly strained. 'The ablest man in the Admiralty,' said
Macaulay a century and a half later. And in 1688, when
Pepys was finishing his *Memoires of the Navy* and retiring from office, he could with honourable satisfaction speak

of his employment wherein 'as an Englishman, and in a Service purely English, I have ever with all simplicity of mind contended, to render this humble Province of mine useful to my Country.'

Pepys took bribes. We think that to take bribes is a bad practice, morally indefensible; and we are right. But, shocking as it may seem to us, there have been generations of national honour and advancement in which our countrymen were not of the same opinion. That our national credit was much advanced in the age of the Restoration we cannot pretend, but it was nevertheless an age of great qualities. It was dirty and unhygienic, but it had taste and intelligence. It was something frivolous, but it did not cant. After the great Puritan effort there was for a time a certain moral exhaustion, but it was no more than a momentary exhaustion of a national spirit that had acquired a new significance. In that age, Pepys devoted his energy and talents to putting one of the chief public services in order. He applied himself to the task with a scrupulous pertinacity, and he was in a large measure successful. The honour of the Navy was very dear to him; after all our accidental knowledge of his private life has been weighed, a knowledge of unequalled intimacy, he remains in his moral and intellectual standards a fairly representative Englishman of his time. And we have to recognize the fact that he considered it permissible to accept bribes, even though they were accepted secretly. It is a difference in point of view about which discussion leads us nowhere.

Like Bacon, Pepys could at least claim that although his favours were not above being rewarded, they were not to be bought. The presents that came his way in the course of business were never quite openly given or received. Pepys was always inclined to ingenuous and mostly harmless little self-deceptions. His solemn bets with himself, his fine-spun self-examinations, and the charming sophistry by which he comforted his mind in indulgence, make agreeable reading in the Diary, but are also significant of character. Pepys suffered from the infirmity, if infirmity it be, that afflicts many men of fine quality. When a problem in affairs presented itself to him, he could see it clearly, equitably, and with firm judgment. When he could consider conduct objectively, he had no patience with neglect of duty or crooked dealing. That is to say, as long as his principles were fortified by external contacts, they were sound. He was the sort of man to whom other men would turn confidently for advice in a difficulty. His opinions of people have a telling air of authority about them, and not the less so because he could change his mind. If a man behaved well to-day, Pepys was very ready to forget that he had behaved badly yesterday. Nor could any man have been less of a humbug than he. There is no affectation in his clearly professed sense of right. So long as he was out in the open, functioning as a social unit, he was a level-headed man of honour, with robust and yet not insensitive value. But in the privacy of his life, in the loneliness that is the daily experience of every man, he was, like every man, very often a poor puzzled fellow. It was so easy to persuade himself that things he knew to be wrong were not so very wrong after all, so humiliating to realise how closely shame walked in the shadow of decency. When we read the intimate and often humorously turned confessions of a man like Pepys, we are apt to regard them with an indulgent smile, to say how humorous it all is and to be a little complacent in our approval of what we take to be nothing graver than amusing triviality. But to read the great Diary in this way is to overlook the fact that it really is a great diary. As a chronicle of incident, and a record of personalities, its merits, we might say without exaggeration, are incomparable. But it is much more than this. We are sometimes told that Pepys is such attractive company because not only does he entertain us with inimitable gossip, but because also we recognise in him our own amiable weaknesses. The estimate is wrong in its reckoning. Pepys was not a man of amiable weaknesses. Certainly, if to like pretty girls and good drink be a weakness, most men are very weak creatures, and Pepys was as weak as any. There were two or

three incidents in his life when the weakness became serious
and got him into some trouble. But these considerations are
after all but a fragment of his Diary, as the Diary itself is
but a fragment of his life. The real weaknesses that Pepys
reveals to us are of a much graver, more deeply rooted
nature, and anything but amiable. He sets them down in
a demure and racy idiom that may easily deceive us. We
may readily fall into the mistake of supposing that things
so ingenuously confessed cannot have been very serious.
But they were serious. The dark squalls of temper, the
angry suspicions, the meannesses, the ugly satisfaction
when a responsibility is ended by death, or a rival comes to
misfortune, the deceptions and the cunning, the oppor-
tunism and the vanity, these are the troubled elements in a
man of courage and integrity. When all is said, we remember that Pepys was a great civil servant, a man of enlightened taste, a good friend, an affectionate husband, and that
in a time of public terror he did not desert his post and
was shocked by those who did. And it was such a man who
was troubled, and deeply troubled, by these evil communications. We have here the stuff of the universal tragedy.
That Pepys writes about it lightly does not really lighten
it. Pepys was never beaten by his own defects, but he was
often lamentably aware of them. Here, indeed, if we have
his claims to credit, we may say that we recognise ourselves.
Most of us, as we watch Pepys come through his trials of
character smiling and unembittered, may hope for nothing
better than that we too may follow him in this. For the
trials, and just such trials, we almost certainly must endure.
And as we see them glooming behind the debonair manner
of the Diary, we know them for what they are, and no
longer titter at them as amiable weaknesses.

And so sometimes we pause to ask ourselves whether a
noted passage is not something more than just the good fun
that it seems to be. A grateful captain, with a lively sense
of favours received, already received, be it noted, in Tangier, sends an envelope to Pepys, his benefactor. There is
something hard inside it, and the Clerk of the Acts thinks

it may be money. Indeed, he knows very well that it can be nothing else. Everybody knows that everybody accepts these little attentions, and yet nobody has the face to say so. The Clerk of the Acts has a much smaller salary than his duties would justify; it is tacitly understood that there will be not inconsiderable perquisites. The great thing is to be quiet about it. If one were publicly accused of taking bribes, the world would affect astonishment, and one would be disgraced. That, in fact, everybody from the King and the Duke down knew all about it would not help one in the least. And here is what seems to be a nice bribe in the envelope. The Clerk of the Acts has no fancy for perjury, but he has a fancy for the bribe. If he is questioned about it later he wants to be able to speak the truth. But he also wants to take the Captain's present. And so, after a little deliberation, he opens the envelope, and with his eyes shut spills out the contents, perhaps on to the soft carpet or among some papers. He then reads the Captain's communication, deals with it, and files it. He can say with a clear conscience that he certainly saw no money in the paper, and presently something is found which, as it belongs to nobody else, must belong to him, and his purse is fatter by a gold piece and four pounds in silver.

With a clear conscience. Delightful old rogue, we say affably, as we read the innocent confession, and learn that Pepys thereupon went home to his father and wife, and after dinner found the maid Ashwell a very deft pupil on the tryangle. But perhaps not quite so clear a conscience, not quite so innocent. The incident is worthy of a Scapin, and Scapins in the comedy of a great poet are finely comic, but in real life a man does not play these tricks with himself with an easy mind. Pepys was not a common cheat, and here he was doing something that was precious like cheating. He was cheating himself. The pitiful little pretence with the envelope may amuse us, but we need not suppose that it amused him. It was symptomatic. Pepys in his conduct was in one of the rather desperate corners into which he was frequently being driven, or driving himself. He usually contrived to escape, but usually with some loss of dignity. Loss of dignity, for some reason, often strikes us as being funny in other people, but it is a good deal less funny when it comes our own way, and Pepys's quite real and very deeply esteemed dignity was always getting into messes of this sort. And to realise his character is to know that he felt about it a good deal more deeply than he chooses to tell us in his Diary. Though even in the Diary there are frequent phrases, such as 'I was much troubled' that have much more meaning than we are apt to recognise in our enjoyment of the lightly flowing narrative.

Pepys's salary as Clerk of the Acts was £350 a year. Shortly after his appointment, he further secured by Lord Sandwich's influence a clerkship to the Privy Seal, which meant employment for a month at a time in rotation with the other clerks, with fees amounting sometimes to £3 a day. If we place his annual official earnings in the early years of his career at £500 we shall not be far wide of the mark. It is difficult to estimate the precise value of this according to our modern rates. It was computed by Mr. Wheatley thirty years ago in his *Pepysiana,* that money at that time was worth not more than a quarter or one fifth of its value in the latter part of the seventeenth century. Without considering what depreciation has further taken place during the last thirty years, it seems doubtful to me whether upon close analysis these figures could be substantiated. The evidence is conflicting. In 1662, Pepys could complain that his ordinary housekeeping came to £7 a month. We do not know what this included, but in any case it is not easy to believe that a young official of under thirty was receiving a salary equivalent in our money to something under £2,500 a year, or that a young married couple by the same reckoning were spending between £30 and £40 a month in 'ordinary housekeeping.' In the same year, Pepys spent £15 on three dinner parties at his house, attended in all by twenty guests. If the scale proposed is correct, this works out at about £3 a head for a dinner at home, which, even allowing for Pepys's handsome views of hospitality

and the ample appetites of the age, again seems unlikely
for a young man's dinner table. Further, Pepys made such
profitable use of his opportunities that within six years of
his entrance to the Navy Office he could assess himself as
being worth just on £7,000. He had his salary as Clerk of
the Acts, his Privy Seal fees, and for a period of eighteen
months or so he held a temporary post at the Navy Office
with an additional salary of £300 a year. The amount of
his savings make it clear that these sources of income must
have been lavishly augumented, and there is, indeed, plenty
of unblushing evidence in the Diary that this was so. Pepys
had his occasional extravagances, but his habit was thrift.
To find his wife's accounts a few shillings out was sufficient
at any time to provoke high words and a fit of the sulks
afterwards. His behaviour was inexcusable, and he did not
attempt to excuse it. But his tidy mind had a real hatred
of even such petty irregularities. He was frequently re-
proaching himself for wasting his money, and although
repentance was short-lived, his practice throughout his
life was very carefully to husband his resources, and on the
whole he was a steady saver. And to have put by £7,000
was pretty good going for a civil servant of thirty-four,
who had only been at the job some six years. But when we
are asked to believe that by present values this surplus
amounted to something like £35,000 we begin to suspect
that something is wrong with the scale. Two further examples may be given. During September, 1664, Pepys, at
the age of thirty-one, spent £89 'for kitchen and clothes for
myself and wife, and a few extraordinaries for the house.'
That, by the reckoning, would be something over £400 in
the month. And, lastly, we hear of him paying £17 for a
suit and thirty-five shillings for a hat, or something more
than £80 and £8 respectively. Men's clothes, we know, are
not to-day the ceremony that they were then, but none the
less the estimate seems extravagant. On the other hand,
there are figures that show an even greater discrepancy on
the other side of the account. Servants' wages, for example,
as Pepys knew them, need a larger adjustment to bring

them into line with modern usage. He agreed with a cook at £3 a year, and thought she should have taken less. John Evelyn's wife in an estimate of housekeeping expenses made in 1675, and printed in *Pepysiana*, allows an inclusive sum of £48 for the women servants (the number is not mentioned), two lady's maids, a valet de chambre, a footman, and a groom. In respect of these figures the ratio of five to one must be reckoned as insufficient, while over a wider range of expenditure it would appear to be excessive. It remains, as I have suggested, a matter very difficult of precise calculation. Pepys's annual £500 or so at the Navy Office was worth more than £500 in our money, but to call it £2,500 must be to exaggerate. Taking one thing with another, and without being able to confirm the figure in detail, which could hardly be done in any case, I should suppose that if we think of Pepys taking up his new duties with a salary that would to-day be the equivalent of £1,000 or £1,200 a year and a house thrown in, we shall form a reasonable view of his position. It may be noted that for the first four years of his clerkship, Pepys had to pay £100 a year to 'Mr. Barlow, an old consumptive man,' who had established some claim to the office.

Pepys at once settled down to his new work, and the pages of the Diary buzz with industry. Consulting with his fellow-Commissioners, interviewing applicants for all kinds of considerations, disposing of places at a price, seeing to it that the price should be a substantial one, but scrupulous always that there should be no 'wrong to the King's service,' engaging a staff, and placing orders with his brother Tom, who was a tailor too, taking still a diligent interest in my Lord's concerns, and making preparations for the removal of the household from Axe Yard to the quarters that were provided for him at the Navy Office, he had not even time to visit Cambridge to receive his Mastership of Arts, which was conferred on him by proxy. The Navy Office was situated on the east side of Seething Lane, its frontage facing south. The old building was burnt down in 1672 and replaced by the one shown in the print given by Mr. Wheat-

ley in the first volume of the Diary. Pepys knew the later
building, though he had left the clerkship before it was
built, but to-day all traces of the block enclosed by Seething
Lane and Crutched Friars have disappeared. Fortunately,
however, St. Olave's Church, at the corner of Hart Street
and Seething Lane, a few yards away from the old Navy
site, is still standing as when it was the most familiar feature seen by Pepys in the immediate neighbourhood of his
house and office. It was here that he worshipped, here that
he caused a special gallery pew to be erected for the accommodation of himself and his fellow-Commissioners, and
here that he and his wife lie buried under the chancel steps.

For some weeks Pepys had to travel to and fro between
his office and Axe Yard, while the domestic premises in
Seething Lane were being made ready. On July 18th, he
was able to dine in his new house for the first time, while
the carpenters were putting the finishing touches to their
work, and making 'an end of my door out of my chamber
upon the leads,' the leads that were to be a source of much
unneighbourly vexation. The household consisted, besides
Pepys and his wife, of William Hewer, William Wayneman with his sister Jane, and a maid, the first in a long
and disturbing succession. Hewer was a young man who
had recently entered Pepys's service as clerk and now became also a sort of confidential servant in return for his
board and lodging. The connection was to grow into one of
intimate friendship, but in the early days Hewer had some
taste of Pepys's quality as a martinet. In August, 1660,
'I was vexed this night that W. Hewer was out of doors
till ten at night, but was pretty well satisfied again when
my wife told me that he wept because I was angry, though
indeed he did give me a good reason for his being out, but
I thought it a good occasion to let him know that I do expect his being at home.' Two years later, the discipline had
not been relaxed: 'Home, and observe my man Will to
walk with his cloak flung over his shoulder, like a Ruffian.
. . . I did ask him where he learned that immodest garb,
and he answered me that it was not immodest, or some such

slight answer, at which I did give him two boxes on the ears, which I never did before, and so was after a little troubled at it.' And, again, a few weeks later, upon some neglect of duty, 'I struck him, and did stay up till 12 o'clock at night chiding him for it, and did in plain terms tell him that I would not be served so.' Hewer, nevertheless, survived these escapades, and lived to become the most devoted and most treasured of Pepys's friends, rising high in his profession. He might well have found the modest niche in the *Dictionary of National Biography* that has been denied him.

William Wayneman's position in the house was much humbler. He was merely the boy about the place, and a good deal of a young rascal at that. If, however, he was a constant trial to Pepys's temper, he had more than enough trials of his own. The scullery was no very comfortable place for a high-spirited lad in the seventeenth century. But Wayneman systematically made the worst of it, and was continually in scrapes. He stole money, he told lies, he carried on experiments in the house with gunpowder, he ordered cakes and ale outside at his master's expense, he refused to go to church with the maids, and he assaulted other boys in the streets. For these exploits he was methodically rewarded with canings and bastings and was finally dismissed, and in another employment misbehaved to the tune of getting himself shipped off to the Barbadoes. He asked Pepys to help him to a release, but 'I will not out of love to the boy, for I doubt to keep him here were to bring him to the gallows.' Altogether, Will Wayneman was not one of Fortune's darlings.

Jane, his sister, also had her vicissitudes. She was called up at two in the morning to do the washing, belaboured with a broomstick, and roused in the night to minister to her master who had overeaten himself, when she diverted him by running 'up and down so innocently in her smock.' But she remained at Seething Lane for three years and Pepys when she left was 'very much troubled, and myself could hardly forbear shedding tears for fear the poor

wench should come to any ill condition after her being so
long with me.'

Advancement came apace. In September, Pepys was
sworn a Justice of the Peace for Middlesex, Essex, Kent,
and Southampton, was much pleased by the honour, and
confessed himself wholly ignorant of its obligations. He
does not appear to have taken the duties very seriously,
since in December, after going home by water on 'a most
pleasant moonshine night,' and being entertained by bawdy
stories from the watermen, he found his first summons
awaiting him, and feared that much as he might desire it,
he would have no time to obey it. And, indeed, he was now
a very busy man. Work at the Navy Office was no sinecure,
and Pepys spared himself no pains to make himself master
of his calling. Not only had he the routine of his own department to organise, he was also often called in by his
fellow-Commissioners to consultation in general matters of
policy. 'To the office, where Sir W. Batten, Colonel Slingsby, and I sat awhile, and Sir R. Ford coming to us about
some business, we talked together of the interest of this
kingdom to have a peace with Spain and a war with France
and Holland.' On which occasion he for the first time
'drank a cup of tea (a China drink).' His work at the Privy
Seal and his attendance upon Lord Sandwich meant also
frequent excursions to Whitehall. He followed the custom of his day by making these commonly by water, and
we learn from Thomas de Laune's *Present State of London*
that in 1681 the current fares between London Bridge and
Westminster were by oars sixpence and by skull threepence.
But Pepys from the beginning was careful that it should
not be all work and no play, and it was seldom that a day
passed without some diversion at a bookshop, a playhouse,
a friend's table, or with music and hospitable fare at home.
Office hours were at his own discretion, and so long as the
work was done he could suit his times to himself, stepping
down the street at his pleasure to meet an acquaintance for
a pint, or going as far afield as Hyde Park to see Lord
Claypoole's footman beat an Irishman by two miles in a

footrace three times round the park. There were days when his attendance at the Navy Office was not required at all, but these were usually in part devoted to work at Whitehall. Occasionally the journeys about the town were made by coach, and if afoot after dark it was still by link home.

Pepys's chief associates among his colleagues in these early days at the Navy Office were Sir William Batten and Sir William Penn. Like Pepys himself, both had residential quarters in the premises at Seething Lane, although Batten was frequently at his luxurious country establishment at Walthamstow. With both of them Pepys had almost daily business and social contacts, and while he contrived for the sake of domestic peace and his own interests to keep on civil terms with men who were at once neighbours and his seniors in the service, he had little liking for either of them. Batten was an aggressive thick-skinned fellow, whose courage and energy as a seaman had been not untouched by brutality. Risen from humble origins, he had an insecure sense of his dignity, and was none too scrupulous in his dealings. Pepys had perhaps little cause to complain of corrupt practices in other men, but Batten's corruption departed from his own somewhat precarious standards by being insufficiently considerate of the King's interests. Batten, in fact, was often on perilously thin ice, and he may well have been suspicious of a junior colleague to whom inquisitiveness was second nature. Moreover, Lady Batten and Mrs. Pepys could not abide each other, and here again the elder lady may have had not a little to endure from a sharp-tongued young neighbour who stood on no ceremony. Indeed, Elizabeth Pepys on one occasion so far forgot herself as to induce her maid to ridicule her Ladyship over the garden wall. Altogether it was difficult to preserve the amenities of life, and it says something for the good sense and discretion of both Batten and Pepys that somehow or another they did manage to get along without open friction. We know that Pepys said a good many hard things of Batten behind his back while preserving a friendly attitude, and even when he was borrowing from him £40, which

sum, however, was duly repaid within six months. This is
no laurel for the Pepysian garland, but on the other hand
we do not know how well founded were his observations on
Batten, nor what Batten had privately to say of him. And
in any case it is not an easy thing for a young civil servant
to tell a superior to his face that he is a scamp, and Pepys
did pretty well when on one occasion he informed Sir William in high tones that he was unreasonable, 'at which he
was very angry and so was I, but I think we shall not much
fall out about it.'

William Penn, who had been knighted by the King on
board the *Naseby* at the time of the Restoration, was a man
who had served with distinction at sea, and was to serve
again. That he was a brave and capable commander, and
that he had enlightened views on the subject of naval
strategy, there seems to be no question; but these qualities
do not necessarily fit a man for administration, and in the
Navy Office Penn was commonly reported to be rather an
adroit dissembler than a competent official. An affectation
of piety did not add to his graces. As in the case of Batten, the relations between Penn and the young Clerk of the
Board were no doubt inflamed by Pepys's meddling mind.
For that Pepys was a meddler there is sufficient evidence in
the undertones of the official passages in the Diary. He was
a meddler by policy. With all his faults he had a genuine
passion for efficiency in the office, and it was part of his
business to know everybody else's. Penn knew all about the
Navy, but he seems to have had no notable gift for affairs,
nor to have had any great solicitude for the service except
as a fighting man. In Pepys's animosity towards both Batten and Penn some personal jealousy may be read, but the
feeling had worthier origins. Pepys cared very much for his
own interests, but however assiduously he served them, it
can be fairly claimed for him that he did not set them above
the interests of the King and State by whom he was employed. It is questionable whether as much can be said for
either of the senior officials who are so severely handled in
the Diary. The simmering dissatisfaction with which he

regarded Batten was as nothing to his savage indictments
of Penn. At first the connection promised well enough.
Pepys found the Commissioner 'a very sociable man, and
an able man, but,' he adds, 'very cunning.' They visited each
other, drank together, and transacted business without constraint. 'Sir W. Penn and I into Moorfields and had a
brave talk, it being a most pleasant day, and besides much
discourse did please ourselves to see young Davis and Whit-
ton, two of our clerks, going by us in the field, who we observe to take much pleasure together, and I did most often
see them at play together.' All very nice and affable. But
before long they were at loggerheads over departmental
questions in the Office, and Pepys settled down to a steady
and incandescent dislike of Penn and his ways. The Commissioner becomes a coxcomb, an asse, a false and rotten-
hearted rogue, a perfidious knave, a cheating rascal, and
even a coward, which was nonsense. In the privacy of his
Diary Pepys allowed himself what licence he chose, and
he was at no pains to conceal from himself a distaste that
took on strong personal bias. There is even a sigh of satisfaction in being able to record that on going to Penn's
house for supper, 'the dishes were so deadly foule that
I could not endure to look upon them.' Nevertheless, prejudice apart, Penn was an unsatisfactory person to work and
live with. His services against the Dutch at sea in 1665
were duly acknowledged in the Royal Charter granting
lands at a later date to his son, the founder of Pennsyl-
vania. And Pepys himself writes on his return, 'I am gladder
to see him than otherwise I should be because of my hearing so well of him for his serviceablenesse in this late great
action.' But the feud persisted, and Pepys was glad to hear
after the action that whatever his courage might have been,
Penn was considered by the authorities to be 'the falsest
rascal that ever was in the world,' and that the Duke of
Albemarle had called him a cowardly rogue for double
dealing, and swore that he should never go with the Fleet
again. By 1667, the strain had almost reached breaking
point. 'To the office . . . and there a most furious con-

flict between Sir W. Penn and I, in few words, and on a sudden occasion, of no great moment, but very bitter, and stared on one another, and so broke off, and to our business, my heart as full of spite as it could hold, for which God forgive me and him.' Altogether the temper of the Navy Office must have been pretty highly charged. On rare occasions Pepys allowed it to get the better of his nerves, but he usually managed to preserve a diplomatic demeanour, and kept his reflections to himself. He had no mind for jeopardising his own position, and knowing that private broils could have nothing but a bad effect upon public business, he passed from one petty crisis to another, not insensible to provocation, but steadily determined to make himself indispensable in a service that he had very much at heart.

Already, within a year of his appointment, his position was becoming one of considerable family pride. It was with much satisfaction that John Pepys saw a son of his own taking a place in the world that would not be altogether unworthy of the Hinchingbrooke and Cambridgeshire connections. And Samuel for his part preserved a nice balance between natural affection and a somewhat patriarchal patronage. His father now a Merchant Taylor, had come to be a man of some consequence in his parish. As far back as 1649, he had been 'chosen scavenger for the year ensueinge,' an office in those days of some responsibility. The Scavenger's Oath, De Laune tells us is thus:

Ye shall Swear that ye shall Diligently oversee that the Pavements within your Ward, be well and sufficiently repaired, and not made too high in Noyance of your Neighbours; and that the Ways, Streets, and Lanes, be cleansed of Dung, and all manner of filth, for the Honesty of this City. And that all the Chimneys, Furnaces, and Recedoes, be of Stone sufficiently made against Peril of Fire. And if ye find any the Contrary, ye shall shew it to the *Alderman* of the Ward, so that the *Alderman*

may Ordain for the amendment thereof. And thus ye
shall do, as God you help, etc.

John Pepys, however, did not fancy the job and managed to
get himself exempted by the payment of £5 to the Poor
Box. In 1658, his name appears as a sydesman at St. Bride's.
Now, in 1660, he was in his sixtieth year, and beginning to
think of retirement. The opportunity was to come at the
death of his brother Robert a few months later. He was
being helped in the business by his son Tom, two years
younger than Samuel. Tom was a source of constant anxiety
and irritation to his elder brother, drifting about with a
fecklessness that was peculiarly displeasing to Samuel's
methodical mind. He made sporadic efforts to keep himself
in order and earn a living, but he had an incurable habit of
borrowing £20, and was in constant hope of redeeming his
debts by some matrimonial enterprise. John, the youngest
brother, still at Cambridge, was showing promise that came
to nothing much. Samuel was lending a hand in his education, noting on one occasion that he has given his father
forty shillings towards college fees for a half year, and on
another that he has put by a little sum for the purchase of
his brother's books. Paulina, aged twenty, was at present
making herself tolerably agreeable, frequently accompany-
ing her sister-in-law on shopping expeditions, and not yet
alarming Samuel by the prospect of becoming an old maid
on his hands. Her position was an odd one. Nobody seemed
to know quite what to do with her, and when it was proposed that she should enter Samuel's household he was anxious to do well by her, but was concerned for her ill-nature.
At length, there was a family conference, and 'there I told
her plainly what my mind was, to have her come not as a
sister in any respect, but as a servant, which she promised
me that she would, and with many thanks did weep for
joy, which did give me and my wife some content and satisfaction.' Two months later she had joined the establishment,
'But I do not let her sit down at table with me, which I do

at first that she may not expect it hereafter from me.' Pall could be trying; but she must have been considerably tried. Samuel's attitude towards his mother was never a very cordial one, and she seems to have been a sufficiently tiresome old lady. 'So to my father, and there finding a discontent between my father and mother about the maid (which my father likes and my mother dislikes), I staid till ten at night, persuading my mother to understand myself, and to that in some high words, which I was sorry for, but she is grown, poor woman, very froward.' And the next day, 'I found my mother alone weeping, upon my last night's quarrel, and so I left her.'

Pepys's wife, Elizabeth, was not yet twenty-one years of age. Strangely enough, although there are constant references to her in the Diary, she somehow does not take on a very definite aspect or personality. She was said to be beautiful as a girl, but the only portrait we have of her shows a finely but heavily featured face, not very friendly or attractive. The impression is confirmed by a contemporary stoneware bust done by John Dwight of Fulham. On the other hand, the memorial on the tomb at St. Olave's Church, executed under Pepys's close supervision, although it is not easily seen, has a much more prepossessing appearance. On the whole, we may conclude that she was not uncomely by Restoration standards, and on the score of looks, at least, Pepys appears to have been well satisfied, since he compares her to her advantage with the notable beauties of the age. Her character was even more enigmatical. It is reflected from day to day in Pepys's own capricious moods, and achieves little in the way of unity. We do not even learn what he called her. It is worth noting that the one person who most frequently takes the stage throughout the period of the Diary is, of all the figures in that astonishingly rich and varied company, the least convincingly drawn. It may indeed be questioned whether Pepys really had an eye for character. He was birdlike in his quickness for recording the vibrations of conduct, and he could see through dissimulation as shrewdly as any man. What people did for good or bad he could bring on the instant to a precisely drawn account, but there is little evidence that he was much interested to understand in any significant sense what people were. Least of all was he disposed to enquire what a woman was, so long as she was agreeable, pretty, and good company. There is nothing to show that Elizabeth Pepys had depths and nobilities in her character that were worth exploring, but there is also nothing to show that if she had her husband would have been at the trouble to explore them. Pepys was not merely a man of his age in wanting his wife to be a good bed companion, a competent housekeeper, and a credit to his taste and generosity in society. There is no doubt that Pepys was very much in love with Elizabeth. Whatever his behaviour, he always chafes at her absence, and the darkest tempers are nearly always redeemed by some clearly genuine touch of endearment. Their quarrels were frequent, and sometimes ugly, but at least they had the merit of being lovers' quarrels to the end. When she died, Pepys could reproach himself with infidelities, but he at no moment of his married life regretted the choice that he had made. Whatever fugitive appeals might engage him, her own did not stale. The Diary leaves no doubt that this was the nature of Pepys's feeling for his wife, but it is a good deal less explicit on the subject of her feeling for him. It seldom occurred to him to set down what other people felt, and we suspect that it was a question that was but little in his mind even with regard to his own wife. This is not to speak harshly of him; many worthy and responsible and likeable men are made that way. We know that Elizabeth was anxious to have children, and Sir d'Arcy Power, in a learned treatise on the subject, surmises that the incapacity was Pepys's. Beyond that we have no reason to suppose that she did not return the affection of a trying but affectionate husband. That she could be vehemently jealous is beyond dispute, and indicates nothing but itself.

It was this fundamental bond between them that kept the peace at all in what was often a much distracted household. Pepys wanted his wife to be, as a secondary but still highly important consideration, a competent housekeeper, and in this Elizabeth was sadly disappointing. She was untidy, inexact, unpunctual, and casual about the appointments of the house and the table. All this Pepys thought inexcusable, and he did not excuse it. He had continually to be standing over her to see that things got done, and he was constantly finding her clothes, her kitchens, and her accounts in a muddle. His patience was tried almost daily, and almost daily it broke down.

And then among their friends, where he took great pride that she should cut a figure, she could carry herself with an air one day and go draggletail the next. She liked clothes well enough, but her taste and her husband's were not always in accord, and, moreover, she may very well at times have been driven for the moment to a desperate unconcern.

And so a married life of very uncertain fortunes went on. Small dissensions alternated with greater differences, but the sheet anchor somehow remained steady. She was scolded for mislaying half-a-crown, 'but we were friends again, as we are always.' Finding her room in disorder, he kicked 'the little fine basket' that he had brought her from Holland and broke it, and was then very properly ashamed of himself. He began to teach her 'some scale in music,' finding her 'apt beyond imagination.' One day, Pepys having found Mrs. Diana outside his old house at Axe Yard, inviting her in, 'did dally with her a great while,' and then returned home to take great pleasure in 'teaching my wife her music lesson.' He made her an irregular dress allowance, giving her sometimes £5 for a petticoat, £4 for 'lace and other things,' or £15 for joint mourning when the Duke of Gloucester died of smallpox. When she took pains with her appearance, he was ready in approval, noting with pleasure when she first adorns herself with patches, and highly gratified when this day 'my wife put on her black silk gown, which is now laced all over with black gimp lace, as the fashion is, in which she is very pretty,' and observing with satisfaction that in her becoming finery she is made much of by Lady Sandwich. But, fondly as he liked to see

MRS. PEPYS AS ST. KATHERINE

Engraved by HOLLYER after JOHN HALES.

his wife well dressed, he was very unwilling to provide the means. To ask was by no means to receive, and to receive was to be told pretty sharply to look to it. And when the outlay was not to his liking, he could become exceedingly unpleasant. After she had been sitting for her portrait, he liked the picture pretty well, but in the coach on the way home he fell out with her 'very highly about her ribbands being ill matched and of two colours, and to very high words, so that, like a passionate fool, I did call her whore, for which I was afterwards sorry.' The passionate fool was not being very thrifty of his happiness. He was putting a rod in pickle for himself, and very thoroughly pickled it was to be.

It cannot be said that Pepys took life easily. He was an apprehensive, choleric little man, and the Diary is full of suspicions and misgivings. But although trouble of one sort or another was usually brewing in his mind, he had a remarkable faculty for not being demoralised by it when it came. His was not a very profound nature, but it was an acutely sensitive one, and the way in which he summarily dismissed his vexations even in the seclusion of his own thoughts, is due to an instinct for self-protection. Vexations were so plentiful, and it would never do to brood on them. That way life could easily be made a misery, and life was far too full of enchantments for that. The, as yet, not very extensive prospect of his career was already notably peopled. In the near foreground, a wife, a father and mother, brothers and sister, and his clerks and domestic servants; a little further removed, Batten and Penn and the other dignitaries of his office, surrounded by a fugitive company of important personages; in the middle distance, but still easy of access, my Lord Sandwich and his family, familiar friends, but having impressive contacts with those figures in the remoter view, the King, and the Duke, and all the great people of the Court. Pepys, eager to make his way, saw in the prospect, with all its attractions, insecurity at every point. It was a world of sudden favours, and sudden declines, and it was a waste of valuable tissue to allow one's nerves to be rattled. And so Pepys, who was always seeing clouds in the sky no bigger than a man's hand, was never panic-stricken when the weather really came.

In consequence, his life, all things considered, was moving very agreeably. He had his aches and pains, but he had a robust constitution to support the attention of the quacks whom he patronised, and he could at intervals congratulate himself in his notes upon his fitness. 'Myself in constant good health, and in a most handsome and thriving condition.' At this earlier period of his life he ate and drank in prodigious quantities, and 'my head akeing all day from last night's debauch' is a familiar confession. One evening with three friends he drank two or three quarts of wine and ate two hundred walnuts. He was sick next morning. On another occasion, the two Sir Williams made him drink two draughts of sack 'to cure last night's disease.' He was lavish in resolutions to mend his ways, but until he was an older man they seldom survived temptation. There is nothing to show that his excesses did him permanent harm, and he lived to a temperate old age.

He found amusement at every turn. He raced Penn's coach against Batten's, and jumped Mr. Creed, the deputy Treasurer, for a quart of sack; he bought himself a box of carpenter's tools; he watched the Duke of York play Pelemele in St. James's Park, and he took singing lessons of Mr. Goodgroome; he went to all the plays, admiring particularly the boy Kynaston in a woman's part, 'the loveliest lady that ever I saw in my life,' and sometimes took a turn at bowls. One day there would be Dr. Fuller to take for a morning draught, and news of the forthcoming publication of the *Worthies,* and on another, more famously, Sir John Denham to follow unobserved in the press to see the King crowned in Westminster Abbey, the sceptre being suitably carried by my Lord. That night most of London seems to have got drunk, even a lady in Pepys's company disappearing under the table, and he himself confessing that he was foxed, if ever he was. In short, all things very merry, this being 'the present life I lead.'

And he was rising in the world. Mr. Payne Fisher, a poet, proposed to dedicate a book to him, 'with my armes . . . very handsome,' and a fortnight later to borrow a gold piece. He borrowed half a piece. The Clerk of the Acts had an offer of £1,000 for his place, which made his mouth water, but he had the good sense not to take it. He was busy getting the Navy pew built in St. Olave's, and on a visit to Chatham he had great pleasure 'to see how I am respected and honoured by all people.' The visit was an official one, but it was enlivened by the social graces of ladies and music and dancing, in which last diversion, however, Pepys made but 'an ugly shift.' And in such notes as the following, written at the end of 1660, we see progress reported to some purpose:

To Whitehall to Sir G. Carteret's chamber, where all the officers met, and so we went up to the Duke of York, and he took us into his closet, and we did open to him our project of stopping the growing charge of the fleet by paying them in hand one moyety, and the other four months hence. This he do like, and we returned by his order to Sir G. Carteret's chamber, and there we did draw up this design in order to be presented to the Parliament.

CHAPTER III

BRAMPTON. THE NAVY OFFICE. LONDON LIFE

IN OCTOBER, 1660, Pepys called on Lady Sandwich in town, she showing him 'most extraordinary love and kindness, and do give me good assurance of my uncle's resolution to make me his heir.' On other occasions his Lordship, coming up from Hinchingbrooke, had been able to speak hopefully to Pepys of his Uncle Robert's intentions, and he had been using his own influence in favour of his young kinsman. There is an implied intimacy between the great house at Hinchingbrooke and the little house at Brampton that speaks well of Robert Pepys's standing. Independently of his family prospects, Samuel was already cherishing the hope of acquiring a little property for himself at Brampton, that should further establish his ties with the Sandwich family, and to which he might retire when the time should come. In June, 1661, his Uncle Robert offered to secure for him some land adjoining his own, indicating that on his death it would be a convenience for his heir to have one considerable estate intact. In this proposal Pepys was more than hinted at, and was 'exceeding glad.' It was very reassuring. At the beginning of the year his mother had been down to Brampton to see Aunt Anne, who was sick and like to die, and had returned with the disquieting intelligence that she suspected in the event of her death that Uncle Robert would marry again, 'which God forbid.' The proposed purchase referred to land lying in the neighbourhood of the church and including the Rectory, the property of Mrs. Norbury, a connection of the Pepys family by marriage. The price asked was more than could be found by Pepys, who, although he had lately been able lovingly to add one little bag of £100 to another in his chest at home, was not yet in a position to invest in landed property. He was, however, anxious to impress Uncle Robert with his thrift and substance, and to this end adopted an expedient that would seem to have had everything to recommend it, apart from the fact that it would inevitably be exposed. He called on his father, who was about to visit Brampton, and desired him to tell his uncle that he was prepared to 'pay ready money £600 and the rest by £150 per annum, to make up as much as will buy £50 per annum, which I do, though I not worth above £500 ready money, that he may think me to be a greater saver than I am.' This was one of Pepys's best performances.

The occasion of his father's visit was news from Brampton that Robert was not well. John arrived to find his brother's condition serious. On July 1st, Pepys heard that his uncle was 'by fits stupid, and like a man that is drunk, and sometimes speechless.' Three days later, the news was that 'my uncle Robert continues to have his fits of stupefaction every day for 10 or 12 hours together'; and on July 6th, word came by 'a messenger on purpose, that my uncle Robert is dead, and died yesterday morning; so I rose sorry in some respect, glad in my expectations in another respect.' An entry in the Brampton church register reads, 'Robert Pepys, Esq. was buryed the seaventh day of July 1661.' In these circumstances, it is unlikely that Robert Pepys heard of his nephew's ingenious financial designs. By eleven o'clock in the morning on which the news reached London, Pepys was setting out for Brampton by post. The rate for riding post, as De Laune tells us, was threepence for every English mile, with an additional fourpence at every stage to the post-boy for conducting. The two roads from London to Brampton, as shown by Ogilby's maps, passed, the one through Kingsland, Tottenham, Waltham, Ware, Puckridge, Buntingford, Royston, Kneesworth, Paxton, Godmanchester, and Huntingdon; and the other, through Barnet, Hatfield, Stevenage, Baldock, Biggleswade, and Buckden. The distance by either route was approximately sixty miles. On this day Pepys did the journey in ten hours, arriving at Brampton before nine o'clock at night. He found his uncle's coffin 'standing upon joynt-stools in the chimney in the hall'; it was necessary to have it removed, and he had it placed in the yard for the night, watched by two men. His aunt was in bed, 'in a most nasty ugly pickle,' which made him sick to see. Concealing his impatience to inspect his uncle's papers, he shared his father's room for the night, and the next morning, Sunday, they walked in the garden reading the will, dated August 12, 1657. It was not quite all that Samuel had hoped, but it was satisfactory. The property was to come to him, but not immediately. After sundry bequests to the other branches of the family, the provision for the payment of forty shillings to the poor of Brampton, and legacies of £50 to John and Paulina, son and daughter of his brother John, Robert's will provides that all lands and tenements, goods and chattel and cattle, money and plate be held by his said brother John Pepys for his lifetime, with an annuity of £30 to his nephew Samuel, when the working charges of the estate had been cleared. And at John's death the said estate, with specific mention of the dwelling house at Brampton, is to pass to Samuel and his heirs, and, failing such issue, to Samuel's younger brothers Thomas and John, and their heirs alternatively. In the event, as we shall see, Samuel, although he had no children, survived his brothers, and at his death was free to leave the estate to Paulina's son, John Jackson.

Preparations were hastened, ribbands and gloves provided, and on the Sunday afternoon Robert Pepys was borne round the bend of the road for the last time to the church to which he had on so many Sundays walked across the footpath in the fields behind his house. A large company gathered from Huntingdon and the surrounding farms and villages, and Pepys was ashamed of the disorder in which the cakes and wine were served. The rector preached a ser-

mon, describing Robert Pepys as a man of such eminent
virtues as to need no eulogy, and, after a somewhat harassed supper party, quiet fell upon the house that Pepys
was to inherit from the man to whom he had owed so much
kindness.

The following days were beset by contentions and fears.
Robert had left his papers in confusion; important documents were missing, and expectations as to the size of the
estate were not being realised. Also there was much trouble
from 'my aunt's base, ugly humours.' Pepys found the meat
and drink not at all to his liking, the gnats bit him by night,
and, worst of all, it was learnt that the meddlesome fellow,
Tom Trice, was entering a caveat against the will. The protracted law proceedings that ensued muddled Pepys's head,
and to tell the truth he has left but a muddled account of
them in the Diary. In any case, they are of small interest.
Robert Pepys, by a clause in his will, had excluded his wife
from the estate, on the grounds that she had ill-treated him
in the matter of a considerable bond, and 'after she did see
how unworthily I was dealt with, still she would hold what
advantage she had got And so let her hold what she can.
So I do require my Executors to be very civil unto her in
all respects, although she know she hath done me much
wrong.' For a fortnight Pepys remained at Brampton, selling crops, appointing a bailiff, arguing his case before
lawyers, calling in to see the imposing alterations that were
going forward at Hinchingbrooke, making an excursion to
Cambridge to see his brother John, who vexed him by being
abed at eight o'clock in the morning, and plagued still by
his aunt's 'base, hypocritical tricks.' She was at length persuaded to leave the house for a consideration of £10, and
on the 22d, Samuel went back to London, having to buy a
pair of coarse woollen stockings at Biggleswade, it being
an uncommonly cold morning for July. On his return, he
was disturbed to find how proud and idle his sister Pall
was growing, and resolved not to keep her. He was glad to
be at the office again among persons of quality, and in command; 'and I give it out among them that the estate left

me is £200 a year in land, besides moneys, because I would
put an esteem upon myself.'

The will was duly proved on August 22d, and it was
decided that Pepys's father and mother should settle at
Brampton, taking Pall with them. Pepys had some ado to
get his sister off his hands in this way. He had high words
upon the matter with his mother, 'who is become a very
simple woman,' and it was not until after a scene in which
'in great anger' he had positively declared that he would
put up with his sister's moods and graces no longer, that
Pepys got his way. Pepys's father left for Brampton at the
end of August, to be followed a week later by his mother
and his sister: Pall, with much good counsel in her mind
and twenty shillings in her purse from Samuel, crying exceedingly. At this time Pepys wrote to Lord Sandwich, then
at sea, in a letter to be found in the Carte MSS.:

. . . the latest [news] hath beene my uncle the Captaine's
[Robert Pepys was a captain of militia] death, and dis-
posall of what hee had to my father and mee (though
with many Cautions) . . . and lastly my Lady's happy
delivery of a young Lady.

Sandwich replied: 'I am sorry for your Uncle's death, but
very glad he hath dealt soe kindly with you.'

In the meantime, Pepys had found his life not a little dis-
organised by the claims of these family affairs. Aunt Anne
had been duly removed from the Brampton house, and no
one seemed likely to be able successfully to contest his
father's possession of it. But a house without money was
an embarrassing inheritance. On reckoning up his father's
accounts, he found that on leaving St. Bride's Churchyard
he would be worth exactly nothing. Tom Pepys was to take
over the business to make what he could of it, but there was
no question of any payment for goodwill. The ready money
left by Robert was disappointing, something under £500,
and the estate otherwise, which included a number of small
separate properties, was becoming deeply involved in legal

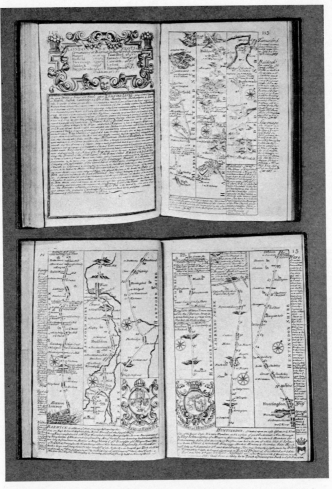

TWO MAPS FROM OGILBY'S *BRITANNIA DEPICTA* (1731)

SHOWING THE ALTERNATIVE ROUTES FROM LONDON TO HUNTINGDON. *Photograph, E. S. Whitney, Huntingdon.*

disputes, to which Uncle Thomas Pepys, the brother between Robert and John, had now become a party. It was,
in fact, more than two years before all claims were settled.
And now, the anxieties and distractions were putting Pepys
off his work, and he was calling himself seriously to order.
'My father gone to settle at Brampton, and myself under
much business and trouble for to settle things in the estate
to our content. But what is worst, I see myself lately too
much given to seeing of plays, and expense, and pleasure,
which makes me forget my business, which I must labour
to amend. No money comes in, so that I have been forced
to borrow a great deal for my own expenses, and to furnish
my father, to leave things in order.' There was some compensation in the importance that he now assumed in the
eyes of his Cambridgeshire relatives, who were people much
esteemed. His family settlements found him at Impington,
where his uncle Talbot lived, and his cousin Roger who was
a member for Cambridge. They took kindly to him, helped
him in his business, and gave him the best chamber in the
house to sleep in. He felt that he belonged to a family
indeed, when on entering church on the Lord's Day 'the
country people all rose with so much reverence; and when
the parson begins, he begins "Right worshipfull and dearly
beloved" to us.'

But, for the moment, Pepys was out of humour with
things in general. He was not queasy, but the licence of the
Court was becoming a little too much even for his stomach.
Pepys was a perfectly loyal subject to his King, even to the
point of admiring his mistresses, but the corrupt and dis-
solute loungers who infested the purlieus of the Court filled
him with indignation. If the King wished to keep a seraglio,
let him, but that he should allow his talents and sometimes
his honour to be seduced by worthless adventurers who
cared for nothing but their own gross indulgences was more
than Pepys could bear. I have attempted elsewhere to examine the moral aspects of the Restoration Court, and need
not reconsider the broader question here. But Pepys's view
of the matter is to our purpose, and like most of his views

it was emphatic and not wholly consistent. The pleasures taken by the King were pleasures for which he had a taste himself. The beautiful women, the fine clothes, the wit, the elegance, and the private wealth, all these were things to excite his admiration, and even his envy. He was never so enchanted as when some stray glance of recognition from the great world of Whitehall and St. James's came his way. The private morals of the Court did not in the least concern him, and he was undisturbed, even though the King himself should choose to bestow lavish favours upon a notorious adventuress or an orange girl. But when the King, or those about him most exalted in rank, belittled the dignity of the State by their public behaviour, Pepys was scandalised. He was not jealous that Lady Castlemaine should receive £20,000, or whatever it might be, from the King, unless, for example, the Navy Office went £20,000 short in consequence, when he was very jealous indeed. And just now, troubled by these voluble lawyers down at the Brampton court, by scenes with Pall and his mother, and by the reflection that an inefficient brother was probably about to get himself into debt at the tailoring business, he viewed the present state of public affairs with alarm. 'We are at our Office quiet, only for lack of money all things go to rack. Our very bills offered to be sold upon the Exchange at 10 per cent loss.' For lack of money all things go to rack—there is real bitterness in the note. Pepys had only been in the service for little more than a year, but he was already genuinely attached to it. He wanted to succeed greatly in it, but he wanted it to be a great thing to succeed in. He was acquiring a sense of his own ability, and it was being frustrated by the cheats and wench-mongers who were demoralising the great people of the Court. At least that was the way he looked at it. It was greatly to his credit that the mood was but a passing one, and that in the coming years no man helped more loyally than he towards mending matters, but for the moment the mood was upon him. And it was aggravated by further vexations of a personal nature. A Benevolence, or a goodwill offering from the grateful subjects of England to their King, was being organised, and he was expected to contribute £20. Moreover, his roof was leaking badly, and doing great damage to his ceilings.

The attention that Pepys was able to give to his Brampton and family affairs is an indication of his freedom to appoint his own times at the Office. Although he complains of official stagnation, and reproaches himself for neglect of business, he must nevertheless have had his hands full in these days. Apart from his work in Seething Lane and the Privy Seal, and his family preoccupations, he was engaged in attending, in an unofficial capacity, to the conduct of the Wardrobe during Lord Sandwich's absence. Since the King's return to England his Lordship had been actively employed as Admiral of the Narrow Seas, and in looking after the safe conduct to and from the Continent of the royal personages who made state visits to St. James's for the Restoration. He had recently been dispatched on a yet more responsible mission. Charles, after many hesitations, had contracted to marry Catherine of Braganza, Princess of Portugal. Portugal was to receive military assistance from us in their differences with Spain, and Bombay and Tangier were to be ceded to this country. Spain was very angry, claimed that Portugal was still her vassal, declared the cession of Tangier to be illegal, and threatened a renewal of war with England. Charles, who, whatever his faults, was the most difficult of men to intimidate, told the King of Spain that he might do what he pleased, but that the marriage was going forward. And in the middle of June, 1661, the Earl of Sandwich was sent as royal proxy to bring the bride away. Before leaving, he instructed Pepys to keep watch upon affairs at the Wardrobe. The Wardrobe Office, which must have been one of the most picturesque establishments in London, was situated on St. Andrew's Hill, off Carter Lane in Blackfriars. Mr. Harris, in his life of the first Earl of Sandwich, has given a vivid account of its activities. 'The knitting, spinning, weaving, lace-making, button-making, and silver winding, gave employment to eight hundred hands.' The King's own clothes, the linens and liveries of the household, furnishings for the royal chapels and apartments, and regimental ensigns, all came under the supervision of the Master, and were renewed and restored at his care. He also had handsome residential quarters on the premises, which the Sandwich family were using as their town house. Pepys was now a welcome visitor at all times. Sandwich had learnt to value him as a competent and trustworthy assistant, was ready to open his mind to him, and even on occasion to take his advice.

Lady Sandwich found in her young cousin a counsellor upon whose sympathy and discretion she could count. His Lordship was a fond and indulgent husband, but his wife had her anxieties. Sandwich's rewards for his services at the Restoration had been splendid, but he had splendid ideas as to the style in which a great position should be supported. Also, he had an intermittent zest for gaming, which sometimes cost more than even his well-filled purse could afford. Lady Sandwich was a thrifty housewife, and always devising means, if not to check, at least to provide for her Lord's extravagances. During his frequent absences she carefully trimmed the household expenditure, so that there should be some reserve to meet the prodigalities that were sure to mark his return. In this prudent guardianship of the family interests she found a willing confederate in Pepys. The two were frequently engaged in amiable little conspiracies to keep the Sandwich exchequer in order and the establishment within bounds. Though they were not always successful, there is no doubt that through their solicitude the fortunes of the Sandwich earldom made a much more auspicious beginning than they would otherwise have done. Here again, Pepys had his own interests to consider, but there was also the inducement of his ever-active instinct for efficiency. Any misfortune to the house of Sandwich would be his misfortune, but it would also be a reflection upon his capacity for affairs. If he was admitted to the confidences of the family, and was so far honoured as to be asked to lend a hand in its management, then his self-

respect demanded that the management should not be mis-
directed. And so Lady Sandwich came more and more to
turn to him in her difficulties. His friendship with her is one
of the most charming and honourable circumstances of his
life. Towards himself and his wife she was liberal in a
hospitality that was never abused. Within a week of the
birth of one of her children, he was admitted to her bed-
side that he might help her in the disposing of a business
difficulty. She could even admonish Pepys where he was
most sensitive without offence. 'Among other things my
Lady did mightily urge me to lay out money upon my wife,
which I perceived was a little more earnest than ordinary,
so I seemed to be pleased with it, and do resolve to bestow
a lace upon her, and what with this and other talk we were
exceedingly merry.' Two days later, Elizabeth took a selec-
tion of laces to the Wardrobe for her Ladyship's approval,
and a choice was made at a cost of £6, 'which I seemed
much glad of that it was no more, though in my mind I
think it too much, and I pray God keep me so to order
myself and my wife's expenses, that no inconvenience in
purse or honour follow this my prodigality.' It may be noted
that during a shortage of ready cash, Pepys had already
been instrumental in borrowing £1,000 for Lord Sandwich
from his cousin Thomas Pepys, on what seems to have been
sufficient security. There was to come a time when he himself would lend her Ladyship £100 in necessity. By the end
of 1661, he could say of a visit with his wife to the Wardrobe that 'my Lady . . . seems to doat every day more
and more upon us,' and six months later, when he called
after an unusually prolonged absence, he found her 'truly
angry and discontented with us for our neglecting to see
her as we used to do, but after a little she was pleased, as
she was used to be, at which we were glad.'

Pepys was also on affectionate terms with the Sandwich
children. 'Back to my wife, and with my Lady Jem and
Pall [*i.e.,* Jemimah and Paulina Montagu] by water
through the bridge, and showed them the ships with great
pleasure, and then took them to my house to show it them,

and we treated them well and were very merry.' And, again, 'I staid and dined with my Lady; but after we were set, comes in some persons of condition, and so the children and I rose and dined with ourselves, all the children and I, and were very merry and they mighty fond of me.' This latter passage may be read in conjunction with three others. In October, 1660, Pepys writes, 'To my Lord's, where I found my wife, and she and I did dine with my Lady, who did treat my wife with a good deal of respect'; in November, 'Here I did leave my wife to dine with my Lord, the first time he ever did take notice of her as my wife, and did seem to have a just esteem for her'; and in the same month, 'To my Lord's . . . where . . . my wife . . . and I dined with him and my Lady, and great company of my Lord's friends, and my Lord did show us great respect.' The relationship is here rather subtly defined, and it has something of a not unpleasing feudal significance. Pepys was intimate with his ennobled and powerful relatives; they were fond of him, they had confidence in him, and they were happy on occasion to acknowledge him and his wife as kinsfolk before their great friends. But the line was not crossed where the graces of ceremony were discarded. It may be difficult in our democratic age to realise how decisive class distinctions were two hundred and fifty years ago— indeed, more recently. It must be remembered that although they came of a common stock, there was a vast difference between the social standing of Sandwich and that of his young cousin. My Lord was a very great personage in the Kingdom, the heir of a highly distinguished house, Commander-in-Chief of the Navy, one of the principal instruments in the King's restoration, Sceptre Bearer at his crowning, a Knight of the Garter, Master of the Wardrobe, and the man now elected to the signal honour of acting as royal proxy to bring a queen to the throne of England. Samuel was the son of an impecunious tailor; by industry and good sense he had raised himself as a boy a little above the entirely undistinguished level of his own family, and had now come to a modest and well-merited elevation in the public service, by the discriminating favour of Sandwich himself. In the circumstances, it says much for Sandwich's character that he admitted Pepys to the courtesies of his public and his social life, with a cordiality so unforced and so free of condescension. And it says no less for Pepys, that while accepting the courtesies worthily and with dignity, he never took them for granted. There is something rather fine about the unaffected and faintly surprised note of satisfaction with which the occasions are recorded, as there is something rather gallant in the instinct that tells him, on the arrival of 'persons of condition,' that it is a suitable moment for him to move with the children to another table. In short, the contacts between Pepys and the Sandwich family, so fortunate and so honourable on both sides, were on both sides conditioned by a nicely balanced chivalry.

The new order of things was settling down, and Pepys was feeling a growing security in his position. The Restoration, once it had been decided to bring the King back, had had to encounter no opposition that mattered, and was now not only firmly established, but popular throughout the country. Sandwich, whose only misgivings had been when he found himself among the judges at certain of the regicide trials, was firmly in favour of the new Court, and his patronage was an assurance about which there could no longer be any doubt. At the end of May, 1662, he returned to England, escorting the pathetic little princess to her ill-starred marriage. He was looking well and happy, and Pepys could say with genuine warmth, 'my soul is glad to see him.' But he was discovered to be £7,000 in debt, and all available ingenuity was once more put to it to steer the family through a serious crisis. The danger passed, although the Sandwich finances seem always to have been in a more or less precarious condition. The same thing might, indeed, almost be said of everybody's finance in those days. No one appears at any time to have known quite how his fortune stood, even in respect of the actual money that he might have on deposit at his goldsmith's. The methodical

Pepys himself was often very indeterminate in his accounting. For example, on September 8, 1661, he tells us that he
was worth £600, and on October 3d following, he has to
borrow £50 on bond 'for my own occasions.' Even allowing
for an intervening proof of a £200 liability to Tom Trice,
the position is not clear. But little by little, his savings
accumulated, and month by month Pepys went steadily forward with his work and his social pleasures. Great events
moved around him, and although his share in them was not
a very conspicuous one, he was near enough to them to find
his interests continually refreshed. In the Diary at this
period he makes two illuminating notes upon his own character. He goes to some public spectacle, 'as I am in all
things curious,' and one night when working at his music,
he 'did try to make a song in the praise of a liberall genius,
as I take my own to be.' Here was the man to whom no
day was tedious. His attention is never at a loss for exercise. A doctor's dog that had killed a hundred cats and
buried them; a new method of shaving with pumice stone,
which made him 'in a suddaine fit cut off all my beard';
Lady Castlemaine's smocks and linen petticoats in the privy
garden at Whitehall; the discontent of his servants because
they were given Suffolk cheese; a woman on the stage in
men's clothes, with 'the best legs that I ever saw'; he is
endlessly diverted by such a variety. If he can be troubled
by graver matters, he has lighter compensations. A little
flown at dinner with a dozen friends, he 'made them a
foolish promise to give them one this day twelve-month,
and so for ever while I live, but I do not intend it.' His
pleasure in the gentler amenities of life is unfailing. He
delights to visit 'Foxall' with his wife and the maids, where
'the wenches gathered pinks.' His music is an almost daily
source of content. He is entranced when a dealer tells him
that his lute is as good as any in England and worth £10,
gets a German expert to play it for him, and rewards him
with a collar of brawn, a mince pie, and some wine for breakfast. He took lessons in composition from Mr. John Berk-
enshaw, and began with modest reason to fancy himself as

a song writer. Sometimes there is a genuinely lyric echo in the mood as it comes to us from the pages of the Diary. 'So to the Temple and by water home, and so walk upon the leads, and in the dark there played upon my flageolette, it being a fine still evening.' He also took lessons in arithmetic from one Cooper, the mate of the *Royal Charles,* exploring for the first time the mysteries of the multiplication table. He records with pleasure the delivery at home of 'my brave vellum covers to keep pictures in,' and he and his wife sit to the paynter Savill for their portraits, Pepys paying £6 for the two, and an additional £3 for a miniature of himself. He took an ever-growing pride in his home, gilding the chimneypieces, beautifying the garden, and was miserable when necessary repairs meant workmen and dirt. He even thought a cellar demanded by his position, and laid in a hogshead of sherry, of which, however, he later repented and sold it to Batten.

His domestic life continued to have its fair days and foul. There were more changes in his staff than he liked, Elizabeth Pepys seldom sharing his opinion of the successive girls whom they employed. Will Wayneman grew no better for his beatings, which were more violent than makes good reading. The domestic arrangements of the household, which presumably were customary at the time, were a little startling. The maid occupied a truckle bed in the matrimonial apartment, but not always, it seems, without some scruples; 'to bed, and this night began to lie in the little green chamber, where the maids lie, but we could not a great while get Nell to lie there, because I lie there and my wife, but at last, when she saw she must lie there or sit up, she, with much ado, came to bed.'

His attachment to his wife continued to survive trials, mostly of his own making. He had indulgent moods, bringing himself to lay out £20 on her for clothes at Easter, and buying her 'a pair of peruques of hair, as the fashion now is for ladies to wear; which are pretty, and are of my wife's own hair, or else I should not endure them.' In October, 1662, he could write, 'we have been for some years now,

and at present more and more, a very happy couple, blessed
be God.' And three weeks later, 'This afternoon my wife in
her discontent sent me a letter, which I am in a quandary
what to do, whether to read it or not, but I purpose not,
but to burn it before her face, that I may put a stop to more
of this nature.' When she went down to Brampton during a
house cleaning at Seething Lane, to his great vexation she
fell at odds with his father and mother; though his father
and mother were much at odds themselves, as he discovered
with much plain speaking when the interminable law business took him down to Brampton himself. On this occasion
he took a 'melancholy walk' with his father to Portholme,
where he found some escape from family cares in seeing
'the country-maids milking their cows there, they being
there now at grass, and to see with what mirth they come
all home together in pomp with their milk, and sometimes
they have musique go before them.' On leaving for London,
he gave Pall ten shillings, but 'have shown no kindness since
I come, for I find her so very ill-natured that I cannot love
her.' Tom Pepys, too, became no less an anxiety. It was
hoped to do for him by marriage what he could not do for
himself by business enterprise, but the favourable match
delayed. Of one lady who was proposed, Pepys wrote significantly, 'considering the possibility there is of my having
no child, and what then I shall be able to leave him, I do
think he may expect in that respect a wife with more
money.'

In his Office, Pepys was mastering his many difficulties
and advancing his reputation. Early in 1662 he was sworn
a Younger Brother of Trinity House, and in August was
made a member of the Tangier Commission. Passing the
Duke of York as his Royal Highness was watching the
wild fowl in St. James's Park, he received very civil recognition, and began to write a brochure, 'The business of striking sayle' or making strangers strike to us at sea, to be
presented to the Duke as 'a good way to make myself
known.' Having to deliver a letter in person to the Lord
Chancellor, Clarendon asked him whether he were not

the son of Mr. Talbot Pepys and spoke to him 'with great respect.' During the year he was so busy that he had to ask the Lord Privy Seal to relieve him of some of his duties. On visiting Portsmouth to inspect the dockyards, he was made a burgess of the town. He took himself very seriously in hand, curbed his excesses and applied himself with increasing diligence to business. He began to be a familiar figure in the naval yards at Deptford, Woolwich, Chatham, and Greenwich. The extravagance and negligence that he saw there infuriated him, and he laboured without stint and without respect of persons to reform them. 'I see it is impossible for the King to have things done as cheap as other men,' but he spared neither persuasion nor invective to make it possible. Exasperated on finding the clerks, who were supposed to be engaged on a survey, playing shuffle-board, he consoled himself with the reflection that Sir William Batten, who was responsible for the enterprise, was 'going down in everybody's esteem.' In October of 1662, he finds himself a 'very rising man,' and at the end of the year he could take stock of his situation thus: he had a comfortable home, £650 in money 'besides my goods of all sorts'; he and his wife were in health; he was acknowledged even by the Duke himself to have 'come to a good degree of knowledge' in his office; and he was conscious of the good opinion of Mr. Coventry, the new Commissioner, of whom more will now be heard. Altogether, at the age of thirty, Pepys had put his talents very prudently to use, and could say without immodesty, 'I doubt not but . . . I shall in a little time come to be a man much taken notice of in the world.'

The following year, 1663, was for Pepys a restless one. During the early months, he was distracted by serious anxieties concerning his wife. After a heated scene, during which she reproached him with the 'retiredness of her life,' he confessed to himself that her complaints were not unreasonable, and resolved to pay more attention to her entertainment. To this end they engaged as companion for Mrs. Pepys a young woman of some accomplishments named

Mary Ashwell, who for a time was a success, more particularly with her master. 'I hope,' he observes on her arrival, 'she will be very good entertainment for my wife without much cost.' Elizabeth, however, was still dissatisfied and irritable, and high words with her husband began to be common. One day he called her a beggar, and she retorted with advantage by calling him a pricklouse. And then Mr. Pembleton, the dancing master, came on the scene, 'a pretty neat black man, but married.' He was engaged to give lessons to Mrs. Pepys, though her husband found that she would 'hardly do any great good at it, because she is conceited that she do well already.' It was then proposed that Pepys himself should prove his paces, and he was well content that Ashwell should be included in the number. But having paid an entrance fee of ten shillings to the class and studied the steps of a Coranto, he began to suspect that the minds of his wife and the instructor were not wholly given to dancing. Within three weeks he was in a high fever of jealousy. He could concentrate on nothing in the office, he made sudden returns to the house, listened furtively through doors and ceilings, asked distractedly ingenuous questions, and even went so far as to spy upon his wife's toilet to see that she was decorously dressed. For some weeks the unfortunate man was truly possessed as by a devil. He saw trespass in a handshake, observed the offending couple leering at each other all through sermon time at church, could write in his 'devilish jealousy' that he knew not 'at this very minute that I now write this almost what either I write or am doing,' and finding them together in the house with the servants out, he made a pretence of going away, returned by stealth, and 'went softly up to see whether any of the beds were out of order or no, which I found not, but that did not content me, but I staid all the evening walking, and though anon my wife came up to me and would have spoke of business to me, yet I construed it to be but impudence.'

We have nothing but Pepys's suspicions to tell us of the circumstances. He, in the manner of his age, while allow-

His Royall Highness James Duke of York & Albany &c

JAMES, DUKE OF YORK

After PETER LELY.

ing himself such liberty as he chose, was exceedingly strict in his views as to how a wife should behave. Elizabeth Pepys was twenty-three, she had French and Irish blood in her veins, and she had a good deal of time on her hands. It is evident that she found the good-looking dancing master attractive, but beyond that we know nothing. The interest of the occasion for us lies in Pepys's attitude towards it. He is plainly not merely jealous because he fears that his possessive rights may be infringed, he is unaffectedly distressed by the possibility that he may be losing hold on his wife's affections. He was making a fool of himself, and knew it, and in view of his own conduct, he appears unimpressively enough as the jealous husband. But as well as being angry, he was deeply stirred, and our impatience may in consequence be modified. After a month the lessons came to an end, and Mr. Pembleton drifted out of the story, but there were long reverberations of the crisis in the Pepys household. For months to come, when Pepys took his wife to church, he looked apprehensively over the congregation, and to see Pembleton was to break out into a sweat. Elizabeth had tasted the pleasures of revolt, and carried herself with a new independence. In the middle of June, Pepys was momentarily driven to exclaim that he wished he had married nobody, but added that, since he had, his choice could not have been bettered. A few days later he had recovered his composure, and we read, 'in the evening our discourse turned to great content and love, and I hope that after a little forgetting our late differences, and being awhile absent one from another, we shall come to agree as well as ever.' Elizabeth the next day set off on a visit to Brampton, and in the evening Samuel dined at Trinity House, where Lord Sandwich asked Sir John Minnes, who was sitting next to Pepys, 'Sir John, what do you think of your neighbour's wife? Do you not think that he hath a great beauty to his wife? Upon my word he hath,' which afforded the anxious husband a great deal of satisfaction.

It is characteristic of Pepys that, while all this was going on, his own susceptibilities were by no means inactive.

He had to admit to himself that he took more pleasure in Ashwell's company than could be agreeable to his wife, and no sooner had Elizabeth left town than he found himself going a little out of his way in pursuit of temptation. There were pretty girls at taverns, there was a carpenter's wife at one of the dockyards, and there was a notorious Mrs. Lane, kind but not slender, who had just sufficient virtue to occasion thanks to God after many assignations that bad had come to no worse. He had more than one misadventure with this lady. Once he was sharing affection and a lobster with her in a tavern, when an indignant onlooker from the street made so bold as to throw a stone through the window, and at another time, when walking with her to take a boat, he had the misfortune to encounter the Lady Jemimah Montagu, who was quick enough to know Mrs. Lane for what she was, and discreet enough to pass on without recognising them, and to say nothing about it afterwards. A little later in the year, when Pepys and his wife were travelling to Brampton, Elizabeth was taken violently ill on the journey, and her husband thinking she would have died was 'in great horror, having a great tryall of my true love and passion for her,' and nursed her with an almost frenzied devotion. And a few days later, back in London, telling his wife that he was called to Deptford, he went instead with Mrs. Lane to Lambeth, and returned with an indisposition which shortly sent him to bed with a posset and the melancholy reflection, 'it is a cold which God Almighty in justice did give me while I sat lewdly sporting with Mrs. Lane the other day with the broken window in my neck.'

On her return from Brampton, Pepys found that his wife had fallen at odds not only with Ashwell, who had accompanied her, but with his father and mother. He was vexed, but kept what silence he could, and patiently set himself to restore amiability in the home, with reasonable success. He took pleasure in teaching her mathematics and the globes, he was solicitous in his attentions, and when a gentleman made advances to her in a shop, he gave him a 'good cuff or two on the chops,' and no retaliation being offered, gave him another. An unsatisfactory balance at the end of the month he attributed to extravagance on clothes, and could record that while he had spent £55 on himself, he at least had also spent £12 on her. He grew to dislike going to entertainments unless she was with him, and finding himself with a friend at Bartholomew Fair, refused to enjoy the sights until he had been home to fetch her. And he describes what they saw, thus:

. . . and so carried her by coach to the fayre, and showed her the monkeys dancing on the ropes, which was strange, but such dirty sport that I was not pleased with it. There was also a horse with hoofs like rams hornes, a goose with four feet, and a cock with three. Thence to another place, and saw some German Clocke works, the Salutation of the Virgin Mary, and several Scriptural stories; but above all there was at last represented the sea, with Neptune, Venus, mermaids, and Ayrid on a dolphin, the sea rocking, so well done, that had it been in a gaudy manner and place, and at a little distance, it had been admirable.

The other members of his family continued in their vexatious courses. Pall lapsed into obscurity at Brampton, but Tom, coming to little good as a tailor, was constant to the refrain of £20, and could not find a wife with the £300 that was considered to be the minimum qualifying figure. He had a new maid in the house, 'a very likely girl,' of whom Samuel expressed the pious hope that he would not 'play the fool with her.' John, having had his Bachelor's cap put on at Cambridge in January, came to stay at Seething Lane, and developed a pronounced taste for loafing, and a distaste for his sister-in-law. It was no repayment to his brother for what had been substantial kindnesses. Old Mrs. Pepys at Brampton was nagging her husband with determination, and once, when he came to London, where he railed at 'the rumbling and ado that is in London over it

is in the country, that he cannot endure it,' a warning was
sent down to her that if she could not promise to mend her
temper, he would not return. The Cambridgeshire connection thrived, but a less desirable one was discovered
when Pepys had to go on family business to Parson's Drove
near Wisbech:

> . . . a heathen place, where I found my uncle and aunt
> Perkins, and their daughters, poor wretches! in a sad,
> poor thatched cottage, like a poor barn, or stable, peeling
> of hemp, in which I did give myself good content to see
> their manner of preparing of hemp: and in a poor con-
> dition of habitt took them to our miserable inn, and
> there, after long stay, and hearing of Frank, their son,
> the miller, play upon his treble, as he calls it, with which
> he earns part of his living, and singing of a country
> bawdy song, we sat down to supper; the whole crew,
> and Frank's wife and child, a sad company, of which I
> was ashamed, supped with us.

Aunt Perkins was his father's sister. After this visit he was
glad to get back to Brampton, where he enjoyed 'the first
and only hour of pleasure, that ever I had in this estate
since I had to do with it,' riding with his wife to gather
nuts in the Brampton woods.

At the Office, Pepys began a new intimacy, that was to
have a deep effect upon his official career, and, indeed, upon
his official character. William Coventry, who was only some
five years older than Pepys himself, joined the Navy Board
as extra Commissioner in 1662, and Pepys's opinion of him
from the first is in strong contrast with that which he held
of his other colleagues. Mr. Wheatley says with some justice that he may be considered as the hero of the Diary.
Coventry, who was knighted in 1665, had been secretary
to the Duke of York, was reputed by Burnet to be the best
speaker in the House of Commons, and 'a man of great
notions and eminent virtues . . . and of the finest and best
temper that belonged to the Court.' Evelyn called him 'a

wise and witty gentleman.' He joined the Navy Office with the fixed intention of repairing its efficiency and putting a stop to its abuses, and in this design he had the whole-hearted support of nobody but Pepys. There was thus created a bond of sympathy between the two men that survived all the many bitter quarrels that frequently made the Council table of the Navy Board a disgrace to the public service. Coventry was something of a statesman, and in this he was distinguished from Penn and Batten and Pepys himself. Penn and Batten were seamen who had strayed into administration; Pepys was an administrator pure and simple and had no desire to be anything else. He enjoyed gossip about policy, but he had no ambition to take any part in it. The purposes for which the Fleet should be used were not his concern, which was to make the Fleet an effective instrument for whatever purpose to which it might be put. Coventry, also, came of a family with high official traditions, his father having been Lord Keeper to Charles I. These circumstances, and his close personal association with the Duke, gave him an authority that Pepys was quick to recognise, and we find the Clerk from the first treating him with respect that he felt for no one else in the Office. Not long after his appointment, he was charged with selling offices, and his reputation was for a time in considerable danger. He did sell offices, and extensively, but his defence was that it was a practice of old standing, that he himself only had employed it on a scale that was well known, and, indeed, fixed by the Duke, that in a great number of instances he refused fees that by precedent he might have taken, and that what he did was without concealment. He made good his case, and although in after years his enemies pursued the charge, even to the point of canvassing a bill against him, they were able to bring it to nothing. He did things that in the public service to-day would be impossible, but that by the standards of his own age he was corrupt, there is no evidence. He was, indeed, singularly high-minded in the business of the State, and Pepys admired his character no less than his ability. At the beginning of their acquaintance Pepys sent to Coventry a complimentary piece of plate; thinking it suitable later to supplement this with another, the gift was returned with a civil assurance that the Clerk's highly valued regard did not need these tangible tokens—an occasion of double satisfaction to Pepys. And that Coventry really did value the regard he lost no opportunities of showing. He told Pepys to his face how much he appreciated his coöperation in the work of the Office, and, better still, he told the Duke of York that in the young Clerk the Navy had a most estimable servant. Pepys, on his side, conceived a regard for Coventry that nothing could shake. Even the fact that the extra Commissioner was on unsatisfactory terms with Sandwich, and was at times one of his most damaging critics, did not alienate Pepys's mind from either of his friends. He believed in both of them, and if they quarrelled on matters of public policy it was not for him to interfere or lessen his regard for either. He cared for Coventry's good opinion, as he did for no other in the service, and at a moment when he fears he may be losing it, he notes as a matter of first importance that he 'must study hard to regain it.' Throughout the Diary Coventry makes a uniformly favourable appearance, and in this he comes down in history with credentials that Pepys awarded to no one else.

Other personalities at the Navy Office with whom Pepys was now coming into contact were Sir George Carteret, Mr. John Creed, and Sir John Minnies. Carteret, Treasurer of the Navy, was turned sixty years of age, and he was an agreeable and not incompetent officer of State, genially inclined towards everyone with the exception of Coventry whose reforming intentions were suspect at a Treasury Office not notable for its discipline. Pepys liked him, but without admiration, thought him a good-natured old gentleman, and after a scene of violent reproaches between Carteret and Coventry in 1667, Pepys, for all his attachment to Coventry, could say that he still regarded Carteret as 'a most honest man.' Pepys commonly spoke of him critically but not disrespectfully; he knew that his favour was worth having, and when the Treasurer's son, Philip Carteret, married Lady Jemimah Montagu in 1665, the favour was advanced to friendship.

John Creed, the Assistant-Treasurer, became secretary to the Tangier Commission, of which Pepys was a member, in 1662. He had been in the service of the Montagu household, and like Pepys he had advanced himself from humble beginnings. Pepys was his senior in the service, but the two men were on more or less level terms socially and officially. They were frequently in each other's company outside the Office, and Creed would sometimes stay the night with Pepys at Seething Yard after an extensive evening out. They made a memorable three-day excursion together to Epsom Wells, where they eat a brave dish of cream, 'the best I ever eat in my life,' played hide and seek in a wood, and spent a whole day looking for a little stray dog that had attached itself to their company. But in spite of these and many such amenities, Pepys liked Creed in the Office no better than he liked Penn or Batten. He called him 'a cunning knave in his heart,' 'a deadly cunning fellow,' and 'so full of policy in the smallest matters' that he was 'made up of nothing but design.' He was, we imagine, a niggling sort of fellow with a long nose, inopportune in his movements. In November, 1663, a passage took place between the two men that is an astonishing comment on the domestic habits of the civil service of the time. Pepys had done Creed some service in getting his accounts passed by Sir George Carteret, and in the ordinary course of business, it seems, expected some return for his trouble. Creed, with much ceremony, sent a parti-coloured Indian gown for Mrs. Pepys, not failing to draw attention to its superior quality. Pepys was not impressed; he gave the boy a shilling and sent the parcel back again. He then took a walk to Ludgate, and there pricing several gowns in the drapers' shops, estimated the present to be worth not more than £15. He considered that he was entitled to something to the value of at least £50, and thereupon wrote to Creed and told him as much in plain terms, with the result that Creed kept the

gown and sent nothing in its place, leaving Pepys to resolve
two months later 'I will have a good fleece out of Creed's
coat ere it be long, or I will have a fall.' The fleece took
yet six months more in coming, and then amounted to but
twenty pieces in gold, 'which I did not refuse, but wish and
expected should have been more. But, however, this is better than nothing, and now I am out of expectation, and
shall henceforward know how to deal with him.' In the
following year, both were elected Fellows of the Royal
Society.

Sir John Minnes, now aged sixty-five, was appointed
Comptroller of the Navy on the death of Sir Robert Slingsby at the end of 1661. He was a Vice-Admiral. He was also
a poet; not a very considerable poet, being part author with
Dr. James Smith of a volume entitled *Musarum Deliciæ*
belonging to the category known politely as facetiæ. A stout
Royalist, he had followed Charles into exile, sharing his
privations, yet, in the words of Anthony Wood, 'always in
a gay, cheerful, and merry condition.' He had been one of
the two royal commanders who had refused to acknowledge
the Earl of Warwick when the Fleet had gone over to the
Parliament, and he had been conspicuously honoured at the
Restoration. He was, in fact, an obscene but not witless
poet, 'An honest and stout man,' to quote Wood again,
'generous and religious and well-skilled in physic and chym-
istry,' and an uncompromising monarchist. But to Pepys
he was a muddle-headed old meddler, who had been put
into the Navy Office when he ought to have been super-
annuated. He was 'the old coxcomb' repeatedly, and Pepys
marvelled 'that so great trust should lie in the hands of
such a fool.' Pepys found him good enough company, but
often a troublesome neighbour at Seething Lane, where,
like Batten, Penn, and himself, Minnes had a house. The
various tenants were continually at odds, among other
things about use of the leads; and other rights of way,
entry, and window spacing, were in constant dispute. In
these conflicts Minnes took a noisy part, chiefly at the expense of Pepys and Penn, Batten being the man, as Pepys

complained, who led the Comptroller by the nose. Minnes played no important part in Pepys's career, but he was a figure in a strangely assorted and vivid community that ran the Navy Office and mostly lived in Seething Lane.

Two others of Pepys's associates may be mentioned here. Peter Pett, who landed in the Tower in consequence of his conduct during the Dutch attack in the Thames in 1667, was the Commissioner Resident at Chatham, and afterwards Assistant-Surveyor to Sir William Batten. He came of a great family of shipbuilders, but Pepys thought him, like Penn and Batten, a knave, and found him a nuisance at the dockyard. There remains Will Howe, who had played his viallin with Pepys on board the *Naseby,* and who in May, 1662, had 'grown a very pretty and is a sober fellow.' Two years later, he had grown 'a little conceited, but will make a discreet man.' He was for some time in the service of Sandwich, and much in Pepys's confidence, until he forfeited it by boasting to acquaintances that the Clerk of the Acts owed his appointment to his interest, 'which makes me wonder that this rogue dare talk after this manner, and I think all the world is grown false.' In 1665, he seems for a brief period to have been Deputy-Treasurer at the Navy Office, but shortly afterwards he fell under suspicion concerning some jewels that were stolen at sea, and fell on difficult times. Like Minnes, he was of no lasting consequence in Pepys's life, but in 1663, their association with Lord Sandwich was to bring them for a moment into rather delicate contact.

In the Navy Office itself, quarrels between the chiefs were of almost daily occurrence. After participating in one of them, Pepys set down in his journal that he was 'ashamed for myself something, and for the honour of the office much more.' The feud between Penn and Batten degenerated into frequent brawls. Minnes stormed about the place, sometimes in his cups, and Pepys, heartily sick of them all, was divided in his delight at seeing them at each other's throats and his concern for the decent conduct of business. Minnes is informed that Penn is to be made joint

Comptroller, 'at which he is stark mad; and swears he will give up his place, and do rail at Sir W. Penn the cruellest; he I made shift to encourage as much as I could, but it pleased me heartily to hear him rail against him, so I do see thoroughly by that they are not like to be great friends, for he cries out against him for his house and yard and God knows what.' And then he adds, 'For my part, I do hope, when all is done, that my following my business will keep me secure against all their envys.' And at intervals the proceedings would be enlivened by the visit of some infuriated sea captain, as when one came in quest of Sir John Minnes declaring that gentleman to be a knave, rogue, and coward, and that he would kick him and pull him by the ears.

But Pepys did not allow the disturbances to interfere with his own industry. He took every occasion to improve his knowledge of naval affairs. 'So to my office, and there till almost 12 at night with Mr. Lewes, learning to understand the manner of a purser's account, which is very hard and little understood by my fellow officers, and yet mighty necessary.' Although he sometimes lay late abed, he could, when his duties made it necessary, cheerfully get up at seven of a December morning, go down by water to Woolwich to see a ship unloaded, get back at noon, and, having dined at home and changed his clothes, go back to the Office and work there till supper time. When he exclaimed, 'to see what a knave Sir W. Batten is makes my heart ake,' he was speaking in a temper that was above personal animosity, and when the Duke told Coventry that in a dispute 'Mr. Pepys and he did stand up and carry it against the rest that were there,' his very natural satisfaction had in it a genuine leaven of public spirit. He did not spare himself on the Tangier Commission, and he read all the naval literature that he could find. He might have two chandlers on his hands, both of whom had given presents to his wife, and with orders to place with neither of them, but in buying £30,000 worth of masts he could say with pride that he had refused profits that he could have taken for himself with safety, and had made the best bargain for the King that the Office had known in twenty-seven years. His success in this particular business provoked an outburst of jealousy from his fellow Commissioners, and in a letter to Sir George Carteret he set out at great length a justification for his action which shows a grasp of technical detail and a liberal view of business policy that were no less than astonishing in a man who had been at the job less than three years. It was not surprising that he heard himself spoken of on 'Change as one who was doing the 'King's business wholly and well.'

During the year 1663 Pepys's relations with Lord Sandwich were put to a severe test. In April, Sandwich, having no present employment at sea, and being little interested in political affairs, had taken an out-of-town lodging at Chelsea. He had, in fact, been indulging, much to Pepys's concern, 'in all sorts of pleasures and vanities, which heretofore he never thought of nor loved.' He had, moreover, been seriously ill, and as he was a sensible man, with a perfectly sane view of life, he decided to be as much as possible away from the unwholesome atmosphere of the Court. His duties at the Wardrobe made little claim upon his time, and often when he could not be as far away as Hinchingbrooke there was no inconvenience in being at Chelsea. After a few months, however, people began to talk. The infrequency of his attendance at Court was noted and spoken of even by the King, and there were whispers that it was not merely love of seclusion that kept his Lordship from the society in which he had been so distinguished a figure. His landlady at Chelsea was one Mrs. Becke, of whose daughter Betty, Pepys began to hear the most unfavourable gossip. His Lordship was said to be playing amorous ditties of a night at her window, and then to be more intimately employed. The scandal grew, and Betty's character steadily deteriorated. Pepys heard that she was a woman of very bad fame and very impudent, a strumpet, and a something else that is indicated by dots in the printed version of the Diary. Pepys was 'ashamed to see my Lord

so grossly play the beast and fool, to the flinging off of all
honour, friends, servants, and every thing and person that
is good, and only will have his private lust undisturbed with
this common . . . his sitting up night after night alone,
suffering nobody to come to them, and all the day too.'
And he resolved 'to speak to him of it if I can seasonably.'
Whatever may have been the truth of the matter, it can
hardly be supposed that Restoration society was scandalised by the fact that Lord Sandwich was keeping a mistress,
nor was Pepys in the least likely to be so bold, or indeed so
impertinent, as to make himself a censor of his patron's
private morals. In point of fact, all the evidence goes to
show that Sandwich was in general a man far less given
to licence of any sort than was common in his time, but it
was a fact, nevertheless, that at this moment he was giving
people an opportunity to talk if they had a mind to, and
he was at the same time, whatever the inducement may have
been, neglecting the Court, and even the offices that were
his maintenance. Certainly, so far as the King was concerned, Sandwich might have had a dozen mistresses if he
wished, but Charles was not a King whose favour was
slighted with impunity. That Sandwich intended any such
discourtesy is highly improbable, but his rewards had
brought him many enemies, and they were not slow to suggest to the King that his Lordship, having gathered his
harvest, was becoming slack in service. The King listened,
and a word of royal displeasure was a train that rapidly
took fire. Justly or not, Sandwich's name was being ill-
spoken in circles of rank and influence, and as Pepys heard
he decided properly that it was no longer a question of
private conduct that was involved. His friend and patron
had strong claims to royal consideration, none stronger,
but the obligations had already been lavishly honoured, and
Pepys knew well enough how easily great eminence could
fall to great ruin. Several conversations that he had with
Will Howe, who was in attendance upon Sandwich, convinced him that there was some serious demoralisation at

work. 'Here I met Mr. Howe . . . he very soberly acquainted me how things are with my Lord, that my Lord do
not anything like himself, but follows his folly, and spends
his time either at cards at Court with the ladies, when he is
there at all, or else at Chelsey with the slut to his great
disgrace, and indeed I do see and believe that my Lord do
apprehend that he do grow less too at Court.' Pepys decided that someone must tell Sandwich the truth about the
situation, and there was no one to do it but himself. On
November 17th, he dispatched a letter, to the composition
of which he had given many days of anxious thought. This
remarkable document reads as follows:

My Lord,—

I do verily hope that neither the manner nor matter of this
   advice will be condemned by your Lordship, when for my
   defence in the first I shall alledge my double attempt,
   since your return from Hinchingbrooke, of doing it personally, in both of which your Lordship's occasions, no
   doubtfulnesse of mine, prevented me, and that being now
   fearful of a sudden summons to Portsmouth, for the discharge of some ships there, I judge it very unbecoming
   the duty which every bit of bread I eat tells me I owe to
   your Lordship to expose the safety of your honour to the
   uncertainty of my return. For the matter, my Lord, it is
   such as could I in any measure think safe to conceal from,
   or likely to be discovered to you by any other hand, I
   should not have dared so far to owne what from my
   heart I believe is false, as to make myself but the relater
   of other's discourse; but, sir, your Lordship's honour
   being such as I ought to value it to be, and finding both
   in city and court that discourses pass to your prejudice,
   too generally for mine or any man's controllings but
   your Lordship's, I shall, my Lord, without the least
   greatening or lessening the matter, do my duty in laying
   it shortly before you.
      People of all conditions, my Lord, raise matter of

wonder from your Lordship's so little appearance at Court: some concluding thence their disfavour thereby, to which purpose I have had questions asked me, and endeavouring to put off such insinuations by asserting the contrary, they have replied, that your Lordship's living so beneath your quality, out of the way, and declining of Court attendance, hath been more than once discoursed about the King. Others, my Lord, when the chief ministers of State, and those most active of the Council have been reckoned up, wherein your Lordship never used to want an eminent place, have said, touching your Lordship, that now your turn was served, and the King had given you a good estate, you left him to stand or fall as he would, and, particularly in that of the Navy, have enlarged upon your letting fall all service there.

Another sort, and those the most, insist upon the bad report of the house wherein your Lordship, now observed in perfect health again, continues to sojourne, and by name have charged one of the daughters for a common courtizan, alledging both places and persons where and with whom she hath been too well known, and how much her wantonnesse occasions, though unjustly, scandal to your Lordship, and that as well to gratifying of some enemies as to the wounding of more friends I am not able to tell.

Lastly, my Lord, I find a general coldness in all persons towards your Lordship, such as, from my first dependance on you, I never yet knew, wherein I shall not offer to interpose any thoughts or advice of mine, well knowing your Lordship needs not any. But with a most faithful assurance that no person or papers under Heaven is privy to what I here write, besides myself and this, which I shall be careful to have put into your owne hands, I rest confident of your Lordship's just construction of my dutiful intents herein, and in all humility take leave, may it please your Lordship,

Your Lordship's most obedient Servant,

S. P.

About this letter we may note, first, that Pepys declared that he does not believe the reports that have been spread. It is clear that this was not true, though Pepys may very well have discredited some of the baser rumours about Sandwich's neglect of his duties, and in any case the assurance was a not inexcusable approach to a very invidious task; secondly, that he attempted no evasions; and last, that he acknowledged to the full his personal indebtedness to Sandwich. Mr. Harris, in his life of Sandwich, seems to do Pepys less than justice in considering his part in the affair. The letter, we read, 'betokens a stout spirit in Samuel Pepys. It was no light matter to reproach the man whose influence gave him the very bread he ate, and a man who held such a position as his patron; but Sandwich could be generous of mind, and he received the letter with a good grace, which does him infinite credit.' That, I think, is a somewhat ingenuous view of the case. Sandwich, in fact, when he read the letter, found that it contained more truth than was agreeable, and in his behaviour to Pepys there was for several weeks something that strongly resembled sulking.

It was not unnatural. Nobody likes to receive a letter of that sort, and least of all if it is justified. Sandwich took a perfectly chivalrous line about the lady, left Chelsea, and began to attend to business. The letter had its effect, and in writing it Pepys did Sandwich an incalculable service at a critical time. But he could hardly expect at the moment much thanks for his pains, and in the weeks following the incident the Diary is full of anxious notes, recording the indications of my Lord's kindness or displeasure. Where Mr. Harris, I think, is mistaken, is in suggesting that Pepys was courageous in writing the letter because he was risking the loss of his friend's patronage, and that when the letter had been received he suffered 'many weeks of unrest' for the same reason. Pepys himself in the letter refers dutifully enough to the bread that he eats, and this was no more than a fitting acknowledgment of the kindnesses by which he had risen in the world. But it must be remembered that by

this time risen in the world he had. He owed his appointment at the Navy Office to Sandwich, but he owed his present authority there to his own industry and talents. Everybody knew that he was an extremely competent official,
and he was highly valued by the Duke of York, Coventry,
and Carteret. If at this time Sandwich had lost control of
himself and had fallen into public discredit, there is not the
smallest reason to suppose that Pepys would have lost his
place or have suffered in his prospects. It is true that a
Sandwich reinvigorated in affairs and reputation was likely
to be of more use to him than a Sandwich with a reputation
lost, but it is important to recognise that considered merely
as a patron Sandwich was no longer a necessity to Pepys's
career. It is therefore a misjudgment to say that he was
alarmed on account of his self-interest after the letter was
written. The truth is, and it seems to be plain enough in
the records, that Pepys wrote it because he felt a deep and
affectionate gratitude towards Sandwich and his family.
And when he had written it, it was not the loss of a patron's
favour that he feared, but the loss of a greatly respected
friend's regard. Mr. Harris, in saying that Sandwich by his
coolness for some time after the incident taught Pepys how
far he might go, does an injustice to both men. It is absurd
to speak of Pepys here as if he had taken some unwarrant-
able liberty. He had very honourably and with exemplary
respect braced himself to tell Sandwich what it was as difficult as it was necessary for somebody to tell him. We
neither know nor wish to know what were the private
morals involved. But Sandwich was in grave danger of a
check in his public life from which recovery would have
been almost impossible, and it was Pepys who made him
realise the danger in time. At the expense of his own feelings, Pepys did what he conceived to be his duty towards
the man whom above all others he loved and honoured.
After the incident, the old cordiality was difficult; but Sandwich, recovering the ordered habit of his life, knew the
loyalty that had served him.

It is worth remarking in this connection that in August of

The Right Hono.ble Edward Lord Mountague Viscount Hinchinbrooke Earle of Sandwich &c of the most noble Order of the Garter, one of his Ma.ties most hono.ble Privy Counsell, Captaine Generall of the Narrow Seas, Vice-Admirall of England, and Grand Master of the great Wardrobe.

EDWARD MONTAGU

FIRST EARL OF SANDWICH. *Engraved by* H. BLOETE-
LING. *After* SIR PETER LELY.

this year, 1663, that is to say three months before the celebrated letter was written, Pepys had returned an old bond for £500 of his own money to Sandwich, and taken up a new one for £700. Pepys could place his money as securely with Sandwich as elsewhere, and there is nothing surprising in the transaction, but there are indications of Pepys's growing independence in the record of an incident at the time of the loan: 'After long discourse with him of the fitness of his giving me a receipt for this money, which I for my security think necessary, and he otherwise do not think so, at last, after being a little angry, and I resolving not to let go my money without it, he did give me one.'

In the midst of all these domestic and official cares, Pepys's curiosity as to the little world about him was never dulled. He has an epicurean satisfaction in telling us of the pleasure of his table.

I had for them, after oysters, at first course, a hash of rabbits, a lamb, and a rare chine of beef. Next a great dish of roasted fowl, cost me about 30s., and a tart, and then fruit and cheese. My dinner was noble and enough. I had my house mighty clean and neat; my room below with a good fire in it; my dining-room above, and my chamber being made a withdrawing-chamber; and my wife's a good fire also. I find my new table very proper, and will hold nine or ten people well, but eight with great room.

And again:

We had a fricasee of rabbits and chickens, a leg of mutton boiled, three carps in a dish, a great dish of a side of lamb, a dish of roasted pigeons, a dish of four lobsters, three tarts, a lamprey pie (a most rare pie), a dish of anchovies, good wine of several sorts, and all things mighty noble and to my great content.

He liked to sit listening to a blackbird that was given to him, one that whistled exceedingly well, but would never finish a tune, he liked to take a walk into the fields 'gathering of cowslipps,' he liked to hear the nightingales sing at Woolwich, and he was concerned to note that an acquaintance was dead of eating cow-cumbers. He went to a cock fight, 'but, Lord! to see the strange variety of people . . . all swearing, cursing, and betting.' And, in spite of repeated vows of abstinence, he continued to go constantly to plays, sometimes two in a day.

That year there was hardly any summer, and heavy frosts came in August. This meant travelling to the City more frequently by coach than usual, a method of conveyance rather more expensive than that by boat, De Laune giving the rates as follows:

That no Hackney-Coach-man so Licensed shall presume to take for his Hire in or about the Cities of London and Westminster above Ten shillings for a day, reckoning 12 hours to the day; and by the hour, not above 18 pence for the first hour, and 12 pence for every hour after; nor for his Hire from any of the Inns of Courts, or thereabouts, to any part of St. James's or Westminster, (except beyond Tuttle-Street) above 12 pence, and the like from the same places to the Inns of Court, or thereabouts; nor from the Inns of Courts, or thereabouts, to the Royal Exchange, more than 12 pence; but if to the Tower, Bishopsgate-Street, Aldgate, or places thereabouts, 18 pence; and so from the same places to the said Inns of Court, as aforesaid.

And, sometimes, he would go abroad on horseback, not always auspiciously. Once he was tempted to stable his own not very imposing mount, and borrow 'a delicate stone-horse' of a captain. He rode it into Hyde Park, where 'it was very troublesome' and began to fight with other horses, and Pepys had much ado to get away in safety. But he was not disconcerted. Indeed, he had a way of taking one thing with another as it came. When a constable knocked him up in the middle of a moonshine night to inform him that his back door was open, he told him to shut it, and went back to bed.

He delighted in strange things, strange news, and strange experiences. When he was told that the Swedish fishermen in winter often brought up swallows in their nets 'out of mudd from under water, hanging together to some twig or other, dead in ropes, and brought to the fire will come to life,' he was surprised but not incredulous; on visiting the Mint he insisted on being shown in detail the whole process of coining, and made an elaborate memorandum of it afterwards; he was enchanted with a present from Mr. Coventry of 'a silver pen to carry inke in, which is very necessary.' He was careful to give no one the opportunity for alarming him as Mr. Christmas had once done; possessing a copy of Seldon's *Mare Clausum,* containing a dedication to the Commonwealth, he discreetly had the page replaced by the new dedication to the King. He grew increasingly careful also of his appearance, and in November, for the first time, had his hair cropped to wear a perriwig. Whatever he might think of the conduct of the Court, its spectacle never failed to charm him.

By and by the King and Queen, who looked in this dress (a white laced waistcoat and a crimson short pettycoat, and her hair dressed *à la negligence*) mighty pretty; and the King rode hand in hand with her. Here was also my Lady Castlemaine rode among the rest of the ladies; but the King took, me-thought, no notice of her; nor when they 'light did any body press (as she seemed to expect, and staid for it) to take her down, but was taken down by her own gentleman. She looked mighty out of humour, and had a yellow plume in her hat (which all took notice of), and yet is very handsome, but very melancholy; nor did any body speak to her, or she so much as smile or speak to any body. I followed them up into White Hall, and into the Queen's presence, where all the ladies walked, talking and fiddling with their hats and feathers, and changing and trying one another's by one another's heads, and laughing. But it was the finest sight to me, considering their great beautys and dress, that ever I did see in all my life. But, above all, Mrs. Stewart in this dress, with her hat cocked and a red plume, with her sweet eye, little Roman nose, and excellent taille, is now the greatest beauty I ever saw, I think, in my life; and, if ever woman can, do exceed my Lady Castlemaine, at least in this dress: nor do I wonder if the King changes, which I verily believe is the reason of his coldness to my Lady Castlemaine.

And all the while he kept his vocation in mind. Picking up an unexpected £3 at the Office, and visiting a bookshop, he could not tell 'whether to lay out my money for books of pleasure, as plays, which my nature was most earnest in'; but, resisting temptation, he rejected Shakespeare, Jonson, and Beaumont for Fuller's *Worthies* and a collection of letters of State 'all of good use or serious pleasure,' allowing himself *Hudibras* as an indulgence, in which, however, he failed to see any wit.

Of his finances he was able to write in November 1663, 'I have got up my crumb . . . to £770,' and at the end of the year he had increased it to a round £800. Making his annual reckoning with himself at the end of December, he found his household 'living now in most perfect content and quiet'; it consisted, besides his wife and himself, of three maids, Will Wayneman having disappeared, and Will Hewer, although still at the Navy Office, having taken lodgings elsewhere. Pepys was advancing in his work, 'though envied to the devil by Sir William Batten, who hates me to death, but cannot hurt me. The rest either love me, or at least do not show otherwise, though I know Sir W. Penn to be a false knave touching me, though he seems fair.' The people at Brampton were at least quiescent, and at the moment were entertaining the young ladies from Hinchingbrooke, where there was smallpox. Disease, indeed, was beginning to disturb the public mind. There were disquieting accounts of the plague in Amsterdam. But for the moment Pepys was happy to know that the little house in Huntingdonshire could afford this neighbourly assistance to the great one. There were other courtesies. Once during the year, when he went to Brampton with his uncle Thomas and his cousin, he was much vexed that they had to be put out to board with Goody Stankes at the Black Bull, although satisfied that the reason was the loan of spare beds to Hinchingbrooke. The year for Pepys had been a stormy one, but it ended quietly and in hope.

CHAPTER IV

THE NAVY OFFICE. DUTCH WAR. THE PLAGUE. THE FIRE OF LONDON

DURING the following eighteen months, that is until the middle of 1665, Pepys was steadily, and on the whole agreeably, engaged in the official and domestic routine of his life. It was a period of somewhat precarious contentment at home, and of growing prestige at the Navy Office. Pepys was making his way in the world in no undecided fashion. His relations with his wife continued to be governed by caprice. Her displays of independence forced from him the confession that they were no less than he deserved. Sometimes the quarrels in the house did not stop short of violence. One morning in bed, Pepys in a temper pulled his wife's nose, and 'the poor wretch took it mighty ill.' On another occasion, he went beyond this and gave her a black eye, whereupon she had sufficient spirit to bite and scratch him to some purpose. There was as usual a speedy reconciliation, in which this time butter and parsley played a part. As we read on through the Diary, it becomes increasingly evident that with all his admirable qualities Pepys had a blind spot in his moral equipment and that the circumstance has to be accepted for what it is worth, though with recognition that we know more about Pepys in these matters than we have the opportunity of knowing about anyone else. It is not merely that he was frail, but that he had a really startling capacity for surprise or indignation when others indulged the frailties of his own habit. If in the anecdotage of Pepys more than enough has been made of his secret emoluments and his infidelities, he has himself to blame.

Up betimes, and find myself disappointed in my receiving presently of my £50 I hoped for sure of Mr. Warren upon the benefit of my press warrant, but he promises to make it good. So by water to the Exchequer, and there up and down through all the offices to strike my tallys for £17,500, which methinks is so great a testimony of the goodness of God to me, that I, from a mean clerke there, should come to strike tallys myself for that sum, and in the authority that I do now, is a very stupendous mercy to me. I shall have them struck to-morrow. But to see how every little fellow looks after his fees, and to get what he can for everything, is a strange consideration.

The simple obtusity of such a passage as this rises above comment. And of Pepys's marital behaviour there is often as little to be said. It is not for us to blame his susceptibilities. There is a genuine cry in the words, 'which is a strange slavery which I stand in to beauty, that I value nothing near it.' And even though his amours were not always fastidious, they were not unintelligible. What is unintelligible, or near it, is the apparently perfect sincerity with which he could be shocked by suspicions of his wife while he was engaged in them. Simultaneous affairs with the incorrigible Mrs. Lane, with Mrs. Bagwell the carpenter's wife, and with Jane Welsh, a barber's maid, became at one time so congested that, in the absurd jargon he adopted for such occasions, he 'did with great content *ferais* a vow to mind my business, and *laisser aller les femmes* for a month, and am with all my heart glad to find myself able to come to so good a resolution, that thereby I may follow my business, which and my honour thereby lies a bleeding.' It might be left at that, were it not that in the meantime Pepys was watching his wife's every movement with unaffected concern, and, so far as can be discovered, without the smallest cause. The sight of Mr. Pembleton in the parish continued to throw him into a flutter of misgivings; if his wife returned home an hour after her appointed time, he considered every possible and impossible explanation; he even grew jealous of Will Hewer. He reproached himself systematically with his own behaviour, but there is hardly a word to show that he regarded it as a reproach upon his attitude to his wife. Had he at any time discovered her in transgression, it would hardly have occurred to him that his own conduct was in any way concerned in the matter. There is evidence that she received advances from more than one suitor of quality, and none that she listened to them. One astonishing proposal made by Pepys's uncle Wight, a freeman fishmonger, had reference to the absence of an heir in two families. Elizabeth at once told her husband, who 'knew not what to think of it of a sudden,' but decided to take no notice until he should have deliberated upon suitable language. He was, in short, jealous of his wife with little right and less reason. Pepys was unaware of his blind spot; to us it is a conspicuous one.

In other respects his household afforded many satisfactions. In spite of fears and differences, he remained in love with his wife and was happy in her companionship. The scholar and the connoisseur found in her a pupil who was at least willing. He read lectures to her in geography, 'which she takes very prettily'; he engaged a drawing master to give her lessons in limning, in which from the first she showed much promise and later came 'to do very finely . . . beyond what I could ever look for.' On the whole the house was well kept and served, though there were the usual shufflings in the domestic staff. These were not always surprising. A small maid, admitting an undesirable Scots woman to the house, was beaten by Mrs. Pepys, shut in the cellar, and kept there all night. A fortnight later another maid, who may well have been unfavourably impressed by this example, went away 'having of all wenches that ever lived with us received the greatest love and kindnesse and good clothes, besides wages, and gone away with the greatest ingratitude.' But in the midst of all distractions

Pepys could write, 'It is a joy to me to see me master of
so much pleasure in my own home,' and on the ninth anniversary of his wedding, he blessed God 'for our long lives
and loves and health together.' Among his other anxieties,
was a suspicion that his wife had leanings to the Catholic
Church. Rumours to that effect were later to cause him serious inconvenience. Apart from the dangers of noncon-
formity to the establishment, Pepys, like a reasonable man,
had no taste for religious controversy. He attended the
services at St. Olave's Church with some regularity, and
he had family prayers at home twice a week. For the rest,
he could wish a man's religion to be his own business.
'While we were talking, came by several poor creatures,
carried by constables, for being at a conventicle. They go
like lambs, without any resistance. I would to God they
would either conform, or be more wise and not be catched.'
A few notes of miscellaneous interest may be taken from
the journal of these months. Going through some old
papers, he found the manuscript of a romance, *Love a
Cheat*, which he had begun ten years before at Cambridge,
and tore it up. He ran in excitement about the streets to
get a good view of a comet that 'appeared again to-night,
but duskishly.' He continued to practice little financial deceptions on himself; spending nine shillings and sixpence on
a book, he paid five shillings forfeit to the poorbox, and
asking Creed to take him to the theatre, lent him the money
for the tickets in order that his vow against the extravagance should not be broken. The judgments on plays, of
which so many appear in the Diary, are always lively, but
seldom of much interest. For the most part, he merely
says in vigorous language that he liked a play or disliked
it. His opinions, particularly his Shakespearean opinions,
surprise us less when we remember that what then passed
for Shakespeare would often have been unrecognisable to
the poet. And Pepys was not seriously concerned with
dramatic criticism. Some plays pleased him, some didn't,
but the theatre was always a delight. He loved it whether
the play was good or bad, and if it was bad there were

compensations. 'To the Duke's . . . all the pleasure of the play was, the King and my Lady Castlemayne were there; and pretty witty Nell . . . and the younger Marshall sat next us; which pleased me mightily.'

In 1665, he was made a Fellow of the Royal Society, and became a constant attendant at the many strange experiments conducted by the institution. He also attended the musical entertainments that even in those days were provided by the Post Office. Hearing the King deliver a formal address, he was of opinion that he spoke 'the worse that ever I heard man in my life.' He had an excellent mastiffe, by name Towser, given him by a chyrurgeon, and he took to carrying a hare's foot in his pocket, to which he attributed his improving health. But an ominous note appears: 'My eyes . . . begin to fail me nowadays by candle light,' and then again: 'even though by day light.' The Brampton business continued to occupy much of his time, and appeared to come no nearer a settlement. We find him negotiating for the sale of a small parcel of land there in the middle of July, 1664, at the end of which month he reckoned himself for the first time as worth about £1,000.

Earlier in the year, Tom Pepys had died, leaving behind him a confusion of debts and illegitimate children. Samuel was involved by both in much delicate negotiation, and although for the credit of the family he had the detrimental young tailor buried in St. Bride's Church, instead of in the graveyard, at an extra cost of ten shillings, he found himself, before the business was concluded, 'Vexed to think what a rogue my brother was in all respects.' The other members of his family were true to form. His wife, visiting Brampton, brought back a report of 'the ill, improvident, disquiett, and sluttish manner that my father and mother and Pall live in.' Pall, receiving an occasional ten shillings, was making no demonstration, but his mother, visiting London, made Seething Lane ring with her complaints, and was with difficulty persuaded to return home at the end of six weeks. During her visit she tried to reconcile Samuel to his brother John, but that young man show-

ing no disposition to do anything for his living, she failed.
Moreover, Samuel had found among his brother Tom's
papers 'several letters of my brother John's to him speaking
very foule words of me and my deportment to him here,
and very crafty designs about Sturtlow land and God knows
what, which I am very glad to know, and shall make him
repent them.' Samuel's father had also come to London, at
the time of Tom's death, a rather weary, harassed man,
old before his time, glad even of so melancholy an excuse
to escape for a while from the squalor and distractions of
Brampton. There is no doubt that Pepys was much more
sincerely attached to his father than to anyone else in his
immediate relationship. Many notes in the Diary reveal
him as sympathetic towards his father's troubles, anxious
for his comfort, and forbearing under many vexations. He
must have known that his mother and sister were uncommonly provoking people to live with, and although he could
speak his mind openly enough to his father when he felt
that family interests were being neglected, his behaviour
for the most part towards one parent at least was that of
a dutiful and considerate son. 'So home, and find my father
come to lie at our house, and so supped, and saw him, poor
man, to bed, my heart never being fuller of love to him,
nor admiration of his prudence and pains heretofore in
the world than now, to see how Tom hath carried himself in
his trade; and how the poor man hath his thoughts going to
provide for his younger children and my mother.' There is
a tenderness here that is not familiar in Pepys, but in this
connection it was not uncommon.

At the Navy Office he was gaining notably in influence;
and not unprofitably. He took his substantial perquisites
with the most ingenuous grace. Receiving £50 from some
aspirant or another, he could assure himself that there was
not 'the least word or deed I have been guilty of in his
behalf, but what I am sure has been to the King's advantage, and the profit of the service.' A contractor having
made a promise to pay £100 on the completion of a certain
business, and failing to make it good at the appointed time,

Pepys innocently asked him if he might borrow that amount, a suggestion that took immediate effect. Having to arrange the Tangier victualling, he did so to his own advantage at the rate of £300 a year, but claimed that his efficiency was effecting a saving of £5,000 a year to the King. And if in these matters his conduct was equivocal, his boasts were not idle. He was bringing economy and organisation into a demoralised service, and everybody knew it.

He continued to furnish his mind with any knowledge that might be useful to his work, spending some time, for example, in reading common law. He was high in favour with the Duke of York, with whom he was now in constant association. He was careful of the good opinion. Passing the royal barge one day on the river, the Duke called out to him to enquire where he was going. 'I told him to Woolwich, but was troubled afterward I should say no farther, being in a gally, lest he think me too profuse in my journeys.' Early in 1665, he was appointed Treasurer to the Tangier Commission, and although he was sensible of the honour and the additional pay, he complained at times that the increased work interfered with what he considered to be the more important business of the Navy Office. He continued, however, to keep pace with his duties in both appointments, and his thirty-second year found him a civil servant of deservedly high standing.

The claims of the Tangier Commission may well have been an embarrassment in view of the growing pressure of work at the Navy Office. As the early months of 1665 went by, the danger of war with Holland became imminent, and a Dutch war meant war at sea. The trade disputes between the two countries had long been in a state of agitation, and the tension clearly was near to breaking point. The origins of the quarrel need concern us as little as they concern Pepys. His single purpose as a naval official was to do everything in his power to put his fighting arm of the service into the highest possible state of efficiency, and he applied himself with restless activity to his departmental work, budgetting for stores and provisions, and inspecting the condition of the dockyards. His zeal was noted even by the King himself. 'Thence to White Hall; where the King seeing me, did come to me, and calling me by name, did discourse with me about the ships in the River: and this is the first time that ever I knew the King did know me personally; so that hereafter I must not go thither, but with expectation to be questioned, and to be ready to give good answers.' And the King in these days was in one of his alert moods, well enough informed as to what was going on in his offices. At a committee meeting of the Council, Lord Annesly exclaimed, 'I think we must be forced to get the King to come to every committee; for I do not see that we do any thing at any time but when he is here.' Upon which Pepys observes, 'And I believe he said the truth: and very constant he is at the council table on council-days.'

But labour as he would, Pepys was full of apprehensions. Nobody knew better than he the deficiencies of the British Navy in man power, in armaments, and in equipment; and none better than he how disastrous to this country would be the by no means improbable event of the command of the sea passing to the Dutch. Early in April, 1665, our Fleet was out, and the issue might be forced by either side at any moment. It was not lightly that Pepys wrote on the 8th, 'We, as high as we make our shew, I am sure, are unable to set out another small fleete, if this should be worsted. Wherefore, God send us peace! I cry.' The weeks went on indecisively, the Dutch under Opdam and the English under the Duke of York and Prince Rupert manœuvring for position in the North Sea. In the meantime, the town was full of daily rumours, the firing of guns was heard from every possible and impossible direction, and strangers accosted each other eagerly with demands for news. London was now beset by a further anxiety. On April 30th, Pepys wrote, 'The fleete, with about 106 ships upon the coast of Holland, in sight of the Dutch, within the Texel.

Great fears of the sicknesse here in the City, it being said that two or three houses are already shut up. God preserve us all!'

It was not until May 23d, that news came of a Dutch movement; and Pepys then heard at the Navy Office that their Fleet was out in full force. On the following day the intelligence was confirmed, and with it the definite announcement that the plague was upon London. It was not until June 8th that Pepys 'met with the great news at last newly come, brought by Bab May from the Duke of Yorke, that we have totally routed the Dutch.' The action had, in fact, been fought off Lowestoft on June 3d, but London knew nothing of it until at least four days after the event. The defeat was a heavy one. Opdam had been blown up in his flagship, the other commanders had been killed or driven to the winds, twenty-four Dutch first-raters had been sunk, and an early estimate placed their losses at six thousand men. The English Fleet was intact, with a casualty list amounting to not more than six hundred. On the wave of public enthusiasm Pepys went to his tailor and ordered a coloured silk ferrandin, which, however, his wife vexed him by saying did not become him so well as his customary black.

The public rejoicings, though natural, were premature. The English victory had been a handsome one, but not decisive. The Dutch Fleet had been swept out of the action, but not off the seas. Even at the moment of the Lowestoft triumph De Ruyter was returning in considerable force from his daring and successful Guinea expedition. His strength had been impaired by disease and hardship, but he had struck heavily at British prestige in the west, and was in high spirits. If he could reach Holland, he was the man to rally Dutch hopes, and bring new life to the crippled Dutch Fleet. Even while the bells were ringing out in thanksgiving for Lowestoft, therefore, the Court, the Admiralty, and the Navy Office knew that the business was by no means done. Unless De Ruyter could be intercepted, the Dutch menace would come again, and De Ruyter was an exceedingly wary and skilful commander. And so, while the English seamen were being fêted, they were preparing also for the next move. In the meantime, there was no reason why the acknowledgment of present mercies should not be generous. The 20th of June was appointed as a thanksgiving day for the Lowestoft victory. Pepys spent the morning very busy by himself at the Office until church time, when he listened to an unsatisfactory sermon, but the day recovered itself: 'Then to the Dolphin Taverne, where all we officers of the Navy met with the Commissioners of the Ordnance by agreement and dined: where good musique at my direction. Our club come to 34s. a man, nine of us.'

In all this business a prominent though somewhat anxious part had been played by the Earl of Sandwich. Since the incident of the famous letter, Sandwich had been civil but constrained towards his cousin. Pepys was troubled by the coolness, but admirably dignified. He neglected no opportunity of serving his Lordship and his family, and was quietly solicitous to regain the old kindness. Little by little Sandwich recovered his humour, but Pepys was careful that it should be at no sacrifice of his own hard-earned independence. There is not a trace anywhere in the connection between the two men that the younger, having established himself in a career, forgot his duties to the patron who had promoted him from obscurity. But it was now nearly ten years since the days when Sandwich could address a letter 'For my Servant Samuel Pepys at my lodgings in Whitehall.' The Servant could now show substantial credentials of his own, and if in the difference that had fallen out between him and his powerful kinsman, he never for a moment forgot his place, he was resolved also that his Lordship should not forget it either. Reflecting upon the difficulty of the position, and confessing how anxious he is for a complete reconciliation, he is determined, nevertheless, to 'stand upon mine owne legs.' Especially was he aware of the delicacy of the situation, in view of the financial transactions that had taken place. 'I do not like,' he says incisively, 'his being angry and in debt both together to me.'

Pepys kept up his contacts with the family, but for a time with a certain stiffness. In February, 1664, we find, 'Went to visit my Ladys Jemimah and Paulina Montagu . . . whom we find at their father's new house in Lincolne's Inn Fields; but the house all in dirt. They received us well enough; but I did not endeavour to carry myself over familiarly with them.' A month later, Pepys was thanking Sandwich for putting him on to the Fishery Committee: ' "Oh!" says he, "in the Fishery you mean. I told you I would remember you in it," but offered no other discourse.' In June of the same year, Pepys was present at a very odd party. Lady Sandwich was on a visit to Dean Hodges, Vicar of Kensington, Rector of St. Peter's, Cornhill, and Dean of Hereford. Pepys calling one day on her ladyship found a considerable company assembled, and among them:

Mr. Becke, of Chelsy, and wife and daughter, my Lord's mistress, and one that hath not one good feature in her face, and yet is a fine lady, of a fine taille, and very well carriaged, and mighty discreet. I took all the occasion I could to discourse with the young ladies in her company to give occasion to her to talk, which now and then she did, and that mighty finely, and is, I perceive, a woman of such an ayre, as I wonder the less at my Lord's favour to her, and I dare warrant him she hath brains enough to entangle him.

'That,' says Mr. Harris, 'was all; poor Betty was approved and whitewashed.' Whitewash, it must be allowed, of a somewhat unusual nature. In the meantime, at Brampton the younger Sandwich children, finding themselves unequal to the ordeals of the Pepys household, had been moved back to Hinchingbrooke 'with great discontent,' saying that though they 'buy good meate, they can never have it before it stinks, which I am ashamed of.' A further incident at the time brought Sandwich and Pepys into more pleasing contact. The Lord Chancellor, in a great temper, complained to Sandwich that his protégé at the Navy Office had ordered a number of trees in Clarendon Park to be cut down without his authority. The occasion in itself is now of no significance, but it brought Sandwich and Pepys together, first in heated dispute and then in a rather pretty scene of reconciliation with Clarendon. 'I think I did thoroughly appease him, till he thanked me for my desire and pains to satisfy him; and upon my desiring to be directed who I should of his servants advise with about this business, he told me nobody, but would be glad to hear from me himself.' Months afterwards, in the Council Chamber, 'My Lord Chancellor passing by stroked me on the head'; on which occasion Pepys also received gracious acknowledgment from the King 'who do now know me so well, that he never sees me but he speaks to me about our Navy business.'

Preparations for the Dutch war brought Sandwich back to active employment, and cleared his mind. With two royal admirals at sea, his was not the supreme command, but the battle order at Lowestoft opened with the Red under James in the centre, the White under Rupert in the van, and the Blue under Sandwich in the rear. During the anxious days of waiting in early June, Pepys under high pressure at the Office found time to call upon Lady Sandwich, 'who, poor lady, expects every hour to hear of my Lord; but in the best temper, neither confident nor troubled with fear, that I ever did see in my life.' When at length the good news came, its edge at first was a little dulled for Pepys by the circumstances that in the general felicitations there was no mention of Sandwich's name. A public news letter, compiled from various sources immediately after the action and imperfectly informed, was concerned less to give a true narration than to load the royal commanders with compliment. Public gossip took the cue, and for the moment it might have seemed that Sandwich had not been in the North Sea at all. But Pepys's genuine anxiety was speedily relieved. On June 9th, he 'met with Mr. Moore, who eases me in one point wherein I was troubled; which was, that I heare of nothing said or done by my Lord Sandwich: but he tells me that Mr. Cowling, my Lord

Chamberlain's secretary, did hear the King say that my Lord Sandwich had done nobly and worthily.' On the 14th, Cowling himself observed to Pepys 'how he finds every body silent in the praise of my Lord Sandwich, to set up the Duke and the Prince, but that the Duke did both to the King and my Lord Chancellor write abundantly of my Lord's courage and service.' The real facts were that Prince Rupert, who in middle age was if anything more irresponsible than he had been twenty years before, when as a cavalry leader he had repeatedly ruined the Royalist cause in the field, had been in the van at Lowestoft only at the first onset, and that Sandwich had held that place of honour through the rest of the day with great distinction, his ship leaving the action with thirty shots in her hull, and 'not one mast whole nor yard.' The King and the Duke of York had their own private opinions of Rupert, but they were not for publication. Sandwich was not unnaturally a little disconcerted that the true facts should be withheld from public knowledge, but that these facts were well known to the King is clear from the following letter written by Charles himself from Whitehall on June 9th.

Whitehall, June 9th, 1665.

My Lord Sandwich,—

Though you have already done me very eminent service, yet the great part you have had in this happy victory which it hath pleased God to send us, adds very much to the former obligations I have to you. I send this bearer, my Lord Hawley, on purpose to let you know more particularly my sense of it; and will say no more myself till I see you, that I may take you in my arms, and give you other testimonies how truly I am

Your affectionate friend,

Charles R.

The crisis proved that the affection between Sandwich and Pepys had survived its test. Before the death of Sandwich seven years later, there was to be a further estrangement,

upon no particular occasion, but rather one that grew in-
sensibly by circumstance. But in the days after Lowestoft
much of the old confident cordiality was resumed, and in
September of 1665, when the Admiral had gone again to
sea, Pepys could write, 'I hear by every body how much
my poor Lord of Sandwich was concerned for me during
my silence a while, lest I had been dead of the plague in
this sickly time.'

It was on June 7th, the day after his considerate visit to
Lady Sandwich, that Pepys for the first time saw, in Drury
Lane, houses marked with a red cross upon the doors, and
'Lord have mercy upon us' there written. For more than a
year the terror had been threatening London. As far back
as June, 1664, over seven hundred people had died of the
plague in a week at Amsterdam, and that sooner or later
the scourge would drift across the sea to an invasion more
dreadful than that of any fleet was a fear that for months
lay heavily over London. The first weekly Bill of Mortality, in 1665, reported nine deaths from the plague. Four
other returns were made that month, the respective figures
being, three, fourteen, seventeen, and forty-three. What
happened thereafter will be shown in a table of figures taken
from De Laune:

	1st week	2nd week	3rd week	4th week	5th week
June	112	168	267	470	
July	725	1089	1843	2010	
August	2817	3880	4237	6102	
September	6988	6544	7165	5538	
October	4929	4327	2665	1421	1031
November	1414	1050	652	333	

The figures diminished week by week until the end of the
year, when the total plague mortality since May was
reckoned at 68,596. In the early days of the epidemic, many
of the great families who had no business ties left London.
By the middle of June, the shops were closing down, the
tradesmen driven away by the danger and lack of custom,

and public servants were moving with their departments into the country. On the 17th of that month, Pepys wrote:

It struck me very deep this afternoon going with a hackney coach from my Lord Treasurer's down Holborne, the coachman I found to drive easily and easily, at last stood still, and come down hardly able to stand, and told me that he was suddenly struck very sicke, and almost blind, he could not see; so I 'light and went into another coach, with a sad heart for the poor man and trouble for myself, lest he should have been struck with the plague, being at the end of the towne that I took him up; but God have mercy upon us all!

A fortnight later he moved his wife to lodgings at Woolwich, and at this time he notes that the Duke of Albemarle and the Lord Chancellor were the only two great statesmen remaining in town. During July London became, with terrible actuality, a city of the dead. Grass began to grow in the silent and empty streets. The hawkers no longer screamed across their barrows; the apprentices put up the shutters of their masters' shops and disappeared. The coaches of fashion and business stood in their sheds unused, and the only regular traffic that the few foot passengers saw as they went like ghosts through the deserted streets was the passing of the death-carts. The awful stillness was broken only by the constant tolling of bells, and sounds of horror from the stricken houses. Upon the whole town lay a sense of inescapable fatality. A few heroic doctors went their rounds, and a few apothecaries dispensed plague waters and quack specifics, but nothing could be done to lift the anguish from the city. It merely had to be endured. While great numbers of people escaped into the country, greater numbers had no means of doing so, and for months a tragic population could do nothing but wait dumbly upon the spectacle of its own destruction.

Throughout the ghastly summer, with pestilence fouling the air, Pepys displayed that most admirable courage of the man who is desperately afraid to do a thing, and does it. The peril was deadly, and he knew it; it was momently impossible not to know it. And yet, with a simple fortitude, indeed without question, he stayed at Seething Lane carrying out his duties as Clerk of the Acts. He went out to Woolwich sometimes to see his wife; occasionally spent a night there. He would make two or three journeys a week down to Hampton Court, whither the royal household, the Court, and many of the State officers, had retired in hope of escaping the terror. But month after month he kept the daily habit of his life in the very heart of the contagion, watching the horrible congestion of the graveyards as he went about his business. There was in Pepys no bland indifference to danger. He was, as we have said before, an apprehensive little man. The slight fever of a cold was enough to throw him also into a fever of fright. On July 21st, he wrote: 'The plague growing very raging, and my apprehensions of it great.' And on the 26th, he recorded that it was now in his parish of St. Olave's, 'So that I begin to think of setting things in order, which I pray God enable me to put both as to soul and body.' There is an air of alarm even in the syntax. But Pepys did not go. He might have done so without loss of reputation. In those distracting days no man could be blamed for refusing to take what must have seemed far less than a level chance with death. Example of the refusal was about him on every hand. If he had said that he too must do his work from Hampton Court, his colleagues in the public services could have made no complaint. There were many in London whose duty could not be done elsewhere, guardians of the town, and doctors, and ministers of religion, who broke under the strain and deserted their posts. And some surely not unheroic stubbornness in this choleric, rather nervy fellow of many sensibilities decided him that in a time when not only was London threatened by the destruction of the plague, but when England was lying under threat of destruction by the Dutch, his place was at the Navy Office in Seething Lane, and at Seething Lane he stayed.

As a man will in such circumstances, he played with himself a curious game of deception. He could not avoid almost daily being brought to a sudden shock of realisation of the danger in which he was living. He even took such precautions as the inadequate medicines of the day afforded. I may perhaps be forgiven for expressing the hope that he was attracted by the following advertisement which appeared in the news-sheets of the time:

Monsieur Angier's famous remedies for stopping and preventing the Plague, having not only been recommended by several certificates from Lyons, Paris, Thoulouse, etc., but likewise experimented here by the special direction of the Lords of His Majesty's most honourable Privy Council, and proved by witnesses upon oath and several Tryals, to be of singular virtue and effect, are to be had at Mr. Drenkwater's at the Fountain in Fleet Street.

But, fears and precautions apart, Pepys disciplined himself to conduct his affairs as though nothing unusual were happening. While the rulers and the commanders were still congratulating each other upon the issue at Lowestoft, it was realised that the Fleet must be at sea again. The Duke of York, an uncongenial man, and later a deplorable king, had confirmed in the battle an already established opinion that he was a very good sailor, but as heir to the throne it was decided that honour had been more than sufficiently satisfied, and that he should take no further risks. Prince Rupert, on the other hand, presented a serious difficulty to the authorities. There was no reason why he should not go to sea again, except that he was an extremely unsatisfactory commander. That he should be overlooked in the new commission was considered undesirable in the interests of policy, and there was no likelihood, in view of his excellent opinion of himself, that he would agree to serve under anyone else. To entrust the fortunes of the Fleet altogether to his care would be manifest folly. The expedient was, therefore, devised, probably by the King in consultation with his brother, of offering him joint command with a seaman of high reputation for level-headed ability. In this respect there was no one with better claims than Sandwich, and he was nominated. Rupert would have none of it, which was, no doubt, what the promoters had anticipated. He suggested that there should be two distinct commands, he and Sandwich to act independently. The proposal was unattractive to the Admiralty, and Rupert was allowed for the time being to discard seamanship for the art of mezzotint engraving, in which he was able to add genuine lustre to a name that otherwise belongs to the tinsel of history. When the Fleet put out upon the extremely delicate task of intercepting De Ruyter, Sandwich was in sole command.

Pepys remained at the Navy Office, jealously guarding his share in the interests of the new venture, and keeping my Lord's business steadfastly in mind. The English Fleet and the house of Sandwich were his concerns, and in attending to them he tried to disregard the dreadful evidence of calamity that was about him in the streets. Proposals were being made for the marriage of Jemimah Montagu with Philip Carteret, and in these negotiations Pepys, to his delight, was accepted as agent by both parties. The choice not only advanced him in social importance, it kept him, with his official calls, more than fully occupied, and that was what his mind needed. The marriage was to take place at Dagenhams in Essex, the seat of Lady Sandwich's sister, Lady Wright. Thither Pepys made several journeys, superintending arrangements on a luxurious scale, and finding some difficulty in the congenial task of persuading Philip Carteret to be less diffident in his love making. At length all was in order, and on July 31st, Pepys, dressed in his 'new coloured silk suit, and coat trimmed with gold buttons and gold broad lace round my hands, very rich and fine,' was at Deptford by six in the morning to meet Lady Sandwich and Sir George Carteret. Missing the ebb at the ferry, they were delayed three hours to their great discontent, 'in the unlucky

Isle of Doggs,' and arrived late for the wedding, meeting
the marriage party coming home from church. But the rest
of the day made amends for the misadventure. Pepys did
not kiss the bride until invited by Lady Sandwich to do so,
and he thought that after the ceremony the young lady
looked 'mighty sad.' At dinner they were all 'very merry
. . . but yet in such a sober way as never almost any
wedding was in so great families,' which Pepys took to be
to the good for everyone concerned. And then:

> At night to supper, and so to talk; and which, methought,
> was the most extraordinary thing, all of us to prayers as
> usual, and the young bride and bridegroom too: and so
> after prayers, soberly to bed; only I got into the bride-
> groom's chamber while he undressed himself, and there
> was very merry, till he was called to the bride's chamber,
> and into bed they went. I kissed the bride in bed, and so
> the curtaines drawne with the greatest gravity that could
> be, and so good night. But the modesty and gravity of
> this business was so decent, that it was to me indeed ten
> times more delightful than if it had been twenty times
> more merry and joviall.

A week later, sending to Lord Sandwich a full report of
the proceedings, Pepys wrote of the match as 'the only
occurrence of all my life I ever met with, begun, proceeded
on, and finished with the same uninterrupted excess of satisfaction to all parties.' The satisfaction to himself was
unbounded:

> . . . it having been the passage of my whole life the most
> pleasing for the time, considering the quality and nature
> of the business, and my noble usage in the doing of it,
> and very many fine journeys, entertainments and great
> company.

As the late summer came on, Pepys was still living at
Seething Lane. He steeled himself against his fears, was

even contemptuous of others who did not. On one of his journeys to Dagenhams, he exclaimed, 'But Lord, to see in what fear all the people here do live would make one mad, they are afeard of us that come to them.' And yet, as fatality became a habit of the city, people acquired the boldness of despair. In many wretched households where hope had perished, a terrible hatred took possession. There could hardly be a more sinister note in history than that in which Pepys tells us how that 'in spite . . . ill people would breathe in the faces (out of their windows) of well people going by.' But there were generosities too. Pepys was co-opted by his parish vestry for the purpose of regulating the ghoulish mobs that began to follow burial processions through the streets, and of taking other measures to prevent the spread of infection. All stricken or suspected houses were closed down, but of one case that came before the vestry Pepys tells us in one of his most sensitive passages.

Among other stories, one was very passionate, methought, of a complaint brought against a man in the towne for taking a child from London from an infected house. Alderman Hooker told us it was the child of a very able citizen in Gracious Street, a saddler, who had buried all the rest of his children of the plague, and himself and wife now being shut up and in despair of escaping, did desire only to save the life of this little child; and so prevailed to have it received stark-naked into the arms of a friend, who brought it (having put it into new fresh clothes) to Greenwich; where upon hearing the story, we did agree it should be permitted to be received and kept in the towne.

This incident took place at Greenwich, to which place the business of the Navy Office was removed on August 19th, by the King's command. At the end of the month, Pepys went to join his wife in lodgings in Woolwich. He stayed in the neighbourhood of desolation until he was ordered to leave it. On August 5th, he had written from Seething Lane to Sir William Coventry:

I have been a good while alone here, the rest having to one place or other provided for themselves out of town. The truth is, few but ticketeers and people of very ordinary errands now come hither, merchants and all persons of better rank with whom we have to deal for provisions and otherwise having left the town; so that I think it will be necessary with respect to them that we remove to some place to which they may be invited to come to us, such as Greenwich or the like. Be pleased to let his Royal Highness's pleasure be signified herein; for though the removal of my particular papers and business be I think impracticable, and so do purpose myself to trust God Almighty and stay in town, yet I would be glad that we might have some place appointed where my fellow-Officers and those we have to do with may think it safe to continue their meeting, without the King's business in a little time will be at a very great stand . . .

The city of London had now fallen into a deathlike trance, broken only by the passing of the dead carts that were now plying by day as well as night, and by a few solitaries who walked about like 'people that have taken leave of the world.'

At Greenwich, Pepys conducted himself in a time of national misfortune with great credit and considerable personal profit. The new expedition at sea under Sandwich had miscarried in its principal aim. De Ruyter had outwitted his pursuers and come safely to port. A project to recover this misfortune by an attack upon the Dutch Fleet at Bergen had failed. The strategy was doubtful, the elements were unkind, and the King of Denmark failed in what Sandwich believed to have been his undertakings. It was a crisis in which the Admiral's credit could have been saved only by some lucky and spectacular stroke of rashness. Sandwich was neither spectacular nor rash: all his successes

had been the outcome of prudent and competent general-
ship, of which the secret had been to reduce hazards to a
minimum before striking. It was a method highly to be
commended, and one that served the State well, as none
knew better than the King. But with De Ruyter back in
Holland, and the Bergen exploit coming to a bad end, the
public mind in England was in no mood for argument. It
was scared by the plague, and it was now more than ever
scared by the Dutch, and its one demand was for a victory.
In the circumstances, no reasonable blame could attach to
Sandwich for his failure, but a scared public is not reasonable. The King and the Duke of York knew that Sandwich
had done everything in his power, but all that the public
cared to know was that he had not beaten the Dutch. And
then, as the English Fleet lay baffled in the North Sea, still
waiting an opportunity, another mischance befell the commander. He captured two East Indiamen, laden with a
cargo representing a vast fortune. It seemed to him that his
losses had been repaired, and had it remained at that all
might have been well. But he decided that no risks must
be taken with prizes so rich, and he brought them into England with the entire Fleet as convoy.

Whether in any case the public would have accepted the
prizes as sufficient compensation for the survival of the
Dutch menace may be doubted, but at all events Sandwich ruined his own credit in the capture by an act of
astonishing misjudgment. Instead of handing over the
oriental wealth in his charge to the Commissioners for regular distribution, he held back the share due to himself and
his flag officers. The story is a long and complicated one,
not to be retold here in detail. There is no question of
Sandwich having taken for himself anything to which he
was not entitled, and it is clear that in counsel with his
officers he was even persuaded that he was doing nothing
amiss in his method of taking it. After the event he obtained
a warrant, and finally a formal exoneration from the King
for his action. But, in fact, an irregularity had been committed, and an inflamed public opinion was quick to interpret

it as something very much more serious. Crowds assembled on the river bank at Erith to see the prizes that angry gossip asserted had been plundered by the Admiral, 'the greatest wealth,' wrote Pepys, 'lie in confusion that a man can see in the world. Pepper scattered through every chink, you trod upon it; and in cloves and nutmegs, I walked above the knees; whole rooms full. And silk in bales, and boxes of copper-plate.' In the wholly ignorant, but not quite unintelligible, outcry, Sandwich's reputation was overwhelmed. He had been outwitted by De Ruyter, and now instead of facing the enemy in the North Sea, he had crept back home with prizes that he had rifled to his own uses. In face of the clamour Sandwich went to explain himself to the King, whose Court was now at Oxford. He succeeded in explaining himself, but he added fuel to the public anger. Why was the Admiral at Court looking after his own interests? Why was he not at sea looking after the Dutch? It was all monstrous enough, but it was effective. The agitation against him made it highly undesirable to send Sandwich back to the Fleet, and he himself wished in the circumstances to be relieved of his command. The King was loyal to the friend to whom he owed so much, but he had a gift for grasping the realities of a situation, and Sandwich was appointed Ambassador to Madrid.

The episode caused Pepys acute distress. It is probable that at first he took Sandwich's own view that there was nothing reprehensible in not handing over the prizes intact. In any case he himself bought an interest in his Lordship's share. We need not plead his moral scruples to say that he would hardly have done this as a knowing party to any grave breach of naval regulations. But he quickly realised his mistake, and anxiously covered up the tracks of his conduct, closing his part in the transaction with unfeigned relief. Much more disturbing than his fear for the consequences of what at most might have been charged against him as an indiscretion, was the deep distress with which he saw Sandwich involved in a public scandal which, while he knew it to be unjust and cruel, he could do little to allay.

With full knowledge of the circumstances, Pepys considered
that Sandwich had been ill advised, but that he was grossly
misrepresented in the public view. He lost no opportunity
of speaking well of the man who was under a cloud; but
the individual testimony of friends was not what Sandwich
needed. If it came to that, he had the unequivocal good
word of the King himself. He was called upon to answer
no specific charges, but was subjected to that elusive kind
of popular hostility that is as dangerous as it is irresponsible. It was countenanced, and even incited, by a few highly
placed personages. Coventry, for example, was not helpful.
One fanatic wanted to move in the House of Commons that
great emoluments should be voted to the Duke of York
and Rupert and half-a-crown to Sandwich. The indignation with which Pepys heard the slanders that were current
is implied in a note made after dining at the Duke of Albemarle's. Monk had married the notorious Nan Clarges,
though there was said to be another husband who had
escaped her celebrated gift for abuse by getting himself
locked up in the Tower of London. It was further said that
the Albemarles gave this gentleman 'two or three hundred
pounds a year to stop his mouth from clamour,' which, as
when they both died in 1670 Albemarle left a fortune of
something like half a million and his wife fifty thousand
pounds of her own, they might very well afford to do.
When Sandwich's appointment to Madrid was announced,
the Duke of York resumed command at sea jointly with
Albemarle, and it was on December 9, 1665, that 'At table
the Duchesse, a damned ill-looked woman, complaining of
her Lord's going to sea the next year, said these cursed
words: "If my Lord had been a coward he had gone to
sea no more: it may be then he might have been excused,
and made an Embassador." ' This, Pepys tells us, made him
mad, which her Grace perceiving she 'Blushed herself very
much.' But a month later, he 'heard the damned Duchesse
again say to twenty gentlemen publiquely in the room, that
she would have Montagu sent once more to sea, before he
goes his Embassy, that we may see whether he will make

amends for his cowardice.' She must, as Pepys later observed, have been a 'filthy woman,' but it went hard with Sandwich to have such things said in the drawing room of the Cockpit even though its mistress was a disgrace to the Billingsgate from which she had risen. The strain told. Attending a Council meeting at Hampton Court, Pepys 'found my Lord Sandwich there, poor man! I see with a melancholy face, and suffers his beard to grow on his upper lip more than usual.' But Sandwich left for Madrid in February, 1666, with an easier mind. He had paid in full measure for his indiscretion, he was acquitted by his friends and his own conscience of all discreditable suspicions, and he carried with him renewed assurances of the King's confidence. The whole story had been a miserable one, in which a brave and honourable man had been played a knavish trick by Fortune. Before sailing, he admitted Pepys again freely to his counsels on the old footing of friendship.

In the meantime, the situation had not only been distressing for Pepys, but also extremely delicate. In all loyalty to Sandwich, he had his own career to consider. He could not afford to offend Coventry, and Coventry took a decidedly unfavourable view both of Bergen and of the breaking of the prize goods. It says not a little for Pepys's diplomacy that he was able to use what influence he had at the Navy Office in Sandwich's interest without endangering his own position. But he was equal to the occasion, and during the months that preceded the Great Fire of 1666 he rose steadily in esteem. In August, 1665, Sir George Carteret told him that his aim was to make himself so indispensable to the Court 'that the King shall not be able to whip a cat, but I must be at the tayle of it,' and then, Pepys adds on his own account, 'meaning so necessary he is, and the King and my Lord Treasurer and all do confess it; which, while I mind my business, is my own case in this office of the Navy, and I hope shall be more, if God give me life and health.' In the following November, Albemarle endorsed his earlier compliment by saying that 'there had been nothing done in the Navy without me.' And then came

a great day in January, 1666, when at Hampton Court
'the King come to me of himself, and told me, "Mr. Pepys,"
says he, "I do give you thanks for your good service all this
year, and I assure you I am very sensible of it." ' At the
end of September 1665, he could write:

I do end this month with the greatest content, and may say
that these last three months, for joy, health, and profit,
have been much the greatest that ever I received in all
my life in any twelve months almost in my life, having
nothing upon me but the consideration of the sicklinesse
of the season during this great plague to mortify mee.
For all which the Lord God be praised!

At the end of the year he found that his diligence had
done much for his reputation, and, further, that it had
increased his fortunes from thirteen hundred to no less than
four thousand four hundred pounds. Being taken home by
an acquaintance to 'a very brave dinner, though no invitation,' he apostrophises himself with 'Lord! to see how I am
treated, that come from so mean a beginning, is a matter
of wonder to me. But it is God's great mercy to me, and
His blessing upon my taking pains and being punctual in
my dealings.'

During its exile at Greenwich in the plague months, naval
society did not languish for want of diversions. Lord
Brouncker, who had joined the Board as a Commissioner
and who kept house with 'an ugly mistress' whom he called
his cousin, made himself socially agreeable, Commissioner
Pett and his wife were of a neighbourly mind, and there
was no lack of colleagues and officers ready for a table at
cards or a turn at music in the evenings. Music there was
in varied plenty. Among others at Woolwich who shared
Pepys's taste was Thomas Hill, an employee at the Prize
Office, and 'a master in most sorts of musique,' with whom
Pepys was constantly in company, even on occasion 'all the
morning at musique, and a song he hath set of three parts,
methinks very good.' There was Edward Coleman, the

opera singer, whose voice now was 'quite spoiled,' though 'when he begins to be drunk he is excellent company, but afterward troublesome and impertinent.' There were Mrs. Coleman and Mrs. Knipp, both of whom learnt to sing Pepys's *Beauty Retire,* and there was Mrs. Pierce, the surgeon's wife, while at home there were Mary Mercer, Mrs. Pepys's maid, and Barbara Sheldon, the landlady's daughter, both with a pretty talent for dancing. In such company Pepys passed many hours to his great content. Tom Hayter and Will Hewer could always be called in to take a part in a madrigal or a turn on the floor to the music of Golding, the Greenwich barber, who was always willing to oblige of an evening for a small fee.

To music, and the beauty of women, Pepys had now become more than ever the confessed slave. On December 6, 1665, he wrote:

Here the best company for musique I ever was in, in my life, and wish I could live and die in it, both for musique and the face of Mrs. Pierce, and my wife and Knipp, who is pretty enough; but the most excellent, mad-humoured thing, and sings the noblest that ever I heard in my life, and Rolt, with her, some things together most excellently.

And three months later, after an evening in Mrs. Knipp's company:

She and I singing, and, God forgive me! I do still see that my nature is not to be quite conquered, but will esteem pleasure above all things, though yet in the middle of it, it has reluctances after my business, which is neglected by my following my pleasure. However musique and women I cannot but give way to, whatever my business is.

It was this faculty for self-knowledge that saved Pepys, when he was becoming confirmed in his habits, from becoming also their creature. And as the pressure of employment and responsibility grew upon him, he grew also in a practical wisdom that gave a shrewd balance to his busy and often difficult life.

I do thinke myself obliged to thinke myself happy, and do look upon myself at this time in the happiest occasion a man can be, and whereas we takes pains in expectation of future comfort and ease, I have taught myself to reflect upon myself at present as happy, and enjoy myself in that consideration, and not only please myself with thoughts of future wealth and forget the pleasure we at present enjoy.

And then again:

The truth is, I do indulge myself a little the more in pleasure, knowing that this is the proper age of my life to do it; and out of my observation that most men that do thrive in the world, do forget to take pleasure during the time that they are getting their estate, but reserve that till they have got one, and then it is too late for them to enjoy it with any pleasure.

Few men have risen to meet each day with keener anticipations than did Pepys in these years of his middle life. His books, his prints, his music, his friends, his work, and his success were all sources of a satisfaction that never lost its freshness. Of an almost unexampled frankness with himself, he was little given to the more dangerous forms of introspection. Any curious phenomenon, such as those that he saw at the meetings of the Royal Society, attracted his attention at once, and he was never at the smallest pains to conceal from himself the caprices or even the misdemeanours of his own character. But from day to day the account was audited and closed. He was not without fears for himself, and knew sometimes that discipline was necessary, as when he made and kept his vow against excessive drinking. But his mind, while subject to fugitive alarms, had no troubled depths. His nature was not a shallow one, still less was it insensitive, but it knew nothing of spiritual darkness or conflict. His eager observation and his penetrating intelligence taught him a great deal about life, but they revealed to him nothing of the labouring passion that informed the Puritan world into which he was born. He was interested in Cromwell as a success, and in Cromwell as a failure, but Cromwell as protagonist meant nothing to him. He had a copy of Milton's poems in his library, but it is unlikely that he read them with more than a casual attention. Apocalyptic adventures of this sort were not at all to his mind. There was enough adventure in addressing himself daily to his two governing ambitions, to be successful and to be happy. The ideal is, after all, a considerable one, and few men have pursued it with a livelier spirit than Pepys. His life, with no wide horizons, and little given to searching speculation, achieved an uncommon degree of intensity. If he was willing to leave the stormier regions of experience and the imagination unexplored, the experience that was within his range has seldom been more acutely known. He was not the man to embarrass his personal anxieties with those of a universal kind, nor would he let his own difficulties escape from terms of plain common sense. To no man would our modern pseudo-psychology have been more wholly unintelligible. He met the experience that came his way, and left the rest to go its own unchallenged. Even in trifles this was his attitude. One day when he was dining at the King's Head at Deptford, a hunting party came in with 'a hare alive and a great many silly stories they tell of their sport, which pleases them mightily, and me not at all, such is the different sense of pleasure in mankind.'

It was during 1665 that Pepys first became intimate with John Evelyn, who at the age of forty-five was living at Sayes Court, Deptford, and was serving as a Commissioner for the sick and wounded. He makes a first agreeable ap-

pearance at Greenwich, 'repeating of some verses made up
of nothing but the various acceptations of *may* and *can,* and
doing it so aptly upon occasion of something of that nature, and so fast, did make us all die almost with laughing.'
A little later he sent his new friend a copy of his *Instructions concerning Erecting of a Library,* which Pepys discovered to be a book 'above my reach.' The two men were
in close sympathy in their efforts to help the wretched seamen whose complaints were making the streets a public
disgrace. On September 28, 1665, Evelyn wrote in his
journal, 'To the General again, to acquaint him of the deplorable state of our men for want of provisions,' and on
October 7th, Pepys in his, 'Did business, though not much,
at the office; because of the horrible crowd and lamentable
moan of the poor seamen that lie starving in the streets for
lack of money.' The victims of the plague and the victims
of the war were indeed everywhere an inescapable reproach.
Says Evelyn, 'I was environed with multitudes of poor
pestiferous creatures begging alms'; and Pepys, 'a whole
hundred of them followed us; some cursing, some swearing, and some praying to us.' On October 24th, the two men
dined together, 'and there merry, yet vexed again at publique matters, and to see how little heed is had to the
prisoners and sicke and wounded.' But Evelyn, for all his
sober gravity, was little more inclined than Pepys to take
the troubles of the world too heavily. Driving about on his
sufficiently heartbreaking errands, he could note, with im-
perturbable temper, that 'This country, from Rochester to
Maidstone and the Downs, is very agreeable for the prospect.' And so the two men, apart from their serious interests in common, found each other attractive company.
Both were connoisseurs, and Evelyn with his wider opportunities had many treasures with which to delight his
younger friend:

. . . made a visit to Mr. Evelyn, who, among other things,
showed me most excellent painting in little; in distemper,
Indian incke, water colours: graveing; and, above all, the

whole secret of mezzo-tinto, and the manner of it, which is very pretty, and good things done with it.

On another occasion, Evelyn delighted his friend by presenting him with an old Navy ledger, containing much curious information. 'He also shewed us several letters of the old Lord of Leicester, in Queen Elizabeth's time, under the very handwriting of Queen Elizabeth, and Queen Mary, Queen of Scots; and others, very memorable names. But, Lord! how poorly, methinks, they wrote in those days, and in what plain and uncut paper.' It has to be recorded that Evelyn lent Pepys some of these letters, and that they now repose in the Pepys Library at Magdalene. But the friendship survived such misdemeanours, and whenever Pepys and Evelyn met there was likely to be 'excellent discourse.' It may be added that Pepys had a high opinion of Evelyn's official capabilities. In October, 1665, he wrote to Sir William Coventry:

. . . I have made it my business this day to visit Mr. Evelyn this afternoon to see in what order his accounts (with respect to our designs) are kept; beyond expectation I find that if the rest of his companions take the same course he doth, they will save the King a very considerable sum in the remedy they will give us to this very evil, for Mr. Evelyn (to instance in one port) shewed me his account of Gravesend, where for every penny he demands allowance for, and for every sick man he hath had under his care, he shews you all you can wish for in columns, of which I have here for your satisfaction enclosed an example, which I dare say you will say with me he deserves great thanks for.

During the plague period Pepys's family affairs were inactive. His wife did not suspect his gallantries, or if she did she said nothing about them. Quarrels were infrequent, and life in the Pepys household was amiably conducted. Pepys in his rising fortunes went so far as to allow his wife to buy a pearl necklace to the value of £80. No unusually distracting news came from Brampton, though negotiations for Pall's marriage were unfruitful. A London upholsterer seemed to be well disposed in the matter, but having asked for £500 as a dowry, raised the figure on second thoughts to £800, which was more than Pepys, who had to find the money, was prepared to give. Benjamin Gawden, the son of a Victualler to the Navy, was then considered, and the match seemed likely to go forward, when a friend pointed out to Pepys that it would 'undo me in all my places, everybody suspecting me in all I do.' A country suitor, by name Ensum, seemed more promising. He demanded £600 down, and £100 on the birth of the first child, but he had imminent expectations of £1,000 'by the death of an old aunt.' He, too, after consideration, raised his figure by £100, but a subsequent compromise was made by which Pepys was to get off with £500 down, with a further £100 upon the contingency aforesaid. The courtship, however, hung fire, and in the Diary six months later its summary conclusion is noted: 'newes this day from Brampton, of Mr. Ensum, my sister's sweetheart, being dead: a clowne.' And so more than another year was to go by before a husband could be provided for the sister, who visiting London in May, 1666, struck her brother as 'a pretty good-bodied woman, and not over thicke, as I thought she would have been, but full of freckles and not handsome in face.'

Shortly after Pepys had left Seething Lane for Woolwich in August, 1665, he wrote in a letter to Lady Carteret, dated September 4th, that he had

. . . stayed in the city till above 7,400 died in one week, and of them above 6,000 of the plague, and little noise heard day or night but tolling of bells; till I could walk Lumber-street, and not meet twenty persons from one end to the other, and not 50 upon the Exchange; till whole families, 10 and 12 together, have been swept away; till my very physician, Dr. Burnet, who undertook to secure me against any infection, having survived the month of his own house being shut up, died himself of the plague; till the nights, though much lengthened, are grown too short to conceal the burials of those that died the day before, people being thereby constrained to borrow daylight for that service: lastly, till I could find neither meat nor drinke safe, the butcheries being every where visited, my brewer's house shut up, and my baker, with his whole family, dead of the plague.

As the year drew towards an end, the violence of the attack abated, though through the winter, and indeed until the time of the fire in the following September, the disease lingered in the city, within and without the walls. But gradually, as the cold weather came on, London began to resume its normal life. At the end of November, Pepys heard from his father 'as great news of joy to them, that he saw Yorke's waggon go again this week to London, and was full of passengers.' In that week the plague mortality numbered 333. In December, Mrs. Pepys returned to Seething Lane, and Pepys himself followed a week or two later. But in the middle of January he writes with great anxiety of an unexpected increase in the figures to 158, 'because of the lateness of the year, and the fear, we may with reason have, of its continuing with us the next summer.' In the same month, however, the Navy Office staff moved back into its permanent quarters, and Pepys began once more to follow the active routine of his London life. Soon after his return, he was laying out £10 on new books in St. Paul's Churchyard, commissioning John Hales to paint portraits of himself and his wife, making 'rendez-vouses' with Mrs. Lane, examining Mr. Evelyn's propositions for public infirmaries, and feasting with the Elder Brothers at Trinity House. Cheerful companies began again to assemble at Seething Lane, being regaled with menus of startling proportions, nobly supported by a cellar which now contained 'two tierces of Claret, two quarter casks of Canary, and a smaller vessel of Sack; a vessel of Tent, another of Malaga, and another of white wine . . .

which, I believe, none of my friends of my name now alive
ever had of his owne at one time.' He was, in fact at ease
in body and mind, as was his habit, save for a momentary
suspicion that he was being tempted again by diversions to
a neglect of business, and his 'being nowadays . . . mightily troubled with my snoring in my sleep, and know not how
to remedy it.'

It was on Sunday, September 2, 1666, that Pepys wrote
in his Diary:

Some of our mayds sitting up late last night to get things
ready against our feast to-day, Jane called us up about
three in the morning, to tell us of a great fire they saw in
the City. So I rose and slipped on my night-gowne, and
went to her window, and thought it to be on the backside of Marke-Lane at the farthest; but, being unused
to such fires as followed, I thought it far enough off; and
went to bed again and to sleep.

This is no place for an extended account of the holocaust
that raged for four days and swept away some fourteen
thousand houses, nearly a hundred parish churches, the city
cathedral, the Royal Exchange, Newgate Gaol, the Guildhall, and a vast number of other public and business buildings, destroying property valued in those days at more than
ten million pounds. Mr. Walter George Bell, in *The Great
Fire of London,* 1666, has given a masterly summary of the
disaster, that was not wholly loss since it burnt out the
festering seed-beds of the plague. Dryden in dedicating his
Annus Mirabilis to the Lord Mayor, Aldermen, Sheriffs and
Common Council of London, paid noble tribute to the 'in-
vincible Courage, and unshaken Constancy' with which the
City had submitted to the Judgments of Heaven, and at the
same time had raised itself in vigour 'above all human
Enemies.' Our interest here is to see the progress of the fire
as it appeared to Pepys. His own narrative is a little classic
in descriptive power. When he rose on the Sunday he found
the news more serious than he had expected, and hurried

anxiously to the Lieutenant of the Tower, from whom he learnt that the fire, which had broken out at the house of the King's baker in Pudding Lane, had already taken dangerous hold. In the City he saw for himself that the damage was already heavy, and, with a high wind blowing, likely to be worse. Going down to Whitehall with his news, he was summoned by the King and Duke of York, and plainly spoke his mind 'that unless his Majesty did command houses to be pulled down nothing could stop the fire.' He was sent off in haste with orders to the Lord Mayor 'to spare no houses, but to pull down before the fire every way.' But Sir Thomas Bludworth, of whom Pepys had written two months earlier that he was a silly man, had lost his head, and 'with a handkercher about his neck' was crying out in Canning Street like a fainting woman: ' "Lord! what can I do? I am spent: people will not obey me." ' Later in the day, watching the fire from the water, Pepys found the river crowded with lighters and boats taking in goods, and valuable property abandoned in large quantities to the tide. The water passengers were in serious peril and terrified by showers of fire drops blown from the burning city. As dark came on, the city shone out 'in a most horrid malicious bloody flame, not like the fine flame of an ordinary fire,' and then later they saw 'only one entire arch of fire from this to the other side the bridge, and in a bow up the hill for an arch of above a mile long: it made me weep to see it. The churches, houses, and all on fire and flaming at once; and a horrid noise the flames made, and the cracking of houses at their ruine.'

Before dawn next morning, Lady Batten sent him a cart to carry away his own valuables to a place of safety, 'Which I did, riding myself in my night-gowne in the cart; and, Lord! to see how the streets and the highways are crowded with people running and riding, and getting of carts at any rate to fetch away things.' During the day, as the destruction went on, the Duke of York rode up and down with his guard to keep order in the city. At night Pepys and his wife slept in quilts on the office floor, all

SAMUEL PEPYS

BY JOHN HALES. *National Portrait Gallery*

their household goods having been removed. The next day he put his office papers in a pit that Sir William Batten was digging in the garden for the purpose of storing his wine, and in the evening he dug himself a pit for the same purpose, and there with his wine put his Parmazan cheese. But as he and Penn sat together in their garden, watching street by street being devoured by the flames, they conceived the idea of importing crews of workmen from the dockyards to protect the Navy Office, the loss of which 'would much hinder the King's business.' They submitted their proposal to the Duke of York, and it was immediately put into effect. On the evening of this day, Tuesday the 4th, William Hewer came in with the news that Paul's was burned and all Cheapside. Before going to bed, Pepys wrote to his father, but finding that the post-house was destroyed also, the letter could not go. 'I lay down in the office again . . . being mighty weary, and sore in my feet with going till I was hardly able to stand.' The next morning, he was awakened at two o'clock by cries that the fire was within a few yards of the end of Seething Lane. He resolved to move his wife to Woolwich, which he did before daybreak, seeing 'the whole city almost' on fire by moonlight. On returning to the Office, he found that the dockmen had isolated it, and that the course of the fire had been deflected from its immediate neighbourhood. During the day, he witnessed an unbroken scene of desolation, 'Fanchurch-streete, Gracious-streete, and Lumbard-streete all in dust.' At night he kept watch at the Office with the workmen, for whom rations of beer and bread and cheese had been provided. The confusions of the time since Sunday so distracted his mind that he could with difficulty remember which day of the week it was. On Thursday, the fire faded away, and as Pepys went home by water from Whitehall, he saw the river banks burnt back into a heap of ashes, from the Tower to the Temple. On the next day, he walked among the ruins, to see the 'miserable sight of Paul's church, with all the roofs fallen, and the body of the quire fallen into St. Fayth's; Paul's school also, Ludgate, and Fleet-street, my father's house, and the church, and a good part of the Temple the like.'

During the following weeks, as the city began to recover from the shock, Pepys continued at intervals to note smaller incidents of the fire. He exclaimed with reason upon one Alderman Starling, 'a very rich man, without children,' who distributed half a crown among thirty dockyard labourers who saved his house, and he was provoked by a Dean, who in a sermon rose to the metaphorical height of declaring that the city was reduced 'from a large folio to a decimotertio.' He agreed with Dryden in saying 'That certainly never so great a loss as this was borne so well by citizens in the world.' On September 15th, he and his wife were back again in their own house, 'But much terrified in the nights now-a-days with dreams of fire, and falling down of houses.' This dread remained with him for months. At the end of the following February he wrote: 'It is strange to think how to this very day, I cannot sleep at night without great terrors of fire, and this very night I could not sleep till almost two in the morning through thoughts of fire.'

CHAPTER V

SOCIAL AND DOMESTIC LIFE. MRS. PEPYS AND DEB. THE DUTCH WAR AGAIN. CLOSE OF THE DIARY

THE burning of London came at a time of great anxiety in Pepys's official career, and during the nine months that followed the anxiety became acute. But while he and his fellow Commissioners were living in daily fear of some major disaster at sea, he found the incidents of his life as absorbing as ever. He could still note on May Day 'the many milk-maids, with their garlands upon their pails, dancing with a fiddler before them'; and 'pretty Nell standing at her lodging's door in Drury-lane in her smock sleeves and bodice'; or record that his wife had gone down to take the air at Woolwich, and 'to gather May-dew to-morrow morning, which Mrs. Turner hath taught her as the only thing in the world to wash her face with.' His curiosity was unresting, but not always well served; visiting the Beargarden, he found it 'a very rude and nasty pleasure.' The trifles of his experience were noted with the utmost nicety.

This cold did most certainly come by my staying a little too long bare-legged yesterday morning when I rose while I looked out fresh socks and thread stockings, yesterday's having in the night, lying near the window, been covered with snow within the window, which made me I durst not put them on.

His moods are defined with the same particularity. His wife dressing one day not to his fancy 'did, together with my being hungry, which always makes me peevish, make me angry, but when my belly was full were friends again.'

It will be suitable at this place to add from the later volumes of the Diary a few more of these strokes of self-portraiture. As Pepys prospered in his career, he enjoyed many little satisfactions of a material kind. He was proud, though not too pleased, to give £40 to the Building Fund of the Royal Society. He was thankful to God when he was able to provide a spare bed for his guests, and he took peculiar delight in ordering from Sympson, the joyner, the handsome book-presses that are now in the Pepys Library at Magdalene. He resolved never to have more books than his presses would contain, finally fixing the limit at three thousand volumes. A devoted bibliophil, he nevertheless read the books that he collected, and formed the habit of carrying one with him for that purpose as he walked from place to place on his business. His occasional notes upon what he read have both candour and intelligence. 'In the barge I took Berckenshaw's translation of Alsted his Templum, but the most ridiculous book, as he has translated it, that ever I saw in my life, I declaring that I understood not three lines together from one end of the book to the other.' His literary enthusiasm is usually of a summary nature. Bringing a copy of Dryden's *Annus Mirabilis* from Westminster Hall at the time of its publication, he had no more to say of it than that it was 'a very good poem.' He read shrewdly by experience. When the Duke of Buckingham was supposed to be under arrest in the Tower, and yet no one in the city seemed to know whether he was there or not, Pepys reflected 'on the uncertainty of all history, when, in a business of this moment, and of this day's growth, we cannot tell the truth.' A word may here be said of Pepys's own quality as a stylist. It has already been suggested that in the shorthand method of the Diary his technical or business entries sometimes become tiresomely involved. But in recording the incidents of his official and social life, he is master always of a manner that precisely serves his purpose. His raciness and his naïveté have for us taken on a pleasing patina

from the years, but he himself can seldom have been wholly
unconscious of a slyly humorous intention as he wrote. And
at times the easy fitness of his style takes on a quite memorable grace. Of his writing in these more exalted moods, one
example may be given, which deserves a distinguished place
in any anthology of English prose:

. . . so the women and W. Hewer and I walked upon the
Downes, where a flock of sheep was; and the most pleasant and innocent sight that ever I saw in my life—we find
a shepherd and his little boy reading, far from any
houses or sight of people, the Bible to him; so I made the
boy read to me, which he did, with the forced tone that
children do usually read, that was mighty pretty, and
then I did give him something, and went to the father,
and talked with him; and I find he had been a servant in
my cozen Pepys's house, and told me what was become
of their old servants. He did content himself mightily in
my liking his boy's reading, and did bless God for him,
the most like one of the old patriarchs that ever I saw in
my life, and it brought those thoughts of the old age of
the world in my mind for two or three days after. We
took notice of his woolen knit stockings of two colours
mixed, and of his shoes shod with iron shoes, both at the
toe and heels, and with great nails in the soles of his
feet, which was mighty pretty: and, taking notice of
them, 'Why,' says the poor man, 'the downes, you see,
are full of stones, and we are faine to shoe ourselves
thus; and these,' says he, 'will make the stones fly till
they sing before me.' I did give the poor man something,
for which he was mighty thankful, and I tried to cast
stones with his horne crooke. He values his dog mightily,
that would turn a sheep any way which he would have
him, when he goes to fold them: told me there was about
eighteen scoare sheep in his flock, and that he hath four
shillings a week the year round for keeping of them: so
we posted thence with mighty pleasure in the discourse
we had with this poor man, and Mrs. Turner, in the

common fields here, did gather one of the prettiest nose-
gays that I ever saw in my life.

As we read the Diary we are aware of a curious lack of
continuity in his conduct and his thought alike. From moment to moment he acts or reflects at the ordering of some
immediate influence, and a single paragraph may reveal a
strange incongruity of motives: 'and so to supper and to
bed, vexed at two or three things, viz.: that my wife's
watch proves so bad as it do; the ill state of the office; and
the Kingdom's business; at the charge which my mother's
death for mourning will bring me when all paid.' He took
a genuine interest, and not only an amatory one, in his servants, and to dismiss one made him wretched. 'It do so
against me to part with a servant, that it troubles me more
than anything in the world,' and again, 'yet I was sorry to
have her go, partly through my love to my servants, and
partly because she was a very drudging, working wench,
only she would be drunk.' And yet, finding that 'Luce, our
cookmayde' had left a door open, he could so far forget
himself as to 'give her a kick in our entry,' and was disturbed only because he was seen to do it by Penn's foot-
boy. When the collector of poll tax came to him with a
demand for £40, he frankly confessed to himself that, although it was a great deal of money, he was being under
assessed, and went to the vestry with the intention of having certain figures included that had been overlooked; but
there 'seeing nobody of our ablest merchants, as Sir Andrew Rickard, to do it, I thought it not decent for me to do
it, nor would it be thought wisdom to do it unnecessarily,
but vain glory.' Being told after dinner one night by Sir
Thomas Crew that members of the House were speaking
handsomely 'of Mr. Pepys's readiness and civility to shew
them every thing,' he was very glad of it, and returning
home to find his wife vexed by his absence, he 'did give her
a pull by the nose and some ill words,' after which she followed him to the office in 'a devilish manner,' and he had

to take her 'into the garden out of hearing, to prevent shame.' But the quarrel, as usual, was soon made up. This was how Pepys met life, being more than most men one who took Fortune's buffets and rewards with equal thanks. When he found himself able to afford a coach of his own, at a cost of £53, he was infinitely delighted with his pair of black horses at a cost of another £50, and the liveries for his boy and coachman. He was a little anxious lest he should be accused by the envious of a display above his station, but was none the less pleased for the Duke of York to see him in his new estate, and he threw restraint to the winds on May-day when 'we went alone through the town with our new liveries of serge, and the horses' manes and tails tied with red ribbons, and the standards there gilt with varnish, and all clean, and green reines, that people did mightily look upon us; and, the truth is, I did not see any coach more pretty, though more gay, than ours, all the day.' And yet when he loses £300 a year by changes at the Victualling Office, he merely remarks that 'we must live with somewhat more thrift' and is anxiously concerned as to how he shall find jobs for two or three clerks who will be thrown out of employment.

Always as he goes about his business there is an eye for unexpected detail. He notes how the summer streets of London become impassable for dust, the difficulty of finding a link at nights because of the danger of passing through the ruins of the fire, or how before a startled crowd a Quaker 'with a chafing-dish of fire and brimstone burning upon his head' ran naked through Westminster Hall, crying, 'Repent! Repent!' And sometimes there is a note of more touching intimacy. A relative comes to see him, 'with her little boy in her armes, a very pretty little boy. The child I like very well, and could wish it my own.' And we could wish it also, for Pepys upon his children would have been a delight indeed. But it was by music that his deepest ardours were evoked. Nothing so soothed the antagonisms with his wife as the progress that she made in her lessons upon the flageolet. And witnessing *The Virgin Martyr* in 1668, he made full confession of the faith that was in him.

But that which did please me beyond anything in the whole world was the wind-musique when the angel comes down, which is so sweet that it ravished me, and indeed, in a word, did wrap up my soul so that it made me really sick, just as I have formerly been when in love with my wife; that neither then, nor all the evening going home, and at home, I was able to think of any thing, but remained all night transported, so as I could not believe that ever any musick hath that real command over the soul of a man as this did upon me: and makes me resolve to practice wind-musique, and to make my wife do the like.

During the later years of the Diary, Pepys's amours, it must be confessed, became wholly unashamed, though retribution was not to seek. Remembering, as we do, that Pepys in confession displays himself to us with unexampled candour, the candour does at times become a little disconcerting. And, to say the least of it, gallantries at the rate of two a day are confusing. It is to be feared that there were occasions when in another age Pepys might have found himself at Vine Street. Turning late into the evening service at St. Dunstan's to hear the sermon, he stood by a 'pretty, modest maid' to whom he began to pay unsolicited attentions; 'but she would not, but got further and further from me; and, at last, I could perceive her to take pins out of her pocket to prick me if I should touch her again —which seeing I did forbear, and was glad I did spy her design.' Such artlessness is disarming. On his way one Sunday to keep a more secular appointment, he met an acquaintance who invited him to a pew in the gallery of St. Margaret's, Westminster, where much against his will he stayed 'in pain while she expected me,' consoling himself by turning his perspective glass on 'a great many very fine women' in the congregation, with which and sleeping he 'passed

away the time till sermon was done,' when he escaped. Of
the childish jargon with which for some reason known to
himself he chose to record his intrigues, the following is
an innocuous example: 'There met Doll Lane coming out,
and par contrat did hazer bargain para aller to the cabaret
de Vin, called the Rose, and ibi I staid two hours, sed she
did not venir, lequel troubled me.'

But Pepys's adventures of the heart came to rude catastrophe with the affair of Deb. Willett. This 'pretty little
girle,' a scholar from Bow School, entered Mrs. Pepys's
service at the end of September, 1667. At first she gave
much satisfaction to her mistress, but by the middle of
October Pepys observed that his wife was 'already jealous
of my kindness to her [Deb.], so that I begin to fear this
girle is not likely to stay long with us.' For a time the
master was circumspect, and it was not until December 22d
(Lord's Day) that he 'first did give her a little kiss, she
being a very pretty humoured girle, and so one that I do
love mightily.' What happened thereafter Pepys for several
months succeeded at least in keeping from the knowledge
of his wife, who took Deb. with her on a visit to Brampton,
and in general seems to have found the girl to her liking.
It was not until October, 1668, that the storm broke. And
then it broke with a pent-up fury of a woman who for
many years had been jealous without precisely realising it,
upon she knew not what occasion; who, moreover, had been
fretting against a discipline that she resented without being
able effectively to dispute it. 'After supper, to have my
head combed by Deb., which occasioned the greatest sorrow to me that ever I knew in this world, for my wife,
coming up suddenly, did find me embracing the girl.'

The scenes that followed make dismal reading. Pepys
made no attempt to justify himself, either to his wife or
in the Diary. And Mrs. Pepys pressed her advantage merci-
lessly. She made her husband promise that he would never
speak again to certain specied ladies of their acquaintance,
and burning a candle in the chimney piece into the small
hours, she made night a torment with her reproaches. For

a fortnight she took no action about the girl, with whom
Pepys in the meantime conspired in a quite futile policy of
denial. Then Deb., under cross-examination, made a full
confession to her mistress, and that night again there was
no sleep until Pepys had undertaken himself to dismiss the
girl, and with no kindness. Two days later this was done,
when Pepys in his wife's presence did 'with tears in my
eyes, which I could not help, discharge her and advise her
to be gone as soon as she could, and never to see me, or
let me see her more while she was in the house.' A few
days' grace were allowed, in which the girl was to find
other work, and during which Mrs. Pepys watched her
husband's every step in the house. Wishing to give his fellow culprit a little over and above her wages, he put forty
shillings into a paper and started off to deliver it in the
kitchen, only to be intercepted by his wife, who 'instantly
flew out into a rage, calling me dog and rogue, and that I
had a rotten heart; all which, knowing that I deserved it,
I bore with.'

Deb. left in the middle of November, three weeks after
the discovery of her offence. And a few days afterwards
Pepys contrived to see her, and to give her twenty (not
forty) shillings and sound advice. Mrs. Pepys got to hear
of the meeting, outdid herself in abuse, and enacted that
thenceforward Pepys should never leave the house but in
the company of herself or William Hewer. Pepys decided
that he had no choice but to accept the condition, or any
other that might be imposed. Hewer proved to be a sympathetic warder, and although conscientious at first after
a little time began to relax his vigilance. The discomforted
husband assured himself repeatedly that never had he been
so happy as in this virtuous reconciliation with his wife.
The night after his clandestine but not secret meeting with
Deb. he began 'to pray to God upon my knees, alone in
my chamber, which God knows I cannot yet do heartily;
but I hope God will give me the grace more and more every
day to fear Him, and to be true to my poor wife.' But the
next day he got a message through to Deb. acquainting her

of certain statements of his own, so that if there should be
further questionings their stories might agree. He then settled into a fond hope that bygones might be bygones. It
was at this time no doubt that his acquaintance with Will
Hewer, who had been giving some dissatisfaction as a
clerk, 'not being able to copy out a letter with sense or true
spelling that makes me mad,' began to ripen into the friendship that was to be so comfortable a feature of his later
years. 'Thence with W. Hewer, who goes up and down
with me like a jaylour; but yet with great love and to my
great good liking, it being my desire above all things to
please my wife therein.' But Mrs. Pepys, in her conscious
and wronged innocence, showed herself uncommonly difficult to please. Upon any or no provocation she returned
to the charge. Not content that Deb. had gone, she determined that her husband should write to the girl, calling her
whore, declaring that he hated her, and that he would
never see her more. All docility, Pepys wrote as he was bid-
den, omitting only the opprobrious word. His wife read the
letter, noted the omission, flew into a rage, and tearing the
paper to pieces made her husband sit down and write again.
A ray of hope came from Hewer, who stood by 'wink-
ing upon me.' Pepys wrote the letter in unexpurgated terms,
and it was given to Hewer to deliver with 'a sharp message'
from Mrs. Pepys, and the young man, finding Deb., discreetly delivered what portions of the letter he thought
proper by word of mouth, and returned the document to
Pepys on the following day.

And so the not altogether convincing, but certainly not
cynical, professions of repentance went on. 'So took our
coach and home, having now little pleasure to look about
me to see the fine faces, for fear of displeasing my wife,
whom I take great pleasure now, more than ever, in pleasing; and it is a real joy to me.' And then a week later,
fresh trouble, Mrs. Pepys having heard that Deb. is going
finely dressed and accusing her husband of supplying the
means. 'I cannot blame her, and therefore she run into
mighty extremes; but I did pacify all, and were mighty

good friends, and to bed, and I hope it will be our last struggle from this business, for I am resolved never to give any new occasion, and great peace I find in my mind by it.' But the poor man discovered that there was no security against the Dæmon that he had raised. Yet a month later his wife broke out again, and threatened him with red-hot tongs as he lay in bed, 'as if she did design to pinch me with them.' By degrees the thing got on Pepys's nerves:

. . . my wife mighty dogged, and I vexed to see it, being mightily troubled, of late, at her being out of humour, for fear of her discovering any new matter of offence against me, though I am conscious of none; but do hate to be unquiet at home. So, late up, silent, and not supping, but hearing her utter some words of discontent to me with silence, and so to bed, weeping to myself for grief, which she discerning, come to bed, and mighty kind, and so with great joy on both sides to sleep.

As time went on Mrs. Pepys quietened in her onsets, but domestically she had achieved the whip hand, and knew it. As time went on, too, and Will Hewer grew less attentive to his charge, Pepys's good resolutions lost some ground at the bidding of old habits. Eighteen months after the crisis there were even further assignations with Deb., but infidelity had received a startling check.

It is needless to moralise the situation at length, but it affords a valuable note on character that we should not neglect. Monsieur Lucas-Dubreton, in his witty French way, can see in the Pepys who emerged from the Willett episode nothing but an eagle, not a very noble eagle perhaps, but nevertheless something of an eagle, with wings and talons clipped. Nothing, it is suggested, is so pathetic, or indeed so ignominious, as a free spirit in confinement, and Pepys, the light-hearted, the gay, the intrepid lover, had lost his liberty. Clearly the professions of repentance must have been made with a wry mouth and with a fallen heart. With this new subjection to his wife the eagerness and the fun of his life went out. Here, henceforth, led by pitiful apron-strings, was a maimed and henpecked gallant of the Restoration. All of which I take to contain a very large percentage, I should say somewhere about ninety, of nonsense. It may amuse Monsieur Dubreton's readers, but it has no relevance to Pepys. It is true that the spectacle of a jealous woman taking it out of a defaulting husband is one of the most unedifying spectacles in the world, and considering this aspect of the case alone, neither Pepys nor his wife make impressive figures. Elizabeth had more than enough reason to be jealous, but reason has never yet made jealousy reasonable. The discovery effected, Elizabeth Pepys behaved like a woman possessed. Pepys does not over-write his narrative, and yet he makes it clear that the scenes during the crisis, and indeed for many weeks afterwards, must have been terrible. On the other hand, Pepys, in bowing patiently to the storm, with hardly a word of protest, certainly makes no hero for a French farce. There is, indeed, something singularly unfunny in the picture of his going to bed and crying about it; and something also, it may be, singularly unheroic. But that the nature of the man was broken by the miserable experience, miserable in all its aspects, there is nothing whatever to show. There is a gloom upon the last months of the Diary, but it is a gloom attributable almost wholly to the fact that he knew his eyesight to be failing. In spite of the scenes, the suspicions, and the constraint, in spite also of desires that were not and never would be wholly dispelled, Pepys quite clearly after the Willett affair did make a genuine and sustained attempt to reëstablish his relations with his wife upon what he earnestly hoped would be durable foundations. And he did so, because he was, as he had always been, in love with her. This again is a circumstance inappropriate to the closing scenes of Parisian invention, but it has the compensating advantage of being the truth.

By the time that the emotions engendered by the incident were losing their bitterness, the married life of Samuel and Elizabeth was within a few months of being brought to an end by death. What would have been its subsequent history no one can tell. That Pepys would ever have become an impeccable husband is unlikely, nor would his wife perhaps have outlived an exacting temper and a scolding tongue. But 'the pretty little girle,' Deb. Willett, had, I think, thrown a solvent into the angrier humours of the household in Seething Lane. The process was at first inevitably attended by violence. But as this subsided, both Pepys and his wife, I cannot but suppose, would have found that they had learnt a lesson. The fact is that Pepys was simply unable to relate his misdemeanours in any way to his affection for his wife. As she was a woman who in jealousy could become ungovernable, there was here a question upon which they were never likely to understand each other. But while Mrs. Pepys, from what we know of her, was not very gifted in seeing round corners, her husband had some talent that way, and after the Willett experience his intention is plainly to adapt himself to necessities. And it is not going too far to say that almost the first necessity of his nature was the domestic companionship of his wife. When, in one of her frenzies, she passed from voluble denunciation of his guilt to a threat of leaving the house for good, he was reduced to the 'most perfect confusion of face and heart, and sorrow and shame, in the greatest agony in the world.' And, although the words were written in the year before the Willett crisis, there is in the following passage a disposition that was likely to survive many shocks: 'But, Lord! to see what a poor content any acquaintance among these people, or the people of the world, as they now-a-days go, is worth; for my part I and my wife will keep to one another and let the world go hang, for there is nothing but falseness in it.' In conclusion of the matter, Elizabeth Pepys died in 1669, and although Samuel lived until 1703 he did not marry again.

In these later years of the Diary there is but little of importance to note concerning the other members of his family. The references to his father show an unabated attachment. He had his portrait painted by Hales, and was rejoiced to have so good a picture of one who 'besides that he is my father, and a man that loves me, and hath ever done so, is also, at this day, one of the most carefull and innocent men in the world.' Disquieting news from Brampton being followed by reassurance, he wrote asking his father to come to town, 'That I may see what can be done for him here; for I would fain do all I can that I may have him live, and take pleasure in my doing well in the world.' His brother John continued to avoid remunerative employment, and it was not until after the date of the Diary that he secured a post at Trinity House on Samuel's recommendation, where he accumulated a debt of £300 which he left to his elder brother as a legacy on his death in 1677. Pall, after many discouragements, found at last a suitor who did not look back. In October, 1667, Samuel at Brampton finding her to grow 'old and ugly,' resolved that something must be done soon to settle her, though when he gave her twenty shillings on leaving, he took her 'to be so cunning and ill-natured, that I have no great love for her; but only she is my sister and must be provided for.' And so, in the following February, a marriage contract was duly made with John Jackson of Brampton, a plain young man, though 'handsome enough for Pall, one of no education nor discourse, but of few words, and one altogether that, I think, will please me well enough.' The suitor, it may be noted, had benefited by the will of his predecessor, Ensum, the clowne. On March 2d, following, Pepys had news 'that my sister was married on Thursday last to Mr. Jackson; so that work is, I hope, well over.' When two months later he went down again to Brampton, he saw his 'sister Jackson, she growing fat, and, since being married, I think looks comelier than before: but a mighty pert woman she is, and I think proud, he keeping her mighty handsome, and they say mighty fond.' In March, 1667, his mother died at Brampton, her last words being, he was told, 'God bless my poor Sam.' The entry in the Brampton register reads: 'Margarett Pepys the wife of John Pepys, gent was buryed the seaven and twenty day of March. Anno Domi. 1667.' Pepys spent £50 on mourning for the family, but did not attend the funeral. The news set him 'weeping heartily,' but on reflecting 'how much bet-

ter both for her and us it is than it might have been had
she outlived my father and me or my happy present condition in the world, she being helpless, I was the sooner at
ease in my mind.' He was, in fact, decently sensible of the
death of a mother between whom and himself there had
never been any deep bond of affection.

The years 1666 and 1668 were eventful ones for the
Navy Office and the Clerk of the Acts. After Sandwich's
departure for Madrid, the Fleet at sea, under the joint command of Albemarle and Rupert, twice came into conflict
with the Dutch during 1666, not without honour, but without any decisive issue. The enemy continued to be a menace
to our coasts, the shortage of money in the naval chest became more and more embarrassing, and Pepys found himself ever more confidently critical of the authorities above
him. Once he came in direct opposition to Rupert, who
'will be asking now who this Pepys is, and find him to be
a creature of my Lord Sandwich's,' which meant danger.
But Pepys's value as an administrator by this time was
generally known. In July, 1666, he could write of himself
'as having the advantage of having had two fleets dispatched in better condition than ever any fleetes were yet,
I believe.' And as misfortune threatened, 'time spending,
and no money to set anything in hand with; the end thereof
must be speedy ruine,' he spared nothing of labour that his
own department at least should not be found wanting.
Various rearrangements of the constitution of the Navy
Board did not affect his position; they rather strengthened
his authority. When he wrote, 'God keep us, for things
look mighty ill,' he wrote not in despair but in determination. And when he wrote further, 'Our enemies French, and
Dutch, great, and grow more by our poverty,' and complained of 'a sad, vicious, negligent Court, and all sober
men there fearful of the ruin of the whole kingdom this
next year,' he still had not lost heart.

But the heart needed to be a stout one, for conditions
were desperately discouraging. Repeated applications,
mostly drawn up by Pepys, were sent by the Commissioners

at the Navy Office to the Duke of York, imploring his Majesty to supply necessary funds. Not only was there an appalling tale of debt, but there was also a complete failure to meet the weekly bills. As one appeal after another was disregarded, the terms in which they were submitted became more outspoken, and always with the same result. At times the pleas almost amounted to a threat that if something was not done the Navy Board would have to retire from responsibilities that they were wholly unable to satisfy. And at a moment when a sum of something like a million pounds was in question, all that the Treasurer could say in respect of one immediately pressing item for two hundred pounds, was that he could by no means meet that figure, but that in view of the urgency he might manage thirty. The discontent among contractors, labourers, and seamen became violent. At the end of 1665, Pepys had written to Coventry:

. . . nay, at this instant while I am writing, the whole company of the *Breda* (which and the *Welcome* have in every point been ready to fall down several days but for the unruliness of the men) are now breaking the windows of our Office and hath twice this day knocked down Marlow our Messenger, swearing they will not budge without money. What meat they'll make of me anon, you shall know by my next. But, Sir, what will the consequence of this be, and how shall it be remedied?

A month or two later he wrote to Pett:

. . . It is now 2 months within 2 days since this Office hath felt one farthing of money for any service, great or small, though to save the life of a man by paying a ticket.

As the months and the years went on, things fell from bad to worse. In March, 1667, the Navy Office received a letter from the Commissioner at Portsmouth, as follows:

Just now is with me a poor oar-maker crying and wringing his hands for money, and desires to be a labourer in the yard to keep him from being arrested, for that he tells me he dareth not go home to his wife any more, for he shall be carried to jail by his timber-merchant; which request of his I granted, and is now entered a labourer, albeit the King oweth him for oars near 300£. But I thank you that you do mind it, and will relieve me as soon as you can.

This morning came a boat loaden with broom into the harbour. Mr. Lucas the shipwright would have bought it, but considering we have six ships to clean and not one broom faggot nor which way else to do it, I seized on the boat of broom and brought her to the yard and is unloaden, the poor man lamenting that he had no money to buy more and was in debt for that, and I having but poor 11£. 14s. 6d. in my custody, was forced to pay him for his broom out of that stock I had to buy me victuals. The sum comes to 8£. 15s., so I have left to supply me 2£. 9s. 6d., which will not find food for my family at the outside above six months.

At the same time the Commissioner at Harwick wrote in despair that he was watching men 'really perish for want of wherewithal to get nourishment. One yesterday came to me crying to get something to relieve him. I ordered him 10s. He went and got hot drink and something to help him, and so drank it, and died within two hours.' In the same month, Pepys wrote in the Diary: 'This day a poor seaman almost starved for want of food, lay in our yard a-dying. I sent him half a crown and we ordered his ticket to be paid.'

It was in such circumstances as these that Pepys, and with him one or two other faithful servants, worked in vain to keep the Navy from the demoralisation that came to an ignominious crisis and almost to capital disaster in the summer of 1667, when the Dutch fleet insulted the defences of the Medway with impunity, and when, had they been accurately informed, they might have delivered a far more crippling stroke. On June 3d of that year Pepys heard from Evelyn that the Dutch were out with eighty men-of-war and twenty fire-ships, and that the French were in the channel manœuvring to join them with another twenty sail, 'which we have not a ship at sea to do them any hurt with.' Two days later there was news of mutiny among the few ships that it had been possible to call into the threatened waters. On the 8th, the Dutch were reported to be off Harwich, and on the 10th they had come up to the Nore. The next day they took Sheerness, and Chatham was in jeopardy. On the 12th, the enemy broke the defensive chain that stretched across the river, and burnt a number of ships, among them the *Royal Charles* that had brought the King back to England. The Commissioners at the Navy Office could do little but exclaim impotently upon a disgrace of which they had given repeated warnings. Pepys and his colleagues, in the face of hopeless difficulties, got a few fire-ships into the river, and were distracted in their efforts to keep the unpaid and starving British seamen from deserting to the Dutch. The ships at sea, totally inadequate in numbers, were almost bankrupt of provisions, powder, and shot, and manned by crews from whom prolonged injustice had driven all notions of discipline. Pepys did the little that he could with the most careful anxiety, but at length even his buoyant spirit was clouded. 'And the truth is, I do fear so much that the whole kingdom is undone, that I do this night resolve to study with my father and wife what to do with the little that I have in money by me, for I give up all the rest . . . for lost.' So he wrote on June 12th, and the next day at two hours' warning he sent them down to Brampton 'with about £1,300 in gold in their night-bag.' Later in the day he sent his clerk, Gibson, after them 'with another 1,000 pieces.' And with that, the best that could be done was to sink our own ships, to which effect 'the King and Duke of York have been below [London Bridge] since four o'clock in the morning,' giving enforced commands that are written on perhaps the blackest page in English naval annals. In fairness to the King, it should be said that while he more than anyone was responsible for the pass to which things had come, he was not lacking in enterprise or personal courage when the blow fell. 'The King and Duke of York up and down all the day here and there: some time on Tower Hill, where the City militia was; where the King did make a speech to them, that they should venture themselves no further than he would himself.'

Fearing that at any moment the city might be overwhelmed, Pepys took the further precaution of carrying £300 in a belt about his body, to meet a last emergency, and among other things which he placed in what he hoped might be safe keeping, were 'my journalls, which I value very much.' 'Never,' so ran the reports that were brought into the Navy Office, 'were people so dejected as they are in the City all over at this day.' The scenes of panic recall those that were witnessed at the Great Fire. On the 14th, the Dutch were reported off Gravesend. Rumour had it that the bankers were 'broke as to ready money,' although one of them alone had had £100,000 in his hands at the first threat of invasion. People went about the streets crying for a Parliament, and Pepys believed, not unreasonably, 'that it would cost blood to answer for these miscarriages.' Pett, the Commissioner at Chatham, was thrown into the Tower on charges of misconduct and incompetence, and Pepys feared that public anger would be turned upon members of the Navy Board without distinction. One report, indeed, went that Pepys himself was already with Pett in confinement. The only remaining hope was that the Dutch would fail to realise how completely they had this country at their mercy, and it was a hope that held. It was not surprising. The Dutch, like ourselves, were great sailors. They had bred a magnificent race of seamen, and their naval administration had been diligent and exacting. In many fierce actions they had learnt to regard the British crews as the equal of their own in courage, the commanders as worthy opponents of the best that they could show, and the administration at Whitehall as a credit to the great Navy that it controlled. It was, therefore, unthinkable to them that there should suddenly be a London supine and incapable of resisting their designs. It is not too much to say that if in June, 1667, the Dutch command had discarded its knowledge of probabilities, and acted merely in the light of immediate appearances, they could have dictated what terms they liked to the British crown and people. But, not believing what seemed to be impossible, they left the Medway, content with an extremely damaging raid, and not pursuing what might have been a crushing victory.

We got off undeservedly, but not so lightly as at first appeared. The Dutch had made havoc of our semblance of a fleet, but since it was no more than a semblance the material damage, although heavy, was not nationally serious. In the ensuing peace, however, the Dutch had learnt enough from their exploit to know, or at least shrewdly to suspect, that we were in no position to be high-handed about terms. And, in fact, they imposed conditions that Pepys and all good Englishmen considered to be to our dishonour. Further discussion of these belongs not to the biography of Pepys but to English history. What concerns us now is the fact that on June 25th, the King, under urgent entreaty from his council, announced that he would call a Parliament in thirty days from that date, and that this Parliament when it assembled addressed itself at once to a rigorous enquiry into the conduct of the Admiralty and of the Navy Office, in the course of which investigation Pepys became an eminent, and for one impressive moment, a national figure.

By October, 1667, it was evident that the enquiry was to be a searching one. It was at first chiefly concerned with payment 'by ticket,' a practice whereby the men were discharged from the ships, not with cash for their wages but with a paper ticket that was redeemable in full at the naval treasury. As, however, the naval treasury was usually in a state of beggary, the system amounted to little more than a convenient method of getting the men quietly away from the port of discharge and throwing them on the streets. In theory, as Dr. Tanner points out, the method was not a bad one, avoiding, as it did, the necessity for continual and dangerous transport of large sums of money down to the docks. But with a defaulting treasury the consequences were disastrous for the wretched crews. The Navy Office were not to blame. They were merely providing for the payment of wages by the most practicable form of draft, and if the draft was not honoured it was no fault of theirs. It was not the function of the Navy Office to supply money, but to send in accounts, which they had done pertinaciously enough. When, therefore, a committee of the House became extremely active in the matter of tickets, Pepys exclaimed with some reason that it was 'a foolery in itself, yet gives me a great deal of trouble to draw up a defence for the Board, as if it was a crime.' In fact, crime was not too strong a word to use, but Pepys was right in disclaiming guilt for his own Office. Parliament, however, was in no mood for these nice distinctions. The Dutch peace had been signed at Breda on July 31st, but it had in it small matter of English honour to soothe the bitter recollections of June. Of the fighting and financial technique of the Navy the House of Commons knew little, but it knew that the Navy had been disgraced, and its displeasure was directed impartially to the Crown, the Admiralty, the Navy Office, and the commanders. The immediate occasion of the tickets was no more than a pretext for a general indictment of the whole naval constitution.

Pepys had no illusions about the matter, but he was determined that Parliament should not be misguided in its censures for want of exact information. He made no attempt to deny that the state of the Navy was rotten, but he had a clear conscience as to his own conduct, and with characteristic vigour he prepared himself to defend it. He knew the peace for what it was worth: 'I do not find the 'Change at all glad of it, but rather the worse, they looking upon it as a peace made only to preserve the King for a time in his lusts and ease, and to sacrifice trade and his kingdoms only to his own pleasures,' and again, 'the nation in certain condition of ruin, while the King, they see, is only governed by his lust, and women, and rogues about him.'

There is a note of deeply wounded pride in words that
Pepys wrote at the moment when the peace was to be
signed: 'I to White Hall [where] . . . I saw the King
(whom I have not had any desire to see since the Dutch
come upon the coast first to Sheerness, for shame that I
should see him, or he me, me thinks, after such a dishonour).' Nor did Pepys for a moment deceive himself as
to the truth of the late engagements: 'Thus, in all things,
in wisdom, courage, force, knowledge of our own streams,
and success, the Dutch have the best of us, and do end the
war with victory on their side.' Nevertheless, he was resolved to preserve the credit of his own department if it
could be done; and for months he applied himself to the
task of convincing the parliamentary committee by elabo-
rately documented argument. At first he was inclined to follow Coventry's advice and present evidence that was slight
and inconclusive, but finding that he had to deal with men
who, if they were not yet well informed, were determined
to be so, he prudently changed his tactics, and whenever
he appeared before the committee did so ready with plain
answers to plain questions. The consequence was that little
by little he won the respect and then the confidence of the
inquisitors. During the months of the enquiry, he was in a
state of deep and continual anxiety, but whenever he was
summoned to the committee room he nerved himself to the
ordeal with a clear head and a secure mastery of detail. It
began to be said that no one in the service was so thoroughly informed as he, and that no one among the witnesses
was as willing to speak candidly and without reservation of
what he knew.

It was not until March 5th that the naval catastrophe
came up for review before the whole House in session. On
that day Lord Brouncker, Sir John Minnes, Sir Thomas
Harvey, and Samuel Pepys were conducted by the mace to
the bar. As they went in it was clear that the House was
in an angry mood. If the Committee had been well impressed by Pepys as a witness, it had come to no favourable
conclusions in its general investigation. Its report upon the

Navy as a unit was an adverse one, and the main body of
the House was indiscriminately out of temper with everyone
in the service. After preliminary remarks to this effect by
the Speaker, Pepys was called upon to present the defence
of the Navy Office in particular. Suddenly the strain of
months relaxed, his apprehension cleared, and 'without any
hesitation or losse, but with full scope, and all my reason
free about me, as if it had been at my own table,' he spoke
for over three hours without interruption, to a House that
listened with growing, and, towards the end, with ungrudg-
ing admiration. It is true that Pepys and his colleagues did
not that day secure the vote of confidence for which after
his speech they reasonably hoped. Some of the members,
finding the address too long, 'had gone out to dinner and
come in again half drunk.' The House at large was openly
persuaded, but two or three inveterate critics used the ab-
sentees as an excuse for postponing a vote which, if taken,
they saw clearly would go in favour of the Navy Office.
But the commanding success of Pepys's speech was universally acknowledged, and it was a very modest estimate
which claimed that 'we have got great ground.' His fellow-
Commissioners were overjoyed, and congratulations were
lavished on him from all sides. Coventry told him that he
ought to be Speaker of the House, the Solicitor-General
said that 'he thought I spoke the best of any man in England,' the Duke of York declared that he had effected a
radical change in public opinion, and the King came up to
him in the Park to say, 'Mr. Pepys, I am very glad of your
success yesterday.' It was the general opinion in Parliament that no such speech had been delivered in the House
in living memory; 'Everybody says I have got the most
honour that any could have had opportunity of getting . . .
Everybody that saw me almost come to me . . . with such
eulogys as cannot be expressed.' Pepys, in short, had risen,
as his habit was, to the occasion. This time the occasion
was, perhaps, the most memorable one of his life, and he
was splendidly its equal. He left the House with his reputation vindicated, and with a shrewd resolution to leave

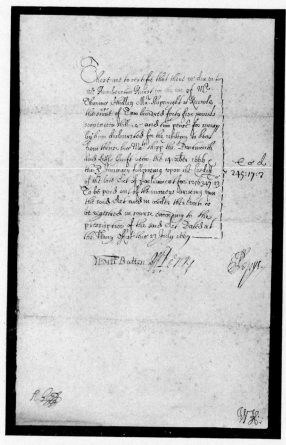

NAVY OFFICE DOCUMENT, 1667

SIGNED BY WILLIAM BATTEN, WILLIAM
PENN, AND SAMUEL PEPYS. DRAFTED AND
INITIALLED BY WILLIAM HEWER. *Photo-
graph, by E. S. Whitney, Huntingdon.*

what was notably well, alone. A week later he had to attend Parliament again, but 'not to make any more speech, which, while my fame is good, I will avoid, for fear of losing it; but only to answer to what objections will be made against us.'

The inimitable Diary has much to answer for. Through it Pepys has achieved a fame incomparable in its kind. But through it also has been created in the popular mind a figure that does not wholly do him justice. How far he himself would have been content with this distribution of effect we cannot tell; though I have a suspicion that it would not have been altogether pleasing to him. However that may be, he has in large measure himself to thank if people have fallen into a habit of thinking of him as an amusing little man, engaged in amusing little adventures, and recording them in a pleasantly scandalous narrative—it is, in fact, a good deal more scandalous than seems commonly to be realised —towards which an agreeable indulgence may be enjoyed. This is well enough so far as it goes, but it is far from being all. It is far from being all even on the evidence of the Diary itself, but, for some perhaps not obscure reason, the impudent daring, or as some would prefer to call it, the human nature of the Diary, has made a far greater impression upon the world than the graver communications in which after all it is no less liberal. It has been said that the appeal of Pepys lies chiefly in his confession of much that his readers have not the courage to confess. We need not dispute this in adding that the appeal is also much more substantially founded. Had Pepys been no more than, like the rest of us, a miserable sinner, we should still have listened to him readily enough. But even the most incorrigible of us does not really get his principal satisfaction from life in miserable sinning, and it is strange that so little attention has been paid to the Pepys who was otherwise employed. On that day in March, it was by no means merely an amusing little man who faced a hostile House of Commons in a national crisis, and by native ability compelled them to listen for three hours to an unanswerable defence to charges of almost capital gravity. On the contrary, this was a man of great talent, judgment, and courage, fortified by years of clear-sighted industry. Let us listen to him, too, when he is speaking elsewhere on serious business, with the authority of his Office. He is writing to Anthony Deane, the shipbuilder:

. . . For the other part of your letter, I will not dissemble with you because I love you. I am wholly dissatisfied in your proceedings about Mr. Browne and Mr. Wheeler.

For the first, you know you were the first man gave me notice of it, and directed me to Wheeler for further information, yet notwithstanding, I have seen a letter of yours to Browne, produced at the Board, wherein you clear him of all guilt, taking it upon yourself notwithstanding Browne himself did confess to us all that which was the occasion of turning him out. But, which is worst of all, it will be proved you have called Wheeler 'informing rogue,' notwithstanding what I said before, you yourself was the first man occasioned the discovery, and which I reckoned a very good service of you.

As for Wheeler's case, he was but newly certified for by you to be a fit man for the place, and since well reported of. Now, all of a sudden, he must be made an idle fellow, an informing rogue, and one fit to be undone, under pretence that his servant was taken with two pieces of slit deal valued by Captain Taylor at sixpence.

The man is to me a stranger, and one for whom Mr. Waith (who you tell me is his friend) nor any person else ever spoke one good word besides yourself and Commissioner Taylor, who at this day gives a very good character of him.

But as much a stranger as he is, I will not to my power see him suffer for well doing.

Mr. Deane, I do bear you still good respect, and (though it may be you do not now think that worth keep-

ing) I should be glad to have reason to continue it to
you. But upon my word, I have not spared to tell the
Board my opinion about this business, as you will shortly
see by a letter we have wrote to Commissioner Taylor.
Wherein I have been very free concerning you, and shall
be more so if ever I meet with the like occasion. The
only kindness I have shewn you in it is, that I have not
acquainted Sir William Coventry with any part of it, and
desire you will give no second occasion of doing it.

You know this hath formerly been my manner of dealing with others, therefore cannot wonder upon the like
case to find me the same man to you, to whom notwithstanding I wish very well. . . .

Here is a letter every word of which repays careful reading. And to it may be added this passage from another,
written at the same time, to the Captain (not the Commissioner) Taylor above mentioned:

I have been very free in telling Mr. Deane my mind, and
believe it will not be unadvisable for him to avoid giving
the Board or me occasion to do the same again.

As to yourself, I bear you very real friendship, and
that which both hath and shall be useful to you if occasion comes, but I must advise you to apply yourself first
to the full mastering of your own business, and then it
will be time enough to employ your observation on other
men's, it being no graceful alteration in you that in so
little time you should contract a friendship with an equal
to the vilifying of a superior officer (and both strangers),
and in a little while after that, magnify the latter as you
do now and quarrel with the former. I doubt not but the
business you were entered newly upon would have found
you better exercise for the time, discourse, and thoughts
this must have required.

I am much a stranger at Harwich, so cannot so well
understand what you propose about storehouses, etc., as

you desire. But be confident I will, when it comes to be discoursed, promote what appears of most use to his Majesty, wherein if you may also have your accommodation I shall receive somewhat the more satisfaction.

It would be difficult to find better examples than these of plain speaking, moderated by justice and personal consideration. Another letter to Deane may here be given as demonstrating Pepys's astonishing capacity for visualising the separate elements of a situation at their proper value. It was, indeed, one of his most remarkable gifts, this faculty for seeing the circumstances of a case as independent factors not to be vaguely summarised in a general judgment. The conduct of his life was governed by much the same method. If a friend behaved well to-day, it was no score against him that he had behaved ill yesterday. The letter is as follows:

I have received a book, and letter along with it, from yourself. The book, which you send me as a present, I do at your desire accept of and give you my thanks for, and the rather for that I am sure you know me so well as not to think I can be tempted by that or anything else to let fall my dissatisfaction, when taken upon such grounds as I declare in my late letter I had done that concerning you. I am sorry to find what I then feared prove so true, that now that league contracted so suddenly with a newcomer, to the dishonouring of the Commissioner and disordering of the yard, is broken, and you left (how justly I know not) to be the subject on which all the miscarriages of the place is laid by them both. What it was that first occasioned my singling you out for my friendship you well know, and so long as the same virtues of diligence and good husbandry remain, I will not fail to continue the good offices I ever did you, but truly when they shall be questioned, I shall not dare to be your advocate.

I am heartily glad to understand the good proof of

your ship, and will rejoice to hear her sailing quality answer to the rest of her good parts . . .

The pains you took about calculating the *Royal Katherine's* draught of water before she was launched I have laid up carefully, and shall be very glad to have the same, in the manner you propose in your letter, about the *Rupert,* which pray send me, because it is a thing of extraordinary practice and speaks more than what I usually find other builders pretend to; it would be of use to you to send me up a certificate from the master of her that her draught of water was so marked out to them before the 169 tons of shot, guns, etc., were put on board.

It is very likely what you desire may be granted about leave to be present at the King and Duke's being on board the *Rupert.*

It is instructive to observe the processes of Pepys's mind as he writes. The book, a matter of no great consequence in itself, he accepts as from one friend to another, but in order that there may be no possibility of misunderstanding, he emphasises the displeasure to which his friend's conduct has given rise, and then condoles with him on the circumstance that the misdemeanour has come home to roost. Having delivered his reprimand where he knew it to be warranted, he then proceeds to generous compliment on work well done, and thanks for services performed to his own office, concluding with a promise of securing a little personal distinction for his correspondent if it can be arranged. It is the letter of a very remarkable man.

Little need here be added to what has been said about Pepys's relations with his fellow-Commissioners at the Navy Office. As his influence increased, he was able to hold his own in any difference of opinion, on one occasion, for example, openly defying Lord Brouncker with success. So convinced did he become of Sir John Minnes's incompetence that he made a formal petition for his removal from office, not, however, with immediate results. Pett, as we have seen, fell into disgrace over the affair in the Medway. During the darkest times at the Office, Pepys was inclined at intervals to better his opinion of William Penn, but the improvement was hardly substantial enough to survive 'a damned venison pasty, that stunk like a devil.' William Batten died in October, 1667, having been the object of Pepys's disapproval to the last. The more he came to know of George Monk, Duke of Albemarle, the less he appears to have liked him, while sensible of his merit: 'I know not how, the blockhead Albemarle hath strange luck to be loved, though he be, and every man must know it, the heaviest man in the world, but stout and honest to his country.' Lady Albemarle he detested: 'I find the Duke of Albemarle at dinner with sorry company . . . dirty dishes, and a nasty wife at table, and bad meat, of which I made but an ill dinner.' Sir George Carteret becomes an inconspicuous figure as the Diary proceeds, but to Sir William Coventry Pepys turned continually for counsel, with perfect confidence in his judgment. The esteem with which he was held by the Duke of York advanced as the years went on, and when Coventry resigned his royal secretaryship Pepys was spoken of as his successor.

Sandwich's absence on his Spanish embassy was fortunate for his reputation. Not only did he escape responsibility for the Dutch misadventures; men began to say that if he had been at sea things would have gone otherwise. At the end of 1666, Pepys was told 'that my Lord Sandwich is called home, and that he do grow more and more in esteem everywhere, and is better spoken of, which I am mighty glad of, though I know well enough his deserving the same before, and did forsee that it will come to it.' But at this time the intimacy between Pepys and his patron fell into a neglect from which it never quite recovered. It had been a distracting time at home, but Pepys was conscious of inattention to an old loyalty. A few days after he had heard the rumour of the Ambassador's recall, he noted: 'Among other things, to write a letter to my Lord Sandwich, it being one of the burdens upon my mind that I have not writ to him since he went into Spain, but now I do intend to give him a brief account of our whole year's actions since he went, which will make amends.' The return was delayed, but nine months later we find Pepys's promise unfulfilled. 'Here was a gentleman . . . lately come from my Lord Sandwich, with an express; but Lord! I was almost ashamed to see him, lest he should know that I have not yet wrote one letter to my Lord since his going.' And still another month passed before in October, 1667, when staying the night at Bishop Stortford on his way to Brampton, he 'fell to write my letter to my Lord Sandwich, which I could not finish before my coming from London; so did finish it to my good content, and a good letter, telling him the present state of all matters.' In the meantime, the King had observed with some satisfaction that in the late misfortunes 'they have been particularly punished that were enemies to my Lord Sandwich,' and in February, 1668, the Ambassador further recovered good opinion by successfully negotiating a peace between Spain and Portugal. The public was again well disposed, the King continued in expressions of goodwill, and Sandwich's friends were reassured, though Pepys for one was sceptical as to the worth of the royal favour, which 'for aught I see, serves very little in stead at this day, but rather is an argument against a man.' It was not until the autumn of 1667 that Sandwich was back in England. In May Pepys had again been uneasy in his conscience: 'another letter from my Lord Sandwich, which troubles me to see how I have neglected him, in not writing or but once, all this time of his being abroad; and I see he takes notice, but yet gently, of it, that it puts me to great trouble, and I know not how to get out of it, having no good excuse, and too late now to mend, he being coming home.' There is a gap in the Diary between September 29th and October 11th of the same year, and it is accounted for by the following entry in Sandwich's journal. On September 29, 1668, leaving his ship off Portsmouth, Sandwich went to the house of his friend Colonel Norton at Southwick on the

Sussex coast, and on September 30th he wrote: 'I received a letter from Mr. Pepys of the Navy Office and a credit for £500.' On the next day, October 1st, we find, 'my sonne Hinchingbrooke, my sonne Sydney, Mr. Jo. Seymor, and my Cosen Samuell Pepys, came to Southwicke to me at night with 2 coaches and 6 horses from London.'

In November Pepys was again waiting upon my Lord at Whitehall, but with 'little encouragement . . . because of the difficulty of seeing him, and the little he hath to say to me when I do see him, or to any body else, but his own idle people about him, Sir Charles Harbord, etc.' In February, 1669, Sandwich's second daughter, Paulina, 'mighty religious in her lifetime; . . . but . . . always a peevish lady' died, at which 'I went to my Lord's lodgings, but he is shut up with sorrow and so not to be spoken with.' This might well be an occasion to refuse even the most intimate friend, but Pepys had lost the old personal contact. Charles Harbord was a young man who now had been in Sandwich's confidential service for some three years, and the tone of Pepys's reference explains itself. In January, 1669, Sandwich proposed Harbord's father to the Duke of York as Paymaster for Tangier, and the incident caused some heat. The Duke told Sandwich:

. . . that it was fit to have Mr. Pepys satisfied therein first, and that it was not good to make places for persons. This my Lord in great confidence tells me, that he do take it very ill from the Duke of York, though nobody knew the meaning of these words but him; and that he did take no notice of them, but bit his lip, being satisfied that the Duke of York's care of me was as desirable to him, as it could be to have Sir Charles Harbord; and did seem industrious to let me see that he was glad that the Duke of York and he might come to contend who shall be the kindest to me, which I owned as his great love, and so I hope and believe it is, though my Lord did go a little too far in this business, to move it so far, without consulting me. But I took no notice of that, but was glad to see this competition come about, that my Lord Sandwich is apparently jealous of my thinking that the Duke of York do mean me more kindness than him.

Walking together after this conversation, Pepys invited my Lord to dine, and on January 23d, Sandwich for the first time sat down to Pepys's hospitality in Seething Lane, in company with Lord Peterborough, Lord Hinchingbrooke, Sir Charles Harbord, Sir William Godolphin, and Mr. Sidney Montagu:

And after greeting them, and some time spent in talk, dinner was brought up, one dish after another, but a dish at a time, but all so good; but, above all things, the variety of wines, and excellent of their kind, I had for them, and all in so good order, that they were mightily pleased, and myself full of content at it: and indeed it was, of a dinner of about six or eight dishes, as noble as any man need to have, I think; at least, all was done in the noblest manner that ever I had any, and I have rarely seen in my life better anywhere else, even at the Court. After dinner, my Lords to cards, and the rest of us sitting about them and talking, and looking on my books and pictures, and my wife's drawings, which they commend mightily; and mighty merry all day long, with exceeding great content, and so till seven at night; and so took their leaves, it being dark and foul weather. Thus was this entertainment over, the best of its kind, and the fullest of honour and content to me, that ever I had in my life: and shall not easily have so good again.

And thus pleasingly, although with a note here and there of constraint, the record in the Diary of a memorable friendship comes to a close. If there was in some sense an estrangement, it was not dishonoured by bitterness, nor did it lessen the esteem in which Pepys was held by the rest of the Sandwich family. Indeed, whatever his personal feelings may have been, he never forgot generously to recog-

nise the obligations of his youth. In December, 1667, Lord
Hinchingbrooke wrote to Pepys urgently asking assistance
in the matter of a £250 debt, and concluding: 'If you can
with any convenience do it, you will do a great kindness to
my father and me, who am Dear cousin, your most affectionate cousin and humble servant, Hinchingbrooke.' Pepys,
with some reluctance, arranged the matter, lending part of
the money himself. On September 29, 1668, on the eve of
his departure to meet Sandwich at Southwick, he excused
himself until the time of their meeting from

> . . . troubling your Lordship with any other present mat-
> ters, than that being yesterday made acquainted by my
> Lord of Hinchingbrooke, and Mr. Sidney Montagu, with
> the straights they found themselves under of providing
> a sum of money for the answering your Lordship's pres-
> ent occasions and, being unwilling your Lordship should
> want what part thereof I could by any shift supply, I
> undertook, for the present, furnishing your Lordship
> with 500£.

And always between Pepys and Lady Sandwich there was
maintained the gentle confidence of which we find a note in
October, 1667, when at Hinchingbrooke:

> . . . a thousand questions my Lady asked me, till she could
> think of no more almost, but walked up and down the
> house with me. But I do find, by her, that they are re-
> duced to great straits for money, having been forced to
> sell her plate, 8 or £900 worth; and she is now going to
> sell a suit of her best hangings, of which I could almost
> wish to buy a piece or two, if the pieces will be broke.
> But the house is most excellently furnished, and brave
> rooms and good pictures, so that it do please me infinitely
> beyond Audley End. Here we staid till night walking and
> talking and drinking, and with mighty satisfaction my
> Lady with me alone most of the day talking of my Lord's
> bad condition to be kept in Spayne without money and

at a great expense, which (as we will save the family) we must labour to remove. Night being come, we took leave with all possible kindness.

In May, 1668, she had to turn to him for £100, which he supplied. In an unpublished letter among the Hinchingbrooke papers, dated May 30th, Lady Sandwich wrote to her husband: 'We are in great straits for money . . . and therefore am forced to borrow from my cousin Pepys £100.' We find in this letter a further example of the liberties taken in spelling Pepys's name; in an earlier paragraph her Ladyship has already referred to 'my cousin Sam Pepes who was in the country the last week, his wife being at Brampton.'

Through the later part of the Diary, Pepys is troubled by a double anxiety; for the security of his position, and for the preservation of his eyesight. But the old natural zest and curiosity remain. In June, 1668, he took a short holiday, visiting Oxford, 'a very sweet place,' Abingdon, where he found 'some pretty good musick, and sang and danced till supper: 5s,' and Stonehenge, 'over the Plain and some great hills, even to fright us. Come thither, and find them [the stones] as prodigious as any tales I ever heard of them, and worth going this journey to see. God knows what their use was! they are hard to tell, but yet may be told.' Sending his wife down to Cambridge for Sturbridge Fair at the invitation of Roger Pepys, he was much vexed to find a friend following her two days later, 'the more because I fear he do know that Knepp did dine with me to-day.' He had a cast of his face made, which afforded him much satisfaction, as did also his commission as Captain of the *Jersey*, made out in order that he might be qualified to sit on a court martial. His taste for play-going was continually indulged, and his notes, of no great critical consequence, are always lively.

But so great performance of a comical part was never, I believe, in the world before as Nell do this, both as a

mad girle, then most and best of all when she comes in
like a young gallant; and hath the motions and carriage
of a spark the most that ever I saw any man have.

But a week later, seeing Miss Davis dance a jig in boy's
clothes, 'the truth is, there is no comparison between Nell's
dancing the other day at the King's house in boy's clothes
and this, this being infinitely beyond the other.' And in November, 1667, 'Nell's ill speaking of a great part made me
mad.' He was always ready for a visit to the prize ring, a
cock fight, or foot racing, but gambling had no attraction
for him. Being taken to a gaming house, he found it a 'pro-
faine mad entertainment.' And as he walked about the street
on his business and social errands, he watched with the
unaffected pride of a good citizen a brave new London rising from the ruins.

But Pepys, while pulling no long face about his troubles,
was anxious. Already in 1666, before he was thirty-four
years of age, he was recognising the possibility of being
turned out of office, and spent an hour one evening talking
in the garden with his wife of retirement to the country,
consoled to think that he had 'wherewith very well to sub-
sist.' At frequent intervals the thought returned to his mind.
In October of the same year, with naval affairs in confusion,
he had 'cause to bless God that I am so well, and shall be
contented to retreat to Brampton, and spend the rest of
my days there.' And, again, a few days later: 'Nothing but
distraction and confusion; which makes me wish with all
my heart that I were well and quietly settled with what
little I have got at Brampton, where I might live peace-
ably, and study, and pray for the good of the King and my
country.' A year later, a few months after the Dutch had
been in the Medway, he was down at Brampton, happy in
the house with its garden, 'especially the little parlour and
the summer-houses in the garden, only the wall do want
greens upon it, and the house is too low-roofed; but that
is only because of my coming from a house with higher ceilings. But altogether is very pretty; and I bless God that

I am like to have such a pretty place to retire to.' This was
the time, October, 1667, of the celebrated adventure of his
buried money. When he had sent it down into the country
during the Dutch scare, his father and his wife buried it in
the garden, and now with a lantern on a dark night they

. . . went about our great work to dig up my gold. But,
Lord! what a tosse I was for some time in, that they
could not justly tell where it was; that I begun heartily
to sweat, and be angry, that they should not agree but
by and by poking with a spit, we found it, and then begun
with a spudd to lift up the ground. But, good God! to
see how sillily they did it, not half a foot under ground,
and in the sight of the world from a hundred places, if
any body by accident were near hand, and within sight
of a neighbour's window, and their hearing also, being
close by: only my father says that he saw them all gone
to church before he begun the work, when he laid the
money, but that do not excuse it to me. But I was out of
my wits almost, and the more from that, upon my lifting
up the earth with the spudd, I did discern that I had
scattered the pieces of gold round about the ground
among the grass and loose earth; and taking up the iron
head-pieces wherein they were put, I perceive the earth
was got among the gold, and wet, so that the bags were
all rotten, and all the notes, that I could not tell what
in the world to say to it, not knowing how to judge what
was wanting, or what had been lost by Gibson in his coming down: which, all put together, did make me mad;
and at last was forced to take up the head-pieces, dirt
and all, and as many of the scattered pieces as I could
with the dirt discern by the candle-light, and carry them
up into my brother's chamber, and there locke them up
till I had eat a little supper: and then, all people going
to bed, W. Hewer and I did all alone, with several pails
of water and basins, at last wash the dirt off of the pieces,
and parted the pieces and the dirt, and then begun to tell
[them]; and by a note which I had of the value of the

whole in my pocket, do find that there was short above a hundred pieces, which did make me mad; and considering that the neighbour's house was so near that we could not suppose we could speak one to another in the garden at the place where the gold lay—especially my father being deaf—but they must know what we had been doing on, I feared that they might in the night come and gather some pieces and prevent us the next morning; so W. Hewer and I out again about midnight, for it was now grown so late, and there by candle-light did make shift to gather forty-five pieces more. And so in, and to cleanse them: and by this time it was past two in the morning; and so to bed, with my mind pretty quiet to think that I have recovered so many. And then to bed, and I lay in the trundle-bed, the girl being gone to bed to my wife, and there lay in some disquiet all night, telling of the clock till it was daylight. 11th. And then rose and called W. Hewer, and he and I, with pails and a sieve, did lock ourselves into the garden, and there gather all the earth about the place into pails and then sift those pails in one of the summer-houses, just as they do for dya-monds in other parts of the world; and there, to our great content, did with much trouble by nine o'clock (and by the time we emptied several pails and could not find one), we did make the last night's forty-five up to seventy-nine: so that we are come to about twenty or thirty of what I think the true number should be; and perhaps within less; and of them I may reasonably think that Mr. Gibson might lose some: so that I am pretty well satisfied that my loss is not great, and do bless God that it is so well. . . .

His father later found another guinea, but so far as is known, the remainder of the gold pieces are still there for the finding somewhere in Brampton soil. The search, how-ever, would be a forlorn one. I may say that careful enquiry has revealed no trace of the original Brampton deeds, nor does there appear to be any means of ascertaining what

was the extent of the garden land attached to the house
when Pepys knew it. It seems likely that both at the front
and the back of the house was a great deal more land than
is indicated by the surviving marks. The talk of summer-
houses suggests something fairly considerable, and Pepys
speaks of being overheard by the neighbours. The probability is, as there is no house of that period within earshot
of the present front garden, that the scene of the nocturnal
search was in a part of the garden that then lay on the far
side of the road, adjoining the house now known as The
Old Bell.

Once on a country excursion near London, Pepys, antici-
pating a modern habit, decided that he did not wish to have
a country house, but 'to keep a coach, and with my wife
on the Saturday go sometimes for a day to this place, and
quit to another place; and there is more variety and as little
charge, and no trouble, as there is in a country-house.' But
in less tranquil moods, the pressure of London set him constantly daydreaming of Brampton. At the time when he was
preparing the Dutch papers for the Parliamentary Committee, Coventry told him that if there was another war
'they should not find a Secretary; "nor," said I, "a Clerk of
the Acts," for I see the reward of it; and, thanked God!
I have enough of my own to buy me a good book and a
good fiddle, and I have a good wife.' There were to be
quiet days at the end. But when the dream came true,
neither Brampton nor his wife were in it.

In November, 1667, Pepys was complaining that the
nights were too long, 'longer than I can sleep out,' his eyes
now curtailing his evening work. He had already taken to
spectacles, which, however, had eased without arresting the
trouble. Sir d'Arcy Power, in an interesting paper printed
in the second volume of the *Pepys Club Transactions,* has
shown that Pepys was at no time in danger of actual blindness, and that modern optics could without difficulty have
afforded him permanent relief. He even shows that, with
a little luck, Pepys with his inventive mind might easily have
discovered for himself the means of correcting the deficiency

in his own glasses. But the luck refrained, and throughout
the last eighteen months of the Diary the fear was repeatedly expressed that his sight would fail him altogether.
In July, 1668, he 'was let blood, and did bleed about fourteen ounces, towards curing my eyes.' A fortnight later he
was trying an experiment with paper tubes. On Christmas
Eve of the same year, 'I begin this night to put on a waistcoat, it being the first winter in my whole memory that
ever I staid till this day before I did so. So to bed in mighty
good humour with my wife, but sad in one thing, and that
is for my poor eyes.' Five months later, he was compelled
to send in a petition to the Duke of York for leave of
absence. For twelve months past he had not been able to
write or read without great pain; not having been absent
for more than a week during his 'whole nine years' service,'
and submitting that the affairs of the Navy Office are now
well ordered,

. . . he therefore in all humility prays,
    That by the favour of his Majesty and your Royal
Highness, your Petitioner may be indulged a vacation for
three or four months this summer. In which his sole aim
being the relieving of his eyes by such a respite from their
present labour, your Petitioner is ready during this time
to embrace any other service on which his Majesty or
your Royal Highness shall think to command him, either
at home or abroad.
    And your Petitioner, as in duty bound, shall pray, etc.

The Petition is dated May 19, 1669, and on the same day
Pepys found opportunity of presenting it to the Duke, who:

. . . took me to his closet, and received my petition, and
discoursed about my eyes, and pitied me, and with much
kindness did give me his consent to be absent, and approved of my proposition to go into Holland to observe
things there, of the Navy; but would first ask the King's
leave, which he anon did, and did tell me that the King

would be a good master to me, these were his words, about my eyes, and do like of my going into Holland, and do advise that nobody should know of my going thither, but pretend that I did go into the country somewhere, which I liked well.

It was not, however, till the late summer that he was able to leave the country, and in the meantime, on May 31, 1669, he made his last entry in the Diary. He spent the morning with his accounts, dined at home, and in the afternoon went by water to Whitehall, on the way calling upon one of his flames, and here 'je did baiser elle,' but had not opportunity 'para hazer some with her as I would have offered if je had had it.' Then there was a conference with the Duke of York at Whitehall, and a turn in the Park, 'Thence to "The World's End,"' a drinking-house by the Park; 'and there merry, and so home late.' And then, with sudden and startling pathos:

And thus ends all that I doubt I shall ever be able to do with my own eyes in the keeping of my Journal, I being not able to do it any longer, having done now so long as to undo my eyes almost every time that I take a pen in my hand; and, therefore, whatever comes of it, I must forbear: and, therefore, resolve, from this time forward, to have it kept by my people in long-hand, and must therefore be contented to set down no more than is fit for them and all the world to know; or, if there be any thing, which cannot be much, now my amours to Deb. are past, and my eyes hindering me in almost all other pleasures, I must endeavour to keep a margin in my book open, to add, here and there, a note in short-hand with my own hand.

And so I betake myself to that course, which is almost as much as to see myself go into my grave: for which, and all the discomforts that will accompany my being blind, the good God prepare me!

S. P.

CHAPTER VI

THE DIARY. DEATH OF ELIZABETH PEPYS. SANDWICH. PARLIAMENT. POPERY. THE ADMIRALTY

TO CLOSE the great Diary is to close a document about which there remain certain elements of mystery. We may remember that in March, 1669, Pepys told Coventry that he had been keeping a Journal 'these eight or ten years.' He had, in fact, at that time been keeping it nine. The statement may, on the face of it, be taken as sufficient evidence that he had kept no journal before the famous entry of New Year's Day 1660: 'Blessed be God, at the end of the last year I was in very good health, without any sense of my old pain, but upon taking cold,' and so on. Nevertheless, readers of the Diary cannot help noting in this entry a somewhat curious feature. Thenceforth for over nine years, Pepys was to make an almost daily record of his life, with a zest, a particularity, and a skill which have become classic in their kind. When, according to the book, he began, he was in full command of his technique, and he said not a word upon the occasion of his undertaking a work to which he was to devote so much care and ingenuity. This, to say the least of it, is odd. It is clear in the light of what happened that he must have addressed himself to his Journal with serious intentions, and yet he says nothing to suggest that he is upon a new venture. On the first page of his book he takes stock of his own affairs and of those of the State, in the way that was to become his yearly practice. In short, the beginning of the Diary does not read like a beginning. When we consider its close, there are yet stronger reasons for speculation. In the last entry, quoted above, he states explicitly that although his eyes make it impossible for him to write his Journal up as heretofore, he is resolved 'from this time forward' to dictate it to someone else. The habit is plainly one that has become of a good deal more than minor importance in his life. Day by day he has learnt to experience what is hardly less than the artist's satisfaction in putting concisely into shape the crowding events that in his own way he, too, 'recollects in tranquillity.' When the Diary, as we know it, closes, Pepys is still a young man of thirty-seven. And in view of his manifest delight in keeping it, and his express intention of continuing it, I can see no satisfactory explanation of what in this respect appears to be his subsequent silence.

It is true that in the period immediately following the last surviving entry, there were reasons why for a time he might well have neglected his usual practice. We do not know who besides his wife accompanied him on his continental tour, and it may have been that there was nobody with him to whom he could suitably dictate. At this time, too, he developed parliamentary ambitions, and these made further claims upon his attention. Certainly the death of his wife in November of the year 1669 would for a time distract his private habits, though there is nothing to show that the routine of his life was more than temporarily disturbed, and in recovering it nothing would seem more likely than that he also resumed its record.

Against the supposition that there may have been more of the Journal than we possess, is the plain fact that we do not possess it. Pepys left his shorthand manuscript, carefully bound in six volumes, among the books that are now in the Magdalene Library. He duly entered them in his catalogue, and nowhere says anything to lead us to suppose that they are not the first and last of the matter. Secondly, the practical difficulty of keeping the Diary would be greatly increased when instead of making the regular entries himself he was obliged to employ an amanuensis. But, even so, the difficulty could not have been insuperable. The obvious person to perform this service was Hewer. He was in daily association with Pepys, most intimately in his confidence, and devoted to a master by whose kindness he was now rising to a very respectable position in the Navy Office. So close was the friendship becoming that before long we shall find the two men keeping house together, with an amiability that survived until Pepys died in 1703. Hewer from the time of Mrs. Pepys's death was unfailingly solicitous for his master's comfort and welfare, and it is difficult to dismiss at least a possibility, I would almost say a probability, that in the many long evenings the two men spent together, Pepys was sometimes engaged in dictating to his younger friend further pages of a work that bears so incontestable a stamp of having given its author as much delight as it has given to generations of readers. There is nothing more tangible than surmise to support the theory, but it is surmise recommended I think by common sense. And if one of these days some lucky investigator made a Pepysian discovery of first-rate importance, I cannot think that it would be very surprising.

There is then the further question as to whether Pepys meant his Diary to be read by anybody but himself. The little evidence that we have is conflicting. When he showed the Journal to his lieutenant friend on the *Naseby* in 1660, we do not learn that he was anxious for secrecy, but when nine years later, on the only other occasion upon which he mentions having spoken of his custom, he confided in Coventry, he immediately regretted having done so. And the nature of the Diary itself makes it sufficiently clear that nothing could have been further from Pepys's mind than that it should in his own time be anything but strictly private and confidential to himself. We do not know how many, if any, members of his household and staff knew that he was keeping it. He seems mostly to have written the Journal in his office, but there were occasions when he did so at home. Although Pepys was a man who could keep his own counsel both in his private and official affairs, it must have needed uncommon luck and adroitness if for a period of nine years he was able to conceal from his wife the fact that he was keeping a daily record of their lives. And yet it seems likely that this is what happened. If Mrs. Pepys knew about it she must have been curious, and sometimes obstinately so, as to what was being said. It was, the Diary tells us plainly enough, a curiosity that could not have been satisfied. If there had been scenes on the subject we should have heard of them from Pepys himself. The conclusion is that the concealment was somehow managed, and although clerks in the Navy Office, for example, must have been suspicious, it seems likely that, apart from one or two unguarded admissions, the Diary while it was being written remained a secret document.

Of Pepys's intentions as to what should happen to it in the future, it is still difficult to form a decided opinion. When he says in his last entry that in dictating his Journal he will have to be more circumspect than he has been in the past, the inference clearly is that he has no scruples as to the indiscretions that he has already committed to its pages, since we must take it he does not intend these pages to be made public in any case until such time as neither he nor the indiscretions can any longer be called to account. In the same way, in February, 1668, having purchased a book which he thought would be an improper addition to his presses, he chose a cheap binding, 'because I resolve, as soon as I have read it, to burn it, that it may not stand in the list of books, nor among them, to disgrace if it should be found.' And the next day it was duly burnt. Here we find that he was ashamed to put the book in his library, where everybody might see it, but not at all uneasy about noting in the Diary that he had read and burnt it, since, again, he knew that this was what nobody would see. It may be added that Pepys had his qualms in this respect on another occasion, when he caused Rochester's book of scandalous poems to be labelled *Rochester's Life,* and kept it in a drawer. The book eventually joined the main collection and is now in Magdalene, where the curious may discover that it is interleaved with a number of manuscript poems in Pepys's own writing, and presumably of his own composition, in which indelicacy is not redeemed by candour from almost unreadable dullness.

On the other hand, while Pepys regarded the Diary as

closed to all eyes but his own, there is the significant circumstance that he took no steps that might lead to its suppression after his death. On the contrary, as we have seen, he had it carefully bound, catalogued it, and bequeathed it to Magdalene College. Although it was in cypher, or shorthand, he left the key with it. As it happened, more than a century was to pass before anyone thought it worth while to investigate its contents, but Pepys at the time of his death could not know but what this might happen at any time. And when it did happen, after a merely accidental neglect, the further accident befell that John Smith, the transcriber, remained in ignorance of the key. If he had but known it, there were ready to his hand in the library pamphlets on shorthand collected by Pepys and indicating at least the elements of the system that he himself employed. Even more helpfully, there was the narrative of Charles the Second's escape from Worcester taken down by Pepys in the same style and translated by himself into longhand. Had John Smith known of these it would immensely have lightened a labour of which he has left a pathetic account in a letter written in 1832 to Lord Brougham, soliciting some relief from his poverty. The letter was privately printed by Magdalene College in 1929. It was written seven years after the first edition of Lord Braybrooke's two quarto volumes in 1825. 'Had not the Almighty graciously raised me up some friends,' he says, 'who have kept me free from debt, I must long since have been in gaol. . . . The original Diary is written in Short-hand, & extends to upwards of 3,000 pages . . . very closely written in an extremely small character. I deciphered the whole, & transcribed it in nearly 10,000 Quarto pages. When I commenced it, I did not know a single character of the Short-hand, wh. varies much in places when Pepys wished to be unusually secret, & it occupied me in incessant labour for three years. . . . My whole remuneration for this labour was £200; & I have received little else but disappointment from it ever since.' Elsewhere he tells us that he worked usually 'for twelve and fourteen hours a day, with frequent wakeful nights.' The unfortunate man might have enjoyed the excitement of discovery with little or none of his burden had he been able to follow the tracks that Pepys had been at no pains to cover. On the whole, the probability is that Pepys in preserving the Diary in the Magdalene bequest, did so in the realisation that sooner or later it would be discovered and published. His keen wits can have made no mistake about this, and if he did not like the prospect there was the remedy of destruction. He did not adopt it, and the conclusion is that he was prepared for the secret that he had guarded so jealously some day to become the delight of curious readers. Nor can those same wits have failed to realise how active and how widespread that delight would be. And yet nowhere in his catalogue, his correspondence, his will, nor in any other paper, has been discovered so much as a hint that might direct attention to the treasure that he was leaving behind. Such a man, quietly contemplating the fame that might one day be his, and saying not a word that might hasten its advent, sharing his expectations with nobody, must have possessed his mind with singular mastery.

It is inevitable that we should consider the closing of the Diary as something of a metamorphosis in a life which in fact, though shaken by bereavement, was unbroken in its continuity. But it so happens that it does mark, in a not precisely definable way, Pepys's full maturity in the public life of his time. He was to remain four more years as Clerk of the Acts at the Navy Office, and to resign the post only on promotion. As the Diary comes to an end, we see him firmly established in authority, assured of his position, secure in the highest favour, and now confidently able to meet any charges that may be made against the conduct of his Office. In his own branch of the service he now knows more than anyone else, and knows that he knows it. He no longer feels the necessity of asserting himself, and he no longer suspects personal danger in every petty official crisis. The terms of his application for leave of absence, and the readiness with which it was granted with every mark of honour, are significant. He makes his request in all duty, but as for a right.

And he is not afraid that any advantage of his own interests will be taken if for a time he leaves his business at the Navy Office to other hands. He has fought his official battles and won them, and he has survived a long and adventurous apprenticeship to become a civil servant of national distinction.

The duration of Pepys's foreign visit in the summer of 1669 cannot be exactly determined. On August 3rd, he informed a correspondent that 'The Duke is at present out of town, and so am not able to signify that from him which I doubt not but I shall at his return, which I expect in a very few days,' which indicates that the writer was then still in London. The first definite information that we have is contained in a letter written by Pepys to Evelyn at the Navy Office on November 2d, begging his friend 'to believe that I would not have been ten days returned into England without waiting on you, had it not pleased God to afflict mee by the sickness of my wife,' which fixes the approximate date of his return as October 23d. Long afterwards he referred to the tour as having taken 'a bare two months,' so that we may conclude that he left England towards the end of August. Here, too, is the first intimation that we have of the illness of his wife, who 'from the first day of her coming back to London, hath layn under a fever so severe, as at this hour to render her recoverie desperate.' Mrs. Pepys, as we learn from the tablet that her husband erected to her memory in St. Olave's Church, died in November 10th, at the age of twenty-nine. The entry in the register reads:

1669. Nov. Elizabeth Pepys Wife of Samuel Pepys Esq. One of his Ma^tes Commiss of ye Navy obit x Novem^r & buryed in ye Channcell xiii Instant.

On the 25th of that month, writing to the Commissioners of Accounts, he offers as an excuse for some delay the claims of 'the other parts of his Majesty's service calling for my daily attendance,' and 'the sorrowful interruption lately given me by the sickness and death of my wife.' More than three months later, on March 3, 1670, he writes to

THE REVEREND JOHN SMITH

Artist Unknown.

Captain Elliott, who had been active in his Aldeburgh interests:

CAPTAIN ELLIOTT—I beg you earnestly to believe that nothing but the sorrow and distraction I have been in by the death of my wife, increased by the suddenness with which it pleased God to surprise me therewith, after a voyage so full of health and content, could have forced me to so long a neglect of my private concernments; this being, I do assure you, the very first day that my affliction, together with my daily attendance on other public occasions of his Majesty's, has suffered me to apply myself to the considering any part of my private concernments.

It was a tragic conclusion to what must have been a happy holiday. The expedition 'so full of health and content' was never forgotten by Pepys. More than thirty years afterwards he wrote to Evelyn of 'a tour that I, by your instructions, when time was, and with my wife, dispatched . . . to a degree of satisfaction and usefulness that has stuck to me through the whole of my life since.' The journey taken was through France and Holland, and in both countries there was ample diversion for the connoisseur and instruction for the naval student. There were other advantages for a man given to making the most of his opportunities. There is a note of personal experience in the advice written seven years later to a young friend, to make himself 'master of the French and Dutch languages, which are with much more facility to be obtained abroad, and without which no man under any public character can, as the world goes, support himself in any public charge, either here or in any foreign Court.' Away from home, too, with 'my amours to Deb. over,' we can see Pepys well content in his wife's society, eagerly explaining to her points of interest as they travelled. It was, in fact, a time of reconciliation, full of engaging incident, congenial to active minds, and soothing to the tired eyes. And then, without warning, at the end of it, the blow falling with 'the suddenness with which it pleased God to surprise me.' There had been no premonitory symptoms. On reaching London, Elizabeth Pepys must have contracted one of the diseases with which the city, even after its purging, was infested. Sir d'Arcy Power surmises that it was typhoid fever.

On December 5, 1668, Pepys being in his mind 'most happy, and may still be so but for my own fault, if I be catched loving any body but my wife again,' had announced his 'great design' of seeking parliamentary election. In the following June, the death of Sir Robert Brooke, one of the burgesses for Aldeburgh, who as a member had been actively interested in the Navy, presented an opening. On the 29th of the month Sandwich wrote to Lord Hereford bespeaking his interest in the forthcoming election for 'my near kinsman, Mr. Samuel Pepys,' and two days later the Duke of York wrote in the same strain to Lord Howard, afterwards Duke of Norfolk, supporting the Clerk of the Acts, 'one in an especial manner qualified,' in his candidature. At the same time Pepys submitted himself to Captain Elliott, one of the Aldeburgh bailiffs, announcing that he did so under the Duke of York's patronage, engaging, if he should be successful in his design, 'not only myself singly, but the whole body of this Office, upon all future occasions to press their sense of your kindness shown to one of its members,' and not doubting but that he should have opportunity of showing himself 'a faithful and useful servant to the corporation.' On July 8th, he further wrote to Lord Howard acknowledging the promise of his influence. On the 10th, the Duke of York wrote to Howard to the same effect, and on the 16th he forwarded a strong recommendation of 'Samuel Pepys, Esq, one of the Commissioners of the Navy,' to the town of Aldeburgh. This was followed on the 22d by support, also addressed to the town, from Lord Howard on the eve of his departure on an embassy to Morocco.

I have been always desirious to preserve your liberties, especially in elections of Parliament. But such hath been my affection to you, and my expectation of a respect from you which I have found on many occasions, that I have sometimes thought fit to propose one to you worthy of your choice; which I do at this time also in Mr. Samuel Pepys, one of the Commissioners, and an active and able Officer, for the managing the affairs of the Navy. I may with some assurance say that it will not be easy for you to find a person every way so qualified for this choice, whether you consider his great and known abilities, or his capacities of serving you, or the inclinations of the Duke our Admiral. . . . And now I well believe that you will find reason to have the same fair opinion of this gentleman as I have, by the extraordinary character many ways given to me of him. . . .

In spite, however, of powerful patronage, Pepys's candidature did not prosper. Other political interests in the town made capital of his being a stranger to the corporation, and unacquainted with its needs. Pepys answered this easily enough by saying that Sir Robert Brooke had been no better informed in this respect, and that his present opponents were in the same case. But more damaging rumours followed. It was basely suggested that the letters from the Duke of York and Lord Howard were fabrications, 'a calumny so scandalous that I am sorry to find such indirect means used to prevent the Duke in his desire. . . . But since they have done it, I shall find a way to give my friends satisfaction in such a manner as I hope shall not only clear that doubt but give them to see what dealings they are to expect from persons that will serve themselves by such unfair helps as these.' At the same time, a report which was to have alarming consequences gained ground, that Pepys was a papist. Again he had no difficulty in showing that the charge was irresponsible, alluding decisively to the duty of his Office, 'which obliges me not only to take the Oaths of Allegiance and Supremacy but to administer it myself to every man that takes the charge as master of any of the King's ships.' The Duke's party took up the fight in

good earnest, sharp reminders of royal displeasure were
sent to leaders of the opposition, and Howard's agents were
insistent and even threatening in their appeals. But the
libels, although they could not for a moment survive examination, had their effect upon electioneering temper, and
when the writ was issued on October 19th, it is probable
that Pepys was in any case pledged to a losing cause. But
whatever chance of success he may have had was further
diminished by the sudden illness of his wife, which entirely
absorbed his attention, and kept him away from Aldeburgh
at the time of the election. He was not returned to Parliament, and on March 3d, he wrote to Elliott apologising for
his neglect of all the arrangements that had been made for
his reception, assuring the bailiff of his gratitude, and taking his defeat with a composure that has in it the suspicion
of a sting: 'having no reason to receive any thing with dissatisfaction in this whole matter, saving the particular disrespect which our noble master, the Duke of York, suffered
from the beginning to the end, from Mr. Duke and Captain
Shippman, who, I doubt not, may meet with a time of seeing their error therein.'

Although the Navy Office had survived parliamentary
inquisition without irreparable damage to its credit, it was
clearly enough recognised by the authorities themselves that
all was not well with its administration. In 1668, Pepys
had been the Duke of York's agent in calling all the members of the Navy Board to an account of their conduct,
with specific charges to answer, and in the reckoning then
made the Clerk of the Acts himself was the sole official to
suffer no loss of prestige. The Commissioners could plead
with justice that their efficiency had been gravely impaired
by lack of proper funds, but most of them were forced to
acknowledge that work had been neglected and regulations
disobeyed. The Duke of York, as Lord High Admiral, administered a firm but gentle rebuke, and the incident, which
was within walls, was closed. But at the end of 1669, a
more public charge had to be met, when the Commissioners
of Accounts accused the Board of mismanagement in gen-

eral during the late war. His colleagues entrusted Pepys with their defence, and the Clerk addressed to the Commissioners of Accounts an elaborate and convincing answer from the Board as a body, and supplemented it by a further defence of his own conduct in particular. 'For what respects my diligence,' he says in the latter:

as no concernments relating to my private fortune, pleasure, or health did, at any time (even under terror of the plague), divide me one day and night from attendance on the business of my place, so was I never absent at any public meeting of the board, but on the special commands of the Lord High Admiral and that not thrice during the three years of the war. To which let me add, that in my endeavours after a full performance of my duty, I have neither made distinction of days between those of rest and others, nor of hours between day and night, being less acquainted during the whole war with the closing my day's work before midnight than after it.

He adds, with obvious reference to the Diary, that he is able to account on oath for his manner of employing any day during the term of his service at the Office. The offences with which the Commissioners of Accounts charged the Board were chiefly those of ineffective control of the lower commissioned ranks during the war, purchase of goods at exorbitant prices, failure to insist on punctual delivery, and placing of contracts by interest. The first of these Pepys was able to show by the records of disciplinary action to be unfounded. The second and third, which were in fact one, he excused by the unanswerable argument that you could not compel contractors, who were on the verge of ruin because the country would not pay its bills, either to be prompt in delivery or moderate in prices. He could be free with instances of goods offered at one figure for cash, and bought at half as much again on credit. So far the defence was satisfactory. When it came to the question of placing contracts by favour, he was on dangerously thin ice. As Dr.

Tanner points out in his masterly examination of the naval manuscripts of the Pepysian Library, there is evidence in the Diary that Pepys himself must have been skating at this moment with a very uneasy conscience. But he skated with just sufficient agility for safety, and when he was called by the Commissioners of Accounts to justify his written defence in person at the Council Board, he again came through the ordeal with an enhanced reputation. From that time until his promotion in 1673, the Clerk of the Acts was securely established in his Office. While he now grew cautious in the matter of irregular emoluments, accepting only such larger perquisites as were recognised to be his right, he had no objection to receiving smaller courtesies, and his influence is indicated by the standing of the people who offered them. A consul from Leghorne, thanking Pepys for his sympathy in some official trouble, has sent by one messenger a 'bundle of musical cards, which I hope will prove to your entire satisfaction, having sent to Venice on purpose for them'; and by another, 'one of the best guitars this country affords.' The Duke of Richmond, British Ambassador at Copenhagen, bespeaking the Clerk's attention in the matter of a yacht, sends him at the same time 'an aume of Rhenish wine of the year sixty.' Mr. Hill, merchant and amateur of music, being in Lisbon, begs his friend's acceptance of 'a few gammons, and some of our hams.' Sometimes the Clerk's interest is desired without such inducements. The Earl of Anglesey, Treasurer of the Navy since 1667, in succession to Sir George Carteret, having at one time treated Pepys somewhat shabbily, now turns to him for assistance in a crisis, with the assurance that 'I and my estate shall be your pledge, and you shall for ever oblige Your affectionate friend and servant.'

In 1673, Pepys and the Navy Board were burnt out of Seething Lane, and for a time he took a house or lodgings in Winchester Street, being allowed a sum of £80 a year by the Treasury for rent until a new official residence was provided for him at the end of 1674. In June, 1673, a reconstruction of naval control took place by which Pepys was

further advanced in influence. But in the meantime he had
suffered a second great personal loss. Since his return from
Madrid, Sandwich had again been attacked on the four-
year-old business of the prize goods, and Pepys had been
helpful in framing a defence against charges that gradually
lost their impetus and were finally discarded. Sandwich for
a year or two did useful work in civil life, becoming President of a Select Council for Foreign Plantations, but the
revival of the old scandal, malicious though it was, had
been unfortunate. When, therefore, in 1672 a third naval
war with the Dutch was imminent and the King called Sandwich back to service at sea, the Admiral, whom fortune had
used none too handsomely, returned to his command with
a chivalrous sense of some reparation due to his own honour. It was nobly made. This is not the place to tell the
story of the indecisive Battle of Solebay. All accounts
agreed that Sandwich fought the *Royal James* magnificently
through the heat of one of the fiercest actions of the century, and he was the last man seen alive on the flagship
before she was abandoned to the flames that destroyed her.
When his body was washed up, on it was found the ribbon
of the Garter, which is still an heirloom at Hinchingbrooke.
Only forty-seven years of age at his death, Sandwich had
made a heroic end. On June 24th, his body was brought to
London and borne in a procession of barges, the King's,
the Queen's and the Duke of York's among them, up the
river to Westminster steps. In the Great Hall, a second procession was in waiting to conduct the coffin to the Abbey.
Led by the Earls of Manchester, St. Albans, and Oxford, a
company of great English nobles were followed by the pall
bearers, by the standard bearer, and by the Great Banner;
and then came 'six Bannerolles,' the first of whom was Mr.
Samuel Pepys. There had in these later days been less than
the old intimacy; no more than a recommendation to the
burgesses of Aldeburgh or a suggested line of defence
against calumniators. But between Pepys and the kinsman
to whom he was performing this last service, there had been
great obligations, much kindness, and deep affection. For-

tune had led them both through strange adventures since
the time twelve years ago when together they had brought a
Stuart back to the English throne. Sandwich had founded a
great and historic house, Pepys had risen from the obscurity of a tailor's shop to an eminence from which he
was to set a lasting mark upon the conduct of naval affairs
in England. Also, he had written a Diary. And now the
older man was dead in his prime, and among his mourners
none can have walked with tenderer recollections than his
cousin Samuel. There must have been a sense, too, of something less than even jestice in my Lord's fate. In the public
life of that time, few men so honest had been so baited by
faction. After the end a story had reached London that at
a Council meeting before the fight, the Duke of York had
used unfortunate words on certain measures of prudence
recommended by Sandwich. And on the morning of Solebay, the Admiral of the Blue, dressing himself with extreme care and wearing the decoration of the Garter, was
reported to have said to his secretary that he had been
charged with lack of courage, and to have left his cabin
at the opening of the action with the words, 'Now, Val, I
must be sacrificed.' Thomas Flatman, who painted minia-
tures, and wrote verses good enough to earn a place among
Dr. Saintsbury's Caroline Poets, must have known with
some intimacy the circumstances of Sandwich's life, when
he wrote in his elegy on the dead Admiral:

> But since thou find'st by thy unhappy fate,
> What 'tis to be unfortunately great,
> And purchase Honour at too dear a rate. . . .

Pepys at one time, as we learn from his *Naval Minutes,*
contemplated writing the life of his friend and patron, but
the project came to nothing. Lady Sandwich survived her
husband by but four years, and with her death in 1674 the
last page of one of the most personal chapters in Pepys's
life was turned.

JEMIMAH, COUNTESS OF SANDWICH

In 1673, the King, harassed on one side by the notorious
Cabal, on the other by a Parliament that stubbornly declined to forget the lessons of 1628 and 1641, and tired of
all disputes, consented, probably against his own inclination,
to the passing of the Test Act, by which all persons who
refused to conform to the English Church were excluded
from holding office under the Crown. Among these was the
Duke of York, and he was called upon to resign his place
as Lord High Admiral, which he had held since the Restoration. Charles, instead of appointing a successor, put
the Admiralty into commission, to which were admitted
Prince Rupert, the Dukes of Buckingham, Monmouth,
Lauderdale, and Ormonde, the Earls of Shaftesbury, Anglesey, and Arlington, Sir George Carteret, Henry Coventry, and Edward Seymour. The Duke of York, in spite of
his exclusion, continued to exercise a powerful influence
upon naval affairs, and was even able to retain the Admiralty of Scotland and Ireland. But the change in administration was an important one. The fighting arm of the service was no longer directed under the King by a Lord High
Admiral, but by Lords of the Admiralty. And when by the
King's personal choice the Clerk of the Acts was sent for
from the Navy Office to become Secretary to the new Commissioners, it was as Secretary of the Admiralty that Pepys
took up his promotion. He was able to reflect that of the
men who had taken over naval control in 1660, he was
the only survivor in office. On June 25, 1673, William
Coventry, who in earlier years had been to the Lord High
Admiral what Pepys was now to the Admiralty, but had
since fallen from favour, wrote to his friend: 'You may
reasonably imagine, when you see a letter from mee, that it
is to congratulate your new employment, which I persuade
my selfe you will as easily beleeve mee to rejoyce at, as any
man whatsoever,' and then recommends a servant who
would like to become a purser, and adds: 'I am very unlikely ever to make you a returne, unless you have occasion
to keepe a running horse at Burford, in which case I offer

you my diligence to overlook him.' Pepys had fairly earned
his advance by merit. Also he enjoyed the King's goodwill;
in 1670, having quarrelled with the Swedish Resident, he
received direct instructions from the King 'neither to send'
any challenge to the said Resident of Sweden, nor to accept
of any from him.' If the unprofitable sparks of Whitehall
chose to take risks of the kind, that was their business, but
Charles was not going to have a first-rate public servant
wasted in such fashion.

It was natural that Pepys should be able to hand on his
appointment at the Navy Office to Thomas Hayter, a clerk
of proved ability, but it is not a little surprising that even
his influence was able, further, to have the Clerkship of the
Acts converted into a post of double tenure, to be held
jointly with Hayter by his brother John. We know nothing
of John's character to suggest that he would assist his colleague either by talents or by industry. Shortly after his
death in 1677, his brother Samuel wrote to a young
protégé:

. . . having provided you a commission that entitles you
to the trust and business of a man, my kindness to you,
as well as justice to myself, will not let me longer withhold my giving you the same cautions which I should with
more severity give a child of my own (and did to my
only brother to the last day he lived in the Navy),
namely, that you do never entertain one thought of any
indulgence from me under any neglects of business, and
much less under any misdoings therein, for I am one that
will never be guilty of contributing to the advancement of
any man that will not be contented to rise by the same
steps of diligence and faithfulness which have (by God's
blessing) raised me to this capacity of doing good offices.

From which we may gather that John had, if precariously,
managed to retain his brother's indulgence to the end. But
after his death Samuel found his private and his business
papers mixed in alarming confusion, and being unable to

verify a demand presented by the Master of Trinity House, requested that institution to

> . . . take the trouble of estimating (to your own satisfaction) what his layings-out upon Trinity Dinners, or any other occasions of disbursements within your view, to the time of this his account, may, with the arrears of his salary, arise unto. And whatever you shall thereupon judge he may upon the balance stand indebted in to your Corporation, I will forthwith deposit it in your hands, to remain there for the use of the poor, without interest, so long as my brother's said accounts shall lay unadjusted.

The sum involved and duly paid by Pepys was, we remember, £300.

When Pepys took up his new duties in the middle of June, 1673, he was again engaged in parliamentary ambitions. In August 1672, he was informed that the Duke of York, hearing that Sir Robert Paston, member for Castle Rising, was to be raised to the peerage, had again secured a promise of Lord Howard's interest on behalf of Pepys, though somewhat, it appears, to his Lordship's embarrassment. 'I had this morning,' wrote Thomas Povey to Pepys, 'full discourse with the Lord Howard, who was telling mee how hee finds himself oppressed with his prerogative of recommending on elections; and how hee stands engaged to the King for Sir Francis North, to the Duchess of Cleveland for Sir John Trevor, hir councill and feoffee, and to the Duke for you; telling me by what circumstances the Duke attacked him: and I find not that hee hath any hesitation in the complying with the Duke on your behalf; though hee bee in much distraction how hee shall accomodate the other 2 persons.' When, however, Sir Robert Paston was created Earl of Yarmouth Pepys's candidature went forward strongly supported by Howard, who in the meantime had succeeded from the Barony of Castle Rising to the Dukedom of Norfolk. 'You may depend upon it,' he wrote to Pepys from Norwich on August 15, 1673, 'as done, though unluckily the mayor (a perfect creature I could depend upon) dying, will put us to a little trouble extraordinary; but I think 'tis so well provided for since I was there, as nothing can start to disturb it, with all which I beg of you to acquaint his Royal Highness.' The writ was issued in October, and Pepys duly achieved his ambition of becoming 'a parliament man.' But he was to learn that the troubles of an election did not necessarily end on declaration of the poll. Already, it seems, a year before the contest, he had found it necessary to deal again with damaging rumours about his religion, as the following paper from his manuscripts testifies:

These are to certify the Mayor and Burgesses of Castle Rising, and all other persons whom it may concern, that we whose names are here subscribed, are sufficiently assured, both by the full testimony of other persons of credit and worth, to whom Samuel Pepys, Esq., Secretary of the Admiralty, is personally known, and also by the particular testimony of Mr. Daniel Mills, minister of that parish in London in which he hath long inhabited, that the said Samuel Pepys, Esq., is both otherwise a worthy person, and particularly that he hath constantly manifested himself to be a firm protestant, according to the rites of the Church of England, and a true son thereof.

William Walkner, Preacher at St. Nicholas, in King's Lynn.

Mordaunt Webster, Vicar of Lyn-All-hollows.

Richard Salter, Preacher at St. Margaret's in Lyn Regis.

November 3, 1672.

The certificate was sufficient for immediate purposes, but after the election, Richard Offley, the unsuccessful candidate, taking advantage of the suspicions that had been roused, entered a petition against his rival and secured from the Committee of Privileges a declaration that Pepys's election was void. The decree never took effect, since Parliament was prorogued before the matter came to a vote in the House, leaving Pepys in possession of the seat that he held until 1679. But the enquiry in committee and the debates in the House had brought into public notice a dispute which was later to involve Pepys in serious misfortune.

The religious controversies of the age were highly charged with danger. With a King of strong Catholic sympathies, an heir to the Crown openly professing allegiance to Rome, and a popular sentiment suspicious of every papist whisper, the course of every sensible citizen was to say as little of his private beliefs as possible. The very ambiguity of the King's position made any private unorthodoxy additionally hazardous; Charles was himself too suspect to risk popular disfavour by protecting a subject who might be suspect also. So that Pepys, however valid his answer to such charges might be, knew well enough that the charges though factious were of an exceedingly vexatious nature. They might even be a good deal worse than that. At the time of his domestic crisis in the affairs of Deb. Willett, his wife had terrified him by declaring that she was a Roman Catholic. She was, in fact, nothing of the sort, but at the moment she wanted to terrify him, and knew that there was no surer way of doing it. And now Anthony Ashley, recently created Earl of Shaftesbury, who had a strong taste for heresy hunting, lent his powerful influence to the attack as Pepys upon his election was challenged by the House. 'A person of quality,' it seemed, had seen in Pepys's house at Seething Lane, 'an Altar with a Crucifix upon it.' Whereupon, 'Mr. Pepys, standing up in his place, did heartily and flatly deny that he ever had any Altar or Crucifix, or the image or picture of any Saint whatsoever in his house, from the top to the bottom of it.' The accusing members were called upon for the name of their informant, and refused 'to declare it without the order of the House; which, being made, they named the Earl of Shaftesbury.'

They also named Sir John Banks. A deputation, of which Coventry was a member, was sent to ask Shaftesbury for precise information, and Banks was ordered to attend at the Bar of the House. When Shaftesbury was questioned, he hedged. Not sure that he had hedged securely enough, he sent a letter after the deputation as they left Exeter House, on February 10, 1674. It was, he would like to point out, 'some years' distance since I was at Mr. Pepys his lodging,' and he could not positively say that he had taken 'so exact notice of things inquired of as to be able to remember them so clearly as is requisite to do in a testimony upon honour or oath, or to so great and honourable a body as the House of Commons.' But he must confess that if he had really seen so striking an object as an Altar, he must have remembered it, which he did not. And on February 13th, the deputation reported to the House to this effect. In conversation Shaftesbury, although he disowned the altar, seemed to remember something of a crucifix, but was not sure whether it was painted or carved, and, in fact, 'his memory was so very imperfect in it, that if he were upon his oath he could give no testimony.' On the 16th, Sir John Banks made his appearance, and afforded even less comfort to the prosecution. He had been acquainted with Mr. Pepys for several years, had known him intimately both at the Navy Office and his house, he had never seen an altar or a crucifix, he did not believe him to be a papist, nor 'that way inclined in the least, nor had any reason or ground to think or believe it.' In order further to clear himself, Pepys obtained from his brother-in-law, Balthasar St. Michel, a long letter giving an account of the family's religious history, and concluding: 'And now, sir, I do declare from my very soul, and am extremely well satisfied that you kept my dear sister in the true protestant religion till her death.'

The irresponsible character of the persecution, for it was nothing else, need not be emphasised. His wife had shown some disposition towards Rome, but it came to no more than that, and in so far as he suspected it at all, he did so with alarm. In 1666, he had bought a varnished picture of a crucifix, 'very fine,' and Hales's portrait of his wife showed her in the character of St. Catherine. It was on no better evidence than this that his political opponents lodged a wholly frivolous charge against a man who at no time showed any sign of Catholic sympathies, and who was notably insensible to the allurements of martyrdom. But in view of what was to follow, it must be allowed that frivolous is an inadequate word. Shaftesbury's biographer claims that in not supporting 'a formal charge, involving important results' which 'was founded on his loose private conversations,' he was acting scrupulously towards Pepys. Mr. Wheatley properly sees nothing scrupulous about it, pointing conclusively to the fact that Shaftesbury had said very damaging things about Pepys in conversations which he meant to be reported. But he was far too astute a person to give evidence on oath that he knew could not stand cross-examination directed by so good an advocate as Pepys. There is no reason to suppose that when the affair started Shaftesbury had any strong personal animus against the Secretary of the Admiralty. What happened no doubt was that his political bigotry saw suitable quarry in Pepys. When he felt that he was going too far he discreetly held his hand, but it was with a sense of frustration not at all pleasing to one of the most inveterate intriguers of his time. Success in his attack upon Pepys would have meant little to him, but failure was not to be forgotten.

A full account of Pepys's activities as Secretary of the Admiralty is to be found among the manuscripts of the Pepysian Library at Magdalene. In the Admiralty journals and letter-books there preserved we find an almost daily record of Pepys's work from his appointment in 1673 until his final retirement from the Admiralty in 1679. It has been left for Dr. Tanner to reduce the huge bulk of these to a form that makes them accessible to anything short of the many years of industry that he had himself devoted to the task. In volumes II and III of the *Catalogue of the Pepysian Manuscripts* he gives précis of just on four thousand letters in chronological order covering the years 1673 to 1677, and he makes for himself a just and modest claim 'that nothing of any conceivable value to the students has been omitted.'

These précis alone amount to over eight hundred printed pages. They establish once and for all Pepys's rare qualities and eminent ability as a civil servant. The reading of them leaves an impression of dispatch, attention to detail, firmness of discipline, fair dealing, and personal courtesy that show the Secretary of the Admiralty in a very favourable light. It is true that he was acting as the mouthpiece of the Lords, but strictly official as his correspondence in almost every instance is, it is constantly enlivened by touches that leave no doubt that while the substance of a communication may have been decided in Council, its manner was left largely to the discretion of the Secretary. For Pepys's business was business, and his official correspondence properly contains no more than an occasional echo of the vivacity that graces the Diary. But at any moment the driest official tone may be relieved by a personal note of warning or advice or encouragement. It was Pepys's boast that during his long period of service he used all his exertions to better the discipline of the Navy, and that the boast was no idle one these letters bear continual witness. But they also tell us that however exacting the demands of discipline might be he never forgot that even the hard-bitten seamen of the seventeenth century were also men.

It should be added that these letters speak well not only for Pepys but for the Admiralty Board as a body. Certain abuses in the Navy persisted in spite of all efforts at correction. Commanders went on plying for private hire, pursers continued to manipulate their accounts, and the officers' roll was still encumbered by unnecessary young gentlemen whose only recommendation was that they were well born. Worst of all, there was the perpetual lack of money, attributable in part to domestic extravagance at Whitehall, but substantially to the incurable Stuart contempt for the parliamentary system. Nevertheless, there

was a steady improvement in all these respects under the
new Admiralty Board. The captains did begin to realise that
they were not merchantmen, the pursers that their accounts
would be strictly audited, and the sailors that wages were
not wholly mythical. Dr. Tanner's promised book is to deal
on an ample scale with these wider naval considerations.
We may here look over Pepys's Admiralty Letters with a
view to seeing what they tell us of the man.

In matters of discipline he is direct, but where possible
the severity is tempered. He allows that the commander
of a sloop had a good excuse for wishing to come to town,
'Yet it is a practice very unfit to be allowed that commanders should on any occasion take the liberty of leaving
their ships without express permission from this board.' A
captain who has neglected his orders to give 'frequent notice to the navy board of all his wants' has thereby missed
his sailing with the fleet, a failure 'which the king and lords
will not be well pleased with,' and a benevolent Secretary
'therefore earnestly advises him to recover it by being gone
with all possible speed.' A purser has come to the office
complaining of ill-usage from a lieutenant on his ship, declaring himself to be no longer 'able to bear the wrong';
and the captain of the ship is duly warned that 'If true no
little part of the blame will reflect upon him, whose duty
it is to support his inferior officers against any injuries
offered them from their superiors.' Pepys, in fact, has inter-
viewed the purser himself, and is backing his own judgment of character. The commander of the *Dragon*, taxed
with dilatoriness and ordered to give an account of his
movements, has been riding a high horse, and the Secretary
informs him: 'I shall always be found walking by that rule
that shall both make and keep me a friend to every worthy
man, and particularly to yourself under that character, and
as such do expect you will excuse me in saying that the king
must be reckoned very hardly used when his officers shall
declare their being weary of his services for his asking them
but once how they spend their time whilst in his service and
wages.' Another captain, who is to proceed on a special

mission, would prefer to do so only as its chief. The King
(happily we may suppose) is this morning gone to Newmarket, otherwise the Secretary fears that he 'would have
been very little satisfied with your desire of having no body
put over your head, nothing rendering a man [the Secretary is sure] in his Majesty's opinion more fit to command
than the being found willing to be commanded.'

Any reasonable appeal to the Secretary is sure of a sympathetic hearing, and on occasion he is ready to take responsibility for granting favours on his own authority. A captain writing to inform him that his wife is sick 'to the
despair of her life,' Pepys takes upon himself 'in the absence of the King and Lords to give him leave to come to
town for a few days.' A meritable man who has not pushed
himself forward, having been proposed by the Navy Board
for promotion, Pepys is happy to announce his appointment
and hopes that they will continue to find such candidates, he
himself having 'met with too much reason to fear that the
want of some such recommendations hath hindered the
modest men, who keep strictly to their duty on board, from
the preferment due to them, whilst others more solicitous
in the getting of certificates, and less scrupulous of spending
their time on shore, have carried it away from them.' On
the other hand, when he suspects a candidate's qualifications
he can say so with admirable point. 'Some persons of quality
at court' desiring him to find employment for a friend who
as an amateur at sea has already behaved himself 'like a
gentleman and an understanding man,' the Secretary turns
to a more reliable source for information, 'for as no man
living can be more inclined than myself to favour a gentleman that is a true seaman, so neither is there any man
more sensible than (after many years' observation) I am,
of the ruinous consequences of an overhasty admitting persons to the office and charge of seamen, upon the bare consideration of their being gentlemen.'

The same note of ironic humour is always the Secretary's
to command. A third-rater having been blown up by accident, an austere Commissioner attributes the mishap to an

excessive use of brandy at sea. Pepys is disposed to agree; too much brandy is drunk, and 'the observation seems very seasonable'; nevertheless, the general opinion on this occasion inclines to blame 'the carelessness of the gunner in his leaving of loose powder about the ship.' And when one Simon Trout complained that the boatswain of the *Holmes* owes him £8, 'which he refuseth to pay,' the Secretary informs the debtor that if he supposes 'his present employment' to secure him against the discharge of his proper liabilities, he will find himself very much mistaken, and desires him to pay the £8 to avoid further unpleasantness.

Strict as he was, Pepys in the exercise of his duties was unfailingly reasonable in his judgments, and liberal in action. Determined to stop the irregularity of pursers in presenting their books, he nevertheless adds: 'There is nothing from which I can sooner expect any amendment of it than the putting of that sort of people into a condition of living honestly in their employments (which as they have been hitherto used I could never think they were), and then correcting them with all severity for what they shall be found falsifying their trust in.' He sharply orders Sir Robert Robinson of the *Assurance* to discharge two youths from his ship, 'neither of them above 16 years of age, and both of them schoolboys belonging to the Charterhouse . . . the same being seduced from Southwalk Fair and shipped against their wills.'

The pressing of men for the Navy is a subject of frequent discussion in the letters. It was not for Pepys to question a practice that was a tradition of the service, but he writes of it with no enthusiasm, and we seem to detect an undertone of satisfaction on many of the occasions when he was to reprimand officers for pressing protected men. A captain, who has apparently allowed his zeal in the matter to be sharpened by rewards, is to be told that while the necessity of the Fleet 'justifies all the industry that can be made use of towards the supplying it,' nothing can excuse 'his taking of moneys.' But, in general, Pepys writes in this connection merely as the Secretary issuing instructions, and

we need but note a few examples of the official attitude towards the operations of the press masters. In August, 1673,
the Mayor of Bristol is ordered immediately to dispatch all
the men there pressed by him to Portsmouth: 'Those that
fail to appear are to be prosecuted.' The following September, the Secretary is sorry to hear that Captain Grant's
lieutenant 'has had so little success in pressing,' and the
commander of a dogger is 'to use all care possible to prevent the running away of his men.' Press warrants are enclosed to him to enable him to replace with others the men
who have already escaped, but he is to be careful of 'unnecessary spending of time in the impresting of men to the
offence of the country.' Early in 1674, the Governor at
Dover expresses a similar misgiving. Having lately heard
of 'dissatisfaction which the Parliament hath expressed
touching our method of pressing of men' he declines to use
his warrant 'till the business be settled in Parliament, as
being unwilling to expose himself to any censure for his
acting therein,' and Pepys in reporting this refusal to one
of the captains advises him 'to take the best care you can
in keeping and well using the men you have, for I dare not
undertake in what time the business will be so settled as to
leave it safe for us to go on with the pressing of men.'
Press-masters are warned against excuses made by pressed
men that they are serving the King in other capacities, and
to accept nothing but a 'good certificate that they are already entertained on some part of his Majesty's service,
and at that time attending thereon.' Precautions are taken
against popular interference with what was perhaps the
most unpopular practice of the age. Pepys instructs the
Lieutenant of the Tower 'To send a file of musketeers on
board the *Royal Escape* lying near the Tower, to secure men
impressed for the *Cambridge*,' and a month later he for-
wards the King's order to the Secretary of War for the
provision of a military guard to prevent disorders between
the press-masters and seamen 'who are said to assemble
themselves mutinously in bodies from day to day, not only
to the interrupting but assaulting and wounding the said

press-masters in the execution of their duties.' The distribution of pressed men seems to have been of a somewhat casual nature. The captain of the *Gloucester,* applying for reinforcements, is told that 'the Governor of Dover is ordered to imprest 200 able seamen in the parts thereabouts for Captain Rooth's fleet, who on application will doubtless let him have a share of them.' And when moderation was shown it was usually with a prudent reservation. An order goes to Captain Russell of the *Swallow* 'to discharge one John Tarrant, a shipwright on board him who is sick and weakly, on his friends producing an able man to serve in his room.' At the conclusion of peace after the Third Dutch War in 1674, the press warrants, in conformity with the usual practice, were withdrawn. A commander asking for such an authorisation is curtly informed that the Lords 'have not used to give order for the impresting of any men in times of peace.' In the great ship-building programme, however, which was inaugurated after the declaration of peace, the supply of artisans and even of seamen became so precarious that the rule of no-pressing in peace time was suspended by the Admiralty, and limited warrants were issued.

By far the greater part of the correspondence is concerned with the movements of the Fleet, naval supplies, and the discipline and manning of the ships. There was a constant exchange of views between the Admiralty and the Navy Board, and here we find Pepys always bringing a sympathetic understanding to the difficulties by which he knew his old office to be embarrassed. Under the astute guidance of their Secretary, the Lords of the Admiralty proved to be far more accessible to the ideas and necessities of the Navy Board than the Duke of York had been in the aloofness of his office as Lord High Admiral. Not that James was by any means indifferent to the welfare of the Navy; on the contrary, his concern for it was the principal merit of his character. But he was a prince and heir to the throne, and nothing was easier for him than to dismiss an inconvenient application with a shrug and silence.

The Lords of the Admiralty could not behave in this manner, and Pepys was there to see that inconvenient applications were not dismissed merely because they were inconvenient. Not only did he prove himself at this time to be an exceedingly able director of his own department, but he was also peculiarly fitted with his experience to be a highly valuable liaison officer between the two branches of the naval executive.

Correctly official, however, as the correspondence mostly is, we find in it besides the human elements to which reference has been made, many graphic notes on an engaging variety of topics. It is a little startling to read that the Secretary will acquaint the King and Lords with a consul's proposal to buy slaves for his Majesty's galleys at Leghorne, and to read a week later that directions for the purchase are being forwarded to the Navy Board. In January, 1674, an order is issued for two or three files of musketeers to be at Execution Dock at Wapping to assist 'Mr. Joynes, the marshal of the Admiralty, until the execution of the pirates be over.' On September 16, 1674, the *Swan* is to hasten away to Yarmouth as fast as possible 'in regard the herring fishers will be very suddenly at sea.' But in December, on the other hand, the bailiffs of Yarmouth are informed that 'the King takes notice of the great backwardness of the herring fleet, the first part whereof which should have been ready by the middle of November appearing not yet, to his great disappointment and charge by his ships lying full manned in victuals and wages.' The bailiffs will kindly let the Lords of the Admiralty know 'the true state of their fish ships' by the next post. On the 10th of February of the same year, Captain Colt of the *Hunter* is instructed that though the King had intended to dispatch certain ships for the purpose of retaking New York, the peace shortly to be concluded will presumably make this no longer necessary. And in the following August, Captain Griffith of the *Diamond* receives orders to conduct Major Andros, the newly appointed Governor, to New York 'with his lady, retinue, and goods.'

Sometimes our attention is taken by slighter matters. Captain Jenifer, sailing for Lisbon, reads, in a postscript to his final instructions, that the Secretary is 'this evening directed by his Highness [Prince Rupert] to bespeak of you the storing of him with some Spanish onions at your return.' Samuel Baldwin is to be discharged from a ship in order that he may again be able to employ his special talent 'for picking of oysters for his Majesty's particular use.' It was, we imagine, with personal satisfaction that Pepys ordered pay for overtime to the gardeners 'employed in trimming and fitting up the garden belonging to the admiralty office at Derby House,' which was now not only the Secretary's official, but also his private residence. An occasional flash of colour strikes the page, as when a guard is to be placed upon the cargo on board the *Susanna* of Weymouth, 'laden with oranges and lemons,' or when the Queen's ship *Saudadoes* is 'to be furnished with a set of silk pennants, and to be gilded like the *Greyhound.*'

The letters abound in common sense. Writing privately to Sir Thomas Allin, Comptroller of the Navy, during the Third Dutch War, Pepys wastes no time in wishing that we had been more successful in a late engagement, 'for that must be submitted to,' but deplores the consequent disagreements between ourselves 'and our friends the French,' which 'if not quickly taken up may prove matter of infinite prejudice to his Majesty's service.' In the same letter he informs his correspondent that proper care has been taken for the safeguarding of our coasts, but that if colliers choose to go out without convoy they must look after themselves. When troops are being dispatched to deal with the Virginian rising of 1676, the Duke of Monmouth desires that they may be provided with as much and as good brandy as the seamen, and the Secretary of the Admiralty enquires of the Navy Board how much and how good this may be. His sense of propriety sometimes takes a domestic turn. Having secured an appointment as muster-master at Deal for his brother-in-law Balthasar St. Michel, he writes him an admirable letter of advice as to how to conduct himself in

the very delicate business of billeting sick seamen. 'As it
would at no time be thought reasonable, so neither in this
time in particular would it be thought excusable, that those
poor people who have already trusted beyond their strength
should be urged to go on further in trusting, or that others
who observe the evil effects of it to their neighbours should
be pressed by any violence to the exposing themselves to the
like inconveniences by giving entertainment to the persons
you would put upon them without better security of their
being reimbursed.' He charges Balty to refrain from 'doing
or saying anything that shall appear like violence' and
rather find himself discharged from his duty, than continue
it 'upon terms dishonourable to the King, unsatisfactory to
the poor seamen, injurious to your poor neighbours, and
unsafe to yourself'; and again, 'to be as serviceable to the
king and careful of yourself as you can while you are in it,
and unless you can have any reasonable hopes . . . that
matters will go better with you hereafter as to payment,
labour with as much decency, prudence, and speed as you
can to get out of it; and God bless you.' St. Michel over-
came his difficulties, and eighteen months later we find him
being felicitated by Pepys on attending the King and the
Duke of York on a return passage from Portsmouth, 'and
making them the little present of the lamb and fish you mention.'

The occasion was Charles's visit to Portsmouth to be
present at the launching of the *Royal James*. On the 12th
of June, 1675, Pepys had written to the Portsmouth Commissioner of the King's intention to come round by sea for
the ceremony, which took place on June 30th, Pepys being
in attendance. The royal yacht was in some difficulty off
shore, and the King was delayed a night in landing, Pepys
writing to Whitehall that 'in case his Majesty comes not in
by the morning, his Royal Highness purposes to go out
again towards him, to the great discomfort of our land
men, who have had enough of the sea for this bout.' Three
days later, he reports that all has gone off well during the
King's visit, and that the homeward journey is to begin by

sea 'this evening, with this (I hope) better choice in his passage that he will take it on the Harwich to the Downs, where Commissioner Haddock and some others will attend him, to the lessening, though not wholly removing, the apprehensions we were lately under from the too great adventure his Majesty was then running without other security on board him than his own seamanship, and poor Clements's.'

Finally we may note of these Admiralty Letters that everywhere they reveal Pepys as familiarly versed in all the many aspects of naval business. It is impossible to detect him anywhere using equivocal language unless it be dictated by policy. There is never a trace of ambiguity used to conceal ignorance. Whatever the matter in hand, the Secretary is not only fully informed of its circumstances, but we feel that behind his information there is a wide background of experience and knowledge. On all questions of custom, procedure, and regulations, he pronounces quietly and with the authority of the man who knows. As has been said, he frequently goes beyond the present necessity to help the correspondent with observations drawn from the richly furnished resources of his mind. He can even recommend one of the most accomplished shipwrights in the kingdom to consider 'whether it would not render the boat more commodious and give her better quality (she now going much deeper abaft than afore) if her state-room were brought a little more forward; and if you do judge so, pray let it be done.'

A distinguished living statesman, who has held office as First Lord of the Admiralty, has been known to say that his researches among Admiralty records led him to the opinion that the civil service had never given to the Navy an administrator abler than Pepys. To read these Admiralty Letters is to find such an opinion supported. The cumulative impression that they leave is above all of a man who is master of his job. And he is this without dullness or pedantry. It is astonishing to find so voluminous an official correspondence at once so incisive, so readable, and so little marred by the rhetoric of self-importance. And yet, not so astonishing after all. Dr. Tanner, whose services to the right understanding of Pepys are an honour to historical scholarship and need no further praise, may in this matter for once be caught in two minds. In his Introduction to Volume I of his descriptive catalogue, he says that Pepys's 'official style, taken alone would give him a reputation,' and that his Admiralty Letters 'are always saved from being dull or ponderous by the writer's native shrewdness of observation and fine full-flavoured sense of humour.' But in the chapter on the 'Diary as Literature' in his *Mr. Pepys,* he writes, that if the style of the Tangier journal 'has little in common with that of the *Diary,* still less has Pepys's official correspondence preserved in the *Admiralty Letters.* This is always perfectly clear and businesslike, but ponderous and processional.' I do not know why Dr. Tanner should thus in 1925 go back on what seems to me to be so sound a judgment delivered in 1903. For while the subject matter of the Admiralty Letters must, by contrast with the subject matter of the Diary, greatly diminish their popular interest, there is, nevertheless, written all over them, with subdued emphasis indeed but plainly, the character of the man who wrote the Diary. And the idiom, too, necessarily modified by the occasion, is the same. The Letters, it need not be said, can never compete with the Diary in public interest, but I do not think that any intimate knowledge of the Diary could fail at once to establish the authorship of the Letters. In other words, Samuel Pepys, when he daily entered the offices of the Navy Board or the Admiralty, by no means ceased to be Samuel Pepys.

No more than brief reference is in place here to the *Admiralty Journal* edited by Dr. Tanner in his fourth volume of the *Catalogue of Pepysian Manuscripts.* This contains full minutes of over three hundred meetings of the Lords of the Admiralty during the years 1673 to 1679. The fact that they were written out by Pepys himself suggests that the failure of his eyesight had been arrested. As a piece of secretarial work, the Journal is, as Dr. Tanner

claims, 'a monument to the great business mind of its com-
piler.' But it contains little that is to the purpose of this
present study. It makes good, and often absorbing, reading.
It is an invaluable historical document, and Pepys had a
way of redeeming even the driest official minutes from
tedium. But he had not here the opportunity, which he took
so freely in the Admiralty Letters, of adding his own
touches of wit and wisdom to the business in hand. A be-
guiling anecdotage might be compiled from the Journal,
but it would tell us nothing of the Secretary who wrote it.
The human aspect of the Navy comes to light in the questions of discipline and consideration of appeals, in which the
Lords were constantly engaged. There are grim stories of
personal disaster, and surprising revelations of naval procedure. It is instructive to learn that a man who had lost
both arms in action could apply successfully for the cook's
place on the *Sweepstakes*. The Journal also covers in detail
many topics, as for example, the progress of our wars in
the Mediterranean, that do not here call for consideration.

The Admiralty meetings were usually held at Derby
House, though at one period there was a weekly adjourn-
ment to Hampton Court, and on occasion the Board would
move to Newmarket or elsewhere to suit the royal convenience. It may be noted to the credit of Charles II, that during the period of the Journal he was more regular in attendance than any of his Commissioners, having been present
at one hundred and ninety-five out of three hundred and
eight meetings, Monmouth being at the bottom of the list
with seventy-seven attendances. The King, indeed, makes a
very good showing in the Journal. The Lords recognised
that to ask for his opinion was no mere observance of eti-
quette, but to refer to as sound a judgment on naval affairs
in general as was to be found in the country. The principal
complaint against him, urged openly on more than one occasion by Pepys, was that he was too indulgent towards misdemeanours. There was some truth in the charge, and the
Lords were at times able to specify grave consequences of
the royal forbearance. But we like Charles none the less

for it. There is a charming story of a mate who was reported by his captain for having spoken in his cups disrespectfully of the King. His Majesty's pleasure in the matter being desired, he directed that the man should be duly punished for being drunk, but that as he himself did not mind what a mate said of him, he did not know that it need concern anyone else. With which passing notice, the Journal may safely be left to the naval historian.

CHAPTER VII

PROSPERITY. TITUS OATES. THE TOWER. RETIREMENT

IN 1676, Pepys was elected Master of Trinity House, of which he had been made a Younger Brother in 1662, and an Elder Brother ten years later. By its constitution Trinity House was in control of pilotage, buoys, lightships, and lighthouses, and responsible for general supervision of the coast waterways. It surveyed certain ports, ordered the ballasting of ships in the Thames, and could give to aged or disabled mariners licences to row on that river without reference to the Waterman's Company. It was, in fact, an auxiliary though independent branch of the naval service, performing duties that fell outside the immediate jurisdiction of the Admiralty. As such it was in frequent communication with Derby House, where Pepys as Secretary had many calls to make upon its coöperation. Also, it had some disciplinary power over seamen. In 1674, we find Pepys writing to his brother John, who continued to hold his Clerkship to the Brotherhood concurrently with his Clerkship of the Acts, asking him to send 'a perfect list of all the present Elder Brethren, with a mark on those who you conceive may be fittest' to serve on a 'commission of oyer and terminer for the admiralty which will shortly be issued.' We may surmise that this innovation was largely due to Pepys, himself then an Elder Brother, and it is evidence of the high importance that he attached to the Brotherhood that he should wish them to be represented on a court for the trial of causes which had hitherto been the Admiralty's prerogative. That Trinity House was sensible of this esteem is suggested by the fact that Pepys was elected to the Mastership 'by a general voice of Elder and Younger Brothers' before he had yet proceeded from a Younger to an Elder Wardenship; so that the chronology of his appointments reads: Younger Brother, 1662; Elder Brother, 1672; Younger Warden, 1675; Master, 1676. Both before and during his Mastership, Pepys freely gave his time and experience to the Brotherhood, and reorganised many of its activities. Among other reforms, he effected an economy in the gastronomic displays at which in younger days he had at Lord Sandwich's invitation been a somewhat too enthusiastic guest. In a paper on *Samuel Pepys and the Trinity House,* in the *English Historical Review* for October, 1929, Dr. Tanner quotes a passage from the Trinity House minutes, in which the Master moves 'that foreasmuch as the charge of those annual entertainments have for some years past amounted to above £120 without the least benefit to the Corporation . . . and whereas the condition of the Corporation in reference to its stock is low . . . he prayed the same might be wholly foreborne for the present year,' which motion was duly carried as 'very seasonable on behalf of the poor and of very good example for the future.' Pepys's first Mastership terminated in June, 1677, and when the scandal of two years later forced him out of the Admiralty, he disappeared also for some eighteen months from the records of the Corporation.

Among other duties undertaken by Trinity House, was the examination of the boys in the mathematical class at Christ's Hospital. In 1657, John Evelyn, visiting the Blue Coat School which had been founded by Edward VI, called it an 'exemplary charity,' and thirty years later he recorded another visit in an enchanting passage of his Diary:

I went this evening to see the order of the boys and children at Christ's Hospital. There were near 800 boys and girls so decently clad, cleanly lodged, so wholesomely fed, so admirably taught, some the mathematics, especially the forty of the late King's foundation, that I was delighted to see the progress some little youths of thirteen or fourteen years of age had made. I saw them at supper, visited their dormitories, and much admired the order, economy, and excellent government of this most charitable seminary. Some are taught for the Universities, others designed for seamen, all for trades and callings. The girls are instructed in all such work as becomes their sex and may fit them for good wives, mistresses, and to be a blessing to their generation. They sung a psalm before they sat down to supper in the great Hall, to an organ which played all the time, with such cheerful harmony, that it seemed to me a vision of angels. I came from the place with infinite satisfaction, having never seen a more noble, pious and admirable charity.

This mathematical class, instituted by Charles II, had been established by Letters Patent in 1673, and was a foundation in which Pepys as Clerk of the Acts had taken a particular interest. It is probable, indeed, that the idea had originated in his desire to have some academy where boys could be trained for the Navy under his own observation, and the 'others designed for seamen,' mentioned by Evelyn, were boys of this class. They were instructed not only in mathematics but in the art of navigation, and they wore on the shoulder a special silver badge designed by John Roettier, bearing a suitable allegorical group and 'two Zephyrs propelling favourably the ships of England.' The following passage from the Admiralty Journal, dated September 12, 1675, brings Pepys happily into contact with the King on Christ's Hospital business.

His Majesty and my Lords being informed by Mr. Pepys in the condition wherein 15 of the Blue Coat boys of his Majesty's Royal Foundation at Christ's Hospital are for being sent abroad from thence to sea, as being the fruits of his Majesty's said Mathematical Foundation, and the improvements of the said children being made known to his Majesty by reading of a certificate signed

by the Master, Wardens, and Assistants of the Trinity
House of Deptford Strand (to whom the examination
of the said children and certifying of their abilities is by
the constitution committed), and the intention of this
motion being that his Majesty would be pleased to consider how far he would think fit to express his further
bounty to the said Foundation by contributing to the support of the said children in their being placed abroad,
either in his own service or otherwise; his Majesty was
pleased to recommend it to my Lords of the Admiralty
to consider of this matter at their next meeting with the
Governors of the Hospital and Officers of the Navy, and
as soon as they shall ripen anything into proportion fit
for his Majesty's view, that the same be reported to him,
giving leave in the mean time to Mr. Pepys to bring the
said children, with some of their Governors, to attend
him to-morrow morning, which was accordingly done,
Sir John Frederick the President, with Sir Richard Ford,
Sir John Sheldon, and several other aldermen and citizens of London, Governors of the said Hospital, accom-
panying the said children to his Majesty and rendering
his Majesty their most humble acknowledgments of his
Majesty's Royal grace and bounty in this his Foundation,
which his Majesty was pleased as graciously to receive
from them and the said children, and to promise his
further care of them.

Pepys had thus an interest in the class both as a naval
administrator and as a Brother of Trinity House. Moreover,
the fragrant seemliness of the charity of which Evelyn gives
so lively an appreciation was no less admired by Pepys, and
it was his pleasure whenever possible to make the interests
of the Blue Coat children his special care. In 1675, he wrote
to Sir John Frederick, President of the Hospital, that the
scheme for apprenticing boys from the mathematical class
to the Navy had been drawn up under his hand and was now
awaiting the authority of the Great Seal: 'A copy of which
memorial I take the liberty of enclosing you, and praying

your accepting it from me on behalf of the said Children
as an earnest of the affection wherewith I shall on every
occasion be ready to serve them, and in them the public, as
my duty both to God and my Royal Master obliges and
your worthy example invites me.' When in 1676 Pepys himself was appointed a Governor of the Hospital the honour
was one that gave him especial satisfaction.

In the following year, 1677, a further public distinction
was bestowed upon the Secretary of the Admiralty. Away
back in 1660 he had taken his wife and Mrs. Pierce to dine
at the invitation of Mr. Chaplin, the victualler, at Clothworkers' Hall, where he found the 'entertainment very
good, a brave hall, good company, and very good music.'
The brave hall was burnt down in the Great Fire, but by
1669 it had been rebuilt, and in April of that year Pepys
had visited the new hall, to dine on 'a good piece of cold
roast beef,' and to see the Lord Mayor and Aldermen
drive by in procession, their wives also in their coaches,
'and, indeed, the sight was mighty pleasing.' Now in 1677,
he found himself elected to the Mastership of the Company, and celebrated the occasion by presenting the livery
with 'an open-work silver cup, with a removable plain gilt
lining,' which may still be seen adorning the banquet table
of the clothworkers. It should be added that it may also be
seen when the club founded in Pepys's memory is the privi-
leged guest of his own Company, to which, as we learn
at Clothworkers' Hall, he also presented two silver tank-
ards. And on December 6, 1677, he received the thanks of
the Court for the gift of 'A large standard having this
Company's arms with Supporters and their Patron and
Crest and a Griffin supporting their arms and the Dragon
supporting the City Arms—and a Banner of his own particular Coat of Arms,' which together cost the sum of £26
10s. On July 4th, in the following year, the Court ordered
that Esquire Pepys's coat of arms should be placed in the
window of the Hall. There is no record in the Company's
books of Pepys having been admitted a Freeman before his
Mastership, and it is significant of his standing in the City

at the time that the influential Clothworkers should have so far departed from their usual custom as to elect a stranger to the Mastership. It may be added that in 1687 William Hewer held the same office, and in a minute of October 3d, Mr. Secretary Pepys was 'intreated' to advise a committee what inscription should be placed under the new Master's coat of arms. As evidence of the liberties that were taken with Pepys's name it may be mentioned that in the clothworkers' records alone it is spelt in no less than seven different ways: Pepys, Peepys, Peepyt, Pepyes, Pepis, Peppes, Pepps.

Pepys's salary as Secretary was £500 a year, but this was handsomely augmented by fees that he was allowed to charge on certain commissions and upon passes issued to ships. There was a wide discrepancy between the value of these as estimated by Pepys himself and as estimated by hostile critics. In any case, his official income was not less than £2,000 a year, and it was alleged in some quarters to be more than four times as much. As Dr. Tanner points out, the records seem to indicate that with this substantial increase in his regular earnings Pepys became far more scrupulous in the matter of irregular profit. It is true that we no longer have the confidences of the Diary to enlighten us, but not only are the Admiralty Letters and his other correspondence free of damaging suggestion, but there is a convincing tone in the following letter written on May 5, 1675, to Captain Howe of the *Phœnix:*

As to your latter letter I find something to take very ill from you, and the more upon account of another letter from one whose hand I know not, not from any unreasonableness in what you ask, it being a thing so just that without your knowledge, much less bespeaking, I had moved his Majesty for and despatched it towards you by his commission of the 25th of April, 1675. . . . But that which I have reason to take amiss from you is your thinking that any consideration of benefit to myself or expectation of reward from you should be of any inducement with me. Therefore pray reserve that sort of argument for such as will be guided by it, and know that your meriting well of the king is the only present that shall ever operate with me, and that it was my belief of your having so done that led me unknown and without your asking to the moving his Majesty for that just kindness.

With this should be read an exchange of letters in 1678 between Pepys and Lord Berkeley of Stratton, who had been one of the extra Commissioners of the Navy in 1660 and at a later date British Ambassador in Paris. His Lordship has made several inglorious appearances in the Diary. In 1663 he had entertained Pepys to 'a fine French dinner,' and two years later, after a heated scene he apologised with the assurance, 'extolling my care and diligence, that he did love me heartily for my own sake.' But such occasional affabilities did not mend Pepys's poor opinion. He found Berkeley 'the most hot, fiery man in discourse, without any cause that ever I saw,' and was by no means displeased on being told that he had 'all along been a fortunate, though a passionate and but weak man as to policy; but as a kinsman brought in and promoted by my Lord of St. Albans, and one that is the greatest vapourer in the world,' and in 1668 there is an entry in the Diary which bluntly accuses Berkeley of swindling the Duke of York, for whose affairs he was a Commissioner, on a wine bill to the tune of £700 a year. It was ten years later that Berkeley, then an old man within a few months of his death, wrote to Pepys from his great new house in Piccadilly, 'or rather Palace' as Evelyn calls it, 'for I am assured it stood him in near £30,000.' It was in answer to a letter in which the Secretary of the Admiralty gave his Lordship a very eloquent piece of his mind. The Berkeley family had solicited Pepys's interest in favour of a Mr. Bonithan, who desired to become a lieutenant in the Navy. Pepys had gone out of his way to do 'not only the most I should have done in the case of a brother, but more than ever I did in any man's case before, or, for his sake, do think I shall ever do again.' He had secured the commission, but upon examination by officers in the Navy Mr. Bonithan made an unsatisfactory impression, whereupon Pepys had taken it upon himself to advise him 'to pass a little longer time in the condition he was then in, under a stricter application of himself to the practice of navigation,' and the commission was given to a more suitable candidate. Since when Pepys had been informed that the ladies of his Lordship's family had let it be known about town that their suit to Mr. Pepys had failed because 'money had been wanting in the case.' And the Secretary now took leave to inform his Lordship that the reproach was one

. . . lost upon me, who am known to be so far from needing any purgation in the point of selling places, as never to have taken so much as my fee for a commission or warrant to any one officer in the navy, within the whole time, now near twenty years, that I have had the honour of serving His Majesty therein—a self-denial at this day so little in fashion, and yet so chargeable to maintain, that I take no pride, and as little pleasure, in the mentioning it, further than it happily falls in here to my defence against the mistake the Ladies seem disposed to arraign me by on this occasion. Besides that, in the particular case of this gentleman, Lieut. Beele, who enjoys the commission designed for Mr. Bonithan, he is one whose face I never saw either before or since the time of his receiving it, nor know one friend he has in the world to whom he owes this benefit, other than the King's justice and his own modest merit: which, having said, it remains only that I assure your Lordship what I have so said, is not calculated with any regard to, much less any repining at, the usage the Ladies are pleased to show me in this affair, for 'tis fit I bear it, but to acquit myself to your Lordship in my demeanour toward them, as becomes their and, my Lord,

Your Lordship's most obedient Servant,

S. P.

Certain fees on commissions were the authorised perquisites of Pepys's office, and in other cases, at least in the past, he had received acknowledgments from officers for making out their papers, but there is little reason to doubt the substantial truth of his statement, and none at all to believe that now or at any time he was capable of recommending a bad officer to the service for the benefit of his own pocket. Berkeley, addressing his reply with some condescension to 'Good Mr. Pepys,' made a handsome disclaimer. 'My wife . . . my daughter Berkeley . . . Mrs. Henrietta' are all greatly concerned that any words of theirs should have caused Mr. Pepys inconvenience; they wish to assure him that their meaning was not all what he has been given to suppose. Mrs. Henrietta, indeed, the youngest daughter, does appear to have been indiscreet, and 'though she did not in the least intend it, yet she begs your pardon,' and for himself, his Lordship, after expressions of personal regard, would like to add:

. . . without flattery to you, and with great sincerity that I believe our gracious master, His Majesty, is so fortunate in employing you in his service, that, if he should lose you, it would be very difficult for His Majesty to find a successor so well qualified in all respects for his service, if we consider both your integrity, vast abilities, industry, and zealous affections for his service; and, if His Majesty were asked the question, I will hold ten to one His Majesty declares himself of my opinion. . . .

Dr. Tanner's assumption is, I think, a fair one, that Pepys mended his ways, not merely because he now earned a larger income by legitimate means, but because in his new responsibility he was so eager for the discipline of the service that he felt that least of all must there be any compromise in his own practice. We know from the terms of his will that when he died he believed himself to be a heavy creditor of the government, and the probability is that during his terms of service at the Admiralty, far from receiving more than his due, he shared the fate of much humbler persons than himself who looked to the naval Treasury as paymaster. A strange light is thrown upon the ethical notions entertained by the Crown in this matter, by an entry made by Pepys himself, apparently in all good faith, in the Admiralty minute-book under date November 14, 1674.

The petition also of a poor woman, Katherine Rawlins, now attending, being read, and praying that in consideration of her husband's being killed in his Majesty's service, and her being left with several children, besides that wherewith she is now big; His Majesty and my Lords, as in a matter for extraordinary charity, were pleased to order the present payment of the wages due on her said husband's ticket.

If the claims set out by Pepys in his will were just, he seems not to have been regarded as an object for such extraordinary charity himself.

That Pepys in his new prosperity was not unmindful of old connections may be shown by one agreeable incident. In 1674, the Duke of Monmouth, a member of the Commission to which Pepys was secretary, was installed Chancellor of the University of Cambridge. In the same year, Thomas Ross, who had been the Duke's tutor in exile, and was now the King's Librarian, wrote to Pepys that his Grace had put forward his request to Dr. Barrow, Master of Trinity, but that he feared for its practicability. The request was that the Duke should exert his influence in obtaining a Trinity Fellowship for John Montagu, Lord Sandwich's son, whom we remember with his twin brother Oliver at Huntingdon Grammar School, now a young man of eighteen. Ten days later, Pepys heard from his young cousin in terms of unmeasured gratitude that the application had succeeded. It was this John Montagu who became Master of Trinity in 1683, Vice-Chancellor in 1687, and Dean of Durham in 1699. His grandniece, Lady Mary Wortley

Montagu, remembered him as 'a venerable figure, meek
and benign in aspect, with silver locks, over-shadowed by a
black velvet cap,' in striking contrast to his elder brother
Sydney, 'seated majestically in his elbow chair, talking very
loud and swearing boisterously at the servants.' John lived
until 1728, and at the close of an honoured career he may
well have remembered with respect the kinsman to whom at
eighteen he had written a little heavily: 'Though I really
believe you are a man of that temper that the expression
of my gratitude to you for your last obligation, if heartily
represented but in one word, will be as significant as if it
were in twenty; yet I would by no means omit a duty which
is requisite in such cases, be the persons never so acquainted
one with another.'

It is pleasant to note that three years after this incident,
Pepys was still careful of the Sandwich interest. Writing in
1677 to the second Earl, now just on thirty years of age,
that he hears of an intended visit to France, Pepys does
not think

. . . it would stand with my duty to let pass such an opportunity of letting your Lordship know that as none owes
so much, so as few shall pay more, either of affection,
honour, or endeavours of service to you and your honourable family than myself; and that therefore if in any
of the circumstances under which it has pleased God to
place me I may be in any sort useful to your Lordship
or it, I beg you will not either overlook your own right
of commanding or deny me the honour and satisfaction
of discharging myself towards your Lordship as becomes . . .

Before reaching the crisis that in 1679 interrupted, and
for a time threatened wholly to ruin, Pepys's career, a few
notes on his personal affairs may be gathered from scattered sources. In 1677, Dr. Burton, a Fellow of Magdalene,
wrote to Pepys: 'Sir—, The foundation of that building in

our College, to which you are pleased to contribute, is now laid, and they begin to want moneys to go on with it.' The new building is now known by the provision of Pepys's will as Bibliotheca Pepysiana and is the present home of his library. In a Master's book at Magdalene, compiled by Daniel Waterland (Master 1713–1740) it is stated that Pepys contributed £60 to the building, which apparently includes a donation of £10 entered in a steward's book of an earlier date.

In 1675 Pepys sent a portrait of himself to his friend Thomas Hill, then in Lisbon. Sir Lionel Cust suggests in his *Notes on the Portraits of Samuel Pepys* that it was a replica of the picture done by Hales in 1666. No other attribution seems to fit the date, though a more recent sitting would seem to be indicated by the recipient's lyrical thanks. 'The picture is beyond praise, but causes admiration in all that see it. Its posture so stately and magnificent, and it hits so naturally your proportion and the noble air of your face, that I remain immovable before it hours together.' In the same year a Mr. Gibbon wrote to Pepys, asking him whether it was true that he had seen a ghost. He hoped that it was so, as such an event would confirm 'the opinions of the ancient Romans concerning their genii,' and confute 'those of the Sadducees and Epicures.' Pepys's reply to this enquiry has unhappily not been preserved. In 1675, too, Pepys wrote to a friend in France asking him for 'one of Gamboust's maps of Paris, which is the best I have seen, either of that or any other city. I would be glad also to recruit myself with what the Fire robbed me of, namely, of all the heads of persons of quality cut by Nanteuil.' He asks the same correspondent for any documents 'either in print or manuscript' concerning the French Navy. He was, in fact, still indulging his tastes as a connoisseur, and he was steadily accumulating material for the great naval history that was constantly in his mind and never to be written. Notes on an immense variety of topics, made in this connection between the years 1680 and 1696, are contained in the *Naval Minutes,* edited by Dr. Tanner.

BIBLIOTHECA PEPYSIANA, MAGDALENE COLLEGE, CAMBRIDGE.

After W. WESTALL. *From* "*History of Cambridge.*"

But that Pepys was cautious in his enlightenments, we learn from another letter of this date. In September, 1675, he recommended a young man, Daniel Skinner, the son of an old friend, to the notice of the British Ambassador at Nimeghen. In November Skinner, who may have been related to the Cyriack Skinner of Milton's sonnet *On His Blindness,* and who in any case had in his possession certain of the poet's Latin manuscripts, wrote from Rotterdam to thank Pepys for his service, and begging his further help. Before leaving England the young man had approached Sir Joseph Williamson, the responsible Secretary of State, for leave to print his manuscripts. Milton's name was obnoxious to authority, and permission was refused. Skinner acquiesced in the decision without question, and further took Sir Joseph's advice not to contemplate doing anything in the matter in Holland, but on arriving in that country he learnt that the Ambassador had been warned of him as a dangerous person who designed to publish the works of one yet more dangerous. In consequence, he found himself cut off from employment, and appealed to Pepys for assistance. Within a week the Secretary of the Admiralty wrote saying that he had called upon Sir Joseph Williamson, and with no very satisfactory result:

. . . such apprehensions do still remain in him of the possible impressions which Mr. Milton and his writings may have wrought in you as that I do not find him to be prevailed with for the absolving you presently of the crime which this inadvertency of yours has exposed you to the suspicion of; and yet I can as little say that I can find the least cause of charging him with any more unkindness towards you than upon the like consideration I think I should myself have had towards my own brother in the same case; my opinion also concurring with his, that some time must be suffered to pass before you can reasonably look to have this unfortunate concernment of yours with Mr. Milton and his writings forgotten or your in-

nocence therein so cleared as that you may recover Sir
J. W.'s fair opinion concerning it.

Milton had been dead two years. It has already been
pointed out that there is nothing to show that Pepys had
any consciousness of the great poet who at the Restoration
had disappeared into obscurity. But it is no credit to a man
with so bright, and on the whole so liberal, a mind, that
he should have regarded Milton merely as a deterimental
agitator against whose influence youth was to be warned.

In 1677, Pepys wrote desiring the Duke of York to bespeak for him the Crown interest in the forfeit estate of a
suicide 'who drowned himself in his own well on Sunday
night last.' The request was conformable to the conscience
of the age, and doubtless it would not occur to Pepys that
it was a barbarous one. We are not told whether it was
granted. Much more agreeable is Pepys's association at this
time with John Locke, the philosopher, a man of his own
age to within a year, already known for his scholarship and
wisdom, but not for twelve years yet to publish *An Essay
Concerning Human Understanding*. In September, 1677,
Pepys wrote to Lady Banks, the wife of the friend who had
served him so well as a witness at the time of the Castle
Rising election, discoursing at large upon her family affairs.
Speaking of his 'pretty countrywoman,' her Ladyship's
daughter, he strongly discourages the prospect of a match
with 'a stranger of so mercenary a courtship as Sir T. M.,
with his pretended £7,000 a year, has shewn himself to be,
to pass her time I know not where, out of sight and hearing in the backside of the kingdom.' As for her son, he
would have him recalled for a short time from Paris, 'for
I am in no wise satisfied that matters either are or are now
likely to come into that posture which I could wish they
were in between him and Mr. Locke [who had been the
boy's tutor in Paris since May]; and I know no so decent
and inoffensive a way of parting them as this of calling
Mr. Bankes into England.' The difference between tutor
and pupil, however, seems to have been composed, possibly

through Pepys's agency, since we find that in the following August he writes an affectionate letter to his young friend, whom he addresses as 'Dear Son,' assuring him that he has 'all along made it my work to shew my most worthy friends your father and mother not only the importance of your travel . . . but the encouragement they have every way met with from you to indulge you all reasonable scope in it under so great a security as they have for its being well used; I mean your own private virtue and the conduct of so excellent a friend and director as Mr. Locke.' He has therefore obtained leave for the travellers to proceed so far as 'Tholouse' but not a step further. 'But truly (child), when I consider how much use one of your application will make of what you have seen, and the anxieties under which I find your poor mother daily to live on your behalf, there is a justice due to her which I think the keeping your back longer upon home would be the offering great violence to.' And by the same post he wrote to Locke informing him of the extended leave, and adding, 'I do think Mr. Bankes may reasonably bound his desire of travel at Tholouse, and from thence make his coming back as delightful and instructive as by your directions he can. . . . For what respects yourself, I have upon ample grounds been long your honourer, making you (with my beloved Mr. Bankes) a great piece of my care.' But a month later he is still writing to his 'Dear Son' that he is trying to persuade his parents to indulge his wish to travel into Italy, though with some misgivings arising 'from pure tenderness towards my poor Lady your mother.' This was on the 26th of September. On the 30th, permission has been granted, and 'credit is sent for money without limitation, both at Genova and Livorne.' Pepys mentions that he has had to make certain undertakings in order to allay maternal anxiety, and on October 10th in a further letter these are specified. The young man is to pay strict regard to his health, if not for his own sake then for his mother's. He is to advise her once a week that he is doing so, and with what success. He is to arrange his journey that in no case shall the promise given by himself, and 'as deliberately declared on the part of my honoured friend Mr. Locke,' to return by the spring be broken. And, finally, he shall in all things, 'what I persuade myself is not more your present practice than your pleasure,' rely 'upon the advice and guidance of Mr. Locke, without whom (in exclusion to all the world besides) I persuade myself it had been impossible to have wrought either upon your father or mother to the point they have been prevailed upon in, nor could I have ever solicited for it with half the satisfaction wherewith I have now done it, so much of our rest concerning you is placed upon our just esteem of his conduct and your regard thereto.' We do not hear what later befell young Bankes. The Italian journey was stopped by bad weather conditions. Nor is there further record of the friendship between Pepys and Locke. In 1694, Evelyn wrote to the former: 'I am told our friend Dr. Locke has made addition to his excellent *Essay,* which may be had without a necessitie of purchasing the whole booke,' which Pepys declares in his reply to be a 'Usefull sample for further reprinters; I hope it will bee folowed, in bookes at least of value,' and in 1699, Pepys, at what he asserts to be the serious request of Lord Clarendon, 'who you know is a great saladist and a curious,' asks his nephew John Jackson in Italy to 'dust your letters to me with Roman lettice-seed; it being what he tells me Mr. Locke . . . used heretofore to do for him.' Locke, who was born a year earlier than Pepys, died a year later. The Bankes episode gives promise of pleasant intercourse between the two men, and Evelyn's 'our friend Dr. Locke' suggests that something came of it, though it cannot have been encouraged by Locke's intimacy with Shaftesbury when in the time now approaching that nobleman returned to his persecution of Pepys.

As member for Castle Rising, Pepys took no conspicuous part in parliamentary affairs, beyond an occasional and effective intervention when naval business was before the House. Such an occasion was the proposal in 1677 to provide £600,000 for the new shipbuilding programme. In a

speech of considerable length Pepys, with a precise mastery
of his material, placed the present conditions and future
necessities of the Navy before the House, and it was largely
due to his presentation of the case that the act voting so
large a sum was passed. He kept on civil if not very intimate terms with his constituency. In 1675, he addressed
a letter of general compliment to the Mayor of Castle
Rising and announced his desire to contribute £50 towards
the repair of the parish church, which sum he had now
placed in the hands of a cousin with local connections, to be
paid on demand. The builders of Rising, however, seem to
have been leisurely folk, for no application was made for
the money until the beginning of 1679, by which time the
current of Pepys's public life was becoming violently disturbed.

At the end of 1678, Pepys may have been a little weary
of the immensely detailed routine of his work. It is clear
from the Admiralty Letters and Journal that his official
responsibility was an extremely heavy one. Although the
Commission of 1673 had acquitted itself with considerable
credit, conflicting interests, personal jealousies, and royal
caprice distracted the councils at which Pepys had to keep
a clear head, of which he had to preserve an exact record,
and to the orders of which he had to give immediate effect.
He was daily faced by the danger of some lapse which a
long record of duties faithfully performed would not condone. And although his clerks, as we know William Hewer
did, may have served him with devoted attention, his responsibility was shared by nobody. He was, to a degree that
is perhaps not possible in the civil service of modern times,
the sole and personal agent through which the decisions of
a great State department were put into operation. But if,
as he was afterwards to declare, the strain at times became
almost intolerable, it was in fact borne by an executive mind
that proved itself equal to all occasions, and although his
Secretaryship brought him great anxieties, it brought him
also increasing honours. And had his way of life not been
suddenly convulsed, he would doubtless have gone on bear-

ing the burdens and reaping the rewards of his place without serious question. But in November of 1678 came the first of a succession of crises that in the following months were to crowd one upon another.

In September, the infamous Titus Oates had sworn before Sir Edmund Berry Godfrey, a magistrate of great ability and strong Protestant convictions, information concerning his alleged discovery of a popish plot to assassinate the King and make England a vassal of the Roman Church. On October 12th, Sir Edmund disappeared, and on the 17th his body was found in a ditch on Primrose Hill. The crime was at once loudly advertised by Oates to be a fresh outrage committed by the papists, and among the persons thereupon arrested was Samuel Atkins, one of Pepys's clerks. Atkins himself was an insignificant object of attention, but Oates in his anti-papist frenzy was like an armed maniac who had run amok. Moreover, his aim was directed through Atkins at more distinguished victims. Oates was encouraged in his criminal fanaticism by Shaftesbury, who was in disgrace at Court and at bitter enmity with the Duke of York. The murder of Sir Edmund Berry Godfrey, which it is by no means impossible had been contrived by Oates himself, terrorised popular feeling, and added fresh momentum to the attack that was being delivered by Oates and his confederates. These Jesuits could brutally destroy a great and respected magistrate who had done no more than listen sympathetically to a case; clearly, they would stop at nothing, and the scene was laid for the panic-stricken orgy in which Oates was to become a paid informer at £40 a month, and some forty innocent persons were to be sent to the gallows.

The charge against Atkins was that of being accessory to the murder; it was alleged that he had been seen with others removing the body from the place of the crime to the ditch where it had been found. The trial did not come on until February, 1679, when Atkins was able to prove so convincing an alibi that the jury accepted it without retiring, and the prisoner was acquitted. But in the meantime a letter from Pepys to his sister Paulina Jackson at Brampton shows how anxiously alive he was to the dangers of the situation. On December 5, 1678, he wrote:

One misfortune there is indeed which has created me much trouble, namely, that by a manifest contrivance one of my clerks (Atkins) has been accused and is now in custody as a party some way concerned in the death of Sir Edmundbury Godfroy; which (though most untrue) cannot be thought to pass in the world at so jealous a time as this without some reflections upon me as his master, and on that score does occasion me not a little disquiet. But I thank God I have not only my innocence to satisfy myself with, but such an assurance of his also as that I make no question of his being able to acquit himself with advantage to him and infamy to his accusers; and that being done, the care which this accident occasions me will soon be over.

In the mean time, pray desire my Father to give no way to any fears concerning me, for that I bless God I have lived so carefully in the discharge of my duty to the King my master and the laws I live under, both towards God and towards men, that I have not one unjust deed or thought to answer for, and consequently neither am myself, nor would pray him to be, under the least doubt or care what can befall me, it being of no use to any man in my place to think of supporting himself by any other means that has such an innocence as mine to rely on, and there, I bless God, lies my comfort, whatever befall me.

The reassuring tone, intended by Pepys to comfort a father whom he loved, is not convincing. He knew, indeed, that Atkins was likely to be provided with an adequate defence, since the witnesses to be called included the officers of a ship who would testify that at the time of Atkins's alleged participation in the crime he was in their company on board. But Pepys knew also that his danger would not be at an end with the acquittal of his clerk. He knew that

the charge had been fabricated in the hope that Atkins
would in evidence say things damaging to himself. Shaftesbury's vindictiveness was not likely to be appeased, and it
was, further, directed not only against Pepys but against a
man whom Pepys had for years regarded with particular
and unfeigned devotion as his master. The Duke of York
better than any man appreciated Pepys's value as a naval
servant, and in his letters addressed to the Secretary there
is a note of what may be said to amount to personal affection. If Pepys could be laid by the heels there was at least
a chance that he might compromise the Duke in his fall,
and as Oates's reign of terror gathered fury the Secretary
knew that he was a marked man. For the time being he
allowed nothing in the conduct of his business to betray his
apprehensions, but he deceived himself with no sense of
false security.

In January the King dissolved Parliament, and writs were
then issued for the summoning of its successor in the following March. Pepys wrote at once to the Mayor and Burgesses of Castle Rising, assuring them 'as I shall always
esteem myself under great obligations for the favour I have
already enjoyed from you, so am I most ready and desirous
of continuing in the quality of your servant in the approaching Parliament.' He encloses the letter to his cousin, asking him to further his interests as he thinks fit, and hoping
that the recollection of his heavy expenses at the previous
election and his promised contribution to the church will
stand him in good stead. He suggests that at his cousin's
discretion the contribution may even be enlarged. Also, it
seems, having bought some property in the town, he has
himself become 'a small burger.' Altogether he has good
reason to suppose that his claims will not be overlooked.
But the Mayor and burgesses of Castle Rising had taken
alarm. They remembered that when they had returned
Pepys to Parliament in 1673 there had been ugly questions
reflecting a little inconveniently perhaps upon themselves.
And now there were reports of further trouble. Samuel
Atkins's arrest might mean nothing; on the other hand it

might mean a great deal. In any case Castle Rising was taking no risks, and on February 1st, Pepys acknowledges a letter from his cousin announcing that his candidature is not to be put forward:

GOOD COSEN,—I do kindly thank you for your letter of yesterday, assuring you that I am not surprised, much less under any disappointment, from the contents of it, I knowing the world too well to expect more than is to be found in it; and I think mine to you did enough shew that what I asked was rather out of respect to the Town of Riseing (as having once been their servant) than from any such advantage I proposed to myself by it as would suffer me to give way to your entering upon any expense for it; I having the good fortune of being so much better understood elsewhere as to have at this time invitations from the Magistracy of no less than three Corporations (of somewhat greater names, though not more in my esteem than that of theirs) to accept of their elections.

The Corporations 'of somewhat greater names' were Harwich, Portsmouth, and an Isle of Wight borough. On February 5th, Pepys wrote to the Governor of the Isle of Wight, saying that he is 'under a firm determination to stand for Harwich, however I be chosen at Portsmouth or elsewhere,' and for Harwich he was duly elected. On March 15th, with the new Parliament in being, Pepys received an application from Castle Rising for his £50 for the church. As the Mayor and burgesses had not only failed even to answer his letter of January 25th, but had given countenance to the renewed scandal against him, they deserved, in a word of Pepys's own usage, 'snuffe' for this, and they got it.

This show of high spirits and his success at Harwich notwithstanding, Pepys at the opening of the new Parliament knew himself to be still in very troubled waters. He preserved his composure; on March 10th he writes to Dr. Gale, the High Master of St. Paul's, asking for a nautical

reference from Lucian, and on the 20th to a surgeon at
Chatham enquiring whether a certain medicine that he had
from him some time since will have retained its virtue, as
he wishes to give it to a lady who has fits which she is
unable to cure by her perseverance in a course of 'Jesuit's
powder.' But in a letter of April 18th to Sir John Holmes,
Commander-in-Chief on the Downs, Pepys returns to his
graver preoccupations. So irksome to those responsible in
the Navy has become the constant application to Parliament for money, and so crippling the lack of it, that:

. . . were the encouragements of my employment ten-fold
what they are or what the world takes them to be, they
should not invite me to hold it one year more upon the
terms I have now done it for several, unless his Majesty's
express commands require it from me, which with bread
and water shall render everything sufferable to me, but
without that, nothing.

Behind this resolution there was much more than appears
in the letter itself. Affairs at the Admiralty were on the eve
of a crisis that Pepys knew could not be long postponed.
The new Parliament was proposing to investigate the state
of the Navy, and already before its assembling the likelihood that this would happen had resulted in high feeling at
the Admiralty Board. In January the Lords had in effect
accused the King of exceeding his prerogative as defined in
the Commission, and had desired him to furnish them
through the Secretary with a report that should enable
them to deal with any charges that might be brought
against them. This the King declined to do, and after a
meeting on April 19th, the Secretary at the end of a lengthy
minute unexpectedly signs his name 'S. Pepys,' as though
marking the termination of a chapter in his life. On the day
before, he had written his letter to Holmes, and now two
days later a new Privy Council was sworn, and with it a
new Commission for the execution of the office of Lord
High Admiral of England. It was a Commission of new

names, but the King proposed to retain the old Secretary.
For the moment Pepys continued to discharge his duties, but
his view of his own position must be told in a notable letter
which he wrote to the Duke of York on May 6th:

. . . How his Majesty has been pleased (among his other
great changes) to dispose of the Admiralty by a new
Commission . . . your Highnesse (I doubt not) has
many days since known; nor shall I think it becoming
mee to interpose any thoughts of mine touching his Majesty's choice therein, more than that (for his and his
service's sake) I could wish his naval action to be for
time such as might allow these worthy gentlemen opportunity of being informed in the work of their great office
before they be urged to much execution in it. . . .

For what concerns my own particular, your Highnesse
was pleased to foretell mee at your going hence what I
was soon after to look for; and it is come to pass. For,
whether I will or noe, a Papist I must be, because favoured by your Royall Highness. . . . But how injuri-
ously soever some would make those just endeavours of
mine towards your Highness inconsistent with Protes-
tancy, neither they, nor any ill usage I can receive from
them for it, shall (by the grace of God) make mee any
more quitt the one than I suspect your Royall Highness
will ever take offence at my perseverance in the t'other.

His Majesty indeed is pleased to express a much more
favourable opinion of me and my slender qualifications
for his service than I dare own any right to, and (as an
instance thereof) has not spared to tell mee how much
weight he is pleased to place upon my experience in the
Navy for supplying, by my Secretaryshipp, what his present choice of Commissioners may possibly be found less
perfect in. Nor shall I think it becoming me to dispute
the giving his Majesty my service on whatever terms he
shall think fitt to require it from mee.

But as your Royall Highness well knows how far I
had not long since made it my humble motion, and

pressed it upon your favour, that after almost 20 years'
continued drudgery in the Navy, to the rendring my selfe
almost blind, and otherwise disabled in health to support it much longer, his Majesty would be pleased to take
the residue of my small service by admitting mee into the
Commission of the Admiralty, so truly (Sir) I have now
upon other considerations purely relative to his service
made the same motion to the King upon occasion of this
change. For if I was truly conscious of being become
less able to bear the fatigue of my office any longer under
a Commission that had many members of it competently
furnished for its execution, besides the easy and help-
full recourse I had at all times had to his Majesty himselfe (and your Royall Highness in matters needing it and
those, as old a Navy-man as I am, not a few), how much
less fitt ought I to think myselfe to goe through this
task when, not only stript of all those helps, but (to say
no worse) charged with a new piece of duty, and that not
a little one, of informing those who should informe and
are to command me, and I remain accountable for all the
ill success that should attend my obeying those commands, though possibly differing from my own advice?

Besides, however fairly some of these gentlemen
seemed disposed towards my continuance in this Secretaryshipp, yet that complyance of theirs I well know to
be grounded upon some opinion they have of the neces-
saryness of my service to them till they have obtained a
stock of knowledge of their own, and then, Farewell.
But others there bee with whom, your Royall Highnesse
knows . . . I have for many years lived in a constant
state of war, they censuring and I defending the manage-
ments of the navy. . . .

Whereto I have humbly to add, what some have not
spared publickly to let fly in opposition to my continuance
in this office, namely, that so long as Mr. Pepys should
be there, his Royall Highness remains in effect Admiral.
In which, though they doe mee a much greater honour
than either I deserve, or their malignity designs mee,

yet, Sir, I cannot but so far consider the importance of having all rubbs removed, which may bee either of impediment to the happy going on of this great part of the King's service or give any unnecessary occasions of keeping alive the jealousies touching your Royall Highnesse, that if his Majesty may as well secure to himselfe the full use of my service, and your Highnesse receive no less content from my being in the Commission than in my present post (which you were pleased, upon my former motion to that purpose, to express your well-likeing of), I see no inconvenience (but to myselfe) likely to arise from his Majesty's giving them the satisfaction of his withdrawing mee from this invidious Secretaryshipp, I being for these reasons not only contented to submitt to, but desire it, and shall bee most ready to give my assistance in this Commission with the same faithfulness and industry (though not with the same fullness of private satisfaction) wherewith I ought, and should, were your Royall Highness your selfe at the head of it.

Which haveing said, I make it my humble prayer to your Royall Highness . . . to enforce from yourselfe this my humble proposal to his Majesty, for my being transferred from the Secretaryshipp into the Commission; your Royall Highnesse well knowing that however bounteous you have always been to mee in your frequent callings on mee to the improvement of your favour to my benefit with his Majesty, I have never to this day done it to the obtaining sixpence from the Crown by any boone extraordinary beyond the plain allowance of my office, and not that neither. . . .

Soe as while the sincerity of my wishes for the weal of his service prompts mee to this voluntary divesting myselfe of my present employment, I should be in very ill condition to bear its not being made up to mee by his Majesty's granting (for his service's sake, as well as in his justice to your Royall Highnesse's mediation and his own promises in my favour) the latter part of my motion for his placeing mee in the Commission, or at least making some other provision for mee, as one super-annuated in his service.

No apology will be deemed necessary for quoting at this considerable length from a letter which is both an admirable example of Pepys's elaborate and yet perfectly controlled ceremony and a document of the highest biographical importance. The sequel to the letter was remarkable. James acknowledged it on May 23d, enclosing a copy of a letter he had the day before addressed to the King recommending Pepys's suit in the handsomest possible terms. To grant it would, he tells his brother, be to the advantage of the Commission and to the honour of the Crown in acknowledging the claims of one in every way so worthy of consideration. He speaks plainly: 'for give me leave to say, your Majesty is bound to do something for him that has spent so many years in your service to your satisfaction.' And to Pepys himself: 'truly I hope His Majesty will do it; I am sure he ought, and it will do more good to reward one old servant than to take off twenty mutineers.' Pepys's answer, written on the 9th, was dated from the Tower of London: 'For what concerns your Royal Highness's particular goodness to me, in your late letter to His Majesty, the condition I am in puts it out of my power to apply it to my benefit; but not so as to make me any thing doubtful of the fruits of it in His Majesty's justice, so soon as the justice I am waiting for from lower hands shall put me into a capacity of asking it.'

Such was the pass to which things had now come. 'For whether I will or no, a Papist I must be, because favoured by your Royal Highness.' On April 28th, a committee had been appointed by the House to conduct the long intended naval enquiry. The chairman was William Harbord, the sitting member for Thetford, in Norfolk, a constituency in the near and in the present circumstances perhaps the dangerous neighbourhood of Castle Rising. He was a son of the family with whom Pepys had already had not very amiable association through their connection with the Earl

of Sandwich, and he was, moreover, freely credited with
the desire himself to become Secretary of the Admiralty.
Whatever his motives, he was a willing party to any designs
against Pepys, and there can be little doubt that he abused
his position as chairman of the newly appointed committee
to admit evidence of the most preposterous kind against the
man whose place he hoped to get. This was readily forthcoming. Two witnesses, of antecedents as to which there
was a prudent silence, appeared before the committee with
a story of fantastic improbability. One of these was John
James, a butler who had been dismissed from Pepys's service. The other was an adventurer named John Scott, who
needs a little more extended notice.

In 1662, he had received from one Major Gotherson
£2,000 for lands which he said that he had bought from
the Indians on Long Island. Five years later, Gotherson's
widow asked the Governor of New York to let her know
the exact condition of her Long Island estate, which it was
proved did not exist. The lady thereupon petitioned the
Duke of York for an enquiry, and Pepys was ordered to investigate Scott's record. It turned out to be one of swindling
on an extensive scale, and Pepys's report exposed him as
no better than a common criminal. An account of his male-
factions is given in G. D. Scull's pamphlet *Dorothea Scott,
Otherwise Gotherson and Hogben,* published in 1882, but
it is not clear how it came about that Scott, although he
was a fugitive from American justice, was able to return
to England without being in danger of arrest in this country. But return he did, and Pepys was warned that it was
with a fixed determination to be revenged. Scott, assuming
the rank of Colonel, associated himself with Oates, and
getting himself called before the committee announced that
it was within his knowledge that Sir Anthony Deane and
Mr. Samuel Pepys had betrayed naval secrets to France,
and conspired with the government of that country to overthrow the Protestant Crown and Church in England.

This precious rigmarole was supported by the needy butler, who confessed a year later on his deathbed that he had

been paid for his evidence by no less a person than William Harbord himself. In April, 1673, Thomas Hill had written from Lisbon recommending to his friend's notice 'a young man, born in Flanders, but bred in Rome, who has a most admirable voice, and sings rarely to his Theorbo, and with great skill. This young man lives with a nobleman, upon a very mean salary; and having been formerly in England, most passionately desires to return thither again.' Eighteen months later, Hill renewed the application, and Pepys replied that 'if you conceive my silent and unemcumbered guise of life will sort with him; and that £30 a-year certain (to be increased as you shall direct, or at my courtesy upon proof of his service), with his lodging and entertainment, will invite him to come to me, he shall not only on his part be welcome, and possibly find me not the most uneasy to be lived with; but myself . . . shall . . . find in him a servant not of less real use by his languages, in reading, writing, translating, or other offices depending thereon, than satisfaction to myself in his excellent qualifications in music, in which my utmost luxury still lies, and is likely to remain so.' More than six months later Hill wrote again: 'I am in great expectation to hear how you approve of my choice in your servant, Cesare Morelli. It would be exceeding satisfactory to me to hear that you like his manner of singing. I think it is well; his ability of performing at sight the most difficult part is to be valued, and I have seldom met with any person that excels him.' Morelli lived in Pepys's house for over two years, but at the end of 1678, Pepys was beginning to realise that the presence of a Catholic in his establishment might be dangerous, and he turned to another merchant friend, James Houblon, for advice. In November of that year, Houblon wrote: 'I have discoursed M. Morelli, and according to your desire, have used all the arguments I could think of against the errors of the Romish Church. . . . But, Sir, I must tell you, I find Morelli so resolved in his religion, that it will be in vain to hope his conversion. . . . I am sorry, Sir, you have not your desires in seeing him a good Protestant. As to the other point, of his necessary removing out of your house, I have propounded to him going to Brentwood, where he would be well received, and upon moderate terms.' But Morelli thought he would prefer to go to Flanders, if Pepys would be so kind as to finance him for that purpose. That he changed his mind, however, we know from a letter written a week later from Brentwood, informing Pepys that he has been received into the house of a most obliging family, that the situation is very pleasant, and the air 'more pure than at London, and consequently favourable to my voice,' which he hopes to improve, without forgetting his lute. He trusts that his departure will have relieved his patron in some part at least of his present difficulties.

Of the accomplished but harmless young musician, great effect was made by John James in his evidence before Harbord's committee. Morelli, it appeared, if the truth had to be told, was almost certainly a Jesuit priest in disguise. Incredible as it may seem, the testimony of this beggarly pair of rascals was reported by the committee to the House on May 20th as being sufficient to convict both Pepys and Deane. In the course of his defence before the house, according to the report in Volume VII of Gray's *Debates,* Pepys was able to state without contradiction that although he had been in attendance upon the committee he had until that moment heard nothing of the accusation brought by Scott and James. Flatly denying every word of the former's evidence in detail, he concluded with the declaration, ' 'Tis Scott's "Yea by report"; 'Tis my "No, before God Almighty." ' And then, 'As for this James, this is an Information of a servant against his master, and a Member of the House, and that Member never called to the Committee to hear it.' The occasion of James's discharge is then revealed, and it must be confessed that it is one towards which Pepys himself cannot have been wholly unsympathetic; indeed, he went so far as to concede that 'It was Sunday three o'clock in the morning (the better day the better deed).'

Subsequently, however, he had 'cause of suspicion that James came within my House at a window, and robbed me.' He then gave the facts concerning Morelli:

As for Morelli, my leisure will not permit me to go abroad for diversion, and I sent abroad for a man of learning and a good musician. A merchant, one Hill, sent me over Morelli. His qualifications are these: he is a thorough-bred scholar, and may be the greatest master of music of any we have. He came to Lisbon, a page to a great man, and my friend Thomas Hill found him out there for me. I have entertained myself harmlessly with him, singing with his lute till twelve o'clock, till it was time to rest. At Lisbon, he was thought so moderate a Catholic that he was under some suspicion. There is a member that knows him so well to be a harmless person, that I need say no more.

The charge of conspiracy with France was so absurd as in any reasonable circumstances to have defeated itself, but reason for the moment had been discarded in public deliberations. Harbord pressed his advantage, though he was driven by the unsatisfactory nature of the evidence before the House to protest heatedly: 'Pepys is an ill man and I will prove him so.' Sir William Coventry informed the House that James had previously been in his employ, and that while he did not 'love to do ill offices to one that has served me . . . his service was not so direct, as to recommend him to a friend.' Sir Francis Rolle observed that Mr. Pepys appeared to be singularly unfortunate in his servants: 'one accused to be in the Plot, another, his best maid, found in bed with his Butler! another accused to be a Jesuit!' Pepys replied that he hoped it was no crime to be so, and added, in a taking phrase, 'that I am unfortunate is my misfortune.'

But the tide of suspicion was running too strongly for such pleasantries to take effect, and Harbord had his way. Pepys and Deane were committed to the custody of the

Sergeant at Arms. On the following day, May 21st, as we learn from the Journals of the House of Commons, the committee was 'empowered to examine the Matter of Fact.' On the 22d, Harbord, offering no evidence, assured the House among other things, that he could prove Pepys to be 'either a papist himself or a great favourer of that Party.' At the close of the debate, Pepys and Deane were removed to the prison of the Tower, and Harbord was instructed to 'acquaint Mr. Attorney General with the Evidence' relating to the charges against them.

Pepys, with characteristic energy, at once set about collecting evidence for his defence. Monstrous as were the charges against him, there was now nothing for it but to meet them clause by clause. Within a week he had made a start, Morelli writing to him on May 29th, acknowledging a favour of five guineas, for which he was infinitely obliged, and naming ten persons of character who could all agree 'in my not having been known at Lisbon as a priest, much less a Jesuit. Had I been such, I should have been obliged, on pain of excommunication, to clothe myself as a priest in Portugal, instead of living at Lisbon four years in the same dress I wear here.' An old friend wrote to Pepys hoping that by the time the letter came into his hands he would 'have weathered that storm, which Satan Scott has so unskilfully conjured to alarm you.' He also hoped that Pepys's virtue would so improve his affliction as to cover his enemies in confusion, and expected 'by the first, to hear you are disentangled of this vexation.' But June 2d was not a day propitious for such confidence, for on it Pepys and Deane were brought to the Bar of the King's Bench, and the Attorney General opposed bail, talking oracularly of more treasonable correspondence with France that was shortly to be produced against the prisoners, who returned in custody to the Tower. On the 4th, Evelyn wrote in his diary: 'I dined with Mr. Pepys in the Tower, he having been committed by the House of Commons for misdemeanours at the Admiralty when he was secretary: I believe he was unjustly charged.' On the 9th, Pepys wrote his let-

ter to the Duke of York, saying that he was now in no
condition to profit by the Duke's application to the King,
but assuring his Royal Highness of his duty and allegiance
to his sovereign, and his gratitude 'which even that Protes-
tancy of mine the world would be thought so doubtful of,
exacts from me towards your Highness, and shall have it to
the last point of my fortune and life.' On the following day
he received a request from a young gentleman who was
expecting a legacy of £1,000, and in the meantime would
like to borrow £50. Pepys replied that as he had come to the
Tower so suddenly, he was short of ready cash himself, and
so could not oblige. During the next month the two friends
were twice again brought to the King's Bench, and twice
again the Attorney General was happy to inform the Court
that startling disclosures would shortly be made. But on
July 9th, after Evelyn on the 3d had again visited Pepys,
to dine on a piece of venison which he had himself sent to
his friend, the Court had had enough of it, and informed
the sanguine Attorney that until he was able to be a little
more substantial in his performances the prisoners would
be released on bail. That the Court nevertheless took a serious view of the matter is clear from the fact that they
fixed the security at no less than £30,000. It was now that
the solid worth of Pepys's reputation among his friends was
manifested. James Houblon brought up his great mercantile
connections, the money was provided on the spot by four
bailors, and Pepys, although not yet a free man, had no
longer to fight for his vindication in the confinement of the
Tower.

In September he was still writing to Morelli, requiring
an exact account that should 'contradict anything that may
happen to be suggested by those who have maliciously in-
vented the story of your being a priest,' asking if he is
sufficiently supplied with wine, and consulting with him
'about the use of the table, which you have given me for
the guitar; for the little knowledge in music which I have,
never was of more use to me than it is now, under the
molestations of mind which I have at this time, more than

ordinary, to contend with.' He proposes an early call to learn more of this, having in the meantime 'nothing remaining in my hands to practise upon, but the Lamentations of Jeremiah.' On October 23d, he appeared again before the Court, asking for a day to be fixed for his trial, but 'found nobody to be heard of to prosecute me, my accuser being withdrawn (or at least absconding) and Mr. Harbord, my old prosecutor, not appearing. So, as all I could have, was to be continued in the state I am in till the end of the term, in expectation of what my adversaries may offer towards prosecution within that time.' His friends were of opinion that at the end of term he would be discharged, but he left nothing to chance. He continued to organise his defence, and on January 6, 1680, he wrote to the Duke of York thanking him for his assistance in securing fresh evidence of 'the artifices of Scott and his patron, Mr. Harbord.' Encouraged by this new information, he forwarded on the same day thirteen specific questions to Mrs. Gotherson concerning Scott, which were answered on the 17th to his complete satisfaction. It was clear that there would be little difficulty in convicting Scott of false pretences, embezzlement, and the abduction of Mrs. Gotherson's son, or in proving that he was now a fugitive from justice. In February, Pepys and Deane were excused their bail but not yet discharged. On the 25th, Pepys wrote to a friend of Harbord's saying that the butler James was on his deathbed and wished to make a confession. A week later, he wrote to a clerical acquaintance bespeaking his attention 'for the sick man, for whose soul's health I am truly concerned, however he has been misled, to the occasioning me much evil.' Before the end of March James the butler was dead, and Pepys wrote to Morelli that it had 'pleased God . . . to bring him to consideration and confession of the wrongs he has been tempted to do towards me and you, which he has largely, solemnly, and publicly done, on receiving the holy sacrament.' The proceedings against Pepys did not finally collapse until the end of June, 1680, and on July 1st he wrote: 'I would not omit giving you the knowledge of

my having at last obtained what with as much reason I
might have expected a year ago, my full discharge from
the bondage I have, from one villain's practice, so long lain
under.'

Throughout his anxieties Pepys had been steadfastly supported by the friend who twenty years before had more
than once had his ears boxed as a boy in the household at
Seething Lane. William Hewer's name was, indeed, popu-
larly associated with that of Pepys in the scurrilous pamphlets provoked by the prosecution. A characteristic passage
may be given from one of these, entitled *Plain Truth or a
Private Discourse between P. and H.*

H.—There is a Purser of a Fourth-rate, that does not love
the Sea, will give me 300 Guinnys for the vacancy of this
first-rate, being he has a mind to stay at home; and then
for the Fourth-rate, I have got one C. that will give
me three score Guinnys for that imploy; and I will take
it, though it be too little.

P.—I will go, and have both the Warrants signed to-night.
But have you the money?

Hewer was not publicly involved in the charges, but close
association with Pepys at the time was dangerous, and it
is to Hewer's honour that he did not for a moment shrink
from the personal risks involved. Among the Rawlinson
manuscripts in the Bodleian Library are a number of
Hewer's letters to Pepys, which show the younger man's
devotion to his friend and master in a very pleasant light.
In 1675, when Hewer was at sea on official business, and,
it seems, in some dejection, he wrote to Pepys, 'I have made
bold to give you a little trouble in a Will left with my
Mother,' and in the event of 'my doing otherwise than well
in this present journey, you will be pleased to afford her
your help and assistance, which will be the greatest Conduct
that can ever be done me.' And in a further note, acknowledging Pepys's promise in case of necessity, he wrote in a
strain that for more than twenty-five years was to be re-

flected in his conduct, 'both myselfe and fortune shall ever be at your command, and . . . liveing or dying I shall remain to the end your faithfull servant.'

When Pepys was released from the Tower in June, 1679, he was a man without employment, and, since his residence had been an official one, without a home. Hewer's profession that not only his devotion, but his fortune, was at his friend's service was not an idle one, since his family seems to have been of substantial means. He was now living with his mother in a house known as York Buildings, taken in his name. It occupied the right-hand corner at the river end of Buckingham Street, Strand, and although the old building has been demolished, the lovely watergate that was known and used by Pepys may still be seen, secluded now by the Embankment from the busy life of which it was once a feature. Within a few weeks of his release from the Tower, Pepys was writing from the house that was for many years to be his home, gratefully acknowledging that he had received from Hewer 'the care, kindliness, and faithfulness of a son.' The house was rented in Hewer's name until 1685, when Pepys took over the tenancy, but doubtless from the time when the charges against Pepys were finally withdrawn in June, 1680, and he was free to make settled arrangements for himself again, the two friends were running and bearing the cost of a joint establishment. At that time Pepys was forty-seven years of age and Hewer nine years younger. To Pepys the new arrangement was a deliverance from what must have been at the time serious domestic anxiety, and we shall see shortly that Hewer regarded it with no less satisfaction.

On February 28, 1679, the King wrote to his brother James the following letter printed by David Dalrymple in 1766, in an Appendix to his edition of the account of Charles's escape from Worcester.

Whitehall, Feb. 28th 1679

I have already given you my reasons, at large, why you should absent yourself for some time beyond sea; as I am truly sorry for the occasion, so you may be sure I shall never desire it longer than it shall be absolutely necessary, both for your good and my service. In the mean time, I think it proper to give you under my hand, that I expect this compliance from you, and desire that it may be as soon as conveniently you can. You may easily believe with what trouble I write this to you, there being nothing I am more sensible of than the constant kindness you have ever had for me. And I hope you are so just to me, as to be assured that no absence, nor any thing else, can ever change me from being truly and entirely yours,

C. R.

So dangerous, indeed, was the Duke's unpopularity that he twice had to withdraw from England for a short period, but in spite of his own insecurity he continued to be of what assistance he could to the man whose public service and private character had earned an esteem of greater warmth than was often stirred in the nature of the last Stuart king. It is true that James had nothing to lose in patronising a Catholic suspect, since his own adherence to Catholicism was publicly known. Charles, on the other hand, as we have pointed out, had much to fear in any such association, but the admirers of that King's many qualities cannot but wish that he had here been stauncher. When in 1667 he abandoned Clarendon, he was guilty of lamentable ingratitude. Clarendon in power had unquestionably become an exceedingly tiresome fellow, but nothing short of plain treason could have justified the King in allowing disgrace to overtake a man who during his exile and restoration had served him with an almost epic loyalty. And when the mind and morals of the public were thrown into a panic by the disgraceful orgies of Oates in 1679 and 1680, Charles has again to be charged with a serious failure in his obligations. There were many cases in which he weakly allowed his terrorised Courts to break men whom he must have known to

YORK BUILDINGS (EXTREME RIGHT)

Engraved after JOHN BOYDELL *from a painting made after the erection of Westminster Bridge in 1750. By courtesy of* ROBSON'S GALLERY.

be innocent, and there is no case in the annals of these persecutions that reflected less credit on the King than that of
Pepys. Charles probably knew the Admiralty Secretary as
intimately as it was possible for any sovereign to know a
subordinate official. He had on several occasions shown his
sense of Pepys's worth by distinguished personal notice. He
must have known the story of Pepys's having sold naval
secrets to France for the infamous invention that it was,
and ten minutes of his time would have been sufficient to
expose the solemn recital about crucifixes and altars as no
less. He would have taken no risks in holding out a helping
hand to a man who was on many scores his creditor, and
he neglected to perform this act of common decency. It is
remarkable that Pepys does not seem to have considered
that he had any such claim upon royal bounty. It must be
remembered that for more than a year he had been in very
grave danger. When in February, 1680, he wrote of his
being involved 'even to the hazard of my life and estate,'
he was not exaggerating. If Harbord had been able to
prove in open court half the things he swore to in the House
of Commons, Pepys would have been uncommonly lucky to
escape with his life. His own knowledge that Scott and
James were rascals was cold comfort. He had to prove
them as such to the world, and he knew very well that this
was going to be no easy matter, no easy matter at least
to get his proofs accepted by a prejudiced Court. Happily
for him, Harbord was unable to induce either of his creatures to face the ordeal of cross-examination, or he may
even have come to his own decision that such effrontery
would overreach itself. But in the meantime, while Pepys
was industriously collecting everything he could in the way
of evidence from the many scenes of Scott's exploits, his
position was desperately precarious. He could, it must seem,
with every propriety have turned to the King in what might
at any moment prove to be his extremity, and he refrained
from doing so. There is in the situation a modest echo of
the splendid loyalty with which Montrose went from

Charles in exile to Scotland, with the understanding that if he miscarried he and not his Prince was to be responsible. The only explanation of Pepys's failure to appeal to the King when a word might have meant so much must be that he regarded the King's convenience as being of greater consequence than his own safety. Perhaps as a devoted subject he was right. But there can be no doubt that Charles was wrong.

CHAPTER VIII

BRAMPTON. SCOTLAND. TANGIER. THE ADMIRALTY AGAIN

WHEN Pepys was discharged in June 1680, he left the Court a free man, but with no express vindication of his character. The prosecution had merely faded away, it had not been answered before the world to the satisfaction of a judge and jury. And while he was able to resume his old relations with the many friends whose respect and affection he had not forfeited, he knew now and for many years to come that danger was in his path, and we find him wary still in his movements, anxious in his precautions against a further crisis. Significantly enough, among his first activities on regaining his freedom was the resumption of his attendance at Court. On September 9, 1679, the *Domestic Intelligence or News from City and Country* published the following notice:

We are informed that the last week Samuel Pepys went to Windsor, having the confidence to think he might kiss the king's hand. But meeting with a person of honour, and acquainting him with his intent, he was told that it was strange he would presume to come to Court, since he stood charged with treason; who, it is said, shewed his innocency was such that he did not value anything he was accused of, which he did not doubt but to make appear at the next Term, at which time it seems his tryal comes on: And thereupon addressed himself to some other persons, and prevailed with them so far as to be introduced into His Majestie's presence; but, however, could not be admitted to the honour he desired.

In two subsequent issues, September 19th and 26th, the Journal was compelled to offer the following apology:

These are to give notice, that all and every part of the relation, published in *Domestic Intelligence* the 9th . . . instant . . . touching Samuel Pepys Esq. is, as to the matter, and every particular circumstance therein mentioned, altogether false and scandalous; there having no such passage happened, nor anything that might give occasion for that report.

The withdrawal was no doubt as warrantable as it was abject, and in March, 1680, that is to say before Pepys had been discharged, but when his relief from bail had already made his discharge a matter of course, he wrote to his father:

I am commanded to attend the King the next week at Newmarket, and, by the grace of God, will go, and wait on you one day, in my going or return, which I presume will be either Tuesday or Saturday next. Designing to set forth hence on Monday, I shall rather choose to call upon you in my going, which will be on Tuesday, for fear lest I should be commanded to accompany the Court to London, where the King designs to be this day sevennight.

We have no evidence that he actually did wait upon the King at Newmarket in March, but we know that he was doing so in October, since on the second of that month he wrote to James Houblon that he was in Newmarket for the purpose of getting some redress 'upon the arrear due to me for my almost twenty years' service'; and complaining that although the ministers were with the King, there was 'not a word of business . . . there seeming nothing now in motion but dogs, hawks, and horses; so that all matters look as if they were left to God Almighty to look after, and much more happy it might have been for us all had they been long ago so.'

It was on the following days, Sunday October 3d and Tuesday October 5th, that Pepys took down from the King's dictation the celebrated account of his Majesty's escape from England after the Battle of Worcester in 1650. Although Pepys himself later transcribed his short-hand notes, the document was not published until 1766, when it appeared under the editorship of David Dalrymple in the volume referred to above. In May 1681, the Duke of York wrote to Pepys: 'Pray send mee a copy of the Relation of his Majesty's Escape from Worcester; 'tis only for my own satisfaction, and I shall let no copys be taken of it.' To which Pepys replied:

For what your Royall Highness is pleased to command from mee touching the Worcester-Paper, my covetous-ness of rendring it as perfect as the memory of any of the survivers (interested in any part of that memorable story) can enable mee to make it, has led mee into so many and distant enquirys relating thereto, as have kept mee out of a capacity of putting it together as I would, and it ought, and shall be, so soon as ever I can possess myselfe of all the memorialls I am in expectation of to-wards it. Which I shall alsoe (for your Royall High-nesse's satisfaction) use my utmost industry in the hast-ning; begging your R[oyal] [Highness] in the mean time to receive this transcript of what I took from his Majesty's own mouth, with a considerable addition I have since obtained to it in writing from Colonel Philips, suit-able to what I am promised and daily look for from Father Hurleston. Which humbly tendering to your R[oyal] H[ighness], I do in all humility remaine, May it please, etc., Your R[oyal] H[ighness]'s most dutifull, faithfull, and obedient servant,

S. P.

In his edition, Dalrymple included Pepys's own notes and those collected from Colonel Philips and Father Hurleston (Huddleston). The narrative was included in the Bohn edition of Grammont's *Memoirs,* and it is described in some detail in my book on Charles II. It does not concern us here, but it is noteworthy as evidence that Pepys was again on terms with the King.

In Pepys's letter to Houblon, dated October 2d, there is a passage that reads strangely in the light of our knowledge: 'What will be my success in it [the business of the arrears], I do not yet certainly forsee; but hope two days more will tell it me, and send me homewards, with a halt of one day only in Huntingdonshire, where I have not yet been.' We have seen that when he proposed visiting Newmarket in March, Pepys had announced his intention of spending a day with his father, and now in October the letter to Houblon suggests that he had had a similar intention. But on the 4th of that month his father was buried at Brampton Church, the entry in the register reading: '1680. Mr. John Pepys gent was buryed ye 4th of October.' The death must have been sudden, and the news of it delayed by having to reach Pepys through London. The domestic circumstances of the event are obscure. Of Pepys's family after the date of the Diary, but scanty information has survived, though it is not difficult to reconstruct with some probability in brief outline the later fortunes of the Brampton household. A little more than a year after Paulina had married John Jackson, Pepys noted in his Diary that they were 'going shortly to live at Ellington of themselves, and will keep malting, and grazing of cattle.' On the same date, walking with his father in the Brampton garden, they consulted as to 'what to do with him and this house when Pall and her husband go away; and I think it will be to let it, and he go live with her, though I am against letting the house for any long time, because of having it to retire to ourselves.' A year later, in May 1669, Pepys found his brother John 'come to town from Ellington, where among other things, he tells me the first news that my sister Jackson is with child.' The will of Pepys's father, which unfortunately bears no date, begins: 'Memorandum. That I, John Pepys of Ellington, in the County of Huntingdon, gent^{n} . . .' which makes it clear that at some period after 1668 the arrangement that John Pepys should live with his daughter in that village was carried out. As the will mentions his son, John, as then living, and as John died in 1677, it must have been drawn up not later than that year. In it, he left forty shillings to the poor of Ellington and five pounds to the poor of Brampton, in the church of which latter parish he desired to be buried. Mr. Whitear, in his highly valuable *More Pepysiana,* is a little doubtful of Wheatley's statement that John Pepys died at Brampton; 'If so,' he says, 'then he must have returned there.' The administration of his estate merely describes him as 'late of Brampton.' But on May 20, 1680, Dr. Turner, the Rector of Eynesbury, of whom we have heard before, wrote to Pepys: 'I give you many thanks for great kindness to me at London. I have been at Brampton. The old gentleman and the rest of the famly have good health; and fewer complaints were made than I have been accustomed to hear from them. I heartily wish you also may have less trouble in that kind. Your father thanks you for the care of his watch.' This shows conclusively that by this date, in any case, John Pepys was back again at the Brampton house. Further, there was no one then living who could be referred to as 'the rest of the family' other than the Jacksons, who now had two young sons, Samuel and John. There is, moreover, a familiar ring about the customary complaints. The likelihood approaches certainty that at a date which cannot be fixed, the Ellington establishment had been closed, its inmates returning as an undivided family to Brampton.

There is further evidence to support this view. On August 26, 1680, Dr. Turner again wrote to Pepys, saying that he had been to Brampton, and assuring him of his assistance 'upon all occasions.' On September 3d Pepys acknowledges this letter, and a later one of August 30th, with 'most faithful thanks for your extraordinary friendship,' and proceeds, 'Since it has pleased God to have put this sickness upon my brother Jackson, I shall respite the offering you any new trouble on that subject till the event of that sickness appears.' Although convinced from the foregoing evidence that John Jackson was living at Brampton at the time of his death, I could find no entry in the Brampton church register to support the theory. In the Ellington register, however, where the burial entries for 1680 are almost indecipherable, the parchment having decayed, careful inspection under a glass revealed the following: '——Jackson——rampt——d September the first.' This undoubtedly is what remains of 'John Jackson [? gent] of Brampton buried September the first.' The only possible meaning of the 'of Brampton' in the entry is that this was his last place of residence, which confirms our deduction. We have seen that in May, 1669, Paulina had moved with her husband to Ellington, and was expecting a child. From an even less decipherable entry among the baptisms in the Ellington register for that year can just be recovered the words: 'Samuel son—John——Jackson.' But in 1673, the following clear record is preserved: 'John sonne of John and Paulina Jackson baptized December the 17.' We know, then, that the Jacksons left Brampton for Ellington not later than 1669, that they were still there in 1673, and that some time between that date and 1680 they returned to Brampton where John Jackson died. It appears from Pepys's letter of September 3d, that the news of this event was two or three days at least in reaching him, but that is a matter for no surprise. It may be mentioned that in the Ellington register there is recorded in 1673 the burial of a John, son of John Jackson, on September 22d, that is to say three months before the baptism above noted. It is possible that Paulina lost an infant son, John, and gave his name to the child born three months later.

Although Pepys was not at Brampton for his father's funeral on October 4th, some time during the month he arrived there for the purpose of settling the family affairs.

Two or three letters that have survived from the later years of his father's life show Pepys lacking neither in consideration, affection, nor a sense of responsibility. In the autumn of 1677, he had called his own London surgeon in to advise on his father's health, and was already showing a concern for the future of his nephews. On September 1st, he wrote:

I hope ere this come to your hand you will have received mine of the 28th of the last, with one enclosed from Mr. Hollyer, to which I much long for an answer, and hope to receive it by Monday's post, that I may understand the present condition of your health, with the effects of his advice and what you shall please to direct me to supply you further with from hence, and particularly about some wine.

With regard to his sister's business he had already in June written to his father, in an unpublished letter, proposing to settle his Brampton estate on his nephews 'in case I die without children as in all probability I shall.' In the letter of September 1st, he added:

I have determined upon taking some advice here more than my own therein, that I may as much as it is possible secure myself against any imputation of doing anything misbecoming an honest man towards my cosens, and prevent my sister and her children's meeting with any occasions of future disputes by my seeing all grounds of dispute removed while I am in being, that may best see it done.

On the 15th of the same month, he wrote again:

I do in the enclosed to Sir John Barnard return you my answer to your desires about our Brampton affair, which, as I hope it will be satisfactory to you and my sister, so

I pray God it may have the good effect to the benefit of her children which you design.

Of the actual disposition of the Brampton property at his death we shall hear later, but now, in October 1680, his father's death revived controversy between various branches of the family, and Pepys was at Brampton for a month or more composing it as best he could. During his absence from London, Hewer, in a series of letters to be found in the Rawlinson MSS., kept him constantly informed as to domestic and public business. Pepys was still adding any useful scraps that he could to his dossier on Scott, and on this and such other delicate topics Hewer wrote to him in cypher. Scott, in fact, was to make a brief reappearance on the scene later, but at the moment he was misbehaving him self most satisfactorily, and in the *Intelligence* of May 20, 1681, where he is described as 'a lusty tall man, squint-eyed, thin-faced, wears a peruke sometimes and has a very h—— look,' it was announced that he had killed a hackney coachman who did not fancy him as a fare. Among other reassuring news at this time, Pepys was informed that a chest containing dangerous documents had been sent to Clapham, where Hewer had now acquired an interest in the house which both men were later to make their home. That Paulina was with her brother at Brampton we know from several messages sent by Hewer, of which the first is in a letter dated October 26th: 'Present my Mothers and owne respecte and service to your Sister.' On the 28th, Pepys was told that a servant at York Buildings, 'Katherine is taken very ill and has kept her bedd this 2 or 3 days, the Coach-man being not yet recovered though it is hoped that he is somewhat better than he was.' On the 30th, Hewer wrote: 'I am glad you have been able to procure a Court to be held at Brampton this day, and that you are in a way of com-pasing the like at Bougden for dispatching your owne & Sister's Affairs relating to those Courts . . . Wee are heartily sorry to understand that your Sister's Ague con-tinues soe strong upon her, wishing that she may be ridd of

it, before the winter comes on too fast.' On November 2d,
Katherine and the coachman were better, though Hewer
was distressed to hear that his friend had been much inconvenienced by the debauchery of another coachman who had
accompanied him to Brampton. But the letter crossed with
one from Pepys announcing: 'Notwithstanding what I
wrote in my last about your coachman, he has made such
submissions and promises of amendment, that I shall not
pursue my resolution of sending him presently up, but will
see if he will keep his word with me.' From a letter of November 6th we learn that Hewer was still in Office employment, he 'haveing spent most parte of the day in attending
on the Comm^rs. for Tanger, and the Lords Comm^rs. of the
Treasury about adjusting some matters relating to Tanger,'
and on the same day upon a motion in Council relating to
Salutes, the King was pleased 'to respite the doeing any
thing therein till they had discoursed you.' On the 9th, the
coachman is of opinion that as the horses at Brampton
have little work to do, 'less corne than what was usually
allowed them here may be enough.' Apart from his family
business, Pepys appears to have been engaged at Brampton in the preparation of some sort of memorandum on his
recent troubles, and on November 11th, Hewer wrote: 'I
am heartily glad to understand, that you have to your
owne satisfaction gone soe farr in the finishing the worke,
you were upon, as to bee able to despatch it by Saturday,
and tho' I beleive upon further consideration you will not
thinke fitt to expose it to publick view just at this time, yet
I doe beleive you will finde it very necessary to furnish some
of your friends with it.'

Pepys, however, in the midst of his anxieties was suffering from no loss of spirits. On November 14th, he wrote
to one of his Houblon friends proposing to keep himself
fresh in remembrance by sending a present of his picture
and 'a small bribe' to everyone in the family to get them
when passing by to 'look upon it; as thus: "Was Mr. Pepys
in these clothes, father, when you used to go to the Tower
to him?" Or thus: "Lord, cousin, how hath this business

of Scott altered my poor cousin Pepys since this was done?"
Or thus: "What would I give for a plot, Jemmy, to get
you laid by the heels, that I might see what this Mr. Pepys
would do for you." ' On the 15th, Hewer wrote to Pepys
that against his return he was providing 'a Mourneing
Chariott for a month's time, and shall meete you at High-
gate with it, in regard it will be, on many considerations
(besides that of the respect you designe to pay the de-
creased), fitte for you to appear in here in towne.' On the
16th, Hewer changed his plans, proposing to meet his
friend at Barnet on the following Friday, the 19th, 'about
11 of the clocke in the morneing, but not with the mourneing chariott, in regard the ways are so badd.' And it was
in this letter that Hewer spoke from his heart of the satisfaction with which he thought of Pepys as his companion
at York Buildings:

And as to the reguard you have, & which you soe kindly
mention in relation to myselfe, as I know nothing can
make my life more uneasie to me, than you makeing any
other place your home, while I have one, soe I am sure,
if it shall not be thought inconvenient for you (to which
for your sake I shall always submitt) your being with me,
can't be any to me, assuring you whatever times shall
come, nothing shall withhold me from makeing you &
your concerne, my owne, while I live, and tho' the Integrity and faithfullness wherewith his Ma^{ty}. and the
publique have for soe many yeares been served by us,
may not at present protect and support us from malitious
Reports & Calumnys of evill men, yet I am satisfyed that
God-Almighty, who is always just, will make it upp to us
some other way to the shame of those who doe now triumph over us, and I thanke God, if I know my owne
heart, I am much more contented in my present condition than I ever was in any.

The letter marks the close of Pepys's visit to Brampton
on this occasion. He was there again in August of 1681,

when he acknowledged a 'most obliging message to me at
Brampton, from whence I have been a week returned.'
Although it is not stated, family business was no doubt the
purpose of his visit. We have no record of his personal association with Brampton after that date. That the house there
remained in the tenancy of his family is clear from a letter
written on April 4, 1682, by Esther St. Michel, Balthasar's
wife. This lady, who makes several appearances in the
Diary, had more than once given Pepys cause for concern.
In the early days of her marriage in 1662, he had noted her
as 'a most little, and yet, I believe, pretty old girl, not handsome, nor has anything in the world pleasing, but they say
she plays mighty well on the Base Violl.' A few months
later, his opinion was modified. He found, indeed, that
she played on the viol 'pretty well for a girl, but my expectation is much deceived in her, not only for that, but in her
spirit, she being I perceive a very subtle witty jade, and
one that will give her husband trouble enough as little as
she is, whereas I took her heretofore for a very child and
a simple fool.' In 1665, she had become 'a pretty little
modest woman,' and in the following year he found her still
improving. In September of 1666, however, Pepys had from
his wife 'an account of great differences between her mother
and Balty's wife. The old woman charges her with going
abroad and staying out late, and painting in the absence
of her husband, and I know not what; and they grow proud,
both he and she, and do not help their father and mother
out of what I help them to, which I do not like, nor my
wife.' And a month later we find Elizabeth Pepys calling to
see her brother, 'who is sick, and she believes is from some
discontent his wife hath given him by her loose carriage,
which, he is told, and hath found has been very suspicious in
his absence, which I am sorry for.' Esther had been only
seventeen years of age when she married Balthasar St.
Michel, so that in 1682 she would be thirty-seven. Her
letter to Pepys is dated from Brampton, and suggests that
she had been keeping house, and keeping it in familiar disorder, during the absence of Paulina, who, as we know from

a letter written by Pepys to his cousin Roger at Impington on March 6, 1681, had been spending some time in London under medical supervision.

HONOURED COUSIN—This comes to kiss your hands, and my cousin your Lady's, with many thanks for her and your last favours at Impington: since which it hath pleased God, by a continued sickness of my Sister's, to prevent my coming to any determination touching my house at Brampton; for that my thoughts therein would be much governed by my having or not having her to reside there, for the better looking after my small affairs, as well as her own, about that place, my dependencies here being still such as will not, I doubt, for some time, give me leisure to retire thither myself; which, as public matters go, without any hopes in my view of their bettering, is the first thing I could wish to compass. But my Sister's illness being become such as our best physicians here, where she has for some months been, can give me no assurance of any speedy recovery, I find it inconvenient for me to delay any longer my taking some resolutions in that matter; and, therefore, remembering, though imperfectly, a motion you were pleased to make to me about this house, when I last waited on you, I thought it becoming me to advertise you so far of it, as may give me the satisfaction of knowing whether, in my proceeding therein, I can have any opportunity of serving you.

From Esther St. Michel's letter which follows, it seems that the proposal to transfer the house to Roger Pepys fell through:

Brampton, April 4, 1682.

HONOURED SIR,
    I have received yours of the 1st instant, wherein you are pleased to let me know of Madam Jackson's return

to your own house at Brampton, which she is mistress of, were it mine.

It will be no trouble to me or straitness, if it proves not so to her, to find your lodgings crowded with people which have not ever had the honour of Madam Jackson's acquaintance, besides the meanness of our capacity in all respects, especially that of entertainment according to her merits, and as your sister. But to that I shall say no more, since your honour hath mentioned it already.

What I have to say to Madam Jackson I shall omit till her return to Brampton. In the mean time I wish her a good and speedy journey, and safe progress in her affairs.

With the dutiful services of my family and self, I remain

> Your honour's obedient servant,
> and ever obliged,
> ESTHER ST. MICHELL.

The date of Paulina Jackson's death seems hitherto to have escaped notice. Mr. Whitear corrects Wheatley's statement that she died in 1680, pointing to the above-noted letter to Roger Pepys as proof that she was alive in 1681. In fact, Esther St. Michel's letter shows that Paulina returned to Brampton in 1682, and we know that she was there at the time of her death in 1689, the Brampton church register for that year containing the entry: 'Mrs. Pauline Jackson was buried 9ber 21.'

The letter to his cousin Roger shows that as late as 1681 Pepys still had thoughts of retiring to Brampton. The house, in accordance with the provisions made by his uncle Robert, passed into his possession at the death of his father, and it was natural that he should think of his own property in this connection. But the eagerness with which he once had thought of moving with his wife to the pleasant little dwelling within ten minutes' walk of Hinchingbrooke had passed. His wife, my Lord and Lady were dead. Hinchingbrooke was occupied by a young earl with whom

he had no ties other than a civil regard for the sake of old
loyalties. The growing intimacy of his relationship with
William Hewer, although it had at present decided nothing as to his future, was already opening up to their part-
nership at York Buildings prospects in which Brampton was
not included. At the moment Pepys was a man of no settled
occupation, but from 1683 he was to be in official employment that continued until the time of his sister's death.
During that period we may suppose that he finally discarded the idea of permanent residence at Brampton. When
she died, Paulina's sons were grown youths, and the elder,
Samuel, appears to have lived on at Brampton, since Pepys
in his will, dated August, 1701, made a bequest, afterwards
revoked in a codicil, 'To my well-beloved nephew, Samuel
Jackson, of Brampton aforesaid, gentleman.' Pepys, therefore, had a continued personal interest in the estate until
the end of his life, and on a trial bookplate, of which the
date, although it cannot be fixed with certainty, is probably
1684, he described himself as 'Samuel Pepys of Brampton
in Huntingdonshire, Esq. Secretary of the Admiralty to his
Ma^ty., King Charles the second: Descended of ye Antient
family of Pepys of Cottenham in Cambridgeshire.' It is
likely that in his later years business necessitated occasional
visits into Huntingdonshire, but once his father's affairs
were settled Brampton became little more for him than a
property to be managed from a distance.

After two hundred and fifty years, Pepys survives, though
but dimly, in the tradition of the neighbourhood that he
once knew so well. The name of his 'antient family' has
long since disappeared from Cottenham, situated sixteen
miles away from Brampton on the outskirts of Cambridge,
but the Manor House that was once its seat still stands,
put now to uses that make it but a dejected memorial of the
past. In All Saints Church, we read upon a panel that 'Mrs.
Catherine Pepys in 1703 gave by will a Commonable House
and £100 since laid out in a purchase of land for a schoolmaster to instruct 16 poor children,' and on another which
has been removed into the church from its original site:

'This school-house being demolished by the Fall of the Steeple A. D. 1617 was rebuilt A. D. 1699 at the charge of Mrs. Katherin Pepys . . .' In the registers of the same church are to be found records of a generation earlier than Samuel's, and here, among entries that commemorate such worthies as Old Father Rush, Old Mother Phillips, Goodman Page, and John Atkins An Ancient Man, we may learn that Uncle Apollo who was baptized in 1575 appears to have set a fashion, since Apollo Badcock appears in 1580. Thomas Pepis was churchwarden in 1604, and Mr. Robert Pepys Sepultus erat 26 martii 1610. In Westrope's *Year Book,* an engaging little annual published by Mr. Westrope at his printing works in Cottenham from 1908 to 1915, a few fragments of Pepysian interest have been preserved. Among the signatories to an agreement between sundry lords of manors and the freeholders of Cottenham in 1596, the name of Pepys, variably spelt, appears seven times, once impressively as Robert Pepis de Norff. Mr. Westrope tells us of 'many old deeds,' in which are cited the 'Seven Men of Cottenham,' overseers of the township, among them George Pepys the elder. But in an undertaking made by leading 'Inhabitants of Cottenham' in 1695 to pay tithes to Dr. Thomas Jekyll the rector, Dr. John Pepys is the sole remaining representative of the family, with a holding of twenty-one acres.

At Ellington, some three miles to the northwest of Brampton, there is no surviving memory of the John Jackson who once went there to 'keep malting, and grazing of cattle,' but a charity is still disbursed to reinforce the yield of five shillings from one field and thirteen and fourpence from another towards the provision of a yearly loaf of bread to every inhabitant of the parish. If this be not the fruits of John Pepys's forty shillings, that humble benefaction has disappeared. It is only in recent times that the Grammar School at Huntingdon has taken to itself any pride in numbering among its scholars not only Oliver Cromwell but Samuel Pepys. At Hinchingbrooke the honour of the obscure kinsman whose fortunes rose with those

of the first Sandwich has never been allowed to fall into dis-
use. The activities, indeed, of one Carte enriched the Bodleian Library at the expense of Hinchingbrooke with many
papers that tell us of the friendship that began when Pepys
was a boy at Brampton and Edward Montagu a lieutenant
of the *Ironsides*. A letter or two and a few references to
Pepys in Sandwich's manuscript Journals are all the memo-
rials in this kind that are to be found in Hinchingbrooke
to-day; but of the place itself, Nunn's Bridge, the walled
terrace, the gatehouse, and many other features, have survived the changes that have befallen the house since Pepys
knew it, and his name is securely cherished in the annals of
the Montagu family.

At Brampton little remains of Pepys's time, but that little is happily not insignificant, although Mr. S. Inskip
Ladds, in a learned and valuable paper on the parish published as recently as 1906 in the *Transactions of the Cambridgeshire and Huntingdonshire Archæological Society,*
could write: 'Of the birthplace of Samuel Pepys in this parish, I can say but little. He mentions it once or twice and
gives an amusing account of a midnight search for some
money he had buried in the garden.' As the Brampton references in the Diary alone amount to something like forty
pages, this notice seems to be inadequate. There are but
three buildings that can be said with certainty to have been
known to Pepys: the church, the Black Bull Inn, and his
own house. The Black Bull, standing a little to the south
of the church on the same side of the road, in Pepys's time
was known as the Bull, under which name it is still licenced,
its later sign notwithstanding. Local tradition has it that
one of its rooms was once a magistrate's court; the parish
stocks are said to have stood at the fork of the road a few
yards away. Certain entries made by Pepys in the Diary
help us to determine with reasonable certainty the tenancy
in his time. When at Brampton in 1662, he had sent to
Goody Stankes for some beer 'very small and fresh, with a
little taste of worme wood, which ever after did please me
very well.' The Stankeses, that is to say, were publicans. A

year later, on September 15, 1663, he was in Brampton again with his uncle Thomas and his cousin, when we remember that owing to a shortage of beds the visitors were sent 'to Stankes's to bed,' and on the next day, after a long sitting in the Brampton court, Pepys went down to see his uncle at the Bull, from which the conclusion is clear that the Bull was kept by Goody Stankes and her family.

In the registers of Brampton Church the burials are recorded, as we have seen, of Robert Pepys, his uncle, Margaret and John, his mother and father, and Paulina, his sister. The only grave of which any trace remains is that of Paulina, to whom there is now an almost indecipherable slab at the west end of the nave. The legible part of the inscription is as follows: 'Here lyeth ye Body of Mrs. Paulina Jackson wid ye last of ye Family of ye Peps in this Parish Dyed November ye 17, 1689.'

The Pepys house has inevitably undergone several structural alterations since his time, but the essential character of the old north wing has been preserved. The internal beams, remarkable for their freshness, the pitch of the roof, and the Tudor brick work of the fireplaces, are all as they must have been in the seventeenth century. There can be little doubt that it was in the large open chimneypiece of what is now the hall, that Pepys saw his uncle's coffin when he arrived from London on that late July evening in 1661. We know that during his lifetime additions were made to the house, and there is at least an even chance that these included the upper room in the east corner of the south wing, which is more than a century later in character than the old building, and has architectural suggestions of the last years of the seventeenth century. What was the extent of Pepys's garden cannot now be told. There are remnants of box that might belong to any age, and there is a strangely formal hedge stretching away into the fields that seems to have no relation to its surroundings and might be a survival of a considerable garden enclosure. Also the sunk fence, now rebricked, may well enough have been a feature known to Pepys. But this is guesswork. It is sufficient that the old part of the house is substantially as it was when Pepys owned it, and that the surrounding landscape has known little or no change since his time. His homes in St. Bride's Churchyard, Axe Yard, Seething Lane, Derby House, York Buildings, and Clapham have disappeared; the little low-roofed house at Brampton, with its 'pretty parlour,' of which at one time he had 'hoped to make a very good seat,' survives alone with reminders of his familiar presence.

Though Pepys was still the mark of his enemies, he had suffered no loss of prestige with his friends, nor, apparently, was his influence considered to have been much diminished. In 1681, we find his interest being sought by applicants for official and academic posts, and in August of that year strong representations were made to him from Cambridge that he should offer himself for election to the vacant Provostship of King's. Although he was informed that his candidature would be welcomed not only by the College but by the whole University and that the King would be inclined to disregard the statute requiring the elected candidate to be in deacon's orders, Pepys at first declined to consider the proposal, there being necessary 'a much greater stock of academic knowledge to the capacitating a man to fill this province . . . than I am furnished with, or, at this time of day, can with any industry ever hope to acquire.' Upon further persuasion, he went so far as to discuss the conditions of his acceptance. He proposed to devote the whole or a large part of the stipend of £700 to public uses in the College, remaining free to employ himself for 'the benefit of the King my master, and the satisfaction of his royal highness the Duke of York, in putting together . . . my collections so many years in the navy and admiralty, which nothing but an entire leisure will ever enable me to do.' He mentions, as another inducement, the proximity of Cambridge to his 'small concernments' at Brampton. The project, however, came to nothing.

With his recovering fortunes, he did not relax in necessary prudence. He continued to assist Morelli, whom we find acknowledging with most hearty thanks seven pounds

PEPYS HOUSE, BRAMPTON

Photograph by E. S. Whitney.

stirling, his wants being 'mighty great, being quite un-
provided of linen and clothes.' But while desiring his protégé to prepare songs which are to be sung with Mrs.
Houblon, he desires that he shall be seen in town as little
as possible, gossip still being active. Mr. Harbord, however, had been discouraged in his persecutions, and he interfered with Pepys no more. He even brought himself to
make civil enquiries of Hewer on meeting him casually at
the House. And as the months went by, Pepys was not without reason in hoping that he might yet again find employment in the service that he had made his life's work. In the
spring of 1682, prospects brightened.

The Duke of York, no longer in exile, but an inconvenient
figure at the Court of St. James's, was at that time sent to
Scotland on a mission of domestic and religious conciliation,
and Pepys was a member of the suite attending him. On
May 6th, Hewer wrote: 'hoping that this will find you in
health, and safely arrived at Edinburgh.' It was by the mere
grace of fortune that Pepys arrived at all. The Duke sailed
on the *Gloucester*. 'Though I had abundant invitation,'
wrote Pepys, 'to have gone on board the Duke, I chose
rather, for room's sake and accomodation, to keep my
yacht, where I had nobody but Sir C. Musgrove and our
servants.' The *Gloucester* was wrecked off the Humber,
and although the Duke was saved many lives were lost.
Writing on May 8th to Hewer from Edinburgh, Pepys
reported his own safety, and also that he had been present
at the scene of the wreck.

Our fortune was, and the rest of the yachts, to be near
the *Gloucester* when she struck; between which and her
final sinking, there passed not, I believe, a full hour; the
Duke and all about him being in bed, and, to show his
security, the pilot himself, till waking by her knocks.

The Duke himself, by the single care of Col. Legg,
was first sent off in a boat, with none but Mr. Churchill
[afterwards Duke of Marlborough] in her, to prevent
his being oppressed with men labouring their escapes:

some two or three, however, did fling themselves after him into her, and my Lord President of Scotland [James, Marquis of Montrose], by the Duke's advice, endeavoured it, but, falling short, was taken up out of the water by him.

Mr. Legg (then) looking after his own safety, got into a boat, and was received on board us with Capt. Macdonnell, Mr. Fortry, one of the Duke's bedchamber, and some poor men unknown: we had also the good fortune to take up Sir Charles Scarborough, almost dead, and others spent with struggling in the water and cold; but were prevented in our doing so much good as we would, by our own boat's being easily sunk by our side, and her men with much difficulty saved. Had this fallen out but two hours sooner in the morning, or the yachts at the usual distance they had all the time before been, the Duke himself and every soul had perished; nor ought I to be less sensible of God's immediate mercy to myself, in directing me, contrary to my purpose at my first coming out, and the Duke's kind welcome to me when on board him in the River, to keep to the yacht; for many will, I doubt, be found lost, as well or better qualified for saving themselves, by swimming and otherwise, than I might have been.

On May 13th Hewer wrote to Pepys in an unpublished letter to be found in the Rawlinson MSS., 'The welcomest Newes I ever received in my Life was what you were pleased to honour mee with by yours of the 8th inst from Edinburgh . . . you cann't imagine in what Consternation all your friends in general were upon the Report of your being cast away,' and on the same date Houblon wrote:

SIR,

Mr. Hewer, bringing last night your letter of the 8th from Edinburgh, was most welcome to all your friends in my family. Before, as you were numbered among the dead by all the City almost, except myself and some others, so no arguments could work on my women and girls to believe otherwise.

Though I assured them . . . that you embarked in the Catherine yacht, they had no faith, and would have you with the Duke. They were sure you loved him so well that you could not be from him. You see . . . what it is to leave us on the sudden, as you did, without asking, or, for all I know, having our prayers; we were all so angry at your going.

The wrecking of the *Gloucester* was due in Pepys's opinion to a pilot's 'obstinate over-winning . . . in opposition to all the contrary opinions of . . . his master, mates . . . the Duke himself, and several others, concurring unanimously in our not being yet clear of the sands.' Houblon reported from the city that the loss of life was imputed to 'the Duke's heat and courage to save the ship,' the men refusing to 'provide for their safety while he stayed with them.' A chronicler of the time, in what sounds like an excess of loyalty, asserts that 'the sinking mariners gave an huzza when they saw the Duke in safety.' The disaster occurred in broad summer daylight and fair weather. It was duly commemorated in a medal bearing the Duke's effigy on the obverse, and on the reverse the figure of the sinking ship with the legend, *'Impavidum feriunt'*—they strike him undismayed.

Pepys in Scotland anticipated in some respects the opinions of Dr. Johnson. Being excused for a time from attendance on the Duke, he made a tour of the country, visiting Stirling, Linlithgow, Hamilton, and Glasgow, which last he found 'a very extraordinary town indeed for beauty and trade, much superior to any in Scotland.' He admired the Scots for their principles of government and 'the order, gravity, and unanimity of their debates,' but their personal habits in 1682 gave him less cause for satisfaction. 'The truth is, there is so universal a rooted nastiness hangs about the person of every Scot (man and woman), that renders the finest show they can make, nauseous, even among those of the first quality.' The Duke's conduct of his mission won Pepys's unstinted praise; authority was maintained 'with so much absoluteness, yet gentleness,' as to render it 'morally impossible for any disquiet to arise in his Majesty's affairs in this kingdom.' Pepys's absence from London lasted little more than a month, and then for a year he was inconspicuously employed in his private affairs, corresponding with his friends, indulging his tastes as a virtuoso, and keeping Harbord and his like carefully under the scrutiny of his intelligence department. But in the middle of 1683, his opportunity came again for public work.

Among the 'others' whose advice the pilot had disregarded when the *Gloucester* was wrecked on the Lemon and Oar sand, was Colonel George Legge, in whose company Pepys subsequently made his Scotch tour. At the age of twenty-two he had been appointed Lieutenant-Governor of Portsmouth, an office which in 1682 he was still holding at the age of thirty-four. He was a favourite of the Duke's and on terms of personal friendship with Pepys. In December, 1682, he was created Baron Dartmouth, and in the early summer was given command of the expedition that was dispatched to Tangier for the purpose of withdrawing the garrison and destroying the Mole. Tangier had for years been a source of anxiety and heavy expense to the government, and Pepys, during the time in which he held the Treasurership to the responsible Commission, made himself familiar with the many problems involved. A letter that he wrote to Evelyn on August 7th from Portsmouth explains itself:

Your kind summons of the 2d. Inst. has overtaken me here, where it cannot be more susprising for you to find me, than it is to me to find myself; the King's command (without any account of the reason of it), requiring my repair hither, at less than eight-and-forty hours' warning: not but that I, now not only know, but am well pleased with the errand; it being to accompany my Lord Dartmouth (and therewith to have some service assigned

me for his majesty) in his present expedition, with a very
fair squadron of ships to Tangier.

What the purpose of the errand was, nor what his share in
it was to be, Pepys had not been informed when he left
London and began his 'Memoranda and general Minutes,
in setting out from London, July 30, 1683, to my departure
from Tangier towards Cadiz, in December following.'
When they were at tea he learnt that he was to be Dartmouth's secretary, and that the evacuation of Tangier was
their purpose. He approved of the undertaking, he liked
Dartmouth, and he told Evelyn that he should be 'in a
good ship, with a good fleet, under a very worthy leader,
in a conversation as delightful, as companions in the first
form in divinity, law, physic, and the usefullest parts of
mathematics can render it, namely, Dr. Ken, Dr. Trumball,
Dr. Lawrence, and Mr. Sheres; with the additional pleasure
of concerts (much above the ordinary) of voices, flutes, and
violins; and to fill up all . . . good humour, good cheer,
some good books, the company of my nearest friend, Mr.
Hewer, and a reasonable prospect of being home again in
less than two months.' Pepys's absence from England lasted
not two but eight months, and it was for him a source of
private pleasure and public credit. It has been usual to com-
pare the Journal that he then kept disparagingly with the
more famous Diary. It is true that now his attention was
more closely confined to business, but the business in itself
was something of an adventure, and his records are not
lacking in zest. And although this later Journal has not
the resilience nor the daring of the earlier masterpiece, it is
by no means deficient in personal interest, and there are
many passages in it which show that the writer's hand had
not lost its cunning. As, like its predecessor, it was kept in
shorthand, it is clear that although his eyes continued to
trouble him they were still not beyond exacting use.
    It was on August 13th, while they were waiting off Ports-
mouth for a favourable wind, that Dartmouth 'broke to me
the truth of our voyage, for disarming and destroying

Tangier.' The news was a surprise, but not a displeasing
one to Pepys. On the following day Dartmouth, who in the
new Journal succeeds Sandwich as 'my Lord,' showed Pepys
his commission under the Great Seal, and the secretary was
entirely satisfied with its contents. On the 16th, Pepys wrote
to Houblon that he was still pledged to silence as to their
intentions, but assuring his correspondent that there was
nothing 'designed in it that may disquiet the Spaniards or
interrupt the peace and security of our merchants with
them.' The voyage was uneventful, and Pepys, although
occasionally inconvenienced by the weather, was able to
enjoy the pleasures of the table, conversation, and music.
Supper might be garnished with 'a sillabub of the milk
brought on board this evening,' and afterwards Pepys, with
a temperance that had now become his habit, could be very
hot in dispute with the theologian about spirits, over a glass
of wine and water. One day he could note 'several thousand
young porpoises swimming by our ship-side,' and on another
he could find in *Hudibras* an escape from the ill-humour of
Dr. Trumbull, the lawyer, by reason of which 'we had no
merry chat these two nights.' Also, there were 'many songs
among the gentlemen and commanders,' and sometimes
'mighty merry music on the flute.' Once there is an echo of
the famous voyage twenty and more years earlier from
Holland to Dover, in the entry under August 30th: 'Thursday.—Up, taking it for Sunday.' There was much talk with
Dartmouth about naval affairs. High spirits notwithstanding, most of it was gloomy. During his Scotch visit Pepys
had heard from Hewer that the Admiralty was distraught
by faction, that the Navy Board was no better, and that
the King's service was going 'to rack, and is at this day
in such a pickle as it never was since I can remember, every
day plainly showing the different management in the Duke's
time and now.' And now Pepys and Dartmouth agreed that
the Duke again at the Admiralty was the only hope,
though, says Pepys, 'I must add, that I doubt whether even
the Duke be now strong enough to mend things.' The
secrecy that was being preserved on board concerning the

Fleet's designs is indicated by the fact that it was not until September 1st that he met Hewer 'by appointment . . . on the quarter-deck [and] communicated, by implication, not in clear words, our business at Tangier, destroying it . . . I told him there were several reasons for doing it, but told him not, then, the particulars.' On the 14th they were in the Bay of Tangier, Pepys exclaiming at first sight, 'But, Lord! how could any body ever think a place fit to be kept at this charge, that, overlooked by so many hills, can never be secured against an enemy.'

On the 17th they landed, and Pepys was at once busily employed by preparations for the task in hand. The Moors were keeping a jealous but not actively hostile watch upon the town, and there were inconveniences of a less formidable nature. Pepys was 'infinitely bit with chinchees' or 'musquittoes,' a mid-day meal was much disturbed by the appearance of 'a great locust left on the table,' and one morning he woke to find in his room 'the most extraordinary spider I ever saw, at least ten times as big as an ordinary spider.' Upon which he reflects: 'With such things this country mightily abounds. But, above all things that was most remarkable here, I met the Governor's lady in the pew; a lady I have long remarked for her beauty: but she is mightily altered, and they tell stories on her part, while her husband minds pleasure of the same kind on his.' He saw few women 'of any quality or beauty' in the place, but he attended Mr. Sheres in his garden for 'harp, guitar, and dance . . . with mighty pleasure.' The Moors, courteous if vigilant, sent in for the entertainment of the strangers a wild boar, 'most admirable grapes and pomegranates . . . and sweetmeats full roasted.' Pepys also described the delights of 'wine in saltpetre,' and found the 'Spanish onions mighty good.' On September 23d, we read: 'Shaved myself, the first time since coming from England.'

As the work went forward, Dartmouth took Pepys into his confidence as to the inadequate provisions with which he had been sent out. On the 24th, Pepys was retiring to bed, having borrowed a mosquito net of his chief, when

Dartmouth himself came into his room, and the two fell
into melancholy talk upon the condition of their enterprise.
They were faced with a serious shortage of victuals, and
when the Fleet should come to know it there was fear of
mutiny as well. The attitude of the inhabitants within the
town and the Moors outside it, when the designs of the
expedition should be disclosed, was an enigma full of dangerous possibilities. Altogether it was one of those hopeless
situations in the successful issue of which about half of
English history has been written. At the end of a long sitting, Pepys, with the privilege of fifteen years' seniority,
advised his commander to submit himself to God Almighty,
while doing all that he could as 'a faithful and diligent
officer . . . in his station, according to his best prudence,
and the best advice he can get.' With which comfort Dartmouth left, and Pepys 'to bed, where I was worse troubled
with biting, than any night since my coming, but the first,
notwithstanding the net.'

In a letter to Houblon written on October 14th, Pepys
wrote that he had never observed in 'any management
. . . greater prudence, justice, and diligence . . . than is
daily shown by my Lord Dartmouth on this occasion,' and
he gave some intimation of his own activities. He and
Hewer were engaged in assessing compensation to the
inhabitants who would suffer by the destruction of the Mole,
and were working 'under a pressure of business equal, at
least, to all that ever you knew us in at Derby-House; yet,
it is to me, a satisfaction, that it is an office wherein I have
it, equally in hand, to serve the King against impostures
from them whose demands are so apt to fly too high, as the
poor proprietors against others, whose want of tenderness
might betray them to making offers of satisfaction too low.
Both my duty and charity meet with a good degree of content.' Pepys liked work, and the content was not feigned;
moreover, he was here relieved of his personal anxieties.
We learn from the Diary that he had with him Samuel
Atkins, the clerk who had been charged with participation
in the murder of Sir Edmund Berry Godfrey, and the two

must have recalled the misadventure with a pleasing sense of security. Enlivening the pages of the Tangier Journal are many turns of the old inquisitive wit. Apart from 'a mighty cold that made me dumb' and was obstinate for two or three weeks, Pepys was well in body and alert in his mind. 'A foolish sermon of Hughes's, but had the pleasure of again seeing fine Mrs. Kirke, better dressed than before, but yet short of what I have known her.' He could lament how 'that the whole business of the navy now abroad is, how to get advantage one of another for private benefit, and how to bring this about by tricks and lies, sacrificing the whole service of the King.' But also he could 'Walk by moonshine in the fields under the wall, thinking of our affairs: a glow-worm shining; very small compared with what we have in England.' He could be roused to indignation by the infamies of the Governor Kirke, who in his dealings with the town had shown himself 'a very brute.' And, having spoken his mind with fitting emphasis on the matter, he could take his man 'Anthony, with my long glass, and therewith entertain myself in the fields, the first time, it being a fine evening. See the whole camp of the Moors, their huts, and manner of walking up and down in their alhagues. They look almost like ghosts, all in white.'

In another letter to Houblon, he announced his complete approval of the policy of 'deserting and extinguishing Tangier.' He had not chosen the service, had indeed not known its nature when he left England, 'But so much I shall never disown of my opinion at this day concerning it, namely, that at no time there needed any more the walking once round it by daylight to convince any man . . . of the impossibility of our ever making it, under our circumstances of government, either tenable by, or useful to, the crown of England.' And then, sententiously, it may be, but with an expedient morality that oddly enough was characteristic of Pepys, 'I would not wish my sweet W. or little Jemmy here; for, with sorrow and indignation I speak, it is a place of the world I would last send a young man to, but to hell. Therefore, on God's account as well as the King's, I think

it high time it were dissolved.' And in a further conversation with Dartmouth at the end of October there was 'a
great deal of good discourse on the viciousness of this place,
and its being time for Almighty God to destroy it.'

The work of destruction went on steadily to its completion, and at the beginning of December, Pepys and
Hewer, having made an end of their assessments, were released in order that they might visit Spain, leaving the
Mole to the attention of the sappers and engineers. It was
the intention of the travellers to return to Tangier within
a few weeks, but on Christmas Day Pepys wrote to Dartmouth that they were weather-bound, and it was not until
the end of February that they were able to rejoin the expedition on the eve of its sailing for England. In the meantime the Journal was continued, but was occupied almost
entirely with reflections upon abuses in the Navy. Many
instances of corruption came under Pepys's notice, and he
made elaborate observations on them for future use. But
there is nothing of personal interest to be gleaned from the
records of these months. On March 5, 1684, he was on
board in Dartmouth's company, sailing out of Tangier Bay.
On the 29th he was off the English coast. Again there was
much talk of present evils in the Navy, and again it was
agreed that the only remedy would be to reinstate the Duke
of York at the Admiralty. By the beginning of April, Pepys
had preceded Dartmouth to London, and was writing to his
chief that the current opinion upon the Tangier enterprise
was favourable. In acknowledging the assurance, Dartmouth added: 'I hope you found his Majesty satisfied in
your service, otherwise I can never hope he will be in mine.'
Dartmouth, indeed, knew how much he owed in the conduct
of his enterprise to the experience and sagacity of his secretary, and on January 11th, in writing from Tangier to
Pepys in Spain, he had enclosed an open order on any ship
'that you may please to put in the commander's name, when
you can come to me; for nothing they can pretend can be
of more service to his Majesty than bringing you hither, in
whose judgment and kindness I have an entire confidence.'

On April 8th, Hewer, still aboard with Dartmouth in the *Downs,* wrote to Pepys complaining that the Admiralty Board, Commissioners, of whose discretion and ability Pepys had had such grave doubts, were behaving towards his Lordship 'with a disrespect and breach of the discipline of the navy in the highest nature.' A letter, however, had been dispatched to them, which would 'make them sensible of their error or ignorance, and learn them how to behave themselves better towards a person of that worth and knowledge as Lord Dartmouth is, whose services I presume are better known to his Majesty and his Royal Highness than to suffer him to be so treated.' That Pepys thought highly of Dartmouth we know; it is true that he had been rather shocked by the circumstance that when in Spain he had received the order 'to take any ship from any other business to bring me,' he had found an exception made in favour of Dartmouth's 'old friend, Williams, who, he understood, had an opportunity of making his fortune by being here.' But when Dartmouth back in London hinted that Pepys might drop a discreet word to the Duke of York, he knew that he was speaking to an influential official whose good opinion he enjoyed.

For in public influence Pepys had more than recovered lost ground. 'But I hope,' wrote Dartmouth on April 8th, 'the Duke will not think it for his service to let me be quite thrown off from the fleet, now he hath an opportunity to serve himself, and protect my future pretensions, in great measure at least; for, on Lord Brounker's death, he hath an opportunity to bring you to the Admiralty; and if my Lord Nottingham can help out Brisbane, Mr. Sheres, with your assistance, may again put some life into the sea-service.' Brouncker, who had joined the reconstituted Admiralty Commission in 1681, had died three days before the date of Dartmouth's letter. A month later preparations were complete for a further reorganisation of naval control, and on May 19, 1684, the office of Lord High Admiral was revived. The urgent representations that had for long past been made by Pepys and others who could claim

something like his own right to speak, had no doubt largely
helped to bring this about. And although the political situation made the appointment of the Duke of York impossible,
it was found that the King, who had nominated himself to
the office, had also made formal provision for the coöperation of his 'royal brother.' By Letters Patent also, a new
office was instituted; that of Secretary for the Affairs of the
Admiralty of England, and to this Pepys was appointed at
a salary of £500 a year and a liberal allowance for expenses.
He held it until James, who himself became Lord High
Admiral on Charles's death in 1685, was dispossessed of his
crown in 1688.

CHAPTER IX

THE ADMIRALTY. JAMES II. DISMISSAL. THE GATE HOUSE

PEPYS'S second term of office at the Admiralty, while it is of high importance to naval history, adds little to our knowledge of the man. The old administrative ability was displayed with ripened powers, and it is hardly too much to say that at this critical period of its evolution Pepys was the brain of the Navy. The measures that he directed, and for the character of which he was often responsible, have been examined authoritatively by Dr. Tanner in his General Introduction to his *Catalogue of the Naval Manuscripts* in the Pepysian Library. We may note that in the Special Commission of 1686, for 'the recovery of the navy,' the constitution and functions of which were proposed by Pepys in an exhaustive report, Balthasar St. Michel was recommended as Commissioner at the Deptford and Woolwich Yards, in consideration of his 'more than twenty years continued service and experience in the navy both at sea and on shore, accompanied with the fullest evidence of his industry, faithfulness, and approved ability.' Our knowledge of 'Balty' leads us to suppose that this ability was somewhat nebulous, but he received the appointment and held it until the crash in 1688. Under the guidance of his brother-in-law he no doubt acquitted himself with sufficient credit to justify what after all was no very flagrant example of family patronage.

Early in 1687, his wife Esther died in childbirth; at the end of the preceding year, Pepys, being seriously troubled by a return of the stone, had warned him not to depend further on his support. But he was happy to have done as

much for his brother-in-law as would be possible were he
'to live twenty years longer in the Navy; and to such a
degree, as will with good conduct enable you both to provide well for your family, and at the same time doe your
King and country good service.' In January, 1689, Balthasar married a second wife.

In the unpublished *Journall or Memoriall* written by
Thomas Baker, his Majesty's Consul at Tripoli in 1684 to
1685, are four letters from Pepys on naval matters of some
importance. These at large do not concern us here, but the
following passage dated from the Admiralty, February 12,
1685, has its interest, showing Pepys in his formal style at
a historical moment.

S[r].,

It having pleased Almighty God to call to his Mercy
Our late Soveraigne Lord King Charles the Second of
Blessed Memorie, and by his decease the imperial
Crownes of England, Scotland, France and Ireland, be-
ing Descended unto the High & Mighty Prince James
Duke of York & Albany, his said late Maj[ties] onely
Brother and Heire; I am by the King's Majes[ties] Com-
and to signifie unto you, the Alterations (upon such
Change) has arisen in the Forme of the Passes given to
the ships of his Subjects Trading into the Mediterranean,
by the Change onely of the word Charles in the Title of
the Passes, into that of James, and these being now at
the Bottome Signed James R. when the others were
Charles R. as you will perceive in the Sample which I
here inclose you in which manner & forme all Passes
hereafter Issued will runn, That is to say all that beare
Date after the sixth day of this Instant February, upon
which day his late Majestie dyed but without any other
alteration in the whole Passe either in words or forme,
Save that onely Change beforementioned.

From a document printed by the Historical Manuscripts
Commission (15th Report. Appendix Part II.) we learn

that Pepys in 1687 was still petitioning for payment of arrears. It is addressed from the King at Whitehall to the Commissioners of the Navy.

1686–7. January 6th, The Court at Whitehall.—Our Will and Pleasure is that, in order to our being rightly informed in the particulars following, and some demands of Mr. Pepys depending thereon, with relation to his past services as Clerke of the Acts of the Navy and Secretary of the Admiralty, you doe forthwith . . . report . . . (1) The value of the yearly sallary enjoyed by Mr. Pepys as Clerke of the Acts of the Navy, and the totalls of his receipts thereon, during the time of his holding that employment.—(2) The value of the yearly sallarys allowed to each of the 2 persons, appointed to the joynt execution of that office, upon Mr. Pepys's removall from the same.—(3) The yearly sallary enjoyed by Sir William Coventry, as Secretary to Us, during our holding the office of Lord High Admirall of England, and as a Commissioner of the Navy, within the same time; with the like of what has been allowed to Mr. Pepys, either as Secretary of the Admiralty, or Commissioner of the Navy, during his sayd Secretaryshipp, and the totall of what his receipts therein amounted to.

As this order appears to have been drafted by Pepys himself, it may be taken that he was in no fear as to the result of the enquiry. It may be added that during his second secretaryship, he for the most part conducted the business of the Admiralty not from Derby House but from York Buildings.

During the time of his service under James II, Pepys's patronage in many kinds was greatly in request. A shipbuilder desiring to represent Rochester in Parliament hoped to gain the Mayor's interest by persuading Pepys against a proposed market at Chatham, which it seems will damage Rochester trade; a Commissioner at Bombay reinforces complaints as to 'swearing, lying, backbiting, and all manner

of villainy' in the place, and as to his own extremely dis-
agreeable condition, with a present of 'a jasper antonia
stone of eight ounces, (very good, I hope: I had it from a
Jesuit of Goa, who makes them,) and fifteen fine little birds
in a small cage,' also 'the finest plain cane I could light of,
having put a head on it,' with an apology that he could find
nothing better to send. A velvet carpet from his lady, however, is added to the gift. Sir Philip Carteret protests from
Jersey 'Your thanks are so far beyond the small present I
made bold to send you, that all the carps and partridges
in this island cannot deserve them. Therefore, the least I
can do is, to offer you all the interest I have in them, and
endeavour, when the season permits, to send you so many
partridges, that you may reserve some for yourself, and
present some to the King, if you think them worthy his acceptance.' One friend, Sir Robert Southwell, would like a
job for a man whom he has redeemed from Algerian
slavery, another, the Reverend Mr. Mills, would like a
place recently vacated by the Reverend Mr. Sill, and the
Duchess of Norfolk would like Pepys to procure for her ten
or eleven pieces of Scotch plaid. Mrs. Evelyn wants a pen-
sion for an unusually deserving widow, Dr. Vincent sug-
gestively needs a book costing twenty-five guineas which
he cannot afford, and Dr. Gale of St. Paul's wonders
whether Pepys could not induce Mr. Houblon to get his
correspondent at Venice to lay out twenty or thirty pounds
on Greek manuscripts. The last was a safe bid, the Houblon family never wearying of doing kindnesses to Pepys or
his friends. In March, 1688, we find James Houblon writing: 'After much-a-do with our tapestry-man, I have
brought him to take 25s. 6d. per ell, which is less by eight
shillings than in ordinary'; and a note by Pepys explains:
'Bought of Gerard Van Heythuyssen 2 pieces of tapestry,
8: 8 ells 4 ells deep, containing 64 ells, at 25s. 6d. . . .
81£. 12s.'

Pepys continued to indulge his enthusiasm as a collector,
adding books and prints to his library, and delighted by
anything that was rare or curious. A letter from a dealer

KING CHARLES II

By a contemporary artist unknown. Photograph by Mansell, Teddington. By permission of the FITZ WILLIAM MUSEUM, *Cambridge.*

informed him that he had a collection of all the medals made by the Roettiers in the finest examples, which he will be pleased to pass on at cost price to one whom he accounted as his 'ancient friend and good acquaintance' although there were several eager applicants on his list. A bookseller, forwarding four volumes with a bill for £1 14s., explained that one had been difficult to come by, but added, 'Without flattery, I love to find a rare book for you, and hope shortly to procure for you a perfect Hall's Chronicle.' Pepys remained in close touch with the affairs of the Bluecoat School, as with those of the Royal Society, of which he was elected President at the end of 1684. In 1685 he was for the second time made Master of Trinity House, and on July 20th, Evelyn notes:

The Trinity-Company met this day, which should have been on the Monday after Trinity, but was put off by reason of the Royal Charter being so large, that it could not be ready before. Some immunities were superadded. Mr. Pepys, Secretary of the Admiralty, was a second time chosen Master. There were present the Duke of Grafton, Lord Dartmouth, Master of the Ordnance, the Commissioners of the Navy, and Brethren of the Corporation. We went to church, according to custom, and then took a barge to the Trinity-House, in London, where we had a great dinner, above eighty at one table.

Of Pepys's family connections in these years but an occasional note remains. In June, 1688, a Richard Pepys, 'humbly praying your Worship's known goodness to excuse the presumption of your meanest vassal,' explained that he came of Buckinghamshire stock, had started life as a goldsmith, and had been 'reduced by an unhappy marriage (the unthinking conduct of a violent passion) to a forced compliance to travel beyond sea for seven years.' Whether his name secured a job for him we do not learn. In a letter to his nephew, John Jackson, written in 1699, Pepys asked for information about the brother Samuel Jackson's affairs,

'never haveing heard any thing of them since my last kinde
expedient to enable him to cleare his debt to mee, which I
would not be thought to have forgott.' Dr. Tanner, in a
footnote to this passage, says that Pepys had quarrelled
with his nephew Samuel, who was disinherited in consequence. But the quarrel did not in fact take place until 1701
at earliest, in August of which year Pepys made the bequests which were afterwards revoked. It is possible that
the debt referred to in the letter of 1699 was in some way
connected with help that Samuel before the date of his
mother's death had received from his uncle by way of train-
ing for the sea. On July 20, 1688, he wrote a letter to
Pepys from the *Foresight* in the Downs, from which we
learn that he had been with Sir John Narborough on the
expedition to St. Domingo for the recovery of treasure from
a wreck. He tells his uncle of Narborough's death on May
26th, refers to his funeral, and proceeds, 'I hope, honoured
Sir, I have made such progress in the art of navigation
. . . that I doubt not to give your honour ample satisfaction.' He recommends to his uncle's favour the gunner and
the yeoman of the powder room of his ship, as having
shown him many kindnesses on the voyage, which liberty he
would not have dared to take 'had not your honour's trans-
cending goodness, and avoiding the sin of ingratitude, been
the chief motives that encouraged me.' What, if anything,
came of his seafaring we do not know.

In 1685, Pepys was again elected as member for Harwich, and one of his last acts before leaving office at the
time of the Revolution was to recommend to the Commissioners the request of the Mayor and Corporation for
the establishment of a custom house in that town. On November 27, 1688, he wrote to the petitioners, that if they
wanted the scheme to go forward they should make haste
with their designs, 'that you may have the benefit and fruit
of your former favours to us [Anthony Deane and him-
self] by our soliciting the settlement and despatch of the
same while we have opportunity.' James was within but a
week or two of disaster when the words were written, and

it could have been with no very resolute heart that Pepys added: 'Not but that I still firmly hope, (cloudy as things at this day look,) that God Almighty has it in his gracious purpose to support the King and his government.'

James Stuart was in many respects a good Lord High Admiral, but he may be said to have been in all respects a bad king. He liked the sea, he was not deficient in physical courage, he was interested in the mechanics of shipbuilding and in the personal detail of the Navy, and he had a sense of admiralty. Under the strain of eulogy in which Pepys as a matter of course always spoke in public of a royal master, there was genuine admiration for a seaman of very considerable parts. His expressed opinion that no one was so well fitted as the Duke for headship of the Navy was inspired not only by the prestige which he knew the Prince's rank would bring to the office, and the high place which he himself held in that Prince's regard, but also by a clear-sighted sense of realities. Pepys, in fact, where the Navy was concerned, was at all times a realist, and Duke or no Duke he would never have lent his voice in favour of a man for whom his own experience could not vouch. If there is nothing in James's character so amiable as his just and steady kindness to Pepys, there is perhaps nothing so greatly to his credit as Pepys's firm conviction of his preëminence in naval service. There was, however, one charge brought against him by his friends on which even Pepys was disinclined to defend him. On the return voyage from Tangier, Dartmouth in conversation reported that it had been said 'that our masters, the King and Duke of York, were good at giving good orders, and encouragement to their servants in office to be strict in keeping good order, but were never found stable enough to support officers in the performance of their orders. By which none was safe in doing them service.' Dartmouth does not seem to have disputed the justice of the observation, which Pepys recorded without comment. That was just the trouble. No man could ever be quite sure where he was with a Stuart. Pepys himself could not complain of inconstancy in James, but he had recently learnt that Charles, the wisest and the least arrogant of his family, could be a faithless master.

Certainly, the cases were not comparable. James, as the executive head of a department, had behaved well to a valuable official, which was easy; Charles, as a King, had not behaved well to a devoted subject in serious political danger, which would have been difficult. And where Charles failed his brother was not at all likely to succeed. James, as chief officer of the Navy, had to maintain a discipline that was clearly regulated by written instructions, and on the whole he did so with justice and discretion. But as King of England his responsibility towards his subjects was of a much more complicated and subtle nature, and he was pathetically deficient in the qualities that it demanded. He might understand the officers of a fleet as such, or even the crew of a ship, but of men he had no knowledge whatever. From the moment he ascended the throne of England the Stuart cause was lost. His bigotry, his self-esteem, and his inability to understand the character of his countrymen, even to recognise that they were his countrymen at all, marked him out for disaster. It is hardly too much to say that the one redeeming feature of his discreditable reign was the steady application to naval reform under the secretaryship of Pepys. There is otherwise but a record of tragic blunders. No one can censure James for his exemplary suppression of Monmouth's miserable rebellion, but nothing can condone his personal treatment of that ill-fated young man at the end, nor the ferocity with which he allowed Jeffreys to close the dreadful account. Most of the bad names in history repay a little friendly advocacy, but Jeffreys simply will not respond to essays in exoneration, and his guilt, in which he was abetted by the notorious Kirke of Tangier, was in effect the King's guilt, since with full knowledge of the facts the King allowed it. Pepys could have had no sympathy with Monmouth's infatuated venture, and in his habitual preoccupation with the business on hand he may well have taken little notice of the Bloody Assize. But even allowing for the ceremony of the age, we could gladly have dispensed with a letter addressed to him by Jeffreys as Lord Chancellor in 1687, asking a favour, and subscribed 'Your most entirely affectionate friend and servant.'

The ineptitudes and misconduct of James's reign belong to history and need not be recounted here. His misreckoning of English character culminated with the Trial of the Seven Bishops in 1688. 'Desirous of confirming his despotic power' says Russell, an engaging though it may be an obsolete historian, 'and inflamed by frantic zeal, James seemed determined no longer to keep any measures with his subjects.' He published a Declaration of Indulgence, his second, and ordered that it should be read by the clergy in all churches after divine service. Everybody knew that this was no measure of toleration, but a direct challenge from Rome. It was a cunning device, and it over-reached itself. Thomas Sancroft, the primate, with six bishops, presented a humble petition that the King should not persist in what they submitted was an infringement at once of their liberty and of the law. The King would have none of it, and called them before the Council, where Jeffreys, the Lord Chancellor, gave an exhibition of his well-known judicial manner. But methods that had terrified illiterate peasants in the west of England now fell disconcertingly flat. The archbishop admitted having written the petition, and the six bishops having signed it. Jeffreys ordered them to find bail for their appearance at King's Bench to stand their trial for seditious libel. They replied that they were peers of England and as such were exempt from finding security on being accused of any misdemeanour. They knew that they were right in this, and that Jeffreys also knew it only served to inflame his notoriously ungovernable temper. With his usual disregard for law, he declared that in default of bail he would commit them to the Tower. They stood firm, a warrant was immediately issued, and to the Tower they were taken.

There were many men living who could remember the impeachment of five members by James's father in 1642, some who could remember the Petition of Right of

1628. And now again a Stuart was threatening English liberty. James was asserting his own right to autocratic government, and denying his subjects' right to petition. Throughout the country the spirit of an earlier generation stirred expectantly. On June 15th, the bishops were brought down by water from the Tower to plead in the King's Court. They were, Sancroft of Canterbury, Lloyd of St. Asaph, Ken of Bath and Wells, Turner of Ely, Lake of Chester, White of Peterborough, and Trelawny of Bristol. They were then released upon their own recognizances, to take their trial on June 29th. Pepys on his return from Scotland had called at Durham, where he found a bishop who seemed 'to live more like a prince of this, than a preacher of the other world.' Here he saw men of a different stamp. As on the appointed morning they went to Westminster Hall, they were accompanied by a great crowd of people, no less than twenty-nine peers joining the procession, as many again awaiting them in the Hall.

The trial was held before the Lord Chief Justice and three other judges, with a jury. It lasted from nine in the morning till past six in the evening. The Chief Justice summed up moderately, and Alibone, a papist, strongly in favour of the Crown, Holloway and Powell in favour of the bishops. At six o'clock the Court adjourned until the following morning, the jury being locked up for the night to consider their verdict. London woke in anxious expectation, and down in the west the country folk were exclaiming in song, 'And shall Trelawny die,' declaring that there were forty thousand Cornish boys would know the reason why. When the Court reassembled, the prisoners, who had been allowed to return to their houses over-night on their own surety, waited until ten o'clock before the jury came into the Hall. And when on the question being put a verdict of Not Guilty was announced, the assembly was shaken by an emotion such as had not been known in England since a majority of eleven passed the Grand Remonstrance through the House of Commons in 1641. 'There was,' says Evelyn, 'great rejoicing; and there was a lane of people from the

King's Bench to the waterside, on their knees, as the Bishops passed and repassed, to beg their blessing.' It is satisfactory to note that the bishops declined to pay any fees to the Lieutenant of the Tower, alleging that he had by no means behaved like a gentleman.

The city was full of bells, and at night there were bonfires in plenty, all of which, as Evelyn naïvely tells us, 'was taken very ill at Court.' The verdict was, in fact, little less than notice for James to quit. When a king issues commands that his people refuse to obey it is time for the king to go. James with his incurable detachment from reality took no heed of the warning. When the news of the acquittal was brought to him he was reviewing his troops at Hounslow, and even the roar of exultation that went through the ranks meant nothing to his mind. If the bishops were acquitted, so much the worse for the bishops, and if the soldiers were glad about it so much the worse for them, so much the worse, also, for the two sympathetic judges, who within forty-eight hours were removed from the Bench. But it was England rejoicing, and that June morning in Westminster Hall was but the opening of a scene that was to close with James's ignominious flight from London less than six months later.

As Secretary of the Admiralty, Pepys was necessarily closely in touch with the events of the revolution of 1688. But this movement was beyond any influence of his, and notwithstanding his personal regard for the King, it is likely that he observed it with political detachment. Pepys was a devoted public servant, but his patriotism was of the kind to believe that England would be England whatever might be the change in government, even the change in monarchy. So far as he was partisan in his mind at all, we may be sure that his lucid realism was sensitive to the profound convictions of the country. He was not the man for a moment to deceive himself that because James had been a good Admiralty chief he had also been a good King. So long as he remained King, Pepys would be his loyal subject; if he had to make way for another, Pepys would trans-

fer his loyalty to the successor without any scruples of conscience. In modified circumstances the position of great
numbers of Englishmen in 1688, and of Pepys among them,
was what it had been in 1660. There had been no prospect of
a stable government in a continuance of the Commonwealth,
and the Stuart House had been brought back as the only
alternative. There was now no prospect of a stable government with a continuance of the Stuarts, and the Stuarts, for
the last time, were turned out. Pepys, moved as no doubt
he was by the misfortunes of a friendly master, can have
been little disturbed by the overthrow of an incapable King.
His own business was to serve the Admiralty, and had William of Orange been unprejudiced enough to take over
Samuel Pepys when he took over a kingdom, he would have
been secure in the loyalty of one of the ablest administrators
in the country.

As events marched Pepys had merely to perform the duty
that shaped itself from day to day. In political developments he had no share. He was called as a witness at the
Trial of the Seven Bishops, but on a matter of fact merely.
His evidence as given in Howell's *State Trials* is brief and
interesting enough to be cited in full. A heated legal argument was going on in Court as to whether the bishops before the King in Council had owned the offending petition
and acknowledged their signatures. The Solicitor-General,
who in a stormy passage with Lord Chief Justice Wright
had been desired to confine himself to what was evidence
and not to waste the time of the Court with what was not,
was examining a difficult witness, when Wright intervened
with a plain question:

L. C. J. I'll ask you, sir John Nicholas, did my lord chancellor ask them this question, is this the petition you delivered to the king?

    Sir J. Nicholas. I do not remember that.

(Then there was a great shout).

    Sol. Gen. Here's wonderful great rejoicing that truth
cannot prevail.

Serj. Pemberton. No, Mr. Solicitor, truth does prevail.

Sol. Gen. You are all very glad that truth is stifled, Mr. Serjeant.

Serj. Trinder. Pray, sir John Nicholas, let me ask you one question; was there any discourse about delivering that petition to the king?

Sir J. Nicholas. Indeed, I do not remember it.

Sol. Gen. There's Mr. Pepys, we'll examine him.

(Mr. Pepys sworn).

L. C. J. Come, I'll ask the questions; were you at the council-board when my lords the bishops were committed?

Mr. Pepys. Yes, I was.

L. C. J. What were the questions that were asked, either by the king, or by my lord chancellor?

Mr. Pepys. My lord, I would remember as well as I could; the very words, and the very words of the question, were, I think, My Lords, do you own this paper? I do not remember any thing was spoken about the delivering; but I believe it was understood by every body at the table, that that was the paper that they had delivered.

L. C. J. Well, have you done now? But to satisfy you, I'll ask this question; Was this question asked, My Lords, was this the paper you delivered to the king?

Mr. Pepys. No, my lord.

Att. Gen. Pray, Sir, do you remember whether the king himself asked the question?

Mr. Pepys. You mean, I suppose, Mr. Attorney, that these were the words, or something that imported their delivering it to the king.

Att. Gen. Yes, Sir.

Mr. Pepys. Truly, I remember nothing of that.

Sol. Gen. Did you observe any discourse concerning their delivery of it to the king?

Mr. Pepys. Indeed, Mr. Solicitor, I do not.

That, so far as we know, was his only public contact at the time with affairs in the wider world outside his own department. As the year moved on, he was engaged in preparing the Fleet for the crisis that seemed to be imminent. In September his friend Dartmouth was appointed by the King to supreme command at sea, and Pepys wrote to Dr. Peachell, the Master of Magdalene at Cambridge, saying that he had been asked to find a suitable chaplain for the flagship, and enquiring whether his correspondent had any liking for the post. Peachell pleaded age and the pressure of his own business in declining. On October 1st Dartmouth's appointment was confirmed by an Order in Council, in which war with Holland was specified as an immediate danger, and Pepys was instructed to draw up necessary instructions for the Admiral. During the following weeks Dartmouth and Pepys were in constant communication as preparations went forward. On October 27th, the Secretary wrote to Captain Langley of Harwich, 'we cannot be long without some considerable action at sea.' Throughout November, as public opinion stiffened and William's intentions became more enigmatical, the gloom at Whitehall deepened, and on the 29th, the King wrote to Dartmouth, 'You will have an account from Mr. Pepys of the ill condition my affairs are in on shore.' It says something for James that even in his extremity he could add considerately, as a sailor, 'I am sorry you have been so roughly used by the winds at sea. This is a bad time for any action on that inconstant element.' On December 10th, James's nerve gave way, and he made his first attempt to escape to the Continent. On the 11th, Pepys was summoned to attend 'The Lords Spiritual and Temporal assembled at Guildhall,' who were sitting as a Committee of Safety while the House of Orange was encompassing the fall of the House of Stuart.

On the same day, Pepys, under orders from the Guildhall, sent instructions to Lord Dartmouth that all popish officers were to be removed from the Fleet, and that hostilities against the Dutch were to cease. James in his flight was intercepted by a fisherman on the Kentish coast, and for a week he was back in London while the turn of events was in the balance. By the 17th, however the provisional government had declared for William, and informed James that his presence in London was an obstacle to settlement. William wisely disregarded extremist proposals that his rival should be placed in confinement. James was allowed to withdraw, ostensibly to Rochester, but, in fact, to the Continent. On the 18th, Evelyn wrote in his Diary: 'I saw the king take barge to Gravesend at twelve o'clock—a sad sight! The Prince comes to St. James's and fills Whitehall with Dutch guards.' On the following day, in the midst of what must have been chaos in the government offices, Hewer, who since 1686 had been one of the Commissioners at the Navy Board, wrote a letter that Pepys might well endorse in his own hand as being 'of great tenderness, at a time of difficulty.'

Honor^d S^r,

I humbly thanke you for yours of this afternoon, which gives me greate satisfaction, and hope this afternoon or evening's audience will prove to your satisfaction, which I doe heartily wish and pray for, if not, I know you will chearefully acquiesce in what ever circumstance God-Almighty shall think most propper for you, which I hope may prove more to your satisfaction than you can imagine; You may rest assured that I am wholly yours, and that you shall never want the utmost of my constant, faithfull, and personall service, the utmost I can doe being inconsiderable to what your kindness and favour to me, has and does oblige me to; And therefore as all I have proceeded from you, soe all I have and am, is and shall be at your service.

I have noe reason to complaine as yet of any hardshipp, but to morrow I shall know the utmost & then I shall waite on you Remaineing in the meane time

Your ever faithfull & Obedient Servant
Wm Hewer.

On the 22d, James escaped from Rochester, though escape is a figure of speech, since he was allowed to depart without hindrance. Three days later he was at St. Germain's in France, and the age of William and Mary had begun.

At the time of his deposition, James was sitting to Kneller at Pepys's request for a portrait of which Wheatley tells an agreeable if speculative story in *Pepysiana*. According to a tradition in the Pepys Cockerell family, James was with Kneller at the moment when news was brought to him of William's landing at Tor Bay, and he dismissed the messenger with the words, 'I have promised Mr. Pepys my picture, and I will finish the sitting.' But true or not, the story has its origins in an intimacy that in the reorganisation of the government could hardly escape unfavourable notice. The final offer of the crown to William and Mary was not made until February 13, 1689, and in the meantime Pepys remained at the Admiralty, superintending with some remnants of authority the adjustment of the Fleet to the new conditions. On December 28th, Dartmouth wrote to him 'I doubt not but utility will help us both, though in this miserable distraction, and the grief I am in for my master, with being at such distance from affairs, and kept so much in the dark by my friends. . . . Pray deny me not your private and friendly advice, by which I shall be glad to govern myself; and I hope we may yet be helpful to one another.' Dartmouth, with the rest of England, transferred his allegiance to William, and for some weeks after James's flight his orders from the Prince were conveyed with due formality through Pepys, while the two friends continued privately to exchange assurances of goodwill. Whatever their personal regrets may have been, it is doubtful whether they regarded the situation as a bad one, and even if they did they were prepared to make the best of it.

But Pepys, whatever his hopes may have been, was in the rapidly closing twilight of his public career. In January, the electors of Harwich failed to elect him to the new Parliament. There was a town demonstration in his favour, and a friendly vicar wrote, 'If we are not by this late defection altogether become unworthy of you, I dare almost be confident [of your return in] the next Parliament,' but he was not to see Westminster again as a member. And when, in the latter part of February, the new sovereign settled his establishments, Pepys's name was omitted from the list of appointments.

He was a discarded servant; but worse was to follow. Jacobitism was a forlorn cause in England from the moment when it acquired its name in 1688. But a king in exile is a much livelier source of anxiety than a dead king to his successor, and also to his friends at home. There is no evidence to show that Pepys carried on any sort of intrigue with James in France, but his partiality was known with disapproval at Court. On May 4, 1689, a warrant was issued against Deane, Pepys, and Hewer, as being 'suspected of dangerous and tresonable practice against his Majestyes Government.' On the following day, Pepys and his friends were arrested, and remained in custody until the 15th of June, on which day they were informed that they could be released on bail for their appearance on the first day of the following term. The bail was found, and on the 18th, a receipt was given to Pepys by one of the messengers of the Privy Chamber for a sum of £14 13s. 4d., being fees due for the forty-two days during which he had been in charge of the 'boddys of Sir Anthony Deane, K T., Samuell Pepys and William Hewer, Esquires.' The charge at the time seems to have been dropped, or in any case suspended until the following year, when Pepys was again in trouble. We may note that it was during this anxious period that his sister Paulina died at Brampton. At the end of October, 1689, shortly before that event, Deane wrote what was endorsed by Pepys as 'a letter of respect and mortification, only to let you know I am alive, and speaking favourably of the grave'; Pepys, who was his friend's senior by some five years, replied that he also was alive, and confident not only of mercies in the world to come, but 'some time or other, even here, [of] the reparations due to such an unaccountable usage as I have sustained in this.' The tone of the letters suggests that the writers were no longer under the restraint of bail, and Pepys clearly, whatever his situation, had lost none of his old resolution. On March 7, 1690, Eve-lyn 'dined with Mr. Pepys, late Secretary to the Admiralty, where was that excellent shipwright and seaman . . . Sir Anthony Deane.' 'Amongst other discourse,' they deplored 'the sad condition of our navy, as now governed by inexperienced men since this Revolution.' In Evelyn again we read, on June 10th:

> Mr. Pepys read to me his Remonstrance, showing with what malice and injustice he was suspected with Sir Anthony Deane about the timber, of which the thirty ships were built by a late Act of Parliament, with the exceeding danger which the fleet would shortly be in, by reason of the tyranny and incompetency of those who now managed the Admiralty and affairs of the Navy, of which he gave an accurate state, and showed his great ability.

But on the 24th, we come to: 'Dined with Mr. Pepys, who the next day was sent to the Gate-house, and several great persons to the Tower, on suspicion of being affected to King James.' On July 14th, however, the Lord President and twelve members of the Council signed an order for Pepys's release, bail being taken for his appearance at the Old Bailey at the August sessions. The occasion of the order was a doctor's certificate 'that Mr. Samuel Pepys . . . is so very ill with an ulcer in his kidneys, that unless he be speedily enlarged from his present confinement he is in danger of death.' And on July 30th, Evelyn wrote in his Diary, 'I dined with Mr. Pepys, now suffered to return to his house, on account of indisposition.' The next we hear of the matter is a letter dated Wednesday evening, October 15, 1690, and endorsed by Pepys: 'A copy of a circular letter to my severall suretys, viz. Sir Peter Palavicini, Mr. James Houblon, Mr. Blackborne, and Mr. Martin; Mr. Hewer being at home with me.'

> Being this day become once againe a free man, in every respect (I mean) but that of my obligations to you and

the rest of my friends to whom I stand indebted for my being soe, I think it but a reasonable part of my duty to pay you and them my first thanks for it in a body; but know not how otherwise to compass it than by begging you (which I hereby doe) to take your share with them and me here to morrow of a piece of mutton, which is all I dare promise you besides that of my being ever, Your most bounden and faithful humble servant,

S. P.

From this date Pepys was for the rest of his life a free if not wholly an unsuspected man.

It is unnecessary to see in these later persecutions the hand of Pepys's old enemies. In 1690, William had to deal on a large scale with persons 'affected to King James' at the Battle of the Boyne. On the day before Pepys's committal to the Gate-house, Evelyn had written 'King William having vanquished King James in Ireland, there was much public rejoicing.' Both at this date and in the year before we may suppose that Pepys's name was conspicuous on the government's general black list. In 1689, in the pressure of business after William's accession, two or three months would doubtless elapse before Pepys's turn came for official attention; and in 1690, with Jacobitism throwing out its serious threat from Ireland, he would again be an obvious mark for government action. That so loyal an Englishman and so valuable a public servant should have been so treated may be deplorable; but there is some reason for thanks that no worse came of it.

CHAPTER X

FINAL RETIREMENT. CLAPHAM. DEATH

PEPYS was now fifty-five years of age. His public career was at an end, and he had lived on into what was a new world; no date in English history more decisively marks the close of an epoch and the coming of a new order than 1688. As he receded from the public life in which he had taken so industrious and so faithful a part, he bore with him no more than memories of the great figures among whom he had moved. The Stuart Kings had gone, Rupert, Albemarle, and Monmouth were dead; dead, too, were Batten, Penn, Carteret and Coventry. The House of Sandwich had passed to a new generation, and of his own immediate family two nephews were all that remained. He was happy in the growing intimacy of a few affectionate friends, the Houblons, John Evelyn, and above all William Hewer. In his retirement he carried on an active correspondence with many acquaintances on erudite and curious topics. We are in the habit of saying that men in that age grew old early, but although Pepys was troubled by the steady inroads of his physical infirmity, his mind lost none of its hungry energy. He was not a great scholar, but he had an immense zest for information, and if his correspondents often outdid him in learning he was always their equal in zeal and pertinacity, while the range of his knowledge made him better company than most specialists. Moreover, in his own subject he was an unrivalled authority. The Navy had not only been the business of his life, but a passion in gratifying which he had gone far beyond the necessities of his office. If John Evelyn had a more cultivated taste than he, and Isaac Newton a far greater intellect, even such men knew how to value his practical enthusiasms. As an amateur of music, indeed, he was able to lead in any company, but in the world of art and learning which was to be the happy refuge of his later years, Pepys was not so much a great man as a man whom great men had good reason for delighting to honour. As he approached the age of sixty he was becoming in the most acceptable sense of the word a venerable figure.

The Remonstrance which Pepys had read to Evelyn on June 10, 1690, was, in fact, the volume which he published in that year entitled *Memoires Relating to the State of the Royal Navy of England, For Ten Years, Determin'd December* 1688. On June 11th, Evelyn wrote to his friend:

So reasonable, so every way generous; in so just, modest, and generous a style; in a word, so perfectly consummate is your excellent remonstrance, and so incontestably vouched! This, Sir, is my sense of it, and I value my selfe upon my judgment of it, that it will stand like a rock, and dash in pieces all the effects and efforts of spitefull and implacable men, who because they cannot bravely emulate, envie your worth and would thus seacretly undermine it.

Readers may find Evelyn's testimony amplified in Dr. Tanner's introduction to the Clarendon Press reprint of the *Memoires.* The little book, in which Pepys displays a detailed mastery of his subject, is implicitly a vindication of his own share in naval government during the period specified. It is a classic of its kind, but for our purposes the gist of the matter may be found in the conclusion.

And having thus summarily brought this Deduction of the last Ten years Home-Transactions of our Navy to the day I first set for its Period, as it also (most wellcomely) proves to my own (now 30 years) Relation to't; wherein (as an Englishman, and in a Service purely English) I have ever with all simplicity of mind contended, to render this humble Province of mine useful to my Country: I close this Paper.

By which paper he has, he hopes, exhibited the validity of these three truths:

1.—That integrity, and general (but unpractic'd) Knowledge, are not alone sufficient to conduct and support a Navy so, as to prevent its Declension into a State little less unhappy, than the worst that can befall it under the want of both.

2.—That not much more (neither) is to be depended on, even from Experience alone and Integrity; unaccompany'd with Vigour of Application, Assiduity, Affection, Strictness of Discipline, and Method.

3.—That it was a strenuous Conjunction of all these (and that Conjunction only) that within half the Time, and less than half the Charge it cost the Crown in the exposing it, had (at the very instant of its unfortunate Lord's Withdrawing from it) rais'd the Navy of England from the lowest state of Impotence, to the most advanced step towards a lasting and solid Prosperity, that (all Circumstances consider'd) this Nation had ever seen it at.

And yet not such; but that (even at this its Zenith) it both did and suffer'd sufficient to teach us, that there is Something above both That and Us, that Governs the World.

To which (incomprehensible) alone be Glory.

In an ironical censure of the *Memoires,* Evelyn submitted that so clearly did its author stand confessed as the fittest man to restore the Navy, that should he fail to apply himself to that task he ought to be exposed as an enemy and betrayer of his country. But as to how Pepys was to come by the opportunity, Evelyn was silent.

About the time of his retirement, an elusive Mrs. Skinner was installed by Pepys at York Buildings as his housekeeper. He describes her in his will as 'the Excellent Lady Mrs. Mary Skyner' and expressed his gratitude for 'her Steddy friendship and Assistances during the whole course of my life, within the last thirty three years.' He was writing in the last year of his life, 1703, and, as Mr. Whitear points out, the term mentioned is exactly that of the interval since his wife's death. There is nothing but negative evidence as to her exact position in Pepys's household. She received liberal bequests in his will, the most important of which was a sum of £5,000, which, however, proved to exist on an unrealised contingency. Her will, which has been recovered by Mr. Whitear, shows her to have been of gentle birth, and Pepys's friends in their correspondence repeatedly convey to her their respectful compliments. A number of letters in the Pepys Cockerell collection which were written by her at Pepys's dictation reveal her as an illiterate scribe, but as much might be said of half the ladies of the nobility at the time. In the correspondence between Pepys and his nephew John Jackson during the young man's European tour, she is constantly mentioned in terms of regard if not of affection, and the traveller is asked to execute for her sundry little commissions. There is no evidence that she was ever married, nor of any romance between herself and Pepys. We do not even know her age. But that she contributed greatly to Pepys's comfort in his later years there is no doubt.

In July 1689, James Houblon wrote to Pepys interceding on behalf of a Mrs. Fane, who, it appears, had been dismissed for domestic wrangling in York Buildings. She confessed to Houblon, who had known her 'from her bib upwards,' that she had often been 'very severe and loud with the servants,' but protested that it was never unreasonably, and only in her employer's interests. Pepys, in his reply, allowed that there could be no more 'knowing, faithful, or vigilant person, or a stricter keeper at home . . . a person more useful in sickness as well as health,' and that as such he should always 'cherish her acquaintance, friendship, and neighbourhood.' But, if Mr. Houblon must know, she always had the very devil of a tongue, and when it was loosened, life in the house became insupportable. Pepys had tried for three years either to get her to mend her ways, or to learn how to endure them, and he had found both tasks impossible. It appears that she had been dismissed once already and had been taken back at Mrs. Skinner's entreaty. That was the truth of it, and Pepys left it to his friend to decide what should be done. Houblon replied, 'Your discourse last night, and forcible arguments, convince me that Mrs. Fane's continuing your servant is to be no more contested,' and begged that Pepys would not impute to him 'officious meddling in your private affairs, in this or any other case. Which I conjure you to do, being averse to nothing so much as to this practice.' Mrs. Fane left, and the probability is that Mrs. Skinner, who evidently was already an influence at York Buildings, succeeded her in control of the establishment. Though it seems to me not certain from the letters that she may not have been already there during Mrs. Fane's employment the latter is definitely spoken of as a servant, while Mrs. Skinner was never regarded in that light.

The most attractive, and with one exception the most voluminous, correspondence of Pepys's later life was with John Evelyn, Pepys's senior by thirteen years. We have already seen the early promises of friendship being fulfilled in Evelyn's solicitude and loyalty during the younger man's misfortunes. At the moment of crisis in 1688, Evelyn wrote on the 12th of December from Sayes Court: 'I . . . send on purpose to learne how it is with you, and to know if, in any sort, I may serve you in this prodigious Revolution. You have many friends, but no man living who is more sincerely your servant, or that has a greater value for you.' Evelyn meant what he said, and Pepys to the day of his death brought no less warmth to the attachment. On the 8th of July, 1689, Evelyn wrote in his Diary, 'I sat for my picture to Mr. Kneller, for Mr. Pepys . . . holding my

Sylva in my right hand. It was on his long and earnest request, and is placed in his Library. Kneller never painted in more masterly manner.' On Easter Monday, 1692, Pepys wrote: 'The last being Confession, this in all good conscience ought to be Restitution-Week,' and proposed to honour the occasion by returning to Evelyn various documents that had been borrowed eleven years earlier. He explained that, owing to the danger of official search, he had not for more than three weeks in three years dared to allow himself access to his papers, which we may presume were safely secluded in the Clapham chest. Later in the same year Evelyn at Wotton has 'been philosophising and world-despising in the solitudes of this place, whither I am retired to passe, and mourne and the absence of my best and worthyest friend. Here is wood and water, meadows and mountaines, the Dryads and Hamadryads; but here's no Mr. Pepys, no Dr. Gale. Nothing of all the cheere in the parlor that I tast; all's insipid, and all will be so to me 'til I see and injoy you againe.' Pepys in his reply written on September 16, 1692, explains the absence which Evelyn laments. He had given out to his friends that he was retiring to the country for the summer, and in order to lend colour to the deception he had hired a house at a cost of £30 'within 4 mile of the towne' and 'but a bow-shott off my friend James Houblon,' whose country house at that period was at Wanstead. In fact, he had stayed in London shutting himself up within this 'lushious towne a whole summer long,' for the purpose of uninterrupted attention to 'a small piece of worke that lay upon my hands which I had noe mind longer to trust futurity with, and less than such sequestration as this (after many attempts) had convinced myselfe would not suffice for.' The nature of this work is revealed in a letter written the day before to Dr. Gale. 'The secret is this. I have (as you know) been every year for now 3 or 4, subject to such a sort of surprizes and disquietings from powers above mee, without any prospect of ever being less soe, that, upon the last trial I had of them, I resolved (when ever that was over) to putt myselfe into

a condition of meeting them with less uneasiness by rid-
ding my selfe quite through of all that might on like occasions give mee any anxietys, and above all in relation
to my papers that I have so many years been tumultuously
gathering and laying by, without a vacancy of hand or head
ever to garble, sort, or putt into order for use either to myselfe or any that come after mee.' He had now succeeded in
putting his house in order, and was recovering from what
reads like an attack of gout, that had kept him to one floor
for a month. He hoped to be civilised again by Saturday
next, when he would, if God pleased, endeavour to meet
Dr. Gale 'in my little parlour at a dish of tripes,' with
hopes that Mr. Evelyn might also be induced to join the entertainment. It does not appear that Evelyn partook of the
tripes, but in the following year he offered in return for the
fatigues of a journey to Sayes Court 'as good beanes and
bacon, and (though but one cow) as good creame as ever
one would wish.'

A few incidents of miscellaneous interest may here be
noted from Pepys's later correspondence. In August, 1689,
a Sir Edward Beash, turned out of his employment and
'a great sufferer, and under straits unfit for one of my birth
to mention' wrote to Pepys as one who 'will willingly contribute and assist a gentleman, though a stranger, for we
are not born only for ourselves,' and earnestly requesting
'the bounty of a *piece* by the bearer.' In 1690, Kneller, having recommended one Cavalier to Pepys as a maker of
portraits in wax, had to adjust what apparently was a disputed charge: 'He did solicit me to do your picture on any
terms. Therefore, being he desired the doing on't, you will
serve him right to pay him three guineas for the wax . . .
Sir, if you do this, you will infinitely oblige me, and make
him civil. All Frenchmen require to be made it, being born
under a slavish government. . . . This man having received so much kindness in Germany, has spoiled him. Being a Frenchman, he should be kept low.' At the same time,
Pepys was using his interest in support of James Houblon's
parliamentary candidature for the City of London; he

could, he said, after twenty years' intimate acquaintance vouch for his friend as 'a most sober, industrious and honest man, and a real and (which renders him not the worse with me) temperate son of the Church of England.' In 1691 he wrote to Sir Robert Howard, the dramatist, reminding him of £400 which he had borrowed in 1676, 'upon an occasion of your going to New-Market,' of which sum only two hundred guineas had been repaid, and assuring him 'that having now nothing coming-in of what I then had, your present ordering me the remainder will be a great pleasure to, Your old humble and most faithfull servant, S. Pepys.'

We hear of another neglected obligation in an exchange of letters between Pepys and the Bishop of London in the same year. The Bishop begs Pepys to submit the case of a deserving applicant to James Southerne, now Secretary to the Admiralty. Southerne had been clerk to Coventry, and at one time had been under Pepys at the Navy Office. In 1662, we learn from the Diary that 'my man Gul [William Hewer] was gone to bed, and upon enquiry I hear that he did vomit before he went to bed, and complained his head ached, and thereupon though he was asleep I sent for him out of his bed, and he rose and came up to me, and I appeared very angry and did tax him with being drunk, and he told me that he had been with Mr. Southerne and Homewood at the Dolphin, and drank a quart of sack, but that his head did ache before he went out. But I do believe he has drunk too much, and so I did threaten to bid his uncle dispose of him some other way.' That had been thirty years ago, and now time had brought in ironical revenges. 'My man Gul' at fifty was the devoted and substantial friend of Pepys's approaching age, while of Mr. Southerne, his successor at the Admiralty, he had now to write to his Grace of London: 'however unnatural it may seem to your Lordshipp, as it does to all who know it, I have been so far from meeting with any marks of Mr. Southerne's remembring himselfe to have been my servant, and by mee (and mee alone) raised to the condition of a Master in the

Navy that, on the contrary, if there bee one man in it that has under his Revolution shewn mee not only most neglect but most despight on all occasions wherein my name has been made use of, it is hee.'

In 1692, a friend, apologising for his long silence, from which Pepys must have expected 'rather to hear of a legacy than a letter,' sent an offering of a 'barne door turky with eggs and a chine of bacon, which epicures call a Bocado de Cardinal, and Pepys in reply, praying for his health, promised to 'pray for your poultry too, and your swinetry, that when all other doores are shutt upon us wee may not want a Barne-door and Pig-sty of our owne to resort to.' In 1692, also, the unfortunate Balty, who had shared his brother-in-law's eclipse after the Revolution, afflicted with 'sickness and tormenting paines all over my body, with the adition of the yallow-jandis and other distempers,' put in a lamentable plea for a bundle of old clothes. In 1693, Pepys propounded to Isaac Newton the following question:

A—has 6 dice in a box, with which he is to fling a 6.

    B—has in another box 12 dice, with which he is to fling 2 sixes.

    C—has in another box 18 dice, with which he is to fling 3 sixes.

    Q—Whether B and C have not as easy a taske as A at even luck?

If any reader should suppose that the problem is a simple one he may turn to Newton's answer, and find that it is not. The great philosopher let himself loose on a computation of chances that gave Pepys a great deal more than he asked for. A Mr. George Tollet, an excise accountant, was drawn into the controversy, and after three months an intoxicated correspondence was still proceeding. By the middle of February, Mr. Tollet was tiring: 'Amongst many faults that are in the paper which I herewith send you, the length of it may justly be complained on; especially the subject being neither profitable, nor yet (by reason of its over-great varietie) so much as moderately pleasant.' Pepys by this time was not tired but under the table, or to use his own figure: 'the much greater part of the learning you lay before mee in this paper lies beyond my depth.' As the figures involved had now amounted to a scale of one hundred million millions, we may sympathise with him; though it was his own fault.

Acknowledging the receipt of a friend's book in May, 1695, Pepys refers to some activity of which we have no other trace: 'I have had a cause in Parliament requiring such attendance on behalf of a friend all the latter part of its Session, as has hardly left me a thought at liberty to any other use.' Pepys was no longer a member, and conjecture has nothing to offer. The following letter, here printed from Braybrooke, is so fresh and sparkling in its charm as to be a fitting example of Pepys's familiar manner at its best in his later years.

September 20, 1695.

MADAM—you are very good, and pray continue so, by as many kind messages as you can, and notices of your health, such as the bearer brings you back my thanks for, and a thousand services. Here's a sad town, and God knows when it will be a better, our losses at sea making a very melancholy exchange at both ends of it; the gentle-women of this, to say nothing of the other, sitting with their arms across, without a yard of muslin in their shops to sell, while the ladies, they tell me, walk pensively by, without a shilling, I mean a good one, in their pockets to buy. One thing there is, indeed, that comes in my way as a Governor, to hear of, which carries a little mirth with it, and indeed is very odd. Two wealthy citizens are lately dead, and left their estates, one to a Blue Coat boy, and the other to a Blue Coat girl, in Christ's Hospital. The extraordinariness of which has led some of the magis-trates to carry it on to a match, which is ended in a public wedding; he in his habit of blue satin, led by two of the

girls, and she in blue, with an apron green, and petticoat
yellow, all of sarsnet, led by two of the boys of the
house, through Cheapside to Guildhall Chapel, where
they were married by the Dean of St. Paul's, she given
by my Lord Mayor. The wedding-dinner, it seems, was
kept in the Hospital Hall, but the great day will be to-
morrow, St. Matthew's; when, so much I am sure of, my
Lord Mayor will be there, and myself also have had a
ticket of invitation thither, and, if I can, will be there
too . . . Bow bells are just now ringing, ding dong, but
whether for this, I cannot presently tell; but it is likely
enough for I have known them to ring upon much fool-
isher occasions, and lately too.

In 1696, Richard Gibson of the Navy Office, who had been
a clerk under Pepys, submitted to his old chief a memorial
that he had drawn up for the King on the present state of
the Navy. The civility was not lost on Pepys, but he had
done this sort of thing himself, and he endorsed the document with a note that 'the proposal there mentioned was
the same with that offered by me upon the subject of the
victualling of the Navy to Sir William Coventry by letter
of the 1st of January, 1665-6.' Later in the year it was
reported to Pepys that the undesirable Scott had returned
to England disguised as a Dutch skipper, that he now 'gott
good cloathes and a perriwig,' and that he had been heard
to order a silver box for a document which he declared to
be his pardon in the affair of the coachman. Further information was desired, but Scott by this time seems to have
lost interest in Pepys, and we hear no more of him.

If Pepys in his retirement had a grievance, he does not
seem unduly to have nursed it. As late as 1699, Dr. Charlett, Master of University College, told him of a conversation with a friend, in which it was agreed that 'It was a
great reproach to the Government that Mr. Pepys was not
at the head of the Navy Board.' Though Pepys at that time
was past what we should call retiring age, he cannot have
lived through the preceding years without a sense of high

abilities wasted. It is a mood given to bitterness, and of that in Pepys we find none. In his *Memoires* of 1690, he had stated his case, not by complaint but by the record of work done and knowledge acquired. The account was closed; he had his diversions and they were sufficient. A short interval must have convinced him that there was no hope of his return to office, and thereafter his only public concern, other than those of good citizenship, was to consolidate his defences against any further attack upon his liberty. It is not unlikely that he also amused himself from time to time by making further memoranda upon his career and upon his fluctuations of fortune. There is a suggestion of something of this kind in the *Six Papers* which in 1699 he sent to Dr. Gale, who responded with: 'You have mett with what was to be expected from men whose education is vile, whose soules never were in the feilds of truth before they came into their bodyes, though Plato sayth all soules spaciate there; nor will, I fear, ever return thether. O seculum infelix! O generations of caterpillars!' It never seems to have been more serious than that.

Among the Pepys Cockerell manuscripts printed by Dr. Tanner, is an interesting paper in Pepys's hand headed 'Home-notes for myself to attend when able.' A clock-pulling was to be mended, keys were to be adjusted, and Dr. Sloane was to be consulted about a benefaction to the Royal Society; enquiry was to be made as to the manner of inspecting eels, heads of Cromwell and Dryden were to be bought, also a new map of London and an eighth book-press. Mrs. Skinner was to be taken to see various manufactures, as card-making, gold-beating, lamp-blowing, and the weaving of silk stockings. His fishmonger, his globe-maker, and his printer, among others, were to be paid. There is a list of books to be obtained from John Bagford, the shoemaker who cobbled books as well as shoes, having a depraved taste, which it is to be feared Pepys shared, for collecting title pages. Dr. Tanner suggests 1698 as the likely date of the paper, but Dryden's *Chaucer*, which is included in this book-list, was not published until 1700.

It is possible that Pepys was merely entering a subscription
for the book, though it is unlikely that he would do so
through Bagford, who was not so much a regular bookseller as a collector who acted on commission for his
friends. In 1699 we find Pepys improving the slight acquaintance of earlier years with Dryden himself. To within
a few months the two men were of an age. On July 14th, the
poet wrote:

PADRON MIO,

I remember last year, when I had the honour of dining
with you, you were pleased to recommend to me the
character of Chaucer's *Good Parson*. Any desire of
yours is a command to me, and accordingly I have put it
into my English, with such additions and alterations as
I thought fit.

Having translated as many fables from Ovid, and as
many novels from Boccace, and tales from Chaucer, as
will make an indifferent large volume in folio, I intend
them for the press in Michaelmas term next. In the meantime, my Parson desires the favour of being known to
you, and promises, if you find any fault in his character,
he will reform it. Whenever you please, he shall wait on
you, and, for the safer conveyance, I will carry him in
my pocket, who am,

My *Padron's* most obedient servant,
JOHN DRYDEN.

On the same day Pepys replied:

You truly have obliged me, and, possibly, in saying so, I
am more in earnest than you can readily think, as verily
hoping from this your copy of one *Good Parson,* to fancy
some amends made me for the hourly offence I bear with
from the sight of so many lewd originals.

I shall, with great pleasure, attend you on this occasion whene'er you'll permit it; unless you would have

the kindness to double it to me, by suffereing my coach to wait on you (and whom you can gain me the same favour from) hither, to a cold chicken and a salad, any noon after Sunday, as being just stepping into the air for two days.

By stepping into the air for two days, Pepys no doubt meant a visit to Hewer's house at Clapham. This had been built in the early sixties by Sir Dennis Gauden, Victualler of the Navy, with whom Pepys and Hewer had been intimately associated. In 1663, before Gauden had been knighted, his credit was so low that Pepys at the Navy Office had been in serious doubts as to whether the victualling fund ought to be placed in his hands without ample security, 'which is a sad thing, that being reduced to this by us, we should be the first to doubt his credit; but so it is.' In 1665, his fortunes had recovered, and on a Tangier account of £8,000 he begged Pepys to keep £500 for himself, 'which in good earnest was against my judgement to do, for I expected about £100 and no more, but however he would have me do it.' A year or so later, in February, 1667, a further £500 changed hands in the same way. In July, 1663, Pepys had written in his Diary:

I resolved to go to Clapham, to Mr. Gauden's, who had sent his coach to their place for me because I was to have my horse of him to go to the race. So I went thither by coach and my Will [Hewer] by horse with me. . . . When I came to Mr. Gauden's one first thing was to show me his house, which is almost built, wherein he and his family live. I find it very regular and finely contrived, and the gardens and offices about it as convenient and as full of good variety as ever I saw in my life. It is true that he hath been censured for laying out so much money; but he tells me that he built it for his brother, who is since dead (the Bishop) who when he should come to be Bishop of Winchester, which he was promised (to which bishoprick at present there is no house), he did intend to dwell here.

But by 1677, Gauden was again in difficulties. In an Admiralty letter of August, 1674, Pepys refers to the 'surprising death of the Earl of Middleton.' Middleton was the Governor of Tangier, and died of a fall down stairs in 'a fit of intoxication.' I have in my possession a discharge given in June, 1677, by Lady Middleton to Samuel Pepys for the sum of £1,000 placed in his hands by Sir Dennis Gauden on her behalf against 'the annexed Bill of Exchange from the L^d. Middleton dated the 13th of May, 1674, for the sum of eighteen hundred eighty five pounds twelve shillings.' The payment is made by a tally 'payable in September next.' Whether the tally was redeemed cannot be said, but in July, Gauden was arrested for debt, and Pepys had considerable difficulty in affecting his release through Admiralty intervention. It was about this time that Gauden seems to have fallen under some financial obligations on account of which Hewer acquired an interest in the Clapham house. Gauden died in 1688, when the property passed into Hewer's sole possession.

A year after the transfer of the York Buildings tenancy from Hewer to Pepys, the former became Commissioner at the Navy Board and would take over an official residence. It is probable that he lived there with his mother from 1686, retiring to his newly acquired house at the time of his expulsion early in 1689; although that he had been there at an earlier date in occasional residence at least, is indicated by a letter from Pepys dated October 2, 1685, regretting that Evelyn had called during his absence on 'a visit to good Mr. Ewer at Clapham.' After 1688, we may be sure that Hewer found open house at York Buildings when it suited him, as we may be sure that Pepys was a welcome guest at Clapham as often and for as long as he liked.

In 1696, Evelyn, urging him to make haste with his naval history, wrote: 'Time flies a pace, my Friend. 'Tis evening with us; do not expect perfection on this side of life.'

Evelyn was then seventy-six, but Pepys at sixty-three did not need the reminder. 'Time and times,' he wrote at this date to a Baron of the Exchequer, 'have together made almost a monk of me; it being months since I have made one stepp over my threshold. Which I begg you to take in excuse for my so long omitting to wait on you, and may yet (possibly) a little longer; for I fear the next swallows and I must sett-out together.' The pretty figure of the swallows may be obscure, but the sense of the passage is plain, and then: 'Not but that the Lady [Mrs. Skinner]you so kindly enquire after . . . will, I hope bring you my compliments sooner, and ask you whether you can still afford an hour for Philosophy and a tansey when the approaching Term shall bee over.' And to another friend six weeks later, he expressed his hopes, 'the hopes I may entertain of waiting on you once more in this town before my infirmitys of age and Jacobitism compell me to leave it.' The date of his final removal to Clapham can be fixed with some certainty. We know from the dates on a continuous series of his letters that he left London at the end of April, 1700, and remained at Clapham until the middle of November in the same year, when he returned to York Buildings. On September 23d, Evelyn 'went to visit Mr. Pepys at Clapham, where he has a very noble and wonderfully well-furnished house, especially with Indian and Chinese curiosities. The offices and gardens well accomodated for pleasure and retirement.' After November, Pepys's letters are dated from London until the following April. There is then an interval until June, on the 7th of which month he wrote to Evelyn that he was ordered by his physician to return to the country 'with some prospect of setting up my future rest there; but 'tis in Surrey, and so not out of the reach of him (my most honoured Mr. Evelyn) whom, of all the surviving world, I would last quit the neighbourhood of.' After that date he did not return to London to live.

The Clapham house was pulled down in the middle of the eighteenth century. Lyson, in his *Environs of London,* wrote in 1792, 'The Mansion House, which was pulled down about thirty years since, was a very magnificent edifice. Some of the rooms were wainscotted with Japan, and a spacious gallery occupied the whole length of the house, both above and below stairs.' In an anonymous volume on *Clapham with its Common,* published in 1841, we are told that 'the site of the house was on the left side of the Chase, leading to the Wandsworth road, with very extensive gardens laid out in the Dutch style . . . with one front to an avenue leading into what is now Wix's Lane. The house formed three sides of a square, the principal front looking on to the Common.'

In his old age, Pepys found a new and delighted interest in the travels of his nephew John Jackson, who set off on a Continental tour at his uncle's expense in October, 1699. The elder brother, Samuel, four years senior to John, was not finally in disgrace at this time, but the letter already quoted shows him to have been in no very high favour. John Jackson appears to have been an excellent nephew, though there is sometimes just a suspicion that his propriety is a little more exact than it might have been if his brother had been more securely fixed in their uncle's intentions. This, however, may be to do him an injustice, and, in any case, a nephew who habitually called his uncle 'honoured sir' is in danger of getting less than his due from a generation that is given to calling its uncle 'old bean.' Nor are we much taken with those critics who complain of the dullness of Pepys's letters to his nephew. They are affectionate and solicitous, they are sensible of the respect due from youth to age, they affect no jocularity, but they are not dull. The objection is one bred of a preoccupation with the engaging indelicacies of the Diary. We here find an amiable but quick-witted old gentleman, rightly anxious that his bounty should be profitably employed, giving sound advice from his liberal experience, generous in his indulgences, and making no claims as a moral inquisitor. If John Jackson was a satisfactory nephew, Pepys was the most eligible of uncles.

We know nothing of John's earlier education. In 1690,

his uncle sent a book in his care to a friend at Cambridge, and a capitation tax receipt for 1697 discovered by Dr. Norman shows that he was at that date a member of the household at York Buildings. He was now, as we know from the Ellington register, twenty-six years of age. He started out with handsome letters of credit and a flourish of introductions in several languages from the house of Houblon. He left home on October 14th, and for some days was weather-bound at Shoreham. Pepys in his first letter specifies by name the friends who are well and send greetings, but proposes in future to confine himself to 'Your friends, etc.' His nephew, however, 'must not bee soe laconique, it being a necessary respect to bee heeded on your side that your friends may finde theyr names mentioned by you, when in proof of it I shall sometimes see it needfull to shew it.' On the 19th, Pepys was missing his nephew, 'haveing ¾ or more of my whole time to spend without any body neare mee, to reade or write word for mee, or know how to fetch mee a booke out of my library or putt it in its place againe when done with; and this, as I grow older, growing lesse supportable.' But the complaint once made was done with. One the same day, Jackson, still delayed at Shoreham, took 'the liberty of sending you a score of bloated herrings, which I thought very well cured.' The civility was not quite a success: 'I thank you for your present of herrings,' wrote Pepys on the 21st, 'but shall in my conscience be more bloated than they, should they reach me before I have tidings of your being gone.'

The traveller with his servant went through Paris to Lyons, on to Geneva, Genoa, Leghorn, and thence to Rome, from which city he wrote on Christmas Day that the Pope was extremely ill, 'and could not do a greater piece of service to the strangers than to dropp off at this juncture, to compleat their shew by a *Sede vacante;* to which some are of opinion will be added a Canonization this Holy Year; and after that I think there would remain nothing more to be wished for by us.' On January 11, 1700, Pepys wrote compliantly: 'There seems little doubt to bee made of a

Sede vacante in a little time, if any reports bee true; and here they begin to talk as much of a Canonization. I wish them both for your own and fellow-travailler's sakes since you are abroad; that you may have nothing more there to wish for when you are come away.' In February, Pepys instructed his nephew to buy him what prints he could, but they must be single prints, 'not books of setts,' and they must be small enough to hang in an ordinary panel of modern wainscotting. With an interval during which a visit was paid to Naples, Jackson stayed in Rome till the end of April. In December Pepys had written that he was 'I blesse God, in perfect health, but willing to spare my eyes in a letter of this length.' But at the end of March, his nephew was writing, 'I am very sorry for the late interruption in your health,' and although he was able to 'bless God for its so happy re-establishment,' Pepys wrote again on April 8th that he had for several weeks been 'bed-rid under an evil so rarely known as to have had it made a matter of universal surprise, and with little less general opinion of its dangerousness; namely, that the cicatrice of a wound occasioned upon my cutting for the stone, without hearing any thing of it in all this time, should after more than fourty-year-perfect cure, all on a sudden, without any known occasion given for it, break-out againe.' Four days later he could report recovery of his strength, 'which my necessary confinement, night and day, with my legs tyed in my bed . . . had unavoidably sunk in a great degree.' In the same letter he was all satisfaction with his nephew's behaviour, the employment of his time, his economy, his attention to requests, and the reports that he was sending home. On the 22d, he noted a further improvement in his health, and he considered that 'your Audience of the Pope will bee little lesse than a Triple Crowne to your journy.' On April 26th, one of the Houblons wrote to Jackson: 'Mr. Pepys lately much discomposed his friends with a dangerous indisposition; he has now pretty well recouverd it. I heartily wish an intire re'establishment of his health, that you may have a joyfull meeting at the end of your journey, for I again assure you he is extreamly delighted with the profitt and improvements you acquire by it.' It was at this time that Pepys moved to Clapham for his first prolonged visit. It was from there that he wrote on May 9th, 'I am, I thanke God, greatly recovered, and in a fayre road towards being perfectly soe.' He also sent news of Dryden's death, 'who will bee buryed in Chaucer's grave.'

A letter two days later to a friend at home confessed that his case had been desperate, and his removal into the country necessary for the preservation of his life. On the 16th, however, he could thank God that he was 'soe farr further profited by the ayre of this place as to have little more left to wish towards a perfect recovery.' His nephew's bills for five hundred dollars had been made good, as should also this new reckoning of one hundred and fifty more, 'But I hope you will bring home some agreeable penny worths for it, beyond what were then in your view.' In this letter we hear of Hewer's association with the East India Company, of which in later years he was to become Deputy-Governor.

On May 23d, Pepys was 'next to perfectly well,' and 'expecting the honour of a visit from my Lord Bishop of London . . . and his dineing with us here to day.' Jackson by now had reached Venice, and during the summer travelled through Mantua, Milan, Bologna, Florence, reaching France again in August, and preparing there for an extension of his travels into Spain. In July he sent home a box containing several books, and amongst other things a pack of Venetian cards, six pairs of gloves in walnut shells, three pots of Naples soap, a set of lute strings, three pounds of best Venice treacle, a broken ivory snush box, and some Turkey pipes.

In October, 1700, Pepys lost James Houblon, the friend who had been unfailing in courtesies and fearless and unsparing in support. 'My best, and near the oldest, of my acquaintance and friends,' he wrote to his nephew, 'is . . . dead . . . I was not in a condition to attend Sir James to his grave, being unable to bear the stone in a coach, and

his funeral being too late for my return hither. But his
sons have remembred me among the closest of his mourners,
as indeed I have a great reason to be, and shall never faile
to testify my memory of it, while I live, by any services I
can pay his family.' Of John Jackson's Spanish tour there
is nothing here for noting. England at the moment had no
minister at Madrid, and Pepys instructed his nephew to improve the occasion by making a full report on public affairs
for discreet distribution at home. 'But herein above all
things'—the letter is in Mrs. Skinner's hand—'lett ther be
nothing trivall or ill founded; nothing of any inferances or
advisess of your owne upon it, but bare maters of act ocur-
ing to you as a traveller; and those as fresh as you can at
the date of your writing, and as soone dispatcht away as
you are able when writen.' Jackson took the admonition to
heart, and the results have no bearing on our story. By the
end of the year he was back in England.

A few trifles may be gleaned from the correspondence of
Pepys's last years. A Scotch peer curiously informed him
that in the Castle of Borthwick he had eaten salt beef
that was two hundred years old; Lord Clarendon wished
his compliments to be conveyed to Mr. Jackson 'for remembring soe small an affair as the lettice seeds, of which my
wife is very proud.' A Lady Harbord, who for decency's
sake we may hope had nothing to do with the offensive William, wrote, with triumphant orthography, 'Sir,—I hope
you will parding my geven you thes trobull and geve me
leve to make an ombull request to you. I am informd that
thes is the time you take in poor celderne in to the ospitall,
and I have won to recomend to youer Carity. She is a
widow, and not abell out of har wagis to keep him and har
self.' Almost the only reprimand administered by Pepys to
his nephew during the Continental tour was on account of
'the ill choice of your wax on all your letters from Mont-
pelier, as being no better than dough.' Wishing to consult
a book in Lambeth that was not allowed to be taken away
from the Palace, Pepys arranged to visit London for the
purpose, but his health and the season being what they

were he enquired might he be accommodated in a lesser
room than the library, with perhaps a small fire?

This modest request was made at the end of 1700, by
which time, for all his assurances to his nephew, Pepys was
daily becoming more conscious of his sickness and the in-
firmities of age. Back in 1694, he had written to Evelyn:

If, as old as you are, you fancy yourself at liberty to do
what you will with yourself, you mistake, for I, and many
more, have too great a stock going in your bottom, not
to insist upon your taking more care on't than to be running out of a warm room into a cold wherry in November, as you did from me on Saturday last, for it is to it
I impute your cold, and would be glad I could as well
ease you of it; but, God be thanked! you have a good
nurse.

And now, in 1700, Evelyn could write to Pepys, also an
old man: 'This, alarme, Friend, is frequently in my
thoughts, intent upon finishing a thousand impertinencys
which I fancy would render my habitation, my library, garden, collections, and the worke I am about, compleate and
easy . . . Let you and I therefore settle on necessary
affaires, and pray we may not be surprized. An easy, comfortable passage is that which remaines for us to beg of
God, and for the rest to sit loose to things below.' That
was in August, and a month later Pepys wrote to Houblon's
son: 'I trust to my friend Mr. Hewer's usual punctuality in
doing right to your house for the moneys my traveller had
received abroad every where upon the credits you have
honoured him with.' He was 'sitting loose to things below.'
In the same month, Evelyn's son, having presented him
with a set of complimentary verses, Pepys demurred with
'But you have long since taught him to make all Mr. Pepys's
geese, swans and let him go on in't till . . . his own judgment will rectify him, though you wont.'

A leisured courtesy was now everywhere the note. Once
it was jarred by contention at home. He had a clerk,

Thomas Henderson, in whose hand many of his later letters are written. In October of 1700, something in the
house was missing, and the servants charged Henderson
with theft. He made an indignant demand for redress, and
later in the same month, he announced from London his
refusal to go out again to Clapham or to take his meals at
York Buildings when Pepys returned to town. He reasonably supposed that such conditions would make his further
employment impossible, but Pepys appears to have molli-
fied him. On July 11, 1701, a correspondent presented his
respects to Mrs. Skinner, who accompanied Pepys on his
removals to and from Clapham, to Hewer, 'and worthy
Mr. Jackson, of whose safe arrival I impatiently long to
heare.' On August 6th, another friend wrote: 'I mightily
congratulate you with Mr. Jackson's happy arrival, and
wish to every one of you all the felicitations of long and
happy life, and the comfortable injoyment of one another.'
The exact date of John Jackson's arrival cannot be more
definitely fixed than that, but on August 2d, Pepys made his
will, naming as executor 'my most approved and most dear
ffriend William Hewer of Clapham in the County of Surry
Esquire.' It is an exceedingly complicated document, but
the principal interest for us lies in the fact that although
John Jackson was treated handsomely, ampler provision
was made for his brother Samuel. It is true that there was a
highly speculative chance in John's favour. Pepys claimed
that a sum which he meticulously specified as £28,007 2s.
1¼d., was due to him from the Crown. On what Pepys
must have known to be the unlikely event of this being
recovered, John was to take a larger share than his brother,
but of Pepys's tangible estate Samuel was nominated as the
principal heir. It is worth noting that in his will Mary
Skinner is not mentioned, and also that Pepys's preamble,
'and as to the little portion of worldly Goods which . . .
God in his providence shall permit me to dy seized or
possessed of,' is repeated almost to a word in her own
will made thirteen years later.

On December 14, 1699, Paul Lorrain, who served Pepys

as amanuensis, and Newgate Gaol as chaplain, wrote to John Jackson, 'I hope you will also honour me with your commands. Those in relation to your brother shall be presently obeyed; I intending to let him know by this very night's post . . . how and where you were the 28 ult.' It is the only clue we have as to the terms existing between the brothers. It suggests that these were not unfriendly, though there may be something in the fact that John sent his message to Samuel not through his uncle but through a clerk. There is a significant circumstance in the will, which leads us to suppose that John knew his brother to be a topic uncongenial to his uncle's mind. At the moment when the will was made, John was returning from his tour in high favour, and had Samuel at that time seriously forfeited his uncle's regard, John would probably have stepped into his place. That Samuel was in fact made chief beneficiary shows that this had not happened. In providing, however, for the laying out of the Crown money if it should be paid, and of his other funds, Pepys directs that this shall be done by trustees appointed by his executor William Hewer and his nephew John Jackson. The inference is that he was placing upon the younger brother the responsibility for which he did not consider the elder to be fit. We can, I think, reconstruct the family position in August, 1701, thus: Samuel Jackson, on employment of his own, was treating his uncle with no particular respect; although he had as yet done nothing that meant disinheritance, he was on dangerous ground, he was being improvident of fortune. John, on the other hand, had a secure hold upon a younger brother's portion, and if Samuel should commit further indiscretions it might fare better with him yet. In due time Samuel obliged.

At this time Pepys conceived the idea of paying a respectful compliment to the University of Oxford. After anxious reflection, he decided that it should take the form of a portrait of John Wallis, the great mathematician, then eighty-five years of age, to be painted by Sir Godfrey Kneller. The episode was marked by elaborate ceremony. Kneller went down to Oxford, Dr. Wallis explaining that he would have been glad to come to London had it not been 'too late to dissemble my being an old man.' He sought, however, to express his sense of this honour so much above his deserts by treating Kneller 'with the respect due to a person of his quality.' Six months later, in March, 1702, Kneller was in a squall of dignity. The portrait was now finished, and Pepys was complaining not that it was finished, but that he had been told nothing of its progress. Kneller replied that definite instructions had been conveyed to him by Dr. Charlett, the Master of University, 'or else I should hardly [have] left my home and busenis for Oxford's conversation sake.' Pepys retorted that although since Kneller first visited Oxford Charlett had twice been to Clapham, on neither occasion had the subject been mentioned; but Kneller was pacified by Pepys's assurance that he was entirely content with the work itself. On May 14th, Charlett wrote that the picture was much commended in Oxford, and that the Doctor was talking 'very fondly of it.' At the end of July, Kneller wrote to Pepys: 'I understand you have a frame a-making, for that picture, which I desire to see put on at my house and all packt together in a case safe . . . I wil . . . send the porters for to fetch it, and varnish it well bevor it goes, and finish all to the utmost of my skill.' In August, Charlett learnt that it was shortly to arrive in Oxford, and in September Pepys was instructed that as it was to be a present to the University it should be directed to Mr. Vice-Chancellor. In the same month Charlett wrote to Pepys that, while he had certainly given no instructions to Kneller, 'I am very glad it is so admirably done, though I doubt not, besides the point of good manners, your judgment might have added to the beauty of the contrivance. But the Paynter's fancy was warm, and his imaginations not to be controled, it seems, with delays.' Pepys replied:

REVEREND SIR,—Sir Godfrey Kneller has (according to what I told you last night) putt his best hand to our picture, and seemes aequally satisfyed concerning it with respect both to the piece it selfe and to the dresse I have putt it into, and soe I hope you and all my learned friends about you will be; at least I have done my best towards it. Nor lett its comeing in a lackered frame lead you to thinke otherwise, for I could have sent it in the same with my Lord of Ormonde's guilt for lesse mony. But I was ledd to it by the advice of Sir G. Kneller's owne man, in consideration of its first luster being nothing inferior to that of gold, and its being for ever kept soe (when time shall tarnish it) at the 20th part of the charge and trouble that gold will. An observation confirmed by 40 yeares experience of my owne. Neverthelesse, if you or any of the gentlemen with you be of another minde, I shall most willingly bee at the charge of having it guilt, either immediately before it bee sett up or at any time hereafter dureing my life, whenever the University shall bee pleased to desire it; which pray make knowne to it as you shall see proper.

On the 13th, he wrote a formal letter to the Vice-Chancellor, begging the University's acceptance of the gift, and on the same day he assured Dr. Wallis 'I shall ever account myselfe your debtor for this opportunity of obliging mankind.' Suitable acknowledgments were made, and on October 29th, Pepys received a Latin diploma from the University, which in English rose to the heights of:

And to Your Praises, Sir, the whole Ocean bears witness; which You covered with such a powerfull Fleet as has been able to defye the rages of its most formidable Enemys as well as of the Waves. You, with a felicity beyond any Daedalus, added such a strength to your Shipping as rendred the Sailor at once safe, and secure of glory. You have truly encompassed Brittain with woodden Walls, and by Your care alone, whether wee would go on

in quest of new Discoverys or to enlarge our Conquests,
wee may extend our Sails to either Pole.

Pepys in his reply alluded to 'the superlative performances
of your Orator therein, whose every period seems to raise
a new world of glory to me out of nothing.' The interlude
closed with his assurance 'that the University has now made
me their creature, and as such, shall never want to the best
effects of my veneration and duty, whenever their kindness
and service shall call for them from mee.'

In such polite though inconsiderable concerns did Pepys
employ his later years. And yet we may pause on the inconsiderable. For the majority of readers, Pepys's life comes
to an end with the last words of the Diary. Scholarship
such as Dr. Tanner's has shown the inadequacy of this
view, but even the more curiously informed have been apt
to regard him after his retirement in 1689 as an ineffective
old gentleman of no importance in his own time, and of little interest to us. Lord Ponsonby, in reconstructing what
he supposes to have been the contemporary view of Pepys,
speaks of him as 'in later days a cast-off official in bad
odour in retirement, said to collect curios, but only seen by
a few in his seclusion.' Having spent several months in such
intimacy with Pepys as I could daily come at, I do not find
in this picture any resemblance to the original. There was
no place for Pepys in William's government, but there is
no evidence whatever to show that he fell into dishonoured
neglect. Official sanction is not everything in this world, and
when Pepys lost it he retained much that generous minds
may most value. As an old man, he had devoted friends,
he was respected by a wide circle of distinguished acquaintances, he was consulted by the learning and even by the
piety of his time, and young men with the world before
them drew upon his wisdom and experience.

But more than all this, Pepys, in his later years, survived with honour one of the most exacting tests of character. When he was turned away from the Admiralty in
1689, he left behind him work that had been not only a

career but a vocation. The break was sudden, and he was under sixty. Deprived thus of an absorbing interest, he might well have drifted into bewildered stagnation. It is not an uncommon spectacle. And he did nothing of the sort. He addressed himself without repining to those same inconsiderable employments, and made them considerable. His books, his prints, his music, his agreeable controversies, and his learned sociability became a sufficient and liberal occupation for a mind that had lost none of its scope and eagerness. As Pepys grew old, he grew neither tedious nor disillusioned. Sensitive though he was to shocks, he was not a man to meet reverses with enduring fortitude; his mind was too fresh, too resilient, to need such defences, and although the misfortunes of 1689 drove him from a calling that he loved, they could not touch the resources of his nature.

In November, 1701, Pepys wrote to Evelyn from Clapham that he was in perfect present ease as to his health, but that his retreat was 'a very burial to me, as to what of all worldly goods I put most price upon, I mean, the few old and learned friends I had flattered myself with the hopes of closing the little residue of my life in the continued enjoyment of . . . Not that I mean this for a final God-b'-w'-you! for, one way or other, I hope we shall see one another before the winter be over.' And Evelyn replied: 'In good earnest, Sir, I passe not by Yorke-Buildings without serious regret.' In December, Pepys wrote to the same friend of the satisfaction he was deriving 'from the little experiment I am just come from making upon your dutifull servant my nephew Jackson,' so much so that 'I shall struggle hard to give him 2 months' leisure within the next summer to finish his travels with Holland.' The following year, 1702, passed gently by, with book-presses continually to be readjusted so that the fixed limit of three thousand books should not be exceeded, with the spoils of his nephew's travels to be arranged, with civilities to be exchanged, and a well-ordered house always to be put in order. In January, 1703, Evelyn, now eighty-three years of age, wrote again: 'I had not defered so long, either from waiting on you, or giving you an account of my impertinent life since I had last the hapynesse to kiss your hands at your Paradisian Clapham, had my owne health . . . permitted me to repay the many kind friends their visits.' And then after a long discourse upon things mundane and celestial, 'In the meane time I feede on the past conversation I once had in York Buildings, and sterve since my friend have forsaken it.' In March an old servant, Mary Ballard, wrote much concerned 'at your honour's continued illness, and should be extremely glad if anything that I could do would contribute to your honour's health . . . if your honour would be pleased to remember that there was many odd things which I now and then used to make which were not only healthfull but pleasing to your stomack, which I am sorry to hear at present is much out of order. If your honour would be pleased to drink jelly broth, sume hartshorn jelly, sego, a whit drink which your honour had, they are all very strenghting. Thir was pills which wee calld ballsumnick pills, which your honour used to take every night, and cordells, powders to take in the ase's milke, and your honour was advised to eat tench and such sorts of fiche, and cray fiche, and many other things I belive madam Skynner may remember.' In April he wrote to Sir George Rooke, Commander-in-Chief of the Fleet, making what he described as 'the first and only request relating to the Navy that I have ever appeared in since my retirement from it. Nor should I have now done it in this, upon any less moving occasion than that of the unhappy bearer. Mr. St. Michel, heretofore one of its Commissioners, who is now addressing himselfe to the Queen for the relief in all time past and at this day universally enjoyed by persons under his circumstances of age and length of service.'

On April 20, 1703, John Jackson wrote a curious letter to Hewer. Reading it in cold blood, it is easy to regard it, as Dr. Tanner does, as being itself rather cold-blooded. But if we can recapture the emotions that dictated it, this judgment may seem to be doing Jackson an injustice. When

SAMUEL PEPYS

By SIR GODFREY KNELLER. *By permission of* MAGDA-
LENE COLLEGE, *Cambridge.*

strangers are admitted to the privacy of domestic correspondence there is always a danger, most pronounced perhaps in the case of love letters, that the niceties of the
writer's intention will escape the reader. There is a sub-
tlety in the personal idiom of such occasions that is often
very difficult to interpret. The charge against Jackson,
which, if it were upheld, would expose him as a shabbier
fellow than we hope he was, amounts to this. On April 19th,
Pepys had asked his doctors to speak frankly of his condition, and had learnt that it was serious. Jackson who, although in constant attendance on his uncle, seems not to
have been living at Clapham, wrote to Hewer on the following day, that in view of this admission, 'in order to the
adjusting some little remains of his temporal affairs, I presume, Sir, you will find him desirous of applying himself
thereto without delay.' He wishes to submit 'what neither
decency nor grief will permitt me to offer to him myselfe,'
that he has no knowledge of any disposition that has been
made of his uncle's affairs, that, whatever provision may or
may not have been made for himself, he is already under
greater obligations than he can ever acknowledge, but that
if it should prove that further benefactions are intended, he
shall strive always to employ them to the honour of his
uncle's illustrious name, and he begs that in such an event
some injunction should be laid upon him as to the future
disposal of his share in the estate if he himself should die
without heirs. There is, finally, a reference to the Crown
money: 'Should he mention any thing like this to you, be-
seech him, if you please, not to let it occasion one anxious
thought in him for what concerns me. For I should with
much more satisfaction succeed to the loss of £20,000 from
a vertue like his, than to twice the summ unduly gained.'
All of which may be said to savour of somewhat clumsily
veiled suggestion. It is possible to read it in that way, but
it is, I think, with greater plausibility possible to read it in
another. Although Jackson might have guessed it, he could
not know that his uncle's will contained elaborate provisions for the succession to his property after his imme-

diate heirs. I see no reason to doubt the sincerity of Jackson's gratitude for past kindness. But he must have known that he was a probable heir to a considerable part at least of his uncle's wealth. He was then thirty years of age, and in his own words, 'from my observations of the world, I may possibly never change my condition.' He was, in fact, to marry Anne Edgely, Hewer's cousin, but of this there was no intention at the time of his uncle's death. The fifteen years of his retreat had made inroads on Pepys's fortune, but it was likely still to be substantial. There is nothing improbable in his nephew's anxiety not to be responsible for a large share of it without instructions as to its future administration. Such a view is consistent with the precise, methodical, rather officious mind that appears in Jackson's letters; and it absolves him of what is not an agreeable, and may well be a quite unfounded, imputation.

What took place behind the scenes during the following three weeks we cannot tell, but on May 12th, Pepys revoked the will of 1701 by a codicil making a complete redistribution of his estate. It opens with a recital of the provisions already made, and proceeds: 'Whereas Since the time of my Signing and declaring my said Will . . . my said Nephew Samuel Jackson has thought fit to dispose of himselfe in marriage against my positive advice and Injunctions and to his own irreparable prejudice and dishonour I doe think my selfe obliged to express the resentments due to such an act of disrespect and imprudence.' Samuel, thereupon, is disinherited in John's favour, 'But for as much as no degree of provocation has been able wholly to extinguish my Affections towards the said Samuel Jackson I doe hereby give devise and appoint unto the said Samuel Jackson . . . One Annuity . . . of forty pounds of Lawfull money of England.' In this codicil Mrs. Mary Skinner appears for the first time as a legatee, receiving an annuity of £200, and here, too, for the first time special provisions are made for the disposal of the Pepysian Library. On the following day, May 13th, an addition to the Codicil defines these provisions in detail, and among other bequests makes a further one of £5,000 to Mrs. Skinner from the crown money.

Pepys was now desperately ill. By his portraits we judge him to have been a portly, rather heavily built man, of less than medium height. Now, as we learn from an autopsy, he was 'very much emaciated,' and disease that he had held in check for over forty years had defeated him at last. His long life had seen the making of an English epic. Born in the heyday of the Stuarts, he had seen the House fall and rise again and pass to its last eclipse. Though not quite that. In 1694, Queen Mary had died, and in March, 1702, her Dutch husband had gone also leaving the throne to yet another and the last of the Stuarts, that touching and obstinate lady, Anne. A contemporary journal opened its review of events for May, 1703, with, 'We find Things in a very peaceable and quiet posture in England under the Administration of the best of Queens.' But for Pepys the zest had gone out of these great things; was, indeed, for the first time going out of life. On the 24th, he was seized with convulsions which lasted through the night. In the morning, he asked for the curtains and windows to be opened to let in the spring day from Clapham Common. He called his nephew, John, who has left an account of the last hours, and Mrs. Skinner to his couch, and placing their hands together, said: 'Be good friends; I do desire it of you.' His nephew offered to kiss him, and 'he turned his mouth and pressed my lips with an extraordinary affection.' Throughout the day, these two and William Hewer, with the physician and his old friend Dr. Hickes, the non-juring Bishop of Thetford, watched the end coming. In the evening he wished them to retire, leaving him to the care of his bed-servants. In the middle of the night, he sent for his nephew, and John Jackson went into his room to find him dying. He noted that 'the exact time of my Unkle Pepys's departure was 47 minutes past 3 in the morning, by his gold watch.'

Under date May 26, 1703, Evelyn entered in his Diary: 'This day died Mr. Samuel Pepys, a very worthy, industrious and curious person . . . he was universally beloved, hospitable, generous, learned in many things, skilled in music, a very great cherisher of learned men of whom he had the conversation. . . . Mr. Pepys had been for near forty years so much my particular friend, that Mr. Jackson sent me complete mourning, desiring me to be one to hold up the pall at his magnificent obsequies; but my indisposition hindered me from doing him this last office.' On the 28th, Jackson wrote to Evelyn: 'I have thought myself extremely unfortunate to be out of the way at that only time when you were pleased lately to touch here, and express so great a desire of taking your leave of my uncle, which could not but have been admitted by him as a most welcome exception to his general orders against being interrupted.' The aged Evelyn steps from his coach with a gentle pathos to pay this last tribute to a long and happy friendship. In the contemporary chronicle before quoted, we read: 'The 4th of June following, Mr. Pepys's Body was convey'd to London, with a decent Pomp, suitable to his Character, and deposited in the same Vault with his Lady, in the church of St. Olave's Hartstreet, in Crutched Friars; being in the Parish wherein he had longest inhabited, upon Occasion of his Employment in the Navy.'

The burial took place at nine in the evening, and was conducted by Dr. Hickes, who had been with him to the end. 'The greatness of his behaviour,' he wrote to Charlett of the University, 'in his long and sharp tryall before his death, was in every respect answerable to his great life; and I believe no man ever went out of this world with greater contempt of it, or a more lively faith in every thing that was revealed of the world to come.' A contempt of this world, no doubt, in the divine intention of the friendly Bishop. But also, we may add, never man left it with a greater love.

LIST OF BOOKS CONSULTED

Chief Sources

THE DIARY OF SAMUEL PEPYS, M. A., F. R. S.
Transcribed from the shorthand manuscript in the Pepysian Library by the Rev. Mynors Bright, with Lord Braybrooke's notes. Edited with additions by Henry B. Wheatley, F. S. A. Eight volumes and Index. London, G. Bell & Sons, Ltd. 1923–1924.

DIARY AND CORRESPONDENCE OF SAMUEL PEPYS.
With a Life and Notes by Richard Lord Braybrooke, 1879. (Volume VI only. The Correspondence.)

THE LIFE, JOURNALS, AND CORRESPONDENCE OF SAMUEL PEPYS, ESQ., F. R. S.
Including a narrative of his voyage to Tangier. Deciphered from the shorthand MSS. in the Bodleian Library. By the Rev. John Smith, A. M. Two volumes. London, Richard Bentley. 1841.

PEPYSIANA.
Edited by Henry B. Wheatley, F. S. A. London, G. Bell & Sons. Ltd. 1923.

MORE PEPYSIANA.
By Walter H. Whitear, F. R. Hist. S. London, Simpkin, Marshall Hamilton, Kent & Co. 1927.

PRIVATE CORRESPONDENCE AND MISCELLANEOUS PAPERS OF SAMUEL PEPYS. 1679–1703.
Edited by J. R. Tanner, Litt. D. Two volumes. London, G. Bell & Sons. Ltd. 1926.

FURTHER CORRESPONDENCE OF SAMUEL PEPYS. 1662–1679.
Edited by J. R. Tanner. London, G. Bell & Sons, Ltd. 1929.

A DESCRIPTIVE CATALOGUE OF THE NAVAL MANUSCRIPTS IN THE PEPYSIAN LIBRARY AT MAGDALENE COLLEGE, CAMBRIDGE.
Edited by J. R. Tanner, M. A. Four volumes. Printed for the Navy Records Society. 1903–1923.

CARTE MSS. 73 and 75.
Bodleian Library. (Printed in part in *The Early Life of Pepys*. By C. H. Firth. *MacMillan's Magazine*. November, 1893.)

RAWLINSON MSS. A.178, A.179, A.183, A.185, A.186, A.190.
Bodleian Library.

Secondary Authorities

THE JOURNAL OF EDWARD MONTAGU, FIRST EARL OF SANDWICH.
Hinchingbrooke MSS.
Also edited by R. C. Anderson, and printed for the Navy Records
Society. 1929.

THE LIFE OF EDWARD MONTAGU, K. C., FIRST EARL OF SANDWICH.
By F. R. Harris. Two volumes. London, John Murray. 1912.

OCCASIONAL PAPERS.
Read by members at meetings of the Samuel Pepys Club. Two
volumes. London. Printed for the Club. 1917 & 1925.

MR. PEPYS.
By J. R. Tanner. London, G. Bell & Sons, Ltd. 1925.

THE DIARY OF JOHN EVELYN, F. R. S.
Edited by William Bray. Two volumes. London, Dent. 1925.

THE GREAT FIRE OF LONDON IN 1666.
By Walter George Bell, F. R. A. S. London, John Lane. 1920.

Books of Occasional Reference

AN ACCOUNT OF THE PRESERVATION OF CHARLES II AFTER THE
BATTLE OF WORCESTER.
London, Printed for William Sandby. 1766.

PEPYS' MEMOIRES OF THE ROYAL NAVY. 1679–1688.
Edited by J. R. Tanner. At the Clarendon Press. 1906.

SAMUEL PEPYS AND THE ROYAL NAVY.
By J. R. Tanner, Litt. D. Cambridge, at the University Press.
1920.

SAMUEL PEPYS'S NAVAL MINUTES.
Edited by J. R. Tanner. Navy Records Society, 1926.

HISTORICAL MANUSCRIPTS COMMISSION. 15TH REPORT.
Appendix Part II. London, H. M. S. Stationery Office. 1897.

STATE TRIALS.
By T. B. Howell. Volume XII. London, Longman. 1816.

DEBATES OF THE HOUSE OF COMMONS. 1667–1694.
Collected by Anchitell Grey. Volume VII. London. 1769.

TRANSACTIONS OF THE CAMBRIDGESHIRE AND HUNTINGDONSHIRE
ARCHÆOLOGICAL SOCIETY.
Volume II.

LEGENDS AND TRADITIONS OF HUNTINGDONSHIRE.
By W. H. Bernard Saunders. London, Simpkin Marshall & Co.
1888.

THE HISTORY OF GODMANCHESTER.
By Robert Fox. London, Baldwin & Cradock. 1831.

A COMPLEAT HISTORY OF EUROPE. FOR THE YEAR 1703.
London. Printed for H. Rhodes. 1704.

BRITANNIA DEPICTA OR OGILBY IMPROV'D.
London, Thos. Bowles. 1732.

THE PRESENT STATE OF LONDON.
By Tho. De-Laune. London. Printed by George Larkin. 1681.

LONDON RE-DISCOVERIES.
By Walter George Bell. London. The Bodley Head. 1929.

SOME CORRESPONDENCE (1831–32) OF THE REVEREND JOHN SMITH.
Privately printed, by the Masters and Fellows of Magdalene College, Cambridge. 1929.

INDEX